The Psychology of Culture Shock
Second Edition

Crossing cultures can be a stimulating and rewarding adventure. It can also be a stressful and bewildering experience. This thoroughly revised and updated edition of Furnham and Bochner's classic *Culture Shock* (1986) examines the psychological and social processes involved in intercultural contact, including learning new culture specific skills, managing stress and coping with an unfamiliar environment, changing cultural identities and enhancing intergroup relations.

The book describes the ABCs of intercultural encounters, highlighting Affective, Behavioural and Cognitive components of cross-cultural experience. It incorporates both theoretical and applied perspectives on culture shock and a comprehensive review of empirical research on a variety of cross-cultural travellers, such as tourists, students, business people, immigrants and refugees. Minimising the adverse effects of culture shock, facilitating positive psychological outcomes and discussion of selection and training techniques for living and working abroad represent some of the practical issues covered.

The Psychology of Culture Shock will prove an essential reference and textbook for courses within psychology, sociology and business training. It will also be a valuable resource for professionals working with culturally diverse populations and acculturating groups such as international students, immigrants and refugees.

Colleen Ward is Professor of Psychology and Head of the School of Psychology, Victoria University of Wellington, New Zealand, **Stephen Bochner** is Visiting Professor at the School of Psychology, University of New South Wales, Sydney and **Adrian Furnham** is Professor of Psychology at University College London.

The Psychology of Culture Shock

Second Edition

Colleen Ward
Stephen Bochner
Adrian Furnham

First published 2001 by Routledge
27 Church Road, Hove, East Sussex BN3 2FA

Simultaneously published in the USA and Canada
by Taylor & Francis Inc
325 Chestnut Street, Suite 800, Philadelphia, PA 19106

Routledge is part of the Taylor & Francis Group

© 2001 by Routledge

Cover design by Sandra Heath
Typeset in Times by RefineCatch Limited, Bungay, Suffolk
Printed and bound in Great Britain by
Biddles Ltd, Guildford and King's Lynn

British Library Cataloguing in Publication Data
A catalogue record for this book is available from the British Library

Library of Congress Cataloging in Publication Data
Ward, Colleen A.
   The psychology of culture shock / Colleen Ward, Stephen Bochner
and Adrian Furnham.
      p.   cm.
   Includes bibliographical references and index.
   ISBN 0–415–16234–3—ISBN 0–415–16235–1 (pbk.)
   1. Culture shock.   I. Bochner, Stephen.   II. Furnham,
Adrian.   III. Title.
GN517 .W37   2001
303.48′2 – dc21
                                                    00–062802

ISBN 0–415–16234–3 (Hbk)
ISBN 0–415–16235–1 (Pbk)

For David, my ever supportive partner, who endured both my absence and presence while writing this book. C.W.

And Benedict, for attempting to help his father concentrate on the really important things in life. A.F.

Contents

Figures

Tables

Foreword

In a world where there are millions of tourists, sojourners, expatriates, immigrants and refugees, it is high time for psychologists to pay attention to the culture shock that these individuals are experiencing.

Three internationally known psychologists, living in Europe, Asia, and Australia, have combined their skills to write this most impressive book that provides an excellent account of culture shock. The level of scholarship is extremely high. It integrates over one thousand references, placing them in a variety of theoretical frameworks, discussing inconsistencies in the findings, and attempting to find the causes of these inconsistencies. The theoretical perspectives are broad and sound.

It is a culturally sensitive psychology, focused on the intercultural encounter. It starts by examining aspects of cultural differences, such as levels of individualism and collectivism, and the outcomes of contact, such as genocide, assimilation, segregation, and integration. It considers both historical and contemporary approaches. It emphasises the need to learn to pay attention to paralinguistics, the local etiquette, and culture specific methods of resolving conflict. Culture contact is likely to be stressful, and an analysis is provided of factors such as personality and social support that can reduce the stress. The role of cultural distance and modernisation in providing gaps that make the contact more stressful is analysed. People in contact might assimilate the other culture, reject it, or change their identity to include both sets of cultural elements. They might even reject both their own and the other culture. Factors that are likely to result in each of these consequences are discussed with sophistication. A distinction is made between within-culture and between-cultures contact, and the different forms of contact associated with these two kinds of contact are examined.

The volume has chapters on specific groups, such as tourists, students, business people, immigrants, and refugees. While the broad theoretical principles discussed in the first section of the book apply to all these groups, each one faces special circumstances and that requires the examination of how the group can be successful in its particular situation. Culture training is then discussed, and the development of bicultural competencies is emphasised. Finally, the ABCs of culture shock are explored.

A special strength of this book is that it treats culture shock as an active process of dealing with change rather than as a noxious event. Also, it distinguishes Affect, Behaviour and Cognitions (ABCs) when people are exposed to another culture. It uses the principle of culture distance to distinguish different kinds of culture shock. It deals with *Affect* by examining stress and coping theories, and the processes involved in culture change. These have affective outcomes that correspond to psychological adjustment. *Behaviour* is changed through learning, and results in the acquisition of specific skills that have behavioural outcomes corresponding to sociocultural adaptation. *Cognitions* are accounted for through social identity theories. They result in the development and change of a specific identity which has implications for self- and intergroup perceptions. All these factors interact.

The discussion draws upon well-established psychological theories and emphasises factors that reduce culture shock. It provides specific suggestions about how people might be selected, trained and supported in other cultures so that the culture shock will be minimal and the experience less punishing, and possibly even rewarding. For example, they suggest how basic social skills might be developed through behavioural training, mentoring, and learning about the historical, philosophical, and sociopolitical foundations of the host culture. Another strand emphasises how people interpret their interpersonal experiences in other cultures, and how people can manage conflicts of values or perceptions. They discuss stereotypes and how they may both facilitate and impede intergroup relations. They face the fact that in some cases prejudicial attitudes toward culturally different individuals and groups can be highly functional for the holder of these opinions, which is why such beliefs are so difficult to change.

The authors argue that culture shock is now understood much better than it was 15 years ago, and is guided by theories taken from various areas of psychology – social, developmental, personality, cross-cultural and health. Thus, psychologists from all these fields will find this book of interest.

Harry C. Triandis
Professor Emeritus of Psychology
University of Illinois in Urbana-Champaign

Preface

The first edition of this book, entitled *Culture Shock*, was published by Methuen of London and New York in 1986. It was a very successful book in terms of citations, sales and reviews. It was reprinted three times, but developments in the field over the last fifteen years made it clear that a substantial revision was required. This slightly retitled book, *The Psychology of Culture Shock*, is the result.

The time period between the first and second editions has witnessed an unprecedented amount of research on all topics relevant to the themes of this book. The increase in the literature has reflected the substantial growth in the movement of people around the world, a process that has placed more and more individuals into contact with culturally unfamiliar persons. The main categories include those claiming refugee status, economic migrants, foreign students, international workers, tourists and holiday-makers. As travel has become easier, cheaper, and faster, many people have taken the opportunity to live, study and seek employment in societies very different from their 'point of origin'. Reactions to this travel have varied from elation to severe distress. The practical issue, discussed in this book, is how to minimise the adverse effects and maximise the positive psychological outcomes of culture contact.

When things go wrong due to culture clashes, the price in both human and economic terms can be quite high. For example, the repatriation of failed expatriate executives is such a costly endeavour that some firms now invest in selection and screening for those posted on assignments abroad. Some organisations, like universities, now routinely provide counselling facilities for those who struggle in a new culture. Health organisations in many countries have had to deal with disoriented and depressed newcomers unable to adapt to, and hence function effectively in, the new culture. Education and employment programmes aimed at particular groups exposed to culturally-induced stress have also become a regular feature of the contemporary scene.

Another major development since the first edition of this book appeared is the accelerated shrinking of the world, even for those who do not travel abroad. The internet and cable and satellite television have meant that rural Third World communities now have a window on the wider world. Globalisation of the workforce has also contributed to the 'small world' phenomenon.

In addition, some of the more isolated places have been 'invaded' by ecotourists and others who are excited by finding authentic indigenous cultures. This is merely an extreme instance of a new form of 'culture shock', that which is experienced not only by the visitors, but by the visited. Many societies are being inexorably changed, not always for the better, by the huge numbers of travellers they attract. In particular, tourists, business persons, aid workers, military personnel and so-called experts leave their mark on the societies to which they sojourn. Even foreign students have an impact, in the sense of distorting local university practices through their economic role as consumers of higher education. These and many other issues related to human cross-cultural contact are the subject of this volume.

The completion of this book is another example of an intercultural enterprise. The authors live and work on three continents, Asia, Australia, and Europe, and we can add to that educational and professional training in North America and Africa. Differences in time zones and travel schedules have sometimes made it difficult to integrate our efforts, but we hope that the diversity of our international and intercultural experiences in our personal and professional lives has broadened our perspective on 'culture shock'.

Finally, we are indebted to many persons and organisations who have supported us during the production of this book. Colleen Abbott has laboured tirelessly on the manuscript, and for this we are grateful. Research assistants and graduate students, particularly Antony Kennedy, Leong Chan Hoong, Andy Ong, Mano Ramakrishnan, Brenda Wee, and Roy Lam also deserve special thanks. Work on this book has been partially supported by grants from the National University of Singapore and Asia 2000 (New Zealand) as well as a Visiting Fellowship at the University of Canterbury, Christchurch, New Zealand, for the first author. We are also indebted to our publisher for enduring patience as we travelled the long road to completion.

Colleen Ward
Stephen Bochner
Adrian Furnham

Part I

The psychology of intercultural contact

The aims of this volume are to describe and explain the psychological consequences of exposure to novel and unfamiliar cultural environments. The book sets out to look at the assumptions people hold about such experiences, to describe the theories that have been proposed to account for the effects of intercultural contact, to present a systematic review of empirical research on the causes and consequences of 'culture shock', and to consider strategies that might be used to diminish the problems associated with intercultural interactions.

These are largely the same aims as those of the original edition of this book, *Culture Shock*, published in 1986. However, much has changed in the intervening years. First, there has been an enormous increase in research on intercultural contact. The rapidly growing psychological literature on tourists, sojourners, immigrants and refugees has been associated with changing demographic, social and political trends, including a worldwide increase in migration, growing numbers of refugees and displaced persons, the expansion of international tourism and education, and globalisation of the workforce. But changes have emerged not only with respect to the quantity of research undertaken. The quality of research has also dramatically improved. More sophisticated theories, more robust research designs, including longitudinal studies, and more powerful statistical analyses, including causal modelling, are now being employed. All of this augurs well for the present and future.

Despite these advances, the theory and research on the psychology of intercultural contact have not been well integrated. The literature on tourists, sojourners, immigrants and refugees has largely emerged in parallel streams with limited cross-referencing or cross-fertilisation. In addition, scholars working within specific social scientific paradigms often appear unaware or ill-informed about alternative theoretical contributions and how these may lead to a more comprehensive analysis of their own works. So, in addition to reviewing theory and research on 'culture shock', we also attempt to provide a broader integrative framework for the study of intercultural contact.

The book is divided into four parts. The first part provides a general introduction to the psychology of cross-cultural interaction. Chapter 1 sets the scene, raising key issues and discussing fundamental concepts that have been used to make sense of this complex area. We start by describing social systems in terms of inputs, throughputs and outputs, paving the way for a later discussion of the antecedents, correlates and consequences of intercultural contact. We also make explicit distinctions between culture contact that occurs between and within societies and discuss how different research traditions have evolved in these domains. In addition, Chapter 1 foreshadows the reasons why intercultural encounters may be difficult – giving particular attention to the role of individualism and collectivism in shaping and influencing intercultural interactions.

Chapter 2 continues with an introductory overview and distinguishes four ways in which the process of intercultural contact can be understood: in reference to the types of groups studied (e.g. tourists, immigrants), relevant situational variables (e.g. purpose, time span and type of interactions), the outcomes of intercultural contact (on both the individual and group level), and the major conceptual frameworks underlying the empirical research. Both the historical and current literature is reviewed, and the major contemporary theories – culture learning, stress and coping, and social identification – are introduced. The chapter concludes with a framework for the study of intercultural contact.

Part II focuses on the major theoretical approaches to understanding and explaining intercultural contact. Here we introduce our ABC model of 'culture shock'. That is, we consider the Affect, Behaviour, and Cognitions relating to intercultural contact and elaborate the theoretical traditions that guide related research. Chapter 3 concentrates on Behaviour. It reviews culture learning theory, emphasising that effective intercultural interactions are often hampered by the fact that participants are unaware of the subtle, culturally-defined rules and regulations that govern social encounters. These include verbal and nonverbal forms of communication as well as etiquette, the use of time, and strategies for resolving conflict. The chapter also includes a discussion of intercultural communication theory, social relations in multicultural societies, and the assessment of sociocultural adaptation.

Chapter 4 is concerned with Affect. It elaborates the stress and coping perspective on intercultural contact, making particular reference to those factors that facilitate and impede psychological adjustment. This approach emphasises the significance of life events and changes, stress appraisal, and coping styles during intercultural encounters. It also makes reference to the influence of personal and interpersonal resources such as self-efficacy, emotional resilience, and social support, as well as culture-specific variables such as culture distance and acculturation strategies.

Social identification theories are reviewed in Chapter 5. Here we assess both inward-looking Cognitions, i.e. how one views oneself in terms of social and cultural identity, as well as outward-looking perceptions, i.e. how an individual perceives and makes judgements about members of other ethnic, cultural or national groups. This chapter includes a discussion of stereotypes, prejudice and discrimination both within and across societies.

Part III distinguishes different types of culture travellers: tourists (Chapter 6), sojourners, particularly international students (Chapter 7) and international business people (Chapter 8), immigrants (Chapter 9), and refugees (Chapter 10). In this section we have attempted to identify the common and the unique aspects of the culture-contact literature across the various groups. For example, immigrant populations have provided us with some of the best on research on intergenerational changes in values; studies of refugees have been heavily concentrated on the effects of premigration trauma and resultant clinical diagnoses; research with tourists has included studies of the impact of cross-cultural travellers on indigenous populations; and international students have offered us access to valuable longitudinal investigations monitoring changes in psychological and sociocultural adjustment over time. Despite the differences in emphases, the material presented here is interconnected with the theoretical underpinnings elaborated in the preceding section. Issues pertaining to culture learning, stress and coping, identity and intergroup relations are interwoven throughout these chapters.

Part IV, the final section, considers applications and evaluations. In Chapter 11 we review strategies that may be used to reduce stress and enhance the effectiveness of intercultural interactions. Again the three theoretical perspectives are revisited; however, the majority of the material in this chapter on selection, preparation and training procedures is derived from culture learning theory and supported by work from industrial and organisational psychology. Although we suggest a model for culture training, including the knowledge, skills, attitudes and abilities required to function effectively in a new cultural milieu, we acknowledge that the majority of culture travellers do not receive systematic assistance. Finally, in Chapter 12 we conclude with a brief review and evaluation of the field, a comparison of past and present research, and a cautious forecast for the future.

1 Introduction and overview: Setting the scene

Contact between culturally diverse individuals is as old as recorded history. People brought up in one culture have always visited other societies to trade with, learn from, or exert influence in foreign lands. Most societies have experienced visitors from abroad, welcoming them if their motives were seen to be benevolent, or resisting the newcomers if they came to invade, pillage, or exploit. The journals of Xenophon, Marco Polo, Columbus, Drake, Captain Cook, Burton, and Lafcadio Hearn provide excellent accounts of what nowadays we would call intercultural contact. They also touch on some of the interpersonal and sociopolitical difficulties such contacts often create. The difference between then and now is merely one of scope, that is, the quantum increase in the movement of people across national and ethnic boundaries due to factors including mass access to jet travel, globalisation of industry, expansion of educational exchanges, increasing affluence supporting a burgeoning tourist industry, and growing migrant, refugee, and foreign worker movements. All of these developments involve some contact between culturally disparate individuals. The aim of this book is to explore the psychology of culture contact, the term we use to refer to the meeting of individuals and groups who differ in their cultural, ethnic, or linguistic backgrounds.

In this chapter we will raise some of the key issues, concepts and distinctions that have been proposed to make sense of what is a complex and often controversial area. The rest of the book is an elaboration of these ideas.

SOCIAL SYSTEMS AS INPUTS, THROUGHPUTS AND OUTPUTS

In the language of systems theory (Emery, 1969) as well as modern computerspeak, social systems and processes are defined by inputs or what starts the process; throughputs, or how the inputs are transformed by various influences; and outputs, or what outcomes are produced by the input-throughput sequence. This provides quite a useful analytic approach and highlights the need to define the outcomes or, in the language of experimental psychology, the dependent variables which constitute the key end-products of intercultural contact. Basically, these include the participants' behaviours, perceptions, feelings, beliefs, attitudes, and self-references.

In turn, these outcome variables are embedded in various theoretical and research traditions, and what particular studies measure is a function of the theoretical predilections of the investigators. Thus cognitive theorists will concentrate on perceptions; social psychologists will attend to attitudes, beliefs and attributions; psychologists with a behavioural bent will study intergroup processes and social skills; communication theorists will concentrate on the verbal and non-verbal messages that participants send and receive; and personality theorists may prefer measures of feelings, states and traits. One of the aims of this book will be to try to integrate these various theoretical domains, because they all have a contribution to make in helping to get a grasp on the phenomena under scrutiny.

On the throughput side, we propose a fairly rigorous definition of what constitutes contact by limiting the term to refer to social interactions that have the characteristics of a critical incident (Flanagan, 1954), that is, an event that matters and is regarded by one or both of the participants as being of some importance and as having a significant, non-trivial impact on their lives.

CULTURE CONTACT WITHIN AND BETWEEN SOCIETIES

Intercultural contacts can be classified into two broad categories: those that occur among the residents of a culturally diverse nation or society and those that take place when a person from one society travels to another country with a particular objective in mind; for example, to work, play, study, exploit, convert, or provide assistance (Bochner, 1982). Most of the research on culture shock has dealt with the latter, between-society category of contact, and this book reflects this emphasis in the literature. However, the incidence of within-society intercultural contacts has become much more frequent in recent years and is now a prolific target of both research and social/political action.

The term 'multiculturalism' is being increasingly used to describe this form of intercultural contact. For instance, Fowers and Richardson (1996) use this term in their description of racial and minority issues in the United States, and most of the references they cite also deal with intra-society intercultural interactions. Although there exist very few, if any, completely monocultural nations today, some societies are obviously more culturally diverse than others. For instance, Japan and Korea are often cited as examples of relatively culturally homogeneous societies (Kashima and Callan, 1994) as contrasted with more culturally diverse societies such as Australia, the United States, or Canada (Berry, 1997; Berry, Kalin and Taylor, 1977; Bochner, 1986; Bochner and Hesketh, 1994; Hesketh and Bochner, 1994; Triandis, Kurowski and

Gelfand, 1994). Underlying themes in this area relate to judgements about the degree of actual or perceived cultural diversity that characterises a particular society, whether such heterogeneity is desirable or undesirable, and whether it leads to positive or negative outcomes. Some of these issues will be referred to later in this book.

The term 'sojourner' has been used to describe between-society culture travellers (e.g. Ady, 1995; Klineberg and Hull, 1979). This label reflects the assumption that their stay is temporary, and that there is the intention to return to the culture of origin once the purpose of the visit has been achieved, assumptions which are often incorrect, as we shall see. People with whom the visitors enter into significant contact have been referred to as host nationals (e.g. Schild, 1962) which draws attention to the imbalance in the power, rights, territorial claims, and role expectations that distinguish temporary sojourners from permanent members of the host nation. Examples of sojourner categories include business people (Torbiorn, 1994), overseas students (Klineberg, 1981), technical experts (Seidel, 1981), missionaries (Gish, 1983), military personnel (Guthrie, 1966), diplomats (Dane, 1981), and even tourists (Pearce, 1982a,b, 1988). Distinctions are often drawn, however, between sojourners and more long term intercultural travellers such as immigrants and refugees. The intercultural literature on all of these groups will be reviewed in more detail later in this book.

Outcomes of contact

There is the need to put some content into the abstract categories we have described. Ady's (1995) extensive review of the literature found that studies of the empirical outcomes of intercultural contact fit quite neatly into the following six categories:

1   The general satisfaction of the sojourners with their new lives, often defined in terms of their well-being (e.g. Dunbar, 1992).
2   Changes in emotional adjustment over time. This conceptualisation goes back to Oberg's (1960) definition of the successful sojourner progressing through four stages of 'culture shock.' Many writers have subsequently extended this idea with some asserting that adjustment follows a U-shaped curve over time. This has been further elaborated as a W-curve if re-entry into the host culture is included in the process (e.g. Bochner, Lin and McLeod, 1980). To foreshadow, more recent empirical findings and theoretical speculation about the nature of time-based changes have been equivocal with respect to the U-curve hypothesis. This issue will be dealt with later in this book.
3   The extent to which sojourners interact with and engage in the host culture. One way of measuring this aspect empirically is to study the social networks of sojourners (e.g. Bochner, McLeod and Lin, 1977).
4   The adverse psychological (or indeed psychopathological) consequences

of failing to adjust to the new culture. This variable also has a long tradition, going back to Stonequist's (1937) discussion of marginality as one of the possible outcomes of culture contact. Contemporary versions use the concept of 'stress' to describe the more extreme negative experiences of some culture travellers (e.g. Ward, 1996).

5   The ability of the sojourner to manage the transition, to 'fit in' (e.g. Black, 1990). This is a major issue and will receive extensive treatment later.

6   The degree of competence sojourners achieve in negotiating their new setting. This idea is more precisely articulated in terms of the construct of culture learning (e.g. Bochner, 1986) and will be developed in much greater detail in this book.

Clearly, there are other ways of cutting this particular cake. For instance, Ward and colleagues (e.g. Ward, 1996) regard culture contact as a major, stressful life event, a view that would be shared by many of the writers in this field. Their particular contribution is to make an explicit distinction between the affective, cognitive, and behavioural responses to contact, which they suggest lead to two distinct types of outcomes, psychological and socio-cultural. This model will be described in greater detail later in this book.

Although it may be somewhat of an oversimplification, the overriding dependent variable in intercultural contact is whether the outcome tends to be positive or negative or, in plain English, whether the participants, as a result of the contact, liked or hated each other; trusted or viewed each other with suspicion; enjoyed each other's company or found the interaction awkward; were willing to work with, play with, or marry the other-culture individual; gained a sense of self-enhancement or humiliation in the company of culturally disparate individuals; and all the other cognitions and emotions that individuals experience when they engage in social interaction, and the behaviours that reflect these feelings.

It is therefore necessary to establish what actually occurs when individuals from different cultural backgrounds meet. Another task is to uncover the determinants of the various outcomes, or in the language of experimental psychology, to identify the independent and mediating variables that contribute to successful or unsuccessful contacts. And finally, attention will be drawn to the concepts and tools that can be used to provide applied psychology with the means to develop theory-based intervention and training programmes to increase the incidence of harmonious intercultural contacts in the so-called 'real world.'

It is also important to distinguish between the processes that define inter-cultural contact and the institutional structures that either support and enhance or hinder harmonious contact (Bochner, 1999). At the national level, these include various normative and regulatory characteristics such as a country's immigration policy; legislation affecting anti-discrimination in employment, education and housing; and a social climate that supports or opposes multicultural living. At the international level, likewise, countries can either favour or discourage positive contact with visitors from abroad through their visa, employment and educational policies. These characteristics tend to be studied by sociologists, historians, political scientists, and journalists working for the quality press, but increasingly, psychologists are beginning to realise the importance of these contextual aspects of contact (e.g. Berry, 1997).

Contact and cultural diversity

As was noted earlier, between-society and within-society contacts are increasing. Between-society contacts are fuelled by the globalisation of industry, entertainment, education and leisure pursuits (Erez, 1994). Educational exchange provides a very good illustration of this trend. The United States is the largest recipient of foreign students. In 1955 there were about 34,000 overseas students attending university in the US. This grew to 386,000 in 1990, and 450,000 in 1996 (Witherell, 1996).

Within-society contacts are increasing due to more and more nation states changing from being predominantly monocultural to multicultural societies, in part a function of increasing levels of migration from poorer to richer countries and by waves of refugees dislocated by civil wars, famines, and other natural and human-made disasters. Russel and Teitelbaum (1992) estimated that there were about 100 million such immigrants, refugees, and asylum seekers, a number that would have significantly increased since those figures were compiled.

Some of the old barriers that stood in the way of cultural diversity are falling or have been dismantled by legal and moral forces (Moghaddam, Taylor and Wright, 1993). Australia is a good example of this trend. From being a predominantly monocultural Anglo-Celt society during the first 150 years of its existence, during the last 50 years Australia has gradually become a multicultural society containing 140 different ethnic groups. One in three of its 19 million citizens were born overseas or are the descendants of persons born overseas in non-English speaking countries (McLennan, 1996). As recently as 1966, Australia had an explicit White Australia policy, and a number of discriminatory practices were still in effect until the election of the Whitlam Labour government in 1972 (Department of Labour and Immigration, 1975; Grassby, 1973). Since then, a series of non-discriminatory immigration laws have been enacted which have led to a substantial increase in ethnic Chinese, Vietnamese, and other non-European permanent settlers.

The United States, Britain, Canada and many of the European countries, such as France and Germany, have experienced a similar development since the end of the Second World War with those societies also transforming themselves into culturally diverse social systems (Bierbrauer and Pedersen, 1996). France takes in about 60,000 immigrants annually (Schnapper, 1995). In West Germany more than 15 million refugees were settled between 1945 and 1990. In 1992 and 1993 Germany had an annual average of 1.4 million immigrants, putting it ahead of the United States with an annual average of 800,000 (United Nations, 1994). Britain accepts about 50,000 immigrants each year (Coleman, 1995). These statistics underestimate the actual number of immigrants present as all these countries contain substantial groups of illegal immigrants that are not counted in the official figures (Bierbrauer and Pedersen, 1996). A literature is emerging to examine some of the problems and issues stemming from such changes (e.g. Pedersen, 1999) and will be reviewed later in this book.

Theoretical accounts of contact

Social contact between culturally disparate individuals is difficult and often stressful. There is an extensive body of empirical evidence in support of that contention, and this literature, which will be reviewed in some detail later, underpins the theoretical principles that explain why culture contact is problematic. Here we provide a brief summary of the key terms and processes that have been invoked to account for the barriers that stand in the way of successful intercultural relations.

A major theoretical principle is the similarity-attraction hypothesis (Byrne, 1969), which predicts that individuals are more likely to seek out, enjoy, understand, want to work and play with, trust, believe, vote for, and generally prefer people with whom they share salient characteristics. These include interests, values, religion, group affiliation, skills, physical attributes, age, language, and all the other aspects on which human beings differ (for a recent review of this literature, see Bochner, 1996). And since cultural identification by definition categorises people according to the idiosyncratic characteristics which distinguish them from other groups, it follows that cross-cultural interactions occur between individuals who are likely to be dissimilar on at least some of these salient dimensions.

An associated idea is that societies can in principle be located on a continuum of how close or distant they are with respect to their (empirically established) sociocultural features (Babiker, Cox and Miller, 1980). Thus for instance, Australia and New Zealand would be culturally closer to each other than Australia and say, Japan, in terms of key structural and value elements such as language, religion, the status of women, individualism–collectivism, attitudes to authority, forms of government, the legal system, and attitudes to the environment (Hofstede, 1980; Williams and Best, 1990). The culture-distance hypothesis predicts that the greater the cultural gap between participants, the more difficulties they will experience. Thus in the hypothetical example above, expatriate Australian business executives should find it easier to work in Auckland than in Taipei, and there is empirical evidence to support this principle (e.g. Dunbar, 1992; Furnham and Bochner, 1982; Torbiorn, 1994; Ward and Searle, 1991; Ward and Kennedy, 1993a,b, 1999).

Other theoretical principles implying that cross-cultural interaction is inherently difficult include the process of social categorisation (Abrams and Hogg, 1990), a term used to refer to the tendency for individuals to classify others as members of a group, in particular whether they belong to their own, in-group, or to some other, out-group. This has consequences for how people so categorised are perceived and treated, the in-group usually (Tajfel, 1970, 1981), but not always (e.g. Bochner and Cairns, 1976) being given preference. The process of stereotyping (Katz and Braly, 1933; Lippman, 1922) also contributes to the dynamics of intercultural contact, in attributing to individuals the traits that allegedly characterise the group that the target person has been assigned to by the perceiver.

A further contextual influence which aggravates what is already a minefield is the process of primary socialisation (Deaux, 1976). This is the process through which persons acquire a set of core values early in their lives, which they then come to regard as reflecting reality and, therefore, as absolutely true, and which, for a variety of reasons, are highly resistant to change. And again by definition, different cultures may and do provide idiosyncratic primary socialising influences. This may result in belief systems that are not universally shared and values that are diametrically opposed but greatly cherished by their respective groups. When members of two such groups come into contact, the potential for conflict is obvious. A contemporary example is the contrast between the status of women in fundamental Muslim societies, on the one hand, and in secular Western societies such as, say, Sweden, on the other. It is unlikely that there would be much agreement on this important social issue should the matter come up in a meeting between members of these two societies.

Cultural syndromes have also been discussed as a source of difficulties in intercultural interactions (Triandis, 1990). Cultural syndromes refer to patterns of attitudes, beliefs, norms and behaviours that can be used to contrast groups of cultures. Triandis (1990) identified three major cultural syndromes that are relevant to the analysis of ethnocentrism: cultural complexity, tight versus loose cultures, and individualism–collectivism. He also considered the implications of these syndromes for effective intercultural relations. For example, people from tight cultures prefer certainty and security. Because they highly value predictability, they are likely to reject people from loose cultures, perceiving them as unreliable and undisciplined. People from complex cultures pay attention to time. Time is seen as money, to be spent, to be saved or, in unfortunate circumstances, to be wasted. When meetings between persons from more and less complex cultures occur, the latter may be perceived as rude, lazy or disrespectful because of operating on 'elastic time'. Of the three cultural syndromes, however, the greatest attention has been paid to individualism–collectivism (I–C). As I–C provides one of the major guiding theoretical frameworks for comparative analysis in cross-cultural psychology (e.g. Hofstede, 1983; Kim et al., 1994; Triandis, 1995a) and is frequently referred to in this book, it is elaborated in the next section.

INDIVIDUALISM AND COLLECTIVISM

There are large cross-cultural differences in the pattern of the reciprocal relationship between the individual and the group. The form of this covenant resonates through most of the social arrangements which regulate daily life because it constitutes an implicit contract defining the balance between the freedom of the person, on the one hand, and the restrictions placed on the individual to achieve common goals, on the other. The structure of the family, the political system, industrial relations, the delivery of health, education and criminal justice services, and the creation and appreciation of art are only some instances of the institutions which are affected by this equation.

It is therefore not surprising that the inquiry into the link between the individual and society has a long history dating back to ancient times, e.g. Plato's *Republic* and the five Confucian relations (Goodman, 1967). With the advent of modern sociology and cultural anthropology in the late nineteenth and early twentieth centuries, the topic soon became a core issue in those disciplines (Allport, 1937; C. Kluckhohn, 1949; F. Kluckhohn and Strodbeck, 1961; G. H. Mead, 1934; M. Mead, 1928; Parsons and Shils, 1951; Riesman, 1964). However, the empirical investigation of culturally linked differences in the balance between the interests of the individual and the group has a relatively recent history. It can be traced to Hofstede's (1980) seminal study of the work values of 117,000 employees of a multinational company with branches in 40 countries, later expanded to include 50 national cultures and three regions (Hofstede, 1983). A major contribution of this study was its explicit aim to demonstrate that the nature of the person–group relationship will vary according to the culture in which it occurs. And because Hofstede adopted an applied perspective, some of the practical consequences of such a finding, particularly with respect to the culture contact process, were also given systematic attention.

An ecological factor analysis of the mean country scores showed that the countries could be classified along four bipolar dimensions (Individualism–Collectivism, Power Distance, Uncertainty Avoidance, and Masculinity–Femininity) although in the intervening years, the construct which received the greatest empirical attention has been Individualism/Collectivism (I–C).[1] This is largely because of its central role in both theory and practice, but also due to the construct's high face validity. Hofstede's original studies found that European and North American countries (and countries with cultures derived from that heritage) emerged as high on Individualism, whereas Asian and Latin American countries tended towards the collectivist end of the continuum. For instance, the United States, Australia, and Great Britain occupied the first three ranks on the I–C dimension, with Canada and The Netherlands tying for fourth position. In contrast, the rank for Guatemala was 50, Ecuador 49, Panama 48, Indonesia and Pakistan tied at 44, and Taiwan 41.

Hofstede's measures explicitly reflected the dominant values of the societies he sampled. Technically, they were expressed in terms of national mean scores. Caution must therefore be exercised about extrapolating his results, based as they were on country means, to the values and beliefs held by individual residents in those states. It is quite likely that within each national sample there will be wide variations with respect to I–C. For instance, some Australians will almost certainly be less individualistic than some Thais. Nevertheless, because of the large sample sizes in Hofstede's studies, the national culture average scores should provide an adequate estimate of the average scores of the individuals in that country. By and large, studies that independently measure I–C find that there is a reasonable correspondence between the values and beliefs of individuals and their Hofstede nationality ranking (Bochner, 1994; Bochner and Hesketh, 1994; Bond, 1988; Kashima, Hardie and Kashima, 1998; Parkes, Schneider and Bochner, 1999; Schwartz and Bilsky, 1990; Singelis *et al.*, 1995; Triandis, McCusker and Hui, 1990; Watkins *et al.*, 1998; Yamaguchi, 1994).

When individuals are studied, research has shown that I–C manifests itself

Table 1.1 Individualism indices of 50 countries (compiled from Hofstede, 1980, 1983)

Country	Individualism index	Country	Individualism index
United States	91	Brazil	38
Australia	90	Turkey	37
Great Britain	89	Uruguay	36
Canada	80	Greece	35
The Netherlands	80	The Philippines	32
New Zealand	79	Mexico	30
Italy	76	Portugal	27
Belgium	75	Yugoslavia	27
Denmark	74	Malaysia	26
Sweden	71	Hong Kong	25
France	71	Chile	23
Ireland	70	Singapore	20
Norway	69	Thailand	20
Switzerland	68	Salvador	19
Germany (F.R.)	67	South Korea	18
South Africa	65	Taiwan	17
Finland	63	Peru	16
Austria	55	Costa Rica	15
Israel	54	Indonesia	14
Spain	51	Pakistan	14
India	48	Columbia	13
Japan	46	Venezuela	12
Argentina	46	Panama	11
Iran	41	Equador	8
Jamaica	39	Guatemala	6

Note: Mean individualism scores are based on 14 items from Hofstede's (1980) work-related values questionnaire.

in three areas: at the personal level, it affects self-construal, or how people define their identity; at the interpersonal or relational level, I–C determines with whom people prefer to interact and how they regulate their social relationships; and at the societal or institutional level, it determines the nature of the association between the individual and the groups to which they belong, and their relationship with authority (Bochner and Hesketh, 1994; Kim, 1995). Large cross-cultural differences have been observed in each of these domains.

Levels of individualism–collectivism

Personal correlates of I–C

I–C influences self-construal – the way people define themselves in relation to others. The core distinction is in terms of whether the self-concept is distinct and separate from other people and groups or whether persons define themselves in terms of their relationships (Parkes, Schneider and Bochner, 1999). The terms 'independent and interdependent selves' are sometimes used to capture the essence of this distinction (Markus and Kitayama, 1991).

Individualists tend to describe themselves in terms of internal characteristics or traits which make them unique from others. For example, 'I am patient, easy-going, determined'. Collectivists are much more likely to think of themselves in terms of their affiliation with other people. This social identity is derived from being a member of a particular group with whom they share a common fate or by fulfilling a particular social role in relation to designated others. For example, 'I am a daughter, a nurse, a Thai'. This is not to suggest that collectivists lack 'personalities'. What it does indicate is that unlike individualists, collectivists do not separate their personal traits from the situations or relationships which make these characteristics salient (Triandis, 1988, 1989).

Interpersonal correlates of I–C

In collectivist cultures, the interests of the group take precedence over the needs of individual members (Hofstede, 1991; Triandis, 1989, 1995a). If there is a conflict between private aspirations and the common good, individuals will be expected to contribute to the group goal even if that involves personal sacrifice. Collectivist societies are characterised by interdependent, cooperative relationships and tight social networks, both among individuals and between individuals and the groups to which they belong. The person's loyalty is rewarded by the group protecting and looking after its members, whether this constitutes an extended family, employer, church, or social association.

In individualistic cultures people are much more loosely tied to other persons and groups. Individualists will expect and demand that their own interests are fulfilled, even if that diminishes the attainment of group object-ives. Individualists tend to function independently, primarily looking after themselves and their immediate families. Competition rather than cooper-ation is valued, often as an end in itself.

Collectivists make a sharper distinction between in-groups and out-groups than individualists (Gudykunst, Yoon and Nishida, 1987). Collectivists belong to relatively few in-groups but are fiercely loyal and committed to them, often on a lifelong basis. Collectivists tend to have a limited number of relationships, but these will be close and intimate. Relationships are regarded as an end in themselves and maintained even at great cost.

Individualists belong to many groups, but their membership tends to be superficial and in many instances transitory. Individualists have many rela-tionships, most of them lacking genuine intimacy. Relationships are a means to an end and abandoned if the costs become too high (Triandis, 1995a).

In collectivist cultures, the maintenance of harmony within the in-group is highly valued, and direct confrontation is avoided. Collectivists are sensitive to the norms and situational constraints regulating behaviour in groups (Argyle *et al.*, 1986). They become expert at reading implicit interpersonal messages and rely on indirect cues to interpret communication style and content (Singelis and Brown, 1995). Individualists are much more direct in how they express themselves. They place a greater emphasis on explicit communication and telling it as it is, even if that may cause pain.

Societal correlates of I–C

In collectivist cultures self-worth is evaluated in terms of being accepted and valued by the person's in-groups. Being successful in achieving and maintain-ing interpersonal harmony is another major source of satisfaction. Family relationships, religious beliefs, loyalty to institutions and authority, being law abiding, and being considerate of the feelings of others are important determinants of self-esteem. Collectivist societies tend to place substantial emphasis on conformity and favour uniformity in beliefs, customs, and prac-tices. In individualistic cultures the self's worth is evaluated in terms of its independence and uniqueness. Self-esteem is based on individual talent, personal achievement, influence and recognition (Watkins *et al.*, 1998; Yamaguchi, 1994). This translates at the societal level into a much more brittle relationship with authority and the law. Less importance is accorded to social cohesion. Diversity in values, behaviours, and practices is accepted and often explicitly advocated.

Antecedents of individualism–collectivism

There is much speculation about the antecedents of I–C, but not much hard data. Theoretically, it is conceivable that the orientation towards either individualism or collectivism originated in the distinction between hunter-gathering and agricultural societies. It has been suggested that people who depend on nomadic hunting for their food supply will need to be self-reliant and concentrate on their own and their immediate family's well-being. By contrast, people living in stable, agrarian settlements will be better served by developing close-knit, cooperative social networks, enabling them to band together to till the soil and protect their villages from invaders. The contemporary version of this distinction contrasts urban with rural settlements, and there is some evidence that rural dwellers are more collectivist in their orientation than individualist (Freeman, 1997; Kashima *et al.*, 1998).

There also appears to be a link between individualism and wealth or socio-economic status (Hofstede, 1991; Triandis, 1995a). A number of studies have found a statistically significant association between a country's rank on I–C and its average national income (Diener and Diener, 1995; Punnett, Singh and Williams, 1994). This relationship is interpreted as indicating support for the survival value of cooperative social structures for people lacking personal power and material resources. With increasing wealth, persons gain access to resources that enable them 'to do their own thing', whereas less powerful individuals depend on their relationship with influential others or their group for support (Parkes, Bochner and Schneider, 1998). This contention has received some confirmation from within-culture studies, which have found that persons in lower income brackets or in occupations with lower prestige have a more collectivist orientation (Freeman, 1997; Lykes, 1985; Marshall, 1997; Merritt and Helmreich, 1996; Reykowski, 1994; Topalova, 1997).

Culture contact consequences of individualism–collectivism

As this review has shown, when individualists and collectivists meet, they bring to the encounter different social attitudes, moral values and behavioural inclinations. Their cognitive styles will differ as will the manner in which they communicate, particularly with respect to how they express their emotions and wishes. How they act, including their non-verbal behaviour, will also differ as a function of their core value orientation.

Some of the consequences of these differences will be discussed in more detail in later sections of this book. The aim here is to make the point that differences in I–C can act as barriers to effective interpersonal communication, particularly in contexts where the outcome depends on achieving at least some mutual understanding, such as in work-related settings. For instance, there is evidence that in culturally heterogeneous work places with personnel who differ on I–C, interactions among workers, between workers and their supervisors, and between workers and their clients or customers may not always run smoothly (Bochner and Hesketh, 1994; Hesketh and Bochner, 1994). This topic will receive further elaboration, particularly in the chapter on culture training.

CONCLUDING REMARKS

Earlier a distinction was drawn between contact processes and contact structures. Although there are identifiable institutional structures whose function is to support within-society intercultural contact, at the international or between-society level very few such structures exist or, if they do, they are not very visible. Indeed, one of the reasons why sojourners experience difficulties is because they are mostly left to sink or swim on their own. Even in the business sector, where one would have thought it would be in the companies' interests to prepare their employees properly for expatriate assignments, the literature reveals that much of the pre-departure training can at best be described as perfunctory, and that ongoing, systematic during-sojourn support tends to be the exception rather than the rule (Hesketh and Bochner, 1994; Triandis, Kurowski and Gelfand, 1994). However, there is some indication that recently more companies are beginning to take cross-cultural preparation seriously (Tung, 1997).

More generally, since the first edition of this book appeared in 1986, there has been a significant increase in the attention given to both theory and practice towards improving interpersonal relationships in culturally diverse work settings. Prominent publications include an entire volume of the second edition of the *Handbook of Industrial and Organizational Psychology* (Triandis, Dunnette and Hough, 1994), and edited books such as Granrose and Oskamp's (1997) *Cross-Cultural Work Groups*, Semin and Fiedler's (1996) *Applied Social Psychology*, and Landis and Bhagat's (1996) *Handbook of Intercultural Training*.

The next chapter will start on the journey of exploring the psychology of intercultural contact, by identifying in more detail the processes that are involved. Concurrently, we will develop an integrated set of theoretical propositions that will provide the conceptual framework for the rest of the inquiry. To foreshadow that task, the model's purpose will be to account for the responses to other-culture influences. As mentioned earlier, there is overwhelming empirical evidence that interacting with culturally different individuals or functioning in unfamiliar physical and social settings is inherently stressful with outcomes ranging from mild discomfort to severe, debilitating anxiety. This finding has led many authors in the field to follow a theoretical model that concentrates on the coping responses to stress, the most general formulation of which assumes that human beings adapt to stressful life events. Included in that formulation is the notion that successful adaptation often involves the acquisition of culturally relevant competencies and skills. Most of the intervention strategies are also based on these assumptions although the actual procedures vary greatly in their emphasis and rationale. This issue will be discussed more fully later in this book.

However, it is appropriate at this stage of the development of the argument to draw attention to one issue that is sometimes overlooked in the rush to facilitate cross-cultural adaptation. Since, as we have said, a major cause of intercultural problems is the cultural distance between the persons in contact, there has been the temptation to solve the problem by reducing or eradicating the differences that separate the participants (Bochner, 1986), usually by encouraging new settlers to assimilate to their host culture. In practice this has meant abandoning those country-of-origin values and customs that differ significantly from mainstream traditions and behaviours.

Two fundamental objections can be raised in connection with this particular form of dealing with the stress of the different. The first is that it contravenes a basic, probably universal value to the effect that cultures, like species, should be preserved and not eradicated, even if in the short term assimilation may lead to a more harmonious society. But even that assumption is probably false. In any case, nowadays most people and groups strongly resist pressures to dilute their cultural identities, which is why world-wide, elected governments no longer overtly pursue assimilation policies. Furthermore, if the analogy from biology holds in the social domain (Poortinga, 1997), it would be unwise to reduce further global cultural diversity which is already under some threat from modern developments, such as commercial globalisation, the internet, and the domination of the film and television industry by a small number of western companies. A monocultural world is neither a desirable nor feasible prospect for a variety of reasons that will be discussed later in this book.

The second objection is that the eradication of differences between participants constitutes a pseudo-solution. It sidesteps the problem, which is how to achieve mutual understanding among people who differ. Making them all the same is clearly not the answer. Still, the policy of abolishing intergroup differences as a way of dealing with intergroup friction has a long and odious history, providing the basis for genocide, apartheid, ethnic cleansing, and at a more mundane level, the justification for exclusivity in clubs, schools, and controlled housing estates. Throughout this book, our approach will be to regard cultural diversity as an absolute given, as highly desirable, and probably an essential condition for the future survival of humankind. All applied interventions aimed at increasing harmony among culturally diverse individuals and groups will be based on that core idea.

CHAPTER SUMMARY

The aims of this chapter were to set the scene and to introduce the major terms, ideas, problems, and controversies in the field. We defined culture contact as the topic of the book, distinguished between various types of contact, and reviewed evidence indicating that meetings between culturally diverse people are inherently difficult. However, we also noted that most of the difficulties can be overcome. We then briefly identified the main psychological barriers to effective intercultural relations, such as the tendency to prefer to interact with similar people; the finding that the greater the cultural distance between the participants, the more difficult the interaction; the in-group bias; the effects of primary socialisation on the development of ethno-centric values and attitudes; and the differences in the relative emphasis on individual versus group or collective aspirations. We concluded by asserting that cultural heterogeneity will not disappear off the face of the globe, nor would it be desirable for that to happen. The challenge, therefore, is to under-stand and manage contact between culturally diverse people and groups in order to reduce the stresses and difficulties that are a normal aspect of such encounters, as well as to enhance the positive effects that cross-cultural encounters can bestow on the participants.

NOTE

1 Not all contemporary researchers regard individualsm–collectivism as a bipolar dimension (e.g. Kâğitçibaşi, 1994), and some have additionally made a distinction between vertical and horizontal individualism and collectivism (e.g. Singelis *et al.*, 1995). The horizontal–vertical dimension concerns itself with hierarchical versus egalitarian relationships and can be said to bear some resemblance to Hofstede's (1980) dimension of Power Distance.

2 Intercultural contact: Processes and outcomes

There are essentially four ways in which the process of intercultural contact can be described, corresponding to different approaches and emphases in the multidisciplinary literature. First, contact research may be categorised by the sorts of individuals or groups who have been studied. For instance, there exist specialist bodies of literature on tourists, foreign students, migrants, expatriate workers, and so forth. Second, it is possible to analyse the contact experience in terms of situational variables, such as purpose, time-span and type of involvement, and the relationship of these variables to particular groups of participants. We have considered both the types of cross-cultural travellers and situational dimensions of intercultural contact in the organisation of Chapters 6–10 on tourists, sojourners, immigrants and refugees. Third, the outcomes of intercultural contact may be discussed. These outcomes may be classified in terms of their impact on the participating groups or the consequences of contact can be described and categorised in relation to individuals. The analyses of micro and macro processes and outcomes are presented in an integrated fashion throughout the book. Finally, the literature on intercultural contact and change can be presented in terms of guiding theoretical frameworks. We have adopted this organisational method in Chapters 3–5, which are devoted to culture learning, stress and coping, and social identification theories, respectively. In this chapter an introduction to four perspectives on intercultural contact is followed by a discussion of intercultural adaptation and a proposed model for understanding cultural contact and change.

GROUPS IN INTERCULTURAL CONTACT

Tourists

The World Tourism Organisation (WTO) defines tourists as visitors whose length of stay exceeds 24 hours in a location away from home and whose main incentive for travel is other than financial. International tourists are short term, voluntary holiday-makers, and they constitute the largest group of cross-cultural travellers. Nearly 600 million people made international trips in 1996, most commonly as tourists, and these numbers are expected to increase over the next two decades. By 2010 the WTO's projected world-wide figures are 940 million tourists per annum (cited in Vellas and Becherel, 1995).

Despite being the largest group of cross-cultural travellers, tourists have been studied less frequently by psychologists than have sojourners, immigrants and refugees. In addition, less is known about the psychological aspects of tourism than about the demographic trends and their social, economic and cultural consequences. Nevertheless, psychology has contributed to our understanding of tourism, particularly in terms of viewing the tourist experience from the individual's perspective and assessing the influences of tourism on intercultural interactions and intergroup relations.

A significant portion of the psychological literature has concentrated on the motives of tourists. This line of research has revealed that there are a range of reasons that people travel abroad, including scenery, nature, sport and sex; however, only a minority of their motives relate to culture learning. Because the intercultural interactions involved in crossing cultures are often difficult to manage and because culture learning is not always of primary interest, many tourists opt for travel where the amount of contact with members of the host culture is limited. They choose to stay with other co-nationals in hotels and resorts where the staff speak their language and accurately anticipate their needs. They are therefore unlikely to experience any genuine or intimate intercultural contact or to have any of the pleasure and pain associated with it. Despite this insulation from members of the receiving society, tourists may still exert influence on host nationals and their indigenous culture.

Research that has considered the outcomes of intercultural contact has revealed that being a tourist can be a very stressful experience. Often the expectations that tourists have are unrealistic, and many react badly when confronted by experiences of 'culture shock'. Indeed, research has suggested that tourists experience more minor health complaints on holiday than before, and mood disturbances increase in the early stages of a vacation (Pearce, 1981).

More extensive research has been undertaken on the effects of intercultural contact between tourists and their hosts on intergroup perceptions and relations. Although many have viewed tourism as a vehicle for promoting international harmony and world peace, there is very little evidence to support this contention. Indeed, studies have demonstrated that contact per se does not improve intergroup relations, and in many cases it leads to the mutual sharpening of negative stereotypes. The nature of the tourist–host interactions, which are typically brief, superficial, and characterised by power imbalances in terms of financial and informational resources, does not bode well for congenial intergroup relations. This is particularly the case for the host nationals who often hold ambivalent attitudes toward tourists and tourism.

There is, however, a potential for improving relations between tourists and their hosts which includes sound planning and development strategies as well as the implementation of training programmes for personnel in the hospitality industry. These and other issues will be addressed in Chapter 6.

Sojourners

A sojourn is a temporary stay, and, therefore, a sojourner a temporary resident. Sojourners voluntarily go abroad for a set period of time that is usually associated with a specific assignment or contract. Thus, a volunteer might take an overseas assignment for a year or two; a business person might accept a foreign posting for between three and five years; a missionary might go abroad for a longer stint, while military personnel are often posted overseas for shorter 'tours of duty'; and international students generally remain overseas for the duration of their diplomas or degrees. In most cases sojourners expect to return home after the completion of their assignment, contract or studies. In Chapters 7 and 8 we will review the literature on international sojourners with emphasis on students and business people, respectively. For a review of the earlier literature on volunteers the reader may wish to consult the 1986 edition of *Culture Shock* (Furnham and Bochner, 1986).

International students

Since the Second World War, governments and foundations have supported a huge number of students and senior scholars, enabling these persons to spend varying lengths of time attending overseas institutions. In addition, many privately funded students have swelled the ranks of academic exchange. Foreign scholars, often a highly visible minority, constitute about 10 per cent of the student population on many campuses throughout the world. At any time there are likely to be over a million students and scholars attending institutions of higher learning abroad, and recent estimates have set the figure at about 1.3 million (Hayes, 1998; Koretz, 1998).

In the major receiving countries such as the United States, Britain, Canada, and Australia, overseas students have become part of the export industry. For instance, it is estimated that in Australia, international students, drawn mainly from the emerging middle classes in Southeast Asia, contribute about A$2 billion annually to the Australian economy. In the larger, metropolitan universities, full-fee paying overseas students can make up to 20 per cent of the student population (Bochner, 1999). In Canada in 1995, there were 72,000 foreign students, contributing C$2.3 billion and 21,000 jobs to that country's economy, while in New Zealand international education, increasing 400 per cent over the previous five years, provided NZ$530 million in foreign exchange – more than the wine and venison industries combined (Smith, 1997). World 'trade' in international education has been estimated at US $28 billion, and many universities throughout the world now derive a substantial portion of their funds from this source.

The psychological literature on international students has, to some extent, reflected the need to sustain the educational export industry, and a significant portion of the contemporary literature has dealt with the problems of international students. More recent research has also concerned itself with the dynamics of the intercultural classroom and the ways in which multicultural education can benefit both international and local students. However, as student sojourners are perhaps the best-researched group of cross-cultural travellers, there is an extensive body of work that has focused on theory testing. This includes studies of: friendship networks and skills acquisition in international students; intergroup perceptions and relations; the prediction of psychological, sociocultural and academic adaptation; fluctuations in cross-cultural adaptation over time; and the process of re-entry to home culture. These topics will be reviewed in Chapter 7.

International business people

While it is difficult to obtain reliable figures on international business relocations, it is apparently the case that the number of business people working abroad is on the increase. Data from 1978 to 1990 record, for instance, a 700 per cent increase in British business people's visits to Japan, a 200 per cent increase to America, and a 100 per cent increase to the Caribbean. Although short term assignments of under one year are becoming more common, having risen to about 16 per cent of overseas postings, the more conventional three to five year contracts are still considered a necessity to ensure effective global operations. Recent data from a survey of United States-based companies estimated that there are about 350,000 overseas assignments, and these numbers are expected to grow in the next few years (Solomon, 1999).

Many big companies are now multinationals, and it is often thought desirable that senior managers should have the experience of managing a foreign subsidiary. It is not uncommon for business people, like diplomats, missionaries and the military, to take their entire family abroad, and they often find that their loyalties are divided among their organisation, their personal career and their family responsibilities. Unfortunately, preparation for employees and their families before overseas relocation is haphazard at best, and the significance of family concerns is commonly underestimated, despite evidence which suggests that spousal dissatisfaction is one of the most common reasons for early repatriation. Research on expatriate families, however, is currently increasing and now includes issues pertaining to women in the labour force as well as dual-career couples.

Of particular interest to multinational organisations is the work performance of expatriate executives, and unlike most other groups of cross-cultural travellers, there exist accessible, objective data to determine expatriate adaptation. Conceptual models of expatriate adjustment have included both work and non-work domains, and a segment of the research has concerned itself with the prediction of cross-cultural adaptation by factors such as predeparture training, motivation, cultural distance, personality, and interactions with host nationals. Within the organisation special attention has also been paid to differences in cross-cultural values and their implications for effective leadership and team-building. Culture learning is considered essential for successful overseas postings, and this has been facilitated by on-site mentoring as well as more formal training packages (see Chapter 11). Both have been shown to diminish the likelihood of premature return.

Like the empirical literature on student sojourners, research on international business people has a very practical component to it, and one topic that has received special attention is the repatriation process. Research has considered changes in the individual and the organisation in addition to how these changes might contribute to readjustment difficulties and dissatisfaction in expatriate employees. This and other topics relevant to expatriate adjustment are discussed in Chapter 8.

Immigrants

World-wide immigration figures are difficult to verify, but it has been estimated that over 100 million people live outside their country of origin (Russel and Teitlebaum, 1992). The United States and Canada alone accept over one million immigrants a year (Citizenship and Immigration Canada, 1999; United States Immigration and Naturalization Service, 1999). Most agree, however, that there has been a massive swell in international migration in the twentieth century and that this will continue to increase over time.

Migrants include those individuals who voluntarily relocate for long term resettlement. They are generally 'pulled' toward a new country by social, economic and political forces. The majority of immigrants are strongly motivated by economic factors and usually move from poorer to richer countries. A smaller number, however, choose to migrate for political, religious or cultural reasons. Nevertheless, migration is not simply an issue of choice for the migrant. Receiving countries have very different and strict criteria for the admission of migrants. Because there are often enormous barriers that must be overcome in the process of migration, aspiring immigrants sometimes resort to illicit means, and the number of illegal entrants is a serious concern for some countries.

Migrants, like sojourners, are an extremely diverse group. There are wide variations in the relative cultural distance between society of origin and society of settlement across immigrant groups. In addition, the amount of contact that immigrants have with other cultural groups, particularly members of the host society, may vary enormously. There is all the difference in the world between a white English speaking South African migrating to Australia and a South Indian or Korean doing the same thing.

Because of interest and research in the topic of migration and mental health dating back over 100 years, there is a rich literature on the experience of migrants. There are moving personal testimonies, mental health hospital admission figures, survey research, self-help group reports and the writings of clinicians interested in helping migrants cope with cross-cultural transition. As we shall see, a great deal is known about the factors which seem to be associated with adaptation and acculturation. The costs and benefits of immigration for cross-cultural travellers and members of the receiving society have meant that this has become a significant applied area of research. As a result, there are a number of contemporary theories that attempt to describe and explain the causes, manifestations, and consequences of 'culture shock' in immigrants.

More recent research has also considered the acculturation process in relation to changes in ethnocultural identity and intergroup perceptions. In addition, immigrants, compared with other groups of cross-cultural travellers, have been more frequently studied over generations. These intergenerational studies can provide insight into salient changes in a specific immigrant group as it evolves into a more established ethnocultural community over time. These issues are discussed in greater detail in Chapter 9.

Refugees

Refugees, as a group, have also played a significant role in the global growth of international migration. The number of refugees has steadily increased over the last 50 years, has approximately doubled between 1980 and 1990, and has recently reached an all time high of 19 million people (Leopold and Harrell-Bond, 1994; UNHCR, 1993). World-wide figures indicate that Africa, the Middle East and South Asia shelter over 90 per cent of the world's refugees; surprisingly, Europe has typically resettled only about 4 per cent of the refugee population, and North America has assumed responsibility for even less (USCR, 1992) although these figures are beginning to rise (UNHCR, 1998). On the country level Croatia has provided shelter and support for approximately 400,000 refugees who account for more than 10 per cent of its total population (Ajdukovic and Ajdukovic, 1993). Similar refugee-to-population ratios are found in countries such as Malawi, Belize, and Armenia (UNHCR, 1993).

What are the origins of these refugees? United Nations figures for 1991–92 indicate a massive movement of refugees, over half a million respectively from Liberia, Somalia, Mozambique, Ethiopia, and Afghanistan (UNHCR, 1993). More recent figures cite Afghanistan, Rwanda, and Bosnia-Herzegovina as the greatest sources of refugees with each displacing over one million persons (UNHCR, 1996), and in the last two years Iraq, Burundi, and Sierra Leone have joined these ranks (UNHCR, 1998).

While these figures may summarise refugee movements within a single year, they do not describe the dramatic and devastating effects of genocide, war and famine on a country and its people over time. In Vietnam, for example, it has been estimated that 900,000 individuals were wounded, 250,000 were killed, and over 100,000 were incarcerated in re-education camps during the war; in addition, 6–10 million people were resettled prior to 1975 (Wiesner, 1988). More recently in El Salvador there have been an estimated 80,000 deaths; up to 40 per cent of the population have been relocated, and 20 per cent of the 5.2 million population have left the country.

While refugees are faced with many of the same issues and concerns of other cross-cultural travellers, they also differ from sojourners and immigrants in several important ways. On the most fundamental level refugees have generally been exposed to premigration trauma including civil war, genocide, famine, imprisonment and torture. Their relocation is involuntary as they are unwillingly displaced from their home countries and 'pushed' into alien environments. This process differs significantly from the experiences of sojourners and migrants who voluntarily relocate, either temporarily or more permanently, because they are drawn or 'pulled' towards the countries of resettlement.

Researchers have been aware of these differences, and the empirical literature has reflected an emphasis on traumatic premigration factors and their subsequent influences on refugee adaptation problems. Much of this research has been conducted by psychiatrists and has a decidedly clinical flavour, describing diagnoses and prognoses in refugee populations. This is not surprising as a significant portion of this research, as well as many intervention projects, have been sponsored by international agencies such as the World Federation of Mental Health (Mollica *et al.*, 1989). National government departments and institutes with interests in health-related matters have also provided support. Examples have included the Canadian Health and Welfare Department (Beiser and Fleming, 1986) and the National Institute of Mental Health in the United States (Rumbaut, 1985).

In addition to the negative consequences precipitated by traumatic premigration stressors, researchers have also noted that refugees, compared with immigrants and sojourners, possess more limited resources for cross-cultural transition and adaptation. Not only do they generally lack tangible financial assets but, in many cases, they also have limited educational and linguistic resources that could assist in adapting to new and culturally different environments. This is particularly noticeable in cases where refugees from rural areas of Asia and Africa are resettled in urban centres in western industrialised nations.

Despite these obvious disadvantages, an emerging body of research has arrived at a somewhat more optimistic conclusion about the stress and coping processes that occur during refugee displacement and resettlement. Recent studies have examined a range of positive personal and historical influences on adaptation outcomes, and researchers have considered broader issues pertaining to culture and identity, values and generational changes. The theories and research on refugee populations are discussed in greater detail in Chapter 10.

DIMENSIONS OF INTERCULTURAL CONTACT

Variables that relate to the personal psychology of individuals in culture contact include: on whose territory the interactions take place (home, foreign, or joint); the time-span of the interaction; its purpose; the type of involvement; the frequency of contact; the degree of intimacy; relative status and power; the numerical balance; and the distinguishing characteristics of the participants. The framework is presented in detail in Table 2.1.

This analysis suggests that within-society cross-cultural interactions and between-society sojourner contacts differ in several important aspects. Permanent members of multicultural societies or those intending to become permanent (such as immigrants) meet on territories that are joint and often include institutional settings such as schools, work places, amusement centres, and legal and administrative bodies. The commitment of the new-comers should be higher because it is long term, and there will be frequent contacts with dissimilar persons, including host members as well as other migrant groups. However, whether these relations attain intimacy will depend on a range of other variables, such as the relative status, distribution, and size of the participating groups.

Table 2.1 Main dimensions of cultural contact

Types of cross-cultural contact and examples	Between members of the same society		Between members of different societies	
Contact variables	Type	Example	Type	Example
Time-span	Long term	Subcultures in multicultural societies	Short term Medium term	Tourists Overseas students
			Long term	Immigrants
Purpose	Make a life in	Subcultures	Make a life in Study in	Immigrants Overseas students
			Make a profit Recreate	Traders Tourists
Type of involvement	Participate in society	Subcultures	Participate Exploit Contribute Observe Convert Serve as a link	Immigrants Traders Experts Tourists Missionaries Diplomats
Summary concept	Majority Minority	White and black Americans	Host sojourners	Overseas students

Source: S. Bochner (1982). *Cultures in contact: Studies in cross-cultural interaction.* Oxford: Pergamon.

The analysis of between-society contacts reveals a somewhat different set of dynamics. These interactions are all affected by the fundamental distinction between the social role of host and the social role of visitor. The expectations and occasionally the dispensations that are associated with the status of visitor/stranger have long been of interest to sociologists (e.g. Heiss and Nash, 1967; Nash and Wolfe, 1957; Rose and Felton, 1955; Schild, 1962). In the present context the main characteristics relate to those individuals having 'come later', in contrast to the established 'owners' of the territory. Thus, the interactions will seldom take place on joint territory but occur instead on home or foreign ground depending on whether the perspective is that of the host or of the visitor. With the exception of immigrants and possibly refugees, the expectation is that the visitors will at some stage return to their countries of origin; hence, their commitment to the host country will be low.

OUTCOMES OF CONTACT

When culturally disparate groups come into contact with each other, they tend to have an impact on each other's social structures, institutional arrangements, political processes, and value systems. The nature and extent of these changes will depend on the conditions under which the contact occurs (e.g. whether peaceful or in conquest), the relative power of the interacting groups, and a wide range of other variables. Likewise, the actual accommodation between the groups can take a great variety of forms. In addition, the individuals caught up in the contact also have an impact on each other.

This complex state of affairs prompted Bochner (1982) to develop a set of principles that can be used to classify all of the empirically observed outcomes of cultural contact within a single overall framework. The principles were developed so that they would have maximum generality. Thus the same principles can be used to categorise contact at the group level, as well as to describe the psychological reactions of individuals caught up in cross-cultural contact. Finally, the framework can be applied to contact between different groups in the same society, as well as to contact between different societies. Table 2.2 presents this schema as it applies at the group level, and Table 2.3 sets out the various categories of responses that exhaust the varieties of individual reactions to contact. A brief discussion of these principles and their applications now follows.

Group outcomes

A historical overview of the various outcomes of intergroup contact shows that they can be classified into four, more or less, mutually exclusive categories. These are genocide, assimilation, segregation, and integration (Bochner, 1979, 1982).

Table 2.2 Outcomes of cultural contact at the group level

Contact outcomes	Between groups in the same society Examples	Between different societies Examples
Genocide of original inhabitants by outsiders	—	Australian Aborigines in Tasmania American Indians
Genocide of newcomers by insiders	Nazi Germany	—
Assimilation of out-groups by in-group	Migrants in 'melting pot' societies	Diffusion of Western innovations 'Cocacolonisation'
Segregation of out-groups by in-group	USA before Second World War South Africa Imperial India	White Australia immigration policy
Self-segregation of out-group	Tribal lands Enclaves in Alaska, the US South-west, Australian Centre	East Germany during Cold War Mainland China during Cultural Revolution
Integration	Emerging pluralistic societies such as Australia, New Zealand, Hawaii	Emerging transnational institutions such as the United Nations, the East–West Centre and 'third cultures'

Source: S. Bochner (1982). *Cultures in contact: Studies in cross-cultural interaction.* Oxford: Pergamon.

Genocide

There are many recorded instances in ancient as well as recent history where one group, usually in the majority or possessing superior technological resources, has killed or attempted to kill all members of another group with whom they came into contact. There can be nothing more terrifying than belonging to an ethnic group being systematically exterminated. The Nazi Holocaust is recalled as the most dramatic and devastating example of twentieth century genocide, but more recent in activities in Bosnia have been a cause for international concern. The refugee movements discussed in Chapter 10 are often a result of attempted genocide, and the effects of premigration trauma are intense and long lasting.

Assimilation

Assimilation is the term used to describe the 'swallowing up' of one culture by another. It was often the approach of colonial powers, taking the form of imposing their cultural values and etiquette on the countries they had conquered. Technically, assimilation refers to the process whereby a group or a whole society gradually adopt, or are forced into adopting, the customs, values, lifestyles and language of a more dominant culture. This can be observed both within societies as well as internationally. Until quite recently, many countries adopted a deliberate policy of assimilation with respect to existing minority groups or newcomers such as immigrants (Bochner, 1999).

At the international level, the post-war years have seen an irreversible push towards global homogeneity in cultural manifestations (Bochner, 1979; Tung, 1997). The dominant influences have come from the West, leading Lambert (1966: 170) to refer to this process as 'cocacolonisation'. The overall effect is that differences between cultures have become eroded, the diversity of life-styles has been reduced, and many traditional patterns have disappeared for good. It is not usually acknowledged that assimilation policies and practices may be racist, implying as they do that the dominant culture is superior in relation to the minority, or 'lower status', group it is swamping. Sometimes, of course, these attitudes are made explicit, e.g. when the culture being absorbed is described as being backward, primitive and overdue to join the twentieth century, a comment made by Inkeles (1975: 323) in relation to the desirability of transferring Western technology to the underdeveloped regions of the world.

Segregation

Segregation refers to a deliberate policy of separate development. Since such policies are usually unsuccessful in practice, their main value in the present context lies in shedding light on the psychology of those advocating such a course. It is thus interesting to note that at the intrasocietal level, the impetus for segregation can come either from the dominant majority seeking the exclusion of certain minority groups from mainstream positions, institutions, and territories, or from the minority groups themselves actively demanding separate states, cultural enclaves, special schools, land tenure based on ethnic background, territorial reserves, sanctions against intermarriage, and so forth. Without doubt, the most sophisticated and notorious instance of seg-regation in modern times has been the policy of apartheid practised by South Africa for nearly 50 years (1948–94). Although other countries have pursued policies of separate development, none have had the sort of legislative backing that made South Africa synonymous with racist segregation.

Similarly, protectionist policies that are aimed at isolating societies from each other are sometimes pursued at the international level. Thus nations so inclined will develop practices designed to keep unwanted people, information and influences out of their countries. They may also place restrictions on their own citizens' travel abroad in order to prevent them from becoming contaminated by foreign ideas.

Although social and ethnic segregation may be achieved, it is becoming increasingly difficult to segregate knowledge, as the world becomes more interdependent and as the flow of information through global radio, satellite, internet and television systems brings the various peoples of the world into almost instant communication with one another. However, the *attitude* towards segregation – that is, the idea, however empirically untenable, that segregation is desirable and possible – has important consequences for cross-cultural relations. As was mentioned earlier, genocide, assimilation and segregation are pseudo-solutions for the problems associated with cross-cultural contact.

Integration

Cross-cultural relations, as a problem to be solved, can only be tackled when it is explicitly acknowledged that human groups differ in their respective cultural identities, that they have a right to maintain their idiosyncratic features if they so wish, and that this principle applies to diversity both within and between societies. But if groups do and should be allowed to differ, what are the consequences of this cultural diversity? Does it necessarily follow that the greater the cultural diversity (whether within or between societies), the greater the resulting friction between them? Or is there no necessary connection between diversity and intergroup harmony? Stated in this way, the issue now becomes an empirical one and also, of course, a theoretical one in the sense of seeking explanations for the observations. If we start with the premise that at least in principle cultural diversity does not inevitably lead to conflict, then this opens the way to research and theorising about the contact conditions that either enhance or impede cross-cultural understanding. Several chapters of this book directly or indirectly deal with this issue.

The contact model that provides a useful conceptual framework for such an approach draws on the principle of integration to describe the structure of culturally pluralistic societies. The term 'integration' is sometimes erroneously used as interchangeable with 'assimilation', but it needs to be emphasised that the two terms have quite different meanings and describe totally different processes. Integration refers to the accommodation that comes about when different groups maintain their respective core cultural identities while at the same time merging into a superordinate group in other, equally important respects.

Individual outcomes

In the preceding sections we considered the outcomes of intergroup contact from a sociological perspective, particularly the varieties of changes in group structure and norms that may occur during and after contact. Next we will briefly describe the various alternative ways in which individuals respond to intercultural contact. Thus the analysis now shifts to the psychology of the individual caught up in a cross-cultural situation, the kinds of responses that individuals have been observed to make and the psychological effect of these different forms of accommodation on the individual as well as on the person's wider society. Four types of response styles describe most of the possibilities, though there may be exceptions, and in the present discussion these styles will be referred to as 'passing', chauvinist, marginal, and mediating.

One dependent variable that we regard as central in any study of second-culture influences is the changes that may occur in people's ethnic or cultural identities. More precisely, the basic idea is that individuals exposed to hetero-geneous cultural influences, whether through birth or circumstances, can either become or resist becoming multicultural. Translated into the sorts of empirical questions that have been investigated in this area, we arrive at the four response styles referred to above: (1) often individuals, particularly in contact situations in which the second culture has higher status, may reject the original culture and adopt the new culture, an effect that is sometimes referred to as 'passing' (Stonequist, 1937); (2) occasionally, though, after coming into contact with a second culture, individuals will reject those influ-ences as alien, retreat back into the culture of origin and become militant nationalists and chauvinists (Tajfel and Dawson, 1965); (3) a third response, also quite common, is for individuals to vacillate between their two cultures, feeling at home in neither, an effect that has been referred to as the 'marginal syndrome' (Park, 1928); (4) finally, some persons seem to be able to synthesise their various cultural identities, the equivalent of integration at the personal level, and acquire genuine bicultural or multicultural personalities. Such individuals are relatively rare, and Bochner (1982) has referred to them as 'mediating persons'.

Before leaving this topic, we should note that other writers have also grap-pled with the problem of how to depict the effects of exposure to new and unfamiliar cultural influences. For instance, Berry's model (Berry, 1990, 1994a, 1997) distinguishes between changes that can occur either at the group or at the individual level; however, his analysis of group effects is broader and has a different emphasis from the framework presented in Table 2.2. By way of comparison, Berry is relatively less concerned with functional issues, such as how different subgroups relate to each other, the changes in group norms, and their effects on intergroup behaviour, while relatively more interested in tracing the changes that occur in the ecology of the society that provides the setting for the contact, particularly cultural, social and institutional factors that influence and interact with the behaviours of individual members of the society. At the level of the individual, for Berry, as in our model, accultur-ation signifies changes in the person's behaviour, attitudes and cognitions. And he also classifies the responses into four categories very similar to ours: Integration, Assimilation, Separation, and Marginalisation.

Where Berry has advanced matters is by suggesting an empirical method that can be used to place individuals into these categories. He achieves this by asking people to respond to questions about two issues: (1) 'Is it considered to be of value to maintain one's cultural identity and characteristics?'; and (2) 'Is it considered to be of value to maintain relationships with the larger society?' (Berry, 1997). If respondents say 'Yes' to both questions, they are integrating. If they answer 'No' to both questions, they are marginalised. If they answer 'Yes' to issue 1 and 'No' to issue 2, they are placed in the separation category. And if they answer 'No' to issue 1 and 'Yes' to issue 2, they are in the process of assimilating. In our scheme as set out in Table 2.2 we ascribed the underlying psychological dynamics to the relative salience of the various reference groups exerting their influences on persons in contact. Berry's approach provides an empirical procedure for ascertaining the differential pull of these issues.

Finally, the effects of culture contact can also be classified in terms of changes in the person's self-concept or ethnic identity, an approach that draws its theoretical sustenance from the growing social identity literature (e.g. Brewer, 1993; Erez and Earley, 1993; Ferdman, 1995; Keefe, 1992). In Bochner's research an adaptation of the Kuhn and McPartland (1954) method has been used to establish empirically people's ethnic identity. The method asks people who they are, by getting respondents to complete 10

Table 2.3 Outcomes of cultural contact at the individual level: Psychological responses to 'second culture' influences

Response	Type	Multiple-group membership affiliation	Effect on individual	Effect on society
Reject culture of origin, embrace second culture	'Passing'	Culture I norms lose salience Culture II norms become salient	Loss of ethnic identity Self-denigration	Assimilation Cultural erosion
Reject second culture, exaggerate first culture	Chauvinistic	Culture I norms increase in salience Culture II norms decrease in salience	Nationalism Racism	Intergroup friction
Vacillate between the two cultures	Marginal	Norms of both cultures salient but perceived as mutually incompatible	Conflict Identity confusion Over-compensation	Reform Social change
Synthesise both cultures	Mediating	Norms of both cultures salient and perceived as capable of being integrated	Personal growth	Intergroup harmony Pluralistic societies Cultural preservation

Source: S. Bochner (1982). *Cultures in contact: Studies in cross-cultural interaction*. Oxford: Pergamon.

open-ended questions beginning with the phrase 'I am . . .' The responses can be coded and categorised in a variety of ways (Bond and Cheung, 1983; Cousins, 1989; Trafimow, Triandis and Goto, 1991), including in terms of ethnic descriptors. Several studies by Bochner (Bochner, 1976, 1981, 1994; Bochner and Perks, 1971) have found that sojourners and immigrants can be classified in terms of whether they describe themselves primarily as belonging to the culture of origin (corresponding to separatism); the host culture (corresponding to 'passing' or assimilation); neither culture (possibly corresponding to a marginal state); or having a bicultural, hyphenated self (corresponding to integration).

A good deal of research has been conducted on the psychological consequences of the four different resolutions to contact pressure. Right from the early days, when Park (1928) and Stonequist (1937) introduced the construct of marginality to the literature, it has been regarded as having adverse effects on the person's well-being. For instance, one of the world's most famous marginal men, J. Nehru, wrote in his autobiography: 'I have become a queer mixture of the East and the West, out of place everywhere, at home nowhere. I am a stranger and alien in the West. I cannot be of it. But in my own country also, sometimes, I have an exile's feeling' (Nehru, 1936: 596).

Separation or exaggerated chauvinism, as we have called it, can also lead to unhappiness and distress, a classic account being a collection of essays by foreign students in Britain aptly called *Disappointed Guests* (Tajfel and Dawson, 1965). The strategy most likely to produce health and well-being is integration (Sam and Berry, 1995; Schmitz, 1992). A fuller account of both the measurement issues involved and the range and categories of outcomes studied will be provided in Chapter 5.

In the next sections we will consider historical and theoretical approaches to 'culture shock' and offer a comprehensive model of culture contact, influenced by current research and theorising in the areas of social identity, culture learning, and stress, coping and adaptation.

THEORETICAL PERSPECTIVES ON INTERCULTURAL CONTACT

Historical approaches

Some of the earliest work relating to intercultural contact arose in the context of research on migration and mental health. Its origins were perhaps more sociopolitical than psychological and can be traced back to the use of early twentieth century census records in the United States. Statistics based on data collected in 1903 from state mental institutions indicated that immigrants constituted 70 per cent of hospitalised patients despite representing only 20 per cent of the population at large. These findings had significant social, economic and political consequences at the time and were subsequently used to support the establishment of immigration screening programmes in the United States (Furnham and Bochner, 1986).

Although the incidence of migrant institutionalisation was undoubtedly inflated in census data due to the failure to control a range of confounding variables (Robertson, 1903), later, more sophisticated epidemiological investigations in the United States also suggested that migrants were over-represented in hospital admissions (Ødegaard, 1932). This stimulated an increase in systematic comparative studies of immigrants and native-borns (e.g. Malzberg, 1936, 1940; Tietze, Lemkau and Cooper, 1942), a line of research that continued for more than three decades and expanded to the international arena. Investigations in the United Kingdom, Australia, Canada, Germany and South Africa consistently supported the association between migration and psychiatric morbidity (e.g. Hemsi, 1967; Murphy, 1973; Stoller and Krupinski, 1973).

The comparative studies cited above, like the majority of research on mental health and migration undertaken during the early to mid-1970s, shared at least three common characteristics. First, the studies tended to be large-scale epidemiological investigations that concentrated on admissions to mental hospitals. Inevitably, the research was very clinically oriented, relied upon medical models, and dealt with the more serious and extreme forms of psychological dysfunction. Second, although there was considerable variation in hospital admission rates across migrant groups, the research was based on the implicit assumption that migration and mental illness are inextricably linked. Third, it was widely held that the association between migration and psychopathology could be adequately accounted for by two reciprocal theories. The first argued that psychiatric morbidity was associated with predispositional factors that precipitate selective migration, i.e. that people who are dysfunctional are more likely to emigrate. The second theory maintained that psychopathology was a probable consequence of the migration experience.

As research on migration and mental health progressed into the 1980s, a number of investigators began to question the uniformly high reported incidence of psychiatric morbidity in immigrants. Indeed, studies began to emerge that documented lower rates of institutionalisation in selected migrant samples (e.g. Cochrane, 1977; Wong and Cochrane, 1989). At the same time researchers began to shift their data bases from archival records on hospitalisation and the diagnosis of psychotic disorders to community surveys of psychological distress, including anxiety, depression, and psychosomatic complaints. The outcomes of these investigations proved to be more variable. Many studies reported no significant differences between migrants and native-borns (e.g. Brewin, 1980; Kim, 1984) and, in contrast to most earlier investigations, some found even lower levels of symptomatology in the migrant groups (e.g. Lasry, 1977). One consequence of this newer wave of critical research was for investigators to progress from asking why migrants have higher rates of psychological disorders to considering in which circumstances the rates differ (Murphy, 1977). More challenging questions, a gradual shift in emphasis from severe psychopathology to more moderate forms of psychological distress, and greater diversity in methods of data collection paved the way for the emergence of new theoretical perspectives on migration and mental health. This work on stress, coping and adaptation is described later in this chapter and will be elaborated more fully in Chapter 4. Changes in research emphases also led investigators to go beyond mental health concerns and to consider other issues relating to migration including changing values, identity, and acculturation strategies. These areas of research are also introduced later in this chapter and will be discussed in more detail in reference to social identification theories in Chapter 5.

While studies on mental health and migration were increasing and diversifying, a second strand of intercultural research began to emerge in the field of international education. As foreign exchange programmes gained momentum in the 1950s, research activities were directed towards the description and analysis of the social and psychological problems experienced by overseas students. Undoubtedly the most important studies of this kind were those supported by the Social Science Research Council and published by the University of Minnesota Press. These studies generally inquired into the adjustment of student sojourners in the United States (Bennett, Passin and McKnight, 1958; Lambert and Bressler, 1956; Morris, 1960; Scott, 1956; Selltiz *et al.*, 1963; Sewell and Davidsen, 1961). Research with similar objectives began to appear in Britain about the same time (e.g. Carey, 1956; Singh, 1963; Tajfel and Dawson, 1965).

Though lacking a strong theoretical base, the early accounts of student adjustment precipitated a veritable flood of research reports. For example, an annotated bibliography compiled by Parker (1965) contained 915 entries, and a selected bibliography by Shields (1968) listed 495 items. The problem with studies of this era, however, was that many of them were atheoretical and used what Brislin and Baumgardner (1971) have called 'samples of convenience' rather than properly constituted representative groups of participants. The preferred methodology was to administer a questionnaire that included a variety of items about the respondents' adjustment problems and attitudes to the host country. Control groups were notable by their absence, and very few of these studies included a host group sample. Consequently, this literature is difficult to interpret and summarise; studies lacked rigour in their designs, and investigations were not usually theory-driven.

Soon recognisable efforts to bring order to this chaotic field began to emerge with the development of theoretical models capable of guiding research and accounting for the findings in a systematic, integrated way. The problem, however, was that many of the theories that were proposed had a rather low level of conceptual sophistication, tending to be more descriptive than explanatory. These early theories of sojourner adjustment concentrated on the noxious aspects of cross-cultural contact. They were preceded and strongly influenced by Stonequist's (1937) *The Marginal Man* which drew on the previous work of Park (1928) and highlighted the problems encountered by persons caught between two cultural systems. They were further reinforced by the migration and mental health literature reviewed earlier, which linked immigration status to psychiatric morbidity, and were additionally comple-mented by evolving psychoanalytic perspectives that emphasised loss, mourn-ing and the anxious, depressive and hostile features of the sojourn experience (Garza-Guerrero, 1974). All in all, the early theories applied to the study of international students were clinically oriented and strongly related to medical models of sojourner adjustment (e.g. Coelho, 1958; Deutsch and Won, 1963; Du Bois, 1956; Gullahorn and Gullahorn, 1963; Jacobson, 1963; Lysgaard, 1955; Selltiz and Cook, 1962; Sewell, Morris and Davidsen, 1954).

Despite these limitations, a positive outcome of these evolving theories was to draw attention to the dynamic nature of the cross-cultural sojourn. This emphasis on process precipitated the gradual movement away from the pre-vailing clinical model with its focus on the negative features of the transition experience and its view of 'culture shock' as a medical problem. In addition, the implicit assumptions that any failures on the part of the sojourner were due to the person's inability to cope or a weakness in character and that the appropriate 'treatment' was counselling and therapy came to be more critically scrutinised and largely rejected (Bochner, 1986).

In the 1980s, a different view of the sojourn was emerging. It was driven by two core propositions. First, it was postulated that the most appropriate model for cross-cultural exposure was a learning experience. The implication of this was that the appropriate intervention was not therapy for the culture traveller, but preparation, orientation, and the acquisition of culturally rele-vant social skills (Bochner, 1982, 1986; Furnham and Bochner, 1982; Klineberg, 1982). The second idea was to consider seriously the view that the sojourn is an ongoing, dynamic experience, not just for the sojourner, but also for members of the host culture.

Shifting emphases in sojourner research laid the foundation for the culture learning approach which will be discussed in greater detail in the following chapter. This approach, along with grief, fatalism, selective migration, value differences, social support networks, and negative life events were offered as competing theoretical frameworks for the analysis of intercultural contact and change in the 1986 edition of *Culture Shock*. Although an impressive array of theories was discussed in that volume, at that time none appeared clearly to dominate or synthesise the field. In fact, after surveying hundreds of empirical investigations of 'culture shock', Furnham and Bochner (1986: 61) concluded that 'there are no grand – or even mini – theories guiding research in this general area' .

Contemporary approaches

In 1986 Furnham and Bochner maintained that the study of 'culture shock' lacked guidance from sound psychological theory. How much have things changed in the last 15 years? Certainly, the volume of empirical research on intercultural contact has significantly increased. Studies of sojourners, refugees, immigrants, expatriate workers and tourists have proliferated over the last two decades. The scope, quality and orientation of empirical investigations have remained varied; however, two specific theoretical approaches have become more firmly established and widely recognised as guiding forces in the field. The first is the culture learning approach that has been more systematically developed over the last 20 years and convincingly articulated in connection with intercultural research and training. The second is linked to psychological models of stress and coping as applied to the study of cross-cultural transition and adaptation.

The culture learning approach has its roots in social and experimental psychology and has been strongly influenced by Argyle's (1969) work on social skills and interpersonal behaviours, which implies that cross-cultural problems arise because sojourners, immigrants or refugees have difficulties managing everyday social encounters. Adaptation, therefore, comes in the form of learning the culture-specific skills that are required to negotiate the new cultural milieu (Bochner, 1972, 1986). Researchers who have adopted a culture learning approach to intercultural contact and change have emphasised the significance of culture-specific variables in the adaptation process. These have included general knowledge about a new culture (Pruitt, 1978; Ward and Searle, 1991), length of residence in the host culture (Ward *et al.*, 1998), language or communication competence (Furnham, 1993), quantity and quality of contact with host nationals (Bochner, 1982), friendship networks (Bochner, McLeod and Lin, 1977), previous experience abroad (Klineberg and Hull, 1979), cultural distance (Furnham, 1983; Furnham and Bochner, 1982; Ward and Kennedy, 1993a,b), cultural identity (Ward and Searle, 1991), acculturation modes (Ward and Kennedy, 1994), temporary versus permanent residence in a new country (Ward and Kennedy, 1993c), and cross-cultural training (Brislin, Landis and Brandt, 1983; Deshpande and Viswesvaran, 1992). Through the 1970s and 1980s and into the 1990s Furnham and Bochner have remained strong advocates of the culture learning perspective as set out in the first edition of *Culture Shock* and as updated in Chapter 3 of this volume.

In contrast to the culture learning perspective, the stress and coping approach conceptualises cross-cultural transition as a series of stress-provoking life changes that draw on adjustive resources and require coping responses. This approach has been strongly influenced by Lazarus and Folkman's (1984) work on stress, appraisal and coping, as well as earlier theory and research on life events (Holmes and Rahe, 1967). The analytical framework is broad and incorporates both characteristics of the individual and characteristics of the situation that may facilitate or impede adjustment to a new cultural milieu. Accordingly, researchers seeking to identify the factors that affect cross-cultural adjustment have examined many of the same variables as those who investigate stress and coping in other domains. These include life changes (Lin, Tazuma and Masuda, 1979), personality factors, such as locus of control, extraversion and tolerance of ambiguity (Cort and King, 1979; Ward and Chang, 1997; Ward and Kennedy, 1992), cognitive appraisals of change (Chataway and Berry, 1989), coping styles (Shisana and Celentano, 1987; Ward, Leong and Kennedy, 1998), and social support (Adelman, 1988) along with related constructs such as loneliness (Neto, 1995; Stone Feinstein and Ward, 1990), homesickness (Pruitt, 1978), marital satisfaction (Naidoo, 1985) and quality of relationships with both home and host nationals (Furnham and Alibhai, 1985). Premigration stressors (Tran, 1993) and personal and demographic characteristics such as gender, ethnicity and employment status (Chung and Kagawa-Singer, 1993; MacCarthy and Craissati, 1989; Nwadiora and McAdoo, 1996) have also been studied. With respect to more culture-specific variables, cultural distance and acculturation status have been considered in sojourner, immigrant and refugee populations (Babiker, Cox and Miller, 1980; Berry and Kim, 1988). There have also been attempts, inspired by the Social Readjustment Rating Scale (Holmes and Rahe, 1967), to quantify the amount of stress experienced and the readjustment required during cross-cultural transitions (Spradley and Phillips, 1972). Theoretical and empirical aspects of the stress and coping model are elaborated in Chapter 4.

At first glance the stress and coping approach may appear to resemble the earlier medical or clinical models of cross-cultural transition and adaptation. There are, however, some major differences between these perspectives. First, unlike the medical model which assumes an inevitable pathological reaction to intercultural contact, the stress and coping approach, though acknowledging that transition and change are stressful events, places a greater emphasis on the coping process and successful adaptation to a new environment. Second, stress and coping approaches are broader than clinical perspectives, as they incorporate the social aspects of the adjustment experience. Attention is directed beyond the individuals in transition to their wider sociocultural environment. Successful adaptation may be achieved in a variety of ways; it is not confined to the one way flow of 'adjusting' an individual to a difficult or stressful situation. Similarly, failures of adaptation may be dependent on a range of factors and are not solely contingent upon person-related variables, as implied by the clinical approaches to 'culture shock'. This more comprehensive view of cross-cultural transition is exemplified in John Berry's influential work on acculturation and acculturative stress (Berry, 1997; Berry and Annis, 1974).

Although the culture learning and stress and coping approaches have dominated contemporary work on 'culture shock', particularly with reference to cross-cultural adjustment, social identification theories have also exerted some influence over the field. Two major conceptual frameworks have emerged from the broader literature on self and identity, and these have been applied to the study of intercultural contact and change. One line of investigation, broadly consistent with personality theory and research, has highlighted aspects of ethnic or cultural identity, and, as such, is linked to studies concerning the definition and measurement of acculturation (e.g. Cuéllar, Harris and Jasso, 1980; Hocoy, 1996). This approach has generally viewed acculturation as a state, rather than a process, and is concerned with measuring the construct at a single point in time and identifying its relevant predictors, correlates and consequences in cross-sectional studies. The second major line of inquiry reflects stronger influences from social psychology and has highlighted the significance of intergroup perceptions and relations. This line of research frequently examines social interactions between members of the host community and various sojourner or immigrant groups and interprets intergroup relations within the context of Social Identity Theory (e.g. Kosmitzki, 1996; Moghaddam, Taylor and Lalonde, 1987; Ostrowska and Bochenska, 1996).

The social identification theories are largely cognitive in flavour and share some common features with scattered pieces of cognitive-based research that have pointed to the significance of attitudes, values (Chang, 1973; Furnham and Li, 1993), expectations (Bochner, Lin and McLeod, 1980; Weissman and Furnham, 1987) and attributions (Brislin, 1981) during cross-cultural transitions and intercultural encounters. There is also related work that has emerged from communication theory and research. Gudykunst and Hammer's (1988) theorising on uncertainty avoidance, for example, similarly reflects a cognitive perspective but also incorporates salient themes found in both the stress and coping and culture learning approaches. Highlighting change, strangeness and unfamiliarity as significant features of the intercultural experience, the researchers have argued that the major task facing acculturating individuals is the reduction of uncertainty which includes the ability 'to predict and explain their own behaviour and that of others during interactions' (Gudykunst and Hammer, 1988: 112). Consequently, Gudykunst and colleagues have considered the role of cognitive variables such as knowledge of the host culture (Gudykunst and Kim, 1984), attitudes toward hosts and hosts' attitudes towards sojourners (Gudykunst, 1983a), cultural similarity (Gudykunst, 1983b), cultural identity (Gudykunst, Sodetani and Sonoda, 1987) and language competence (Gudykunst, 1985) in the prediction of uncertainty reduction and intercultural adaptation.

How do the contemporary approaches to intercultural contact differ from their predecessors? First, theories are more comprehensive – they consider Affective, Behavioural and Cognitive components of the acculturation process and highlight the shift from the negative and reactive features of culture contact towards its adaptive, active coping aspects. Second, there is the explicit recognition that the ABCs of acculturation represent a process that occurs over time. Third, flowing from the preceding point, there is an awareness that the process shares many of the conceptual features of the Holmes and Rahe (1967) life events construct, the idea that any change is intrinsically stressful, even if the event is a positive or desired one.

More significantly, the contemporary literature has concerned itself explicitly with the skills and strategies that sojourners, immigrants and refugees use in adapting to changes in new cultural milieux. The 'shock' part of culture shock is now being discussed in terms of skills deficits (Bochner, 1986) and acculturative stress (Berry, 1994a, 1997). This, in turn, draws attention to the range of mediating and moderating variables that can either attenuate or accentuate the effects of behavioural deficits and psychosocial stressors that sojourners, immigrants and refugees may face. These influential variables can be related to characteristics of the person or the setting in which the cross-cultural transition takes place and can range from personal resources, such as self-efficacy (Bandura, 1986) and cultural knowledge (Ward and Searle, 1991), to situational variables, such as host culture relations (Bochner, 1982) and social support (Harari, Jones and Sek, 1988).

Recent theories and models have also been expanded to consider the broader relationships between migratory and sedentary groups. Studies are now beginning to appear which try to trace the interaction between the acculturation styles of migrants with the acculturation orientation of the host community. A recent example of this may be found in Bourhis and colleagues' (1997) attempt to develop what they call the Interactive Acculturation Model (or IAM) of culture contact.

In addition to these developments, explicit distinctions are now being made between the affective, cognitive and behavioural aspects of adaptation; between physical and social/psychological well-being; and more generally between psychological and sociocultural adjustment (Kealey, 1989; Ward, 1996). These distinctions are reflected in the measures being developed to quantify 'culture shock', leading to a much more rigorous metric than that which was deployed in the past.

Despite these merits, a note of caution is in order. There is a tendency for the models to become exceedingly complex with every conceivable component included. When they are drawn with arrows that depict all of the possible interconnections, it becomes clear that such models are unlikely to be capable of being put to the empirical test. A good example of this theoretical excess is Gudykunst's (1995) Anxiety Uncertainty Management (AUM) model of cross-cultural communication, which contains 94 (yes, ninety-four) axioms. Fortunately, Gudykunst has refrained from drawing a diagram of these axioms, undoubtedly because it would have looked like one of the old Rorschach ink blots and served a similar purpose. The most useful theories will be those that discriminate between core and peripheral influences and include only those predictive, mediating and moderating variables that are crucial to the argument and for which there exist valid and reliable empirical measures.

INTERCULTURAL CONTACT AND ADAPTATION

Despite the emerging theoretical sophistication and coherence in the study of cross-cultural transition, there is still considerable debate about the appropriate criteria for the assessment of intercultural adaptation (Benson,

1978; Church, 1982; Mumford, 1998; Ward, 1996). What are the definitive features of a successful transition? Good relations with members of the host culture? Psychological well-being? Competent work performance? Positive attitudes toward the transition? Identification with host nationals? Diverse indices of adjustment have been reported in the immigrant, refugee, and sojourner literature, and research has incorporated a wide range of outcome measures. These have included self-awareness and self-esteem (David, 1971), mood states (Stone Feinstein and Ward, 1990), health status (Babiker, Cox and Miller, 1980), feelings of acceptance and satisfaction (Brislin, 1981), the nature and extent of interactions with hosts (Sewell and Davidsen, 1961), the acquisition of culturally appropriate behaviours (Bochner, Lin and McLeod, 1979), perceptual maturity (Yoshikawa, 1988), communication competence (Ruben, 1976), acculturative stress (Berry *et al.*, 1987), and academic and job performance (Black and Gregersen, 1990; Perkins *et al.*, 1977).

Controversies surrounding the definition of adaptation and its criterion measures have arisen in connection with both conceptual and psychometric issues. Hammer, Gudykunst and Wiseman's (1978) study of intercultural effectiveness provides an example of the latter. The researchers began by identifying a range of competencies required for successful living abroad. A list of 24 abilities, generated by a sample of North American sojourners and refined by the researchers, was subjected to exploratory factor analysis. The analysis produced a three factor model of intercultural effectiveness: (1) ability to manage psychological stress, (2) ability to communicate effectively, and (3) ability to establish interpersonal relationships. Although the concept of intercultural effectiveness has proven popular in contemporary research, attempts to replicate the factor structure in the original study have produced somewhat varied results (Abe and Wiseman, 1983; Gudykunst and Hammer, 1984; Hammer, 1987). Of course the utility and value of factor analysis as an empirical tool are determined by both the original item pool and the theoretical orientation of the researchers. It is not surprising, then, that factor analytic approaches to intercultural effectiveness and intercultural competence have shared similarities but have also been marked by salient differences (Black and Stephens, 1989; Cui and Awa, 1992; Kealey, 1989; Martin, 1986a; Tanaka *et al.*, 1994).

Because many researchers have relied upon a combination of conceptual and empirical approaches to describe and define adaptation, a variety of analytical frameworks has emerged. Mendenhall and Oddou (1985) discussed affective, behavioural and cognitive components of adaptation including psychological well-being, functional interactions with hosts and the acceptance of appropriate attitudes and values. Taft's (1986) model is based on the distinction of socioemotional adjustment, which refers to a sense of psychological well-being, and psychosocial integration, which is intertwined with the concept of assimilation and includes national and ethnic identity, cultural competence, social absorption and role acculturation. Kealey's (1989) empirical research highlighted both positive and negative psychological outcomes, such as life satisfaction and indicators of psychological and psychosomatic distress, in addition to cross-cultural understanding, contact variables and job performance. Black and Stephens (1989) assumed a more explicitly behavioural approach and identified three facets of sojourner adjustment: general adjustment (managing daily activities), interaction adjustment (relating effectively to host nationals) and work adjustment (accomplishing work-related objectives). A number of other researchers have also concentrated on domain-specific types of adaptation such as work performance and satisfaction (Lance and Richardson, 1985), economic adaptation (Aycan and Berry, 1996) or academic achievement and adjustment to school (Lese and Robbins, 1994). A common theme running through all of these models is the recognition that psychological well-being and satisfaction as well as effective relationships with members of the new culture are important components of adaptation for cross-cultural travellers.

This theme is reflected in work by Ward and colleagues who have maintained that intercultural adaptation can be broadly divided into two categories: psychological and sociocultural (Searle and Ward, 1990; Ward and Kennedy, 1992). Psychological adjustment, based predominantly on affective responses, refers to feelings of well-being or satisfaction during cross-cultural transitions. Sociocultural adaptation, on the other hand, is situated within the behavioural domain and refers to the ability to 'fit in' or execute effective interactions in a new cultural milieu. An evolving programme of research has demonstrated that psychological and sociocultural adaptation are conceptually related but empirically distinct. They derive from different theoretical foundations; they are predicted by different types of variables; and they exhibit different patterns of variation over time.

Situated within a stress and coping framework, psychological adjustment is strongly influenced by factors such as life changes, personality and social support variables (Searle and Ward, 1990; Ward and Kennedy, 1992). Evidence suggests that fluctuations in psychological adjustment are variable over time despite the tendency for problems to peak in the earliest stages of transition. Sociocultural adaptation, interpreted from a culture learning perspective, is more strongly affected by contact variables such as quantity and quality of relations with host nationals (Ward and Kennedy, 1993b; Ward and Rana-Deuba, 2000), cultural distance (Furnham and Bochner, 1982; Searle and Ward, 1990) and length of residence in the host country (Ward and Kennedy, 1996a). Changes in sociocultural adaptation are also more predictable; adaptation improves rapidly in the earliest stages of transition, reaches a plateau and then appears to stabilise (Ward and Kennedy, 1996b; Ward et al., 1998). Given the breadth of the theoretical constructs, their conceptual underpinnings, their empirical foundation, and their potential for application at the intrapersonal, interpersonal, intragroup and intergroup levels, the distinction of psychological and sociocultural adaptation provides a fairly comprehensive yet parsimonious overview of intercultural outcomes.

A MODEL OF THE ACCULTURATION PROCESS

As previously noted, contemporary empirical studies of 'culture shock' consider intercultural contact and cross-cultural transition within the broader framework of acculturation theory. Acculturation refers to changes that occur as a result of sustained first hand contact between individuals of differing cultural origins (Redfield, Linton and Herskovits, 1936). First studied by sociologists and anthropologists in reference to group-level phenomena, acculturation has more recently attracted the attention of psychologists and has been examined as an individual level variable with affective, behavioural and cognitive components (Berry, 1997; Graves, 1967). Acculturation may occur in a wide variety of circumstances. Although it has been most commonly investigated among persons who undertake cross-cultural relocations, such as immigrants, sojourners or refugees, it may also be studied within sedentary communities, such as indigenous peoples or multi-ethnic groups in plural societies. It is important to note, however, that acculturation in these terms is viewed as a dynamic process rather than a static condition.

The model presented in Figure 2.1 has been evolving and continues to be refined with increasing research on intercultural contact and change. The conceptual framework is largely guided by the work of Lazarus and Folkman (1984), draws heavily on the model proposed by Berry (1994b) and is supplemented by theory and research on culture learning by Furnham and Bochner (1986). It integrates both stress and coping and culture learning perspectives on acculturation, distinguishes psychological and sociocultural domains of adaptation and incorporates a range of micro and macro level variables, including social identity, as predictors of the adjustive outcomes. Accordingly, this model offers an organising framework for the synthesis of a large and diverse body of theory and research on the affective, behavioural and cognitive components of cross-cultural transition and intercultural interactions.

The model conceptualises cross-cultural transition as a significant life event involving unaccustomed changes and new forms of intercultural contact. While these experiences may be perceived as stimulating, challenging, confusing or disorientating, individuals are seldom equipped, at least in the earliest stages of transition, to manage or cope effectively with a broad spectrum of demanding situations and novel and unfamiliar patterns of social interactions. Depending upon one's theoretical preference, this state of affairs may be described in terms of either debilitating stress or social skills deficits. In either case, personal and situational factors necessitate appraisal and action. This may involve cognitive, behavioural and affective responses for both stress management and the acquisition of culture-specific skills. The appraisal and action domains, as well as their psychological and sociocultural outcomes, are influenced by both societal and individual level variables. On the macro level characteristics of the society of settlement and the society of origin are likely to be important. Discriminating features may include

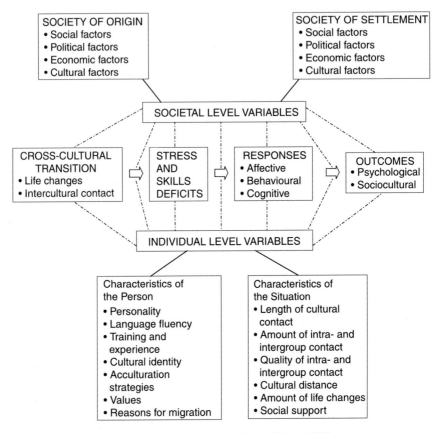

Figure 2.1 The acculturation process (adapted from Ward, 1996)

sociopolitical and demographic factors, such as ethnic composition and salient attitudes toward ethnic and cultural out-groups. On the micro level characteristics of both the person and the situation may prove to be important. This may include factors such as language competence, personality, cultural identity and acculturation strategies on the one hand and friendship networks, cultural distance, intergroup relations or social support on the other. All things considered, the model is particularly efficient for the study of the acculturation process. It permits the incorporation of selected aspects of contemporary work on social identity and the consolidation of theory and research on the prediction of the psychological and sociocultural components of intercultural adaptation.

CHAPTER SUMMARY

Interaction between culturally heterogeneous individuals and groups involves a variety of complex social and psychological processes, and there is a range of approaches that may be taken to describe and explain these intercultural phenomena. The structure of this chapter reflects our decision to start at the most general descriptive and conceptual level and gradually work our way down to both the empirical and theoretical coal-face. At the broadest level, the material can be classified according to the different groups of persons exposed to second-culture influences. These include tourists, international students, international workers and executives, immigrants and refugees. Next, the contact experience can be described in terms of its constituent characteristics. These include the ownership of the territory on which the interaction takes place, its time-span, purpose, frequency and intimacy of contact, the cultural distance between the participants, and all the other demographic and sociocultural characteristics of the individuals and societies concerned.

The effects of intercultural contact were described at two levels, first at the group level and then at the level of the individual. Intergroup outcomes can take one of four different forms: genocide, assimilation, segregation (or separatism), and integration. Only the last-mentioned form can be considered as a genuine resolution to the problem of harmonising cross-cultural relations. The effect of contact on the participating individuals can also take one of four different forms: 'passing', exaggerated chauvinism, marginality, and biculturality. These four different styles reflect changes in the individual's ethnic identity as a consequence of exposure to second-culture influences.

There is general consensus that cross-cultural contact is inherently stressful but considerable debate as to why this should be so, how best to portray it conceptually, and how one should proceed to reduce 'culture shock'. Earlier models were described as having a pseudo-medical flavour in assuming that those unable to cope with cross-cultural experiences had broken down and required therapy and counselling. More recent models have likened cross-cultural adaptation to two broader processes: learning experiences, which assist with the acquisition of appropriate social skills needed to negotiate life in the new setting, and the management of stress-provoking life changes, which requires multiple coping strategies to facilitate psychological well-being. Implied remedial action in the first case involves preparation, orientation, and culture learning, particularly behaviourally-based social skills training. In the second case individuals are expected to draw on personal and interpersonal resources and to engage a wide range of psychological coping mechanisms to adapt or adjust to their new milieux. Both the culture learning and the stress and coping approaches portray persons in contact as actively responding to and dealing in constructive ways with their problems, in contrast to the earlier medical model of culture shock, which regarded sojourners as passive victims in need of outside help. Underlining this change in orientation is a change in terminology, the construct of acculturation being increasingly used as a replacement for the term 'culture shock'.

The stress and coping model draws attention to the affective and emotional impact of culture contact whereas the culture-learning construct has at its centre the behavioural changes that successful sojourners make in order to survive and thrive in their new setting. We have called these psychological and sociocultural adaptation, respectively. Both processes also entail changes in the cognitive domain, which tend to fall into three categories: ethnic identity, self-references, and culturally-related attitudes and values; information about the new culture, including language and communication competence; and the way in which sojourners perceive and interpret their intercultural experiences. Taken together these domains constitute the ABCs of acculturation. The chapter concludes with an attempt to integrate all of these constructs and approaches into a general, complex model of contact.

Part II

Theoretical approaches to culture shock

It seems appropriate at this stage to restate the approach we have taken in organising the material in this book. The theoretical aim is to describe and account for the responses of individuals to novel cultural environments, the core assumption being that culture contact is inherently stressful. And running in tandem with this is a practical strand that looks at how contact-induced stress and skills deficits can be managed and reduced. To use an analogy from medicine, the theoretical analysis aims at achieving an understanding of stress and diagnosing its sources, whereas the practical coverage describes the range of therapeutic interventions available and their effectiveness in dealing with the problem.

The other major feature of this book is that it takes the classic topics of general psychology and explicitly extends them to analysing the culture contact phenomenon. In other words, it is our deliberate intention to treat the subject matter as a special instance of general psychological processes, using constructs that have wide currency in the theoretical literature and substantial empirical support. Cross-cultural psychology is not a substantive area in its own right, but a method or an approach that has special relevance in particular domains (Bochner, Brislin and Lonner, 1975; Lonner, 1997).

Virtually from its inception, psychology has found it useful to distinguish the ABCs (Affect, Behaviour and Cognitions) of human interactions, and we have followed this approach in our treatment of culture contact. We have also paid heed to a second classificatory scheme that characterises modern psychology; that is, the distinction between the individual versus the group as the unit of analysis. These themes underlie much of the general discussion in this book and provide the organisational framework for the chapters in Part II on the major theoretical approaches to culture shock. Chapter 3 describes the culture learning perspective; Chapter 4 deals with stress and coping models, and Chapter 5 discusses social identification theories. The acculturation framework presented in the preceding chapter accommodates all of these theoretical approaches. While it depicts stress and skills deficits as core features of intercultural contact and cross-cultural transition, it also recognises the significance of identity and its influences on acculturation outcomes.

In the following chapters we elaborate the ABCs of 'culture shock'. Chapter 3 concentrates on behaviour. It describes the culture learning approach to intercultural contact, highlighting the social skills required for effective interactions with members of new and unfamiliar cultures. Based on the premise that social interactions are mutually organised and skilled performances, the culture learning approach assumes that behavioural competence is fundamentally dependent upon mastering the intricacies of intercultural communication. Although meetings between culturally disparate persons are, in principle, no different from other social encounters, they are often handicapped by an absence of information about communication conventions. Consequently, the chapter provides material about cross-cultural differences in both verbal and non-verbal forms of communication, including the discussion of topics such as conflict resolution, forms of address, eye contact, gestures, and proxemics. The chapter also considers a range of factors that are more broadly associated with effective culture learning and predict sociocultural adaptation.

Chapter 4 emphasises affect. It assumes a stress and coping approach to cross-cultural transition and highlights emotional aspects of sojourner and immigrant adjustment, particularly psychological well-being and satisfaction. Based on the premise that life changes are inherently stressful, the stress and coping model considers resources and deficits in the adjustment process. Issues arising specifically from intercultural contact (e.g. acculturation strategies or relationships with host nationals) are examined along with generic factors (e.g. social support) that have been shown to enhance or impede psychological adjustment. This approach also includes explicit reference to the experience and appraisal of stress as well as the coping strategies used to manage difficulties associated with intercultural contact and change.

Chapter 5 focuses on cognitions. Social identification theories form the basis of this theoretical approach and are complemented by the inclusion of key constructs from social psychology. Based on the assumption that identity is a fundamental issue for the cross-cultural traveller, social identification theories consider the measurement of and changes in cultural identity. And since self-definition is greatly affected by group membership, this leads to questions about how ethnic identity is maintained or changed, how in-groups and out-groups are defined and perceived, and how self-esteem is affected by acculturative pressures. Subsets of cognitive theory such as social perception and attribution are also invoked to explain some of the recurring findings on intergroup contact – in particular stereotyping, the in-group bias, and prejudice.

How do these broad and unifying frameworks compare and contrast with the seven theoretical explanations of culture shock offered by Furnham and Bochner in 1986? There, selective migration; grief, bereavement and loss; locus of control; expectations; negative life events; social support; value differences; and social skills were examined. These earlier 'explanations' varied in conceptual content, the extent of their theoretical development and the amount of related empirical research. While these perspectives still exert some influence on theory and research on sojourners, immigrants, tourists and refugees, with the exception of the social skills model, which is discussed in the following chapter, none offers a comprehensive theoretical formulation for explaining or predicting culture shock.

Culture learning, stress and coping, and social identification theories represent broad and comprehensive conceptual frameworks for the study of intercultural contact and cross-cultural adjustment. It is easy to recognise that most of the earlier 'explanations' can be readily incorporated into the more contemporary, systematic approaches. This is particularly true for the stress and coping model. Life changes, including personal *loss*, represent a core component of the stress and coping approach to cross-cultural transition and adaptation. Other factors may act as assets or liabilities in the coping process. Personality traits, such as *locus of control*, as well as situational factors, such as *social support*, exert both direct and moderating influences on cross-cultural adjustment. *Expectations* are likewise relevant to the stress and coping model; research described in Chapter 4 indicates that larger discrepancies between expectations and experiences in a new culture are frequently associated with greater psychological adjustment problems. Empirical research has additionally demonstrated that the reasons for migration and the characteristics of the migrating group affect coping and adjustive outcomes. That some ethnocultural groups adapt better than others is in line with the earlier theories of *selective migration*.

The culture learning approach also draws on some of these basic explanations, particularly acknowledging the significance of *expectations* and *values* in intercultural interactions. Accurate expectations may facilitate the development of culture-specific skills, promote more satisfying and effective intercultural encounters, and lead to successful sociocultural adaptation. Value differences, however, are indicative of cultural distance and are likely to be associated with more sociocultural difficulties. These themes are explored in Chapter 3 and further elaborated in Chapter 11 which applies culture learning theory to the selection and training of international students, business people and volunteers.

Theory and research on *values* also have a place in the cognitive-based social identification theories. First, as evaluative beliefs, values in themselves are cognitive constructs. Second, they are intimately tied to self-definition and cultural identity, and they are significantly affected by intercultural contact. Value change, for example, has attracted considerable attention in models and measurements of acculturation. Third, values are linked to perceptions of out-group members. A fundamental principle in social psychology is that we like others who are like ourselves. Consequently, shared values may be seen to promote positive perceptions of out-group members. This applies not only to cross-cultural travellers' views of host nationals, but also to host nationals' perceptions of immigrants, tourists, sojourners and refugees. These themes are discussed in Chapter 5.

We believe that the distinction of affective, behavioural, and cognitive approaches to 'culture shock' is a theoretically sound, comprehensive, yet parsimonious, way to represent conceptual developments in the field over the last 15 years. These approaches draw on theoretical formulations in general psychology and may be systematically applied to the study of intercultural contact and change. As will be seen in following chapters, the ABCs of culture shock provide a solid conceptual base for the empirical research on tourists, immigrants, refugees and sojourners that is described in Part III of this volume.

3   Culture learning

This chapter deals with the behavioural aspects of culture contact – in particular, those acts that typically characterise non-trivial encounters between newcomers and existing members of the receiving society. Culture learning is the process whereby sojourners acquire culturally relevant social knowledge and skills in order to survive and thrive in their new society. We start by presenting a general model of social interaction and then review some of the key elements that regulate interpersonal behaviour. These include various aspects of non-verbal communication, such as proxemics, the use and function of touch, and gestures, all topics which have generated a substantial literature over the past 30 years. More recent work on communication strategies will also be reviewed.

The elements of verbal and non-verbal communication are of central importance to a consideration of the dynamics and effects of culture contact because the evidence indicates that many of these processes vary between cultural and ethnic groups. Furthermore, many of these communication elements are 'hidden' in the sense that the participants are not fully aware of their presence in the background of the interaction until something goes wrong. An analogy is the presence of oxygen in the atmosphere, of which we are not conscious until it suddenly disappears, as when an airplane loses compression at high altitude. The practical implications are that failed social interactions lead to misperceptions, negative stereotypes, and intergroup friction, and that the likelihood of this happening increases with the cultural distance separating the participants (Torbiorn, 1994; Ward and Kennedy, 1999).

SOCIAL INTERACTION

Argyle and Kendon (1967) were among the first to suggest that the social behaviour of persons interacting with each other constitutes a mutually organised, skilled performance. Interpersonal friction arises when this performance breaks down or cannot be initiated in the first place. Research has identified some of the interpersonal skills that socially incompetent persons lack or perform unsatisfactorily, prominent among these being the inter-active elements that regulate social encounters, in particular the non-verbal aspects of social interaction (Burgoon, Buller and Woodall, 1989). These include expressing attitudes, feelings and emotions; adopting the appropriate proxemic posture; understanding the gaze patterns of the people with whom they are interacting; carrying out ritualised routines such as greetings, leave-taking, self-disclosure, and making or refusing requests; and asserting them-selves (Trower, Bryant and Argyle, 1978). These acts tend to define the tenor of the relationship by indirectly conveying feelings such as liking, friendli-ness, dominance, and trust, and the term 'relational communication' has been used to refer to such implicit messages (Burgoon, 1995). There is empirical evidence to indicate that the elements of social interaction listed vary across cultures (Argyle, 1982; Brislin, 1993; Furnham, 1979, 1983; Hall, 1959, 1966; Hall and Beil-Warner, 1978; Leff, 1977) and that many travellers do not easily learn the conventions of another society. More recent research has integrated these behaviours under the general heading of communica-tion style or communication competence, and there now exists a growing literature dealing with communication issues in intercultural encounters (Chen, 1995; Gibson, 1997; Gudykunst and Shapiro, 1996; Wiseman, 1995). This includes the specific problem of what has been called intercultural communication apprehension, or the anxiety that can be aroused by inter-acting with culturally dissimilar people (Gudykunst, 1995; Neuliep and Ryan, 1998).

There are individual differences in the extent to which people exhibit perceptual sensitivity and are prepared to behave flexibly. Socially skilled individuals tend to be sensitive to how others respond to them and to what is going on around them psychologically. They acquire a flexible behavioural repertoire that enables them to respond appropriately in vari-ous social milieux. Thus, socially inadequate individuals may not have mas-tered the conventions of their society, either because they are unaware of the rules of social behaviour that regulate interpersonal conduct in their culture or, if aware of the rules, are unable or unwilling to abide by them. Their performance may also be affected by anxiety about whether their behaviour is being positively evaluated. In this regard, socially unskilled persons behave like strangers in their own land, suggesting that people newly arrived in an alien culture or subculture will be in a similar position to socially inadequate indigenous individuals. It is ironic to note that individuals in this predicament, such as foreign students, business people, or diplomats, often tend to be highly skilled in the customs of their own society and find their sudden inadequacy in the new culture to be par-ticularly frustrating. Competent adults in their home culture come to feel like helpless children in the other.

THE SOCIAL PSYCHOLOGY OF THE CROSS-CULTURAL ENCOUNTER

The advantage of applying the social skills/communication deficit formulation to intercultural contact difficulties is to place the interaction problems of culture travellers within the general literature on communication theory, in effect saying that a meeting between two culturally disparate persons is in principle no different from any other social encounter. There are various ways of conceptualising troublesome social interactions. An early approach (Argyle, 1982; Bochner, 1982) was to regard unsuccessful social episodes as instances of failed verbal and non-verbal communication. This idea still permeates much current research and theorising, particularly with respect to cross-cultural interactions, and is supported by the core finding that a major problem in such encounters is the inaccurate exchange of information and affect. From the point of view of the sender, the intended messages may not have reached the receiver, or if they did, they were incomplete, garbled or distorted. From the point of view of the receiver, the messages may have been difficult to interpret, were ambiguous and, in more extreme cases, offensive. And since receivers are also senders, the spiral of miscommunications can quickly accelerate into a vicious circle of misunderstanding. The rest of this chapter will provide examples and a review of the relevant literature.

CROSS-CULTURAL DIFFERENCES IN HOW PEOPLE COMMUNICATE

Research has shown that there are consistent and systematic cultural differences in the way in which people send and receive information, prescriptions (commands and wishes), and affect (Gallois *et al.*, 1995). One dimension along which members of different cultures vary is the preference for high versus low context communications (Gudykunst and Matsumoto, 1996). Members of low context cultures convey information directly and rely heavily on verbal communication. Members of high context cultures convey limited information in coded messages; they are more apt to be influenced by situational cues and communicate in an indirect and often ambiguous fashion. Other important dimensions of cross-cultural variability include differences in self-disclosure/social penetration (Gudykunst and Nishida, 1986), the importance of face negotiation (Ting-Toomey, 1988), and proxemics (Argyle, 1982). In many cases these dimensions are related to broader social values, particularly variations in individualism and collectivism across cultures (Andersen, 1994).

When persons from two different cultures meet, they will have difficulty in communicating with one another to the extent that their respective 'codes' differ (Fox, 1997). It is also quite possible that they may be unaware that these differences exist. The latter situation is particularly problematic in encounters between two groups that share the same linguistic forms (or at least speak mutually intelligible dialects) because the similarities in language may obscure any differences that might exist in their subjective cultures (Triandis *et al.*, 1972). Consequently, the participants may not realise that they are sending unintended messages and distorting incoming information (Witte and Morrison, 1995).

For instance, when a North American says 'Would you like to . . . ?' (e.g. as in 'write a report on the sales prospect of a particular product'), this is not a question but a polite order; if an Australian subordinate were to answer 'No', the American might be offended and the Australian out of a job. In general, however, the evidence indicates that as differences (including differences in language) between the cultures of the participants increase, so do the difficulties in communication (Levy *et al.*, 1997), due largely to differences in the elements that enter into and regulate interpersonal behaviour.

The psychological literature describing these processes is voluminous, and a comprehensive review is beyond the scope of this chapter. What follows is a brief list of those aspects of interpersonal communication that are known to differ cross-culturally and which contribute significantly to the effectiveness of information exchange. The underlying principle is that both emitted and received/perceived behaviours occur within a complex sociocultural context with particular rules and conventions.

Polite usage: Etiquette

Cultures differ in the extent to which people are direct or indirect, how requests are made, and more importantly, how requests are denied or refused (Dillard *et al.*, 1997; Kim, 1995). For instance, Filipino social interaction is based on smooth interpersonal relationships. Yet Americans assigned to the Philippines as Peace Corps Volunteers were initially told to be perfectly frank in their dealings with the locals, which turned out to be a devastating piece of advice, because the directness of the Americans was regarded as tactless and brutal (Guthrie, 1966). The Chinese use ambiguous forms in communication to a much greater extent than is the case in Western societies, mainly due to a greater emphasis on polite usage and face-saving (Lin, 1997), a direct function of their collectivist, other-oriented, self-concept (Gao, 1998). Turn distribution also varies across cultures, the Japanese taking short turns which they distribute evenly, whereas Americans take longer turns which are unevenly distributed in favour of the participant who has initiated the topic (Gudykunst, 1998a).

In many Asian countries the word 'no' is seldom used, so that 'yes' can mean 'no' or 'maybe'. Rules surrounding invitations and how these are to be extended and accepted are highly culture-bound. There are many stories of Westerners extending an invitation to an Asian acquaintance, receiving what they consider to be an affirmative reply, and then becoming angry when the visitor does not show up (Brein and David, 1971). Triandis (1975) relates how an American visitor asked his Greek acquaintance what time they should come to his house for dinner. The Greek villager replied 'any time'. In American usage the expression 'any time' is a non-invitation that people give to appear polite but which they hope will not lead to anything. The Greek, however, actually meant that the Americans would be welcome any time, because in his culture putting limits on when a guest can come is deemed insulting. Triandis does not reveal how the incident ended, but it is quite likely that the Americans would have taken what they thought was a hint and withdrawn from the engagement, thereby seriously offending their Greek host.

Some cultures use linguistic forms like 'thank you' to show their appreciation, whereas in other cultures 'thank you' is signalled non-verbally. A visitor from a 'linguistic' culture unaware of this custom may come to regard the hosts as rude and uncouth; the hosts, in turn, may wait in vain for the visitor to exhibit the appropriate gesture of appreciation. The intensity with which speech is uttered is also a variable. For instance, Arabs tend to speak loudly which Europeans interpret as shouting. Americans speak louder than the English, to whom they sound brash and assertive. Americans and Japanese differ with respect to the situations that require an apology and the form in which an acceptable apology should be phrased and delivered (Sugimoto, 1998). The are many opportunities for cultural travellers inadvertently to infringe the rules of cross-cultural etiquette (Axtell, 1993).

Resolving conflict

Dealing with embarrassing predicaments and face-saving are additional minefields for culture travellers (Earley and Randel, 1997; Imahori and Cupach, 1994; Ting-Toomey and Kurogi, 1998; Tsai, 1996). For example, in a study of American executives supervising Mexican assembly line workers, the direct manner in which the expatriate manager reprimanded poorly performing workers was found to violate the Mexican cultural norm of saving face and to lead to absenteeism, high labour turnover, and poor morale (Lindsley and Braithwaite, 1996). More specifically, being publicly and openly criticised is regarded as shameful and insulting in Mexican culture, unlike in American work settings where managers regard it as their duty to provide frank feedback on the performance of their staff.

Two cultural dimensions that significantly affect interpersonal communication style and content are individualism–collectivism and power distance (Hofstede, 1980). These highly complex constructs were elaborated in Chapter 1, but they may be briefly summarised as follows. Power distance refers to the extent to which there is general acceptance of status inequality while individualism–collectivism refers to the extent to which the needs of the group predominate over those of individuals (Triandis, 1995a).

Examples of where differences in these values have led to communication difficulties can be found in a 23-nation study conducted by Smith *et al.* (1998)

in various industrial organisations. Their research revealed systematic differences in the handling of disagreements across cultures. In low power distance and individualist nations, managers tended to rely on their own training and experience in resolving conflict and showed a greater readiness to involve subordinates and co-workers. In collectivist countries formal rules and procedures were given more importance. Differences such as these may lead to serious consequences as demonstrated by Orasanu, Fischer and Davison (1997) in their study of safety in the airline industry. In this research the authors found that the unwillingness of first officers to challenge the decisions of airline captains or to use circumspect, indirect language as a means of preserving the captain's face contributed to aircraft accidents, particularly in high power-distance cultural contexts.

Negotiating styles also differ between cultures. Pearson and Stephan (1998) compared Brazilian and American approaches to resolving conflict. Brazilian participants, coming from a collectivist society, preferred a negotiating style that included taking into account the interests of the other party. In contrast, the American participants, reflecting the individualistic orientation of their culture, were more inclined to use negotiating strategies that maximised their own interests at the expense of the other party. A laboratory study comparing the negotiating styles of American (individualist) and Mexican (collectivist) students also found that the Mexicans showed a greater preference for strategies such as accommodation and collaboration, which take an opponent's outcomes into account. In addition, the Mexican participants tended to avoid strategies leading to animosity, conflict and competition (Gabrielidis *et al.*, 1997). There is no doubt that cross-cultural differences in Individualism–Collectivism and power distance may hinder effective intercultural communication, particularly when the interaction occurs between persons of unequal status and when there is a need to achieve agreement on some important issue.

Non-verbal communication

Non-verbal signals play an important role in communicating attitudes, in expressing emotions, and in supporting speech by elaborating what is said. They also provide feedback from listener to sender and assist in synchronising verbal interactions by indicating to the participants when it is their turn to speak, when it is their turn to listen, and when it is appropriate to interrupt (Argyle, 1975, 1980). Although the meaning of some non-verbal signals is universal, many vary across cultures.

Communication elements that have been studied cross-culturally include the face, eyes, spatial behaviour, bodily contact, and gestures (Duncan, 1969; Ekman and Friesen, 1972, 1975; Mehrabian, 1972; Sommer, 1969). For instance, Japanese display rules discourage the use of negative facial expressions (Shimoda, Argyle and Ricci Bitti, 1978), making them relatively 'inscrutable' to members of low context cultures, and Filipinos may smile and laugh when they are very angry (Guthrie, 1975), which could give outsiders a completely false impression of the impact they are making.

Mutual gaze

Levels of mutual gaze vary across cultures. Arabs and Latin Americans display a high frequency of mutual gaze while Europeans display a comparatively lower frequency (Watson, 1970). When persons from high and low-gaze cultures meet, the behaviour of the low-gaze participant may be interpreted as impolite, not paying attention and dishonest while the high-gaze person may be seen as disrespectful, threatening, or insulting (Burgoon, Coker and Coker, 1986). Spatial behaviour also varies across cultures, some groups standing much closer to each other than others (Aiello and Jones, 1971; Baxter, 1970; Brein and David, 1971; Hall, 1959, 1966; Jones, 1971; Scherer, 1974; Watson and Graves, 1966).

Bodily contact

Cultures also vary in the extent to which they allow bodily contact (Argyle, 1982). Contact cultures include Arab, Latin American, and Southern European groups. In non-contact societies, touching is only allowed under very restricted conditions, such as within the family, in brief handshakes with strangers, or in specialised role relationships (e.g. doctors, dentists, and tailors). Contact outside these approved settings can be a source of considerable anxiety. When a high-touch culture meets a low-touch one, the low-contact person is seen as aloof, cold and unfriendly, whereas the high-contact person may be seen as sexually predatory.

Northern Europeans are very sensitive about having their personal space invaded, unlike the Southern Europeans, who prefer to sit and stand much closer to each other. They also engage in much more physical contact than other Europeans, the Italians probably being the most tactile (Collett, 1994). Arab societies are high contact cultures. However, this only applies to same-sex touching. Physical contact between members of the opposite sex in public is rare and regarded as offensive (Feghali, 1997). East-Asian societies, particularly China, Korea, and Japan, tend to be low tactile cultures, the reluctance towards interpersonal touch by members of those societies being ascribed to the influence of Confucianism with its emphasis on prescribed public social deportment (McDaniel and Andersen, 1998).

Immediacy refers to behaviours that invite communication and imply psychological closeness. This is mostly conveyed through non-verbal signals which vary cross-culturally (McCroskey *et al.*, 1996). Complicating the issue further are differences between cultures regarding the extent to which their members welcome psychological closeness. For instance, members of a high-context culture such as the Japanese rely more on non-verbal than verbal communication channels and do not seek psychological closeness. In contrast, a low-context culture such as the United States relies more on verbal than non-verbal means of communicating affect, and its members value psychological closeness (Hinkle, 1998).

Gestures

Gestures and their significance vary widely across cultures (Collett, 1982; Morris *et al.*, 1979). Some gestures are used in one culture and not in others, and the same gesture can have quite diverse, indeed opposite, meanings in different cultures. For instance, in the United States a raised thumb is used as a signal of approval or approbation, and even has a name, the 'thumbs up' signal. However, in Greece the same sign is employed as an insult, often being associated with the expression *'katsa pano'* or 'sit on this'. Another example is the ring sign, performed by bringing the tips of the thumb and finger together so that they form a circle. For most English-speaking people it means 'okay' and is widely known as the 'OK' gesture. But in some sections of France the ring means zero or worthless. In English-speaking countries disagreement is signalled by shaking the head, but in Greece and southern Italy the head-toss is employed to signify 'no'.

Among Europeans, Italians are probably the most intense users of expressive hand movements in conversation. 'As points and arguments fly back and forth, the hands gyrate and puncture the air, throwing cryptic signs in every direction' (Collett, 1994: 65). Other groups who gesticulate a great deal are the French, Eastern European Jews, Greeks, Spaniards, and the Portuguese. Nordic peoples – the Swedes, Finns, Norwegians, and Danes – make very little use of gesticulation. The British, Germans, Dutch, Belgians, and Russians use gestures in moderation, particularly facial expressions such as smiling and gaze (Argyle, 1981).

Social-skills training has always placed a great deal of emphasis on non-verbal behaviours. The complexity and variety of these signals across cultures attest to their importance in effective cross-cultural interaction, and experimental research has shown that culturally congruent non-verbal behaviours are a more powerful predictor of interpersonal attraction than ethnicity (Dew and Ward, 1993). However, it should be noted that some aspects of non-verbal behaviour are more important than others. For instance, facial expressions and gaze play a greater role in communicating affect than does spatial behaviour. Nevertheless, in a specific instance even the smallest variation in non-verbal behaviour may lead to a major failure in communication.

Rules and conventions

Cross-cultural differences in the rules that govern interpersonal behaviour are another major source of difficulty in intercultural communication (Driskill and Downs, 1995). For instance, rules about punctuality vary from culture to culture (Argyle, 1982; Brein and David, 1971; Collett, 1994). LeVine, West and Reis (1980) found that Americans regard someone who is never late for an appointment as more successful than someone who is occasionally late, who in turn is perceived as more successful than a person who is always late. Exactly the opposite is the case in Brazil, where arriving late for an appointment is indicative of success.

In an unobtrusive study of attitudes to punctuality, LeVine and Bartlett (1984) checked the accuracy of clocks in cities in Japan, Taiwan, Indonesia, Italy, England, and the United States. They found clocks to be most accurate in Japan and least accurate in Indonesia. In another aspect of the same study, the walking speed of pedestrians was measured in the same cities. Again, the Japanese were the fastest and Indonesians the slowest strollers. Data such as these can be interpreted to reflect cultural differences in attitudes to pace of life.

Conventions about punctuality are only one example of the many social rules that cross-cultural travellers must take into account. Furnham and Bochner (1982) identified forty routine social situations which sojourners have difficulty in negotiating to varying degrees, partly because the rules regulating these encounters vary from culture to culture and may not be obvious to an outsider. Furnham (1983) administered the Social Situations Questionnaire to African, Indian, and European nurses in Natal, South Africa. He found significant differences in reported difficulty between the three groups, with the Europeans expressing least and the Africans expressing most problems. In this case, although all the subjects were in a sense insiders, black Africans had been kept separate from the dominant sectors of their society and hence had fewer opportunities to acquire and rehearse mainstream socially skilled acts and their respective ground rules.

In a more direct demonstration of the existence and effects of cultural differences in social rules, Noesjirwan (1978) contrasted Indonesia and Australia on three general cultural themes: first, that Indonesians value maintaining friendly social relationships with everyone, in contrast to the Australian preference for a few exclusive relationships and personal privacy; second, that Indonesians value conformity to the group and the community in contrast to the Australian emphasis on individuality; and third, that Indonesians prefer an interpersonal lifestyle that is smooth, graceful and restrained in contrast to the Australian preference for an open, direct social manner. On the basis of these themes, Noesjirwan then generated a number of common social situations, and Australian and Indonesian participants were provided with alternate choices about how they would manage the encounter. The study confirmed that Indonesian and Australian preferences differed in terms of how congruent they were with each culture's rule structure.

Social rules tend to operate below the level of consciousness. Often, people only become aware of the existence of a particular rule if they have broken it. Or rather, their social environment ensures that they realise that they have transgressed. Outsiders lack easy access to such information. Unless they have a host culture friend who can serve as a mentor in this regard, even sensitive sojourners may miss some vital cues and behave inappropriately from their hosts' perspective.

Forms of address

Forms of address vary between cultures, mainly in terms of whether to use first names, last names, and titles. For example, in Germany great emphasis is placed on titles, and a man with two doctorates will be referred to as Herr Doktor Doktor (Collett, 1994). Germans are quick to take offence if they think they are not being addressed properly. Titles are always used when introducing people in countries such as Germany and Italy, often as a way of conveying the person's occupation and educational status. The honorific 'Don' is used in Latin countries to acknowledge a person's position of influence and power. In Mexico a lawyer is addressed as *Licenciado*, a title of some import in that society (Samovar and Porter, 1988).

There is considerable cross-cultural variation in the use of first names. In the United States, people newly introduced very quickly begin to call each other by their given names. However, in other societies, such as Germany, Italy, and to some extent Britain, first names are reserved for addressing close friends and family members (Chaney and Martin, 1995). These differences can lead to sojourner–host friction. For instance, a distinguished British academic psychologist visiting Australia was heard to complain about the rudeness of Australian undergraduates. It turned out that he was referring to a question and answer session in his seminar presentation during which the students called him by his given name. He was only partially mollified when it was suggested that this indicated that the students accepted him and that their informal approach was a mark of respect.

The principle underlying such communication difficulties stems from culturally determined differences in the extent to which importance is attached to rank, title and profession. As Hofstede (1980) and others have noted, power distance varies across cultures. These variations relate to differences in beliefs as to whether people should be regarded as equals irrespective of their birth, position or wealth; or whether individuals in certain social categories (including class, gender and age) should be given greater respect. The use of honorific or respect names indicates a deferential attitude on the part of the speaker and draws attention to the social or occupation role of the person being addressed (Alford, 1988). Societies high on power distance are more likely to employ forms of address that reflect an acceptance or a belief in status differences.

In Japanese culture, where social categories do matter, the business card is used as a means of conveying vital information about the relative status of the participants. This is achieved by including on the card titles, degrees, position in the company, and any other details that in a precise way establish the social standing of the person. Rules about exchanging business cards vary across cultures. The Japanese will carefully read a card presented to them and may comment on it while accepting it. Japanese executives would regard the American practice of a quick glance while pocketing the business card as quite rude (Axtell, 1993; Baldrige, 1993).

In Britain the foreigner has to cope with the custom of people using the surname only in some social contexts, but including titles or first names in other circumstances. A similar difficulty faces sojourners in some Chinese cultures where the surname comes first and the given name last. Ching Lo Chang would be addressed as Mr Ching. In Korea it is customary for women to retain their maiden name when they marry, so that South Korean President Kim Young Sam's wife, Mrs Sohn Myong-suk, should have been addressed as Mrs Sohn by President Clinton when they met on a State visit, rather than as Mrs Kim. This is also the custom in Latin America, where people will often add their mother's maiden name to their surname, which then becomes the name by which they are addressed. Thus Maria Rodrigues Castillo would expect to be called Senorita Rodrigues (Devine and Braganti, 1988).

The problem of when to use first, middle or last names is not restricted to social interactions between culturally disparate individuals. In multicultural societies, government departments face this issue on a daily basis. For example, the Australian Department of Social Security has produced a handbook to assist staff in their dealings with NESB (non-English speaking background) clients (Department of Social Security, 1990). In relation to the Chinese example mentioned earlier, the handbook sternly advises staff that it is 'important to always check the name order in the passport or on travel documents' (Department of Social Security, 1990: 7).

Forms of address play a prominent role in facilitating or hindering inter-cultural communication, because of their high visibility and ubiquity. During most conversations, the participants will at some stage use a form of address. A person incorrectly addressed (from their perspective) will almost certainly notice the error, and depending on the context, may interpret it as an insult, or at best, an indication of ignorance on the part of the other person. At the same time, there are many opportunities for inadvertent misuse of forms of address, due to their variability and the subtleties in the rules that determine them. It is not surprising that this area of culture learning is receiving increasing prominence, both in the scientific literature and in popular guide books for travellers (Braganti and Devine, 1992; Mole, 1990).

INTERCULTURAL COMMUNICATION THEORY: INTEGRATING THE COMMUNICATION ELEMENTS

Probably the most developed communication theory, and the one most relevant to the topic of the present chapter, is the Communication Accommodation Theory or CAT (Gallois *et al.*, 1995), drawing on earlier theories, such as Speech Accommodation Theory, Ethnolinguistic Identity Theory, Ethnolinguistic Vitality Theory, and Social Identity Theory (see Figure 3.1). CAT is

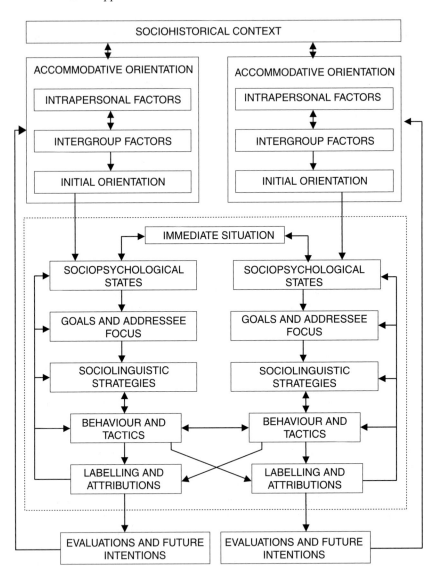

Figure 3.1 The Communication Accommodation Theory in intercultural contexts
(from C. Gallois, H. Giles, E. Jones, A. A. Cargile and H. Ota (1995).
Accommodating intercultural encounters: Elaborations and extensions. In
R. Wiseman (Ed.), *Intercultural communication theory* (pp. 115–147).
Thousand Oaks, CA: Sage).

an extension of pioneering work by Howard Giles (1973) and integrates
aspects of communication strategies, participant motivation and group
membership to explain the dynamics of intercultural interactions. At the core
of the model is the assumption that participants in linguistic encounters will

be driven by one of the following motives: to converge to their conversational partners, that is, make some aspects of their speech more similar, as a means of identifying with the other person and/or gaining the person's approval; to diverge from the partner's style and content, as a way of distinguishing themselves from the other person; or to maintain their own style, which usually means divergence.

More recently, convergence, divergence, and maintenance were renamed as approximation strategies, and the model now includes an explicit consideration of the extent to which speakers are motivated at the outset of an interaction to converge or diverge. Approximation strategies aimed at making the participants closer are called accommodation. Strategies aimed at emphasising interpersonal or intergroup differences are called non-accommodation. Specific elements include taking (or not taking) into account the skills and competence of the partner, leading for instance to slower speech, the use of questions to check understanding, and the choice of familiar topics; discourse management, allowing (or not allowing) the partner to choose topics and how they should be treated; and interpersonal sensitivity to such issues as the use of honorifics. The model is dynamic in regarding the conversation as consisting of a continuous feedback cycle with the reactions of each speaker being contingent on the behaviour of the other, albeit within a general path to a particular goal.

Cynthia Gallois (1988) and her colleagues have extended this model into the specific context of intercultural communication. Additional components taken into account include whether the participants view the encounter as mainly interpersonal or intergroup and the nature of the situation and its context, for instance if it is threatening or benign. The special relevance of this theory to the present discussion is its emphasis on accommodation as a determinant of harmonious intergroup contact. Virtually all of the behavioural elements reviewed in this chapter involve some aspect of accommodation, either explicitly or implicitly. Likewise, intergroup friction occurs when the participants are unwilling or unmotivated to make the necessary accommodation, do not have the skills to do so, or are unaware that their behaviour is non-accommodating. The other contribution to the present exposition is CAT's distinction between the interpersonal and intergroup determinants of accommodation. Accommodation based on group membership is more likely to affect broader, long term behaviours such as newcomers' social networks and language acquisition, and ultimately their cultural identity. Interpersonal accommodation is more likely to function at the level of specific behaviours, such as gesture, gaze, and proxemics.

SOCIAL RELATIONS IN MULTICULTURAL SOCIETIES

Earlier in this book we distinguished culture-contact occurring within multi-ethnic societies from contact taking place between members of different societies. We have been using the term 'sojourner' to refer to the individuals who embody inter-society contact, examples being overseas students and expatriate business persons. In this section we would like to deal briefly with some of the behavioural, culture learning issues that arise in connection with intra-societal contact between culturally diverse groups.

As has already been mentioned, there are very few culturally homogeneous societies in the world today. Most countries have or are becoming culturally pluralistic, either through a deliberate policy of immigration, or inadvertently due to circumstances not entirely to their liking or choosing. The fact remains that many nations contain within their borders sizeable groups of permanent settlers who consider themselves and are seen by others to possess distinct ethnic identities, and whose practices, customs, linguistic forms and often appearance clearly distinguish them from other groups. In most cases, these people can be characterised as belonging to minority groups, distinguishing them from the majority-defining cultural group.

With the exception of the descendants of any aboriginal inhabitants of a particular receiving nation, the minority groups are relative newcomers. Despite official policies based on the principle of integration, in practice immigrants are expected to assimilate to the dominant ethos, at least at the overt, behavioural level. In other words, they are expected to learn the culture of their hosts. However, as was also discussed earlier, this creates various dilemmas for the new settlers. If they simply 'pass' into the dominant society, this will inevitably lead to a weakening or total abandoning of the ties with their culture of origin, something they may not wish to do. On the other hand, if they resist adopting some of the more utilitarian practices of their new society, they may become socially and economically marginalised. Furthermore, most migrants will be members of two cultural social networks, made up of co-national migrants and host culture members, respectively. Children of immigrants are exposed to host-culture influences at school but may live in a family setting which is organised along traditional, culture-of-origin customs and values, including the language being spoken at home, the food eaten, and the child-rearing and disciplinary practices the parents employ. Many migrant workers also live in two separate cultural milieux, one employment related and the other based on family and friendship networks.

Linguists understood this problem long before cross-cultural psychologists came upon it and have studied it under the heading of 'code switching' (Bolinger, 1975), where speakers change their speech style to put themselves closer to their audience as a way of expressing solidarity or exclusivity. Arabic speakers move between different forms of Arabic, as well as French and English, allowing them to select speech that has special connotations or emphasises particular points (Feghali, 1997). In English-speaking countries, minority groups will often use non-standard English among themselves as a means of affirming their ethnic identity (Phinney, 1996) but switch to standard linguistic forms in their interactions with host-culture members (Gallimore, Boggs and Jordan, 1974). Traditional educationalists tend to frown on this practice, but it has the important function of providing an empirical base for supporting the establishment of a bicultural ethnic identity or what Bochner (1999) has called a hyphenated person, as in Greek-Australian. It should also be noted that code switching is a special case of the process of speech accommodation reviewed earlier in the discussion on the CAT model of intercultural communication.

In the present context, a major issue is to facilitate, or better still, systematically inculcate culture learning for bicultural competence (LaFromboise and Rowe, 1983; LaFromboise, Coleman and Gerton, 1993). Very few such programmes of this type exist because most traditional culture training approaches seek to 'adjust' the sojourner or immigrant to the dominant culture. One exception is in the clinical field where influential workers such as Paul Pedersen and Juris Draguns (Draguns, 1997; Pedersen, 1991, 1994a,b; Pedersen *et al.*, 1996; Tanaka-Matsumi and Draguns, 1997) have identified some of the theoretical, practical and ethical difficulties of defining the mental health of minority groups in terms of the values of the dominant majority. This has led to an explicit recognition that a bicultural approach is vital in both conceptualising the goals of psychotherapy and in the counselling practices used in therapeutic procedures with minority groups.

CROSS-CULTURAL TRANSITION AND SOCIAL DIFFICULTY

As this chapter has shown, the culture learning approach provides a broad theoretical framework for understanding 'culture shock'. On the most basic level it recognises that the problems experienced by cross-cultural travellers can be attributed to the absence or distortion of familiar environmental and social cues. Oberg (1960) was not specific about the nature or boundaries of these cues in his original formulation of the culture shock hypothesis, and indeed, Furnham and Bochner (1982) have criticised his propositions as being too broad and not amenable to empirical testing. They have noted, for example, that unfamiliarity with any or all aspects of a new society (physical, technological, climatic, political, legal, educational, linguistic and socio-cultural) may contribute to 'culture shock', but have argued that the most fundamental difficulties experienced by cross-cultural travellers occur in social situations, episodes and transactions. Consequently, they have emphasised the significance of social skills and social interactions and have concentrated on the acquisition of those culturally relevant behavioural skills required for sojourners, immigrants and refugees to survive and thrive in their new societies. Salient aspects of these social skills and their variations across cultures, including differences in etiquette, conflict resolution, forms of address, non-verbal communication, and rules and conventions, have been discussed in detail throughout this chapter.

The culture learning approach suggests that skill deficits should be

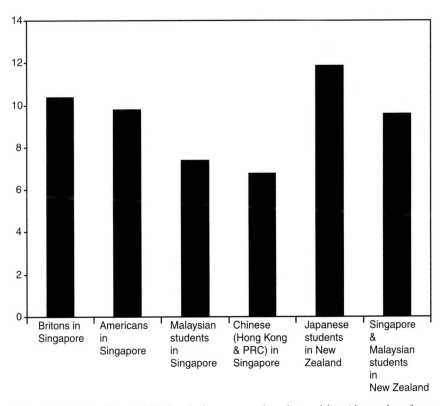

Figure 3.2 Sociocultural difficulty during cross-cultural transition (data taken from Ward and Kennedy, 1999)

home. This is in line with Furnham and Bochner's (1982) point that sojourners are relatively unskilled when they enter a new environment.

4   *Does sociocultural adaptation vary across sojourning groups?* Figure 3.2 gives a selection of comparative findings (Ward and Kennedy, 1999). These results suggest that cultural and ethnic similarity is generally associated with fewer sociocultural difficulties. Mainland Chinese and Malaysian sojourners in Singapore, for example, adapt more readily than Anglo-European ones. Similarly, Malaysian students in Singapore experience less difficulty than Malaysian and Singaporean students in New Zealand. In addition, Japanese students in New Zealand report more sociocultural adaptation problems than their Southeast Asian counterparts, most likely reflecting the greater English fluency in the latter group.

The culture learning model has offered a valuable theoretical perspective on 'culture shock'. Furnham and Bochner (1982) have contributed methodological advancements for its empirical analysis, and Ward and colleagues have extended research on social difficulty to intercultural encounters. These developments provide a useful background for and basic introduction to the topic of culture training, which will be discussed in Chapter 11.

CHAPTER SUMMARY

The theme of this chapter followed the argument that the distress that many culture travellers experience is largely due to their lacking the social and behavioural skills of the new society. This creates barriers to effective communication between visitors and hosts and sows the seeds for a vicious circle of misunderstanding, friction and hostility. Social interaction can be regarded as a mutually organised, skilled performance. The synchronisation that is the hallmark of an effective and satisfying encounter results from the participants having a shared, although often only implicit, understanding of the bases of the interaction. These include the method of signalling turn-taking, the appropriate manner in which to effect self-disclosure, what gestures signify, and the correct interpersonal distance within which to conduct the encounter. Intercultural communication competence depends on mastering the intricacies of these processes. The evidence indicates that these forms are not universal but that there are systematic cross-cultural differences in communication patterns and that how people send and receive information, express emotion and influence each other tend to be culture bound. The rules and conventions that regulate interpersonal encounters also vary between cultures.

The communication patterns and social conventions of a given society are usually taken for granted by its members. Consequently, people tend to be unaware of the operation, or even the very existence of these rules which often only come into prominence after they have been broken either inadvertently or by someone not familiar with them. What has been called the hidden language of interpersonal interaction is a major source of cross-cultural misunderstanding and friction. In an intercultural encounter the greater the difference that exists in the respective, culturally determined communication patterns of the participants, the more difficulty they will have in establishing a mutually satisfying relationship.

Finally, in multicultural societies, successful culture learning for newcomers involves acquiring bicultural communication competence, to enable these permanent settlers to function effectively in both their co-national and host-national social networks. Bicultural communication competence also sustains the development of an integrated, bicultural identity which contributes to the mental and physical well-being of the settlers.

4   Stress, coping and adjustment

The previous chapter described theory and research on culture learning. It emphasised behavioural aspects of intercultural contact and suggested that a social skills interpretation of the difficulties that arise during cross-cultural transition provides a sound conceptual framework for understanding the acculturation process. This chapter focuses on the affective components of intercultural contact. In particular it examines the psychological well-being and satisfaction of immigrants, sojourners, and refugees by applying a stress and coping model to the study of cross-cultural transition and adjustment.

The stress and coping approach was preceded and influenced by earlier epidemiological studies that highlighted the negative emotional reactions to culture contact and change and focused on the incidence and severity of psychopathology in migrant populations (Eitinger and Grunfeld, 1966; Ødegaard, 1932). While contemporary approaches to intercultural contact also reflect a concern for the psychological consequences of cross-cultural transition, prevailing views on this issue have changed considerably over the last two decades. Conceptual frameworks are now guided by psychosocial rather than medical models, and in contrast to emphases on 'culture shock' and psychopathology, current approaches discuss intercultural contact and change in terms of coping with stress.

The shift in theoretical direction has been accompanied by substantial methodological advances. More diverse and varied investigations have been conducted, incorporating not only a wider range of adjustment indicators (e.g. mood disturbance, self-esteem, and psychosomatic complaints), and predictor variables (e.g. social, economic, historical, and political factors), but also a more varied selection of migrant groups (e.g. tourists, aid workers, and diplomats). Survey research based on self-report questionnaires has become more prominent. Increasingly complex research designs, including longitudinal studies, and more powerful methods of data analysis, such as multiple regression and causal modelling, have become commonplace. Attention has also moved from describing patterns of migrant mental health and sojourner psychological well-being to explaining and predicting them via sophisticated hypothesis-testing. These recent theoretical and methodological advances along with contemporary empirical research on stress and coping are described in the remainder of this chapter.

THE STRESS AND COPING FRAMEWORK

The stress and coping framework highlights the significance of life changes during cross-cultural transitions, the appraisal of these changes, and the selection and implementation of coping strategies to deal with them. The framework fits neatly within the general model of acculturation that was presented in Chapter 2, the core assumptions being that the experience of intercultural contact and change occurs in a sociopolitical and economic context and is influenced by the characteristics of the migrant's society of origin and society of settlement. The changes associated with this contact are viewed as precipitating stress, which results in affective, behavioural and cognitive coping responses. Both stress and coping are mediated by characteristics of the individual and characteristics of the situation, and, in turn, affect adjustive outcomes.

A similar, but more explicit and elaborated, stress and coping model of immigration, acculturation and adaptation has been presented by John Berry (1997) in his recent review. As can be seen in Figure 4.1, this model also highlights stress and features the central flow of life events, appraisal, coping and short and long term outcomes. Berry's (1997) framework considers the acculturative experience as a major life event that is characterised by stress, demands cognitive appraisal of the situation, and requires coping strategies. These processes, as well as their psychological outcomes, are likely to be influenced both by societal and individual level variables. On the macro level characteristics of the society of settlement and society of origin are important. Discriminating features of these societies may include social, political, and demographic factors, such as ethnic composition, extent of cultural pluralism, and salient attitudes towards ethnic and cultural out-groups. On the micro level characteristics of the acculturating individual and situational aspects of the acculturative experience exert influences on stress, coping and adaptation. Berry also distinguishes between influences arising prior to and during acculturation. In the first instance, factors such as personality or cultural distance may be important; in the second, acculturation strategies or social support may be more relevant.

FACTORS AFFECTING STRESS, COPING AND ADJUSTMENT

A stress and coping approach to understanding and interpreting the acculturative experience recognises that the factors affecting cross-cultural adjustment are much the same as the factors involved in adapting to other

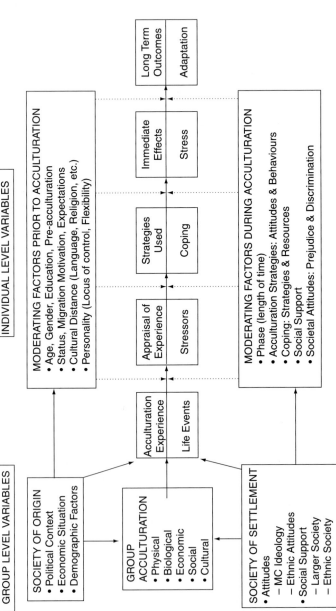

Figure 4.1 Stress and coping framework for acculturation research (from J. H. Berry (1997). Immigration, acculturation and adaptation. *Applied Psychology: An International Review*, 46, 1–30. Reprinted by permission of the International Association of Applied Psychology.)

transitional experiences. Consequently, researchers who have adopted this perspective on 'culture shock' have acknowledged the relevance of the life events literature to the acculturation experience, noting the vast array of changes confronted by immigrants, sojourners, refugees, and even tourists (Furnham and Bochner, 1986; Spradley and Phillips, 1972). In line with conventional stress and coping research, investigators have examined the influences of life changes (Lin, Tazuma and Masuda, 1979), pre- and postmigration stressors (Nicassio *et al.*, 1986), cognitive appraisals of change (Chataway and Berry, 1989), personality (Ward and Kennedy, 1992), and social support (Adelman, 1988) on acculturation outcomes, particularly physical and mental health.

In addition to these general stress and coping factors, researchers have also considered variables that are specific to cross-cultural transition and adjustment. Investigators have gone beyond the assessment of life changes, personality and social support to consider factors such as cultural distance, acculturation strategies and acculturation status. Both types of factors, the general and the specific, are discussed in this chapter.

Life changes

The stress and coping perspective on the acculturation process conceptualises cross-cultural transitions as entailing a series of stress-provoking life changes which tax adjustive resources and necessitate coping responses. Consequently, the measurement of salient life events is an important feature of this approach. Reference is frequently made to Holmes and Rahe's (1967) Social Readjustment Rating Scale (SRRS) as a functional index of life changes. The instrument provides standardised Life Change Units (LCUs) for 43 life events including a selection of life changes that are particularly likely to be experienced during migration. The SRRS is scored by summing the LCUs of events experienced within a certain time period (e.g. six months, one year), and research has indicated that a greater number of LCUs is reliably associated with increased physical and mental distress (Monroe, 1982). Indeed, Furnham and Bochner (1986) previously noted that the combined total of SRRS life events which are frequently connected with migration, such as change to a new line of work, change in living conditions, change in social activities, and change in residence, exceed 300 LCUs. Holmes and Holmes (1970) have indicated that exposure to 200–299 LCUs within recent months carries a 50 per cent risk of major illness and exposure to over 300 LCUs is associated with an 80 per cent risk factor!

Holmes and Rahe's (1967) general work on life changes and social readjustment has inspired attempts to construct a more specific assessment tool for cross-cultural relocation. Along these lines Spradley and Phillips (1972) developed the Cultural Readjustment Rating Scale (see Table 4.1). They began with the identification of 33 life changes associated with cross-cultural transition and sampled Peace Corps volunteers, Chinese students in

Table 4.1 The Cultural Readjustment Rating Scale

1. The type of food eaten.
2. The type of clothes worn.
3. How punctual most people are.
4. Ideas about what offends people.
5. The language spoken.
6. How ambitious people are.
7. Personal cleanliness of most people.
8. The general pace of life.
9. The amount of privacy I would have.
10. My own financial state.
11. Type of recreation and leisure activities.
12. How parents treat children.
13. The sense of closeness and obligation felt among family members.
14. The amount of body contact such as touching or standing close.
15. The subjects which should not be discussed in normal conversations.
16. The number of people of your own race.
17. The degree of friendliness and intimacy between married and unmarried women.
18. How free and independent women seem to be.
19. Sleeping practices such as amount of time, time of day, and sleeping arrangement.
20. General standard of living.
21. Ideas about friendship – the way people act and feel towards friends.
22. The number of people of your religious faith.
23. How formal or informal people are.
24. Your own opportunities for social contacts.
25. The degree to which your good intentions are misunderstood by others.
26. The number of people who live in the community.
27. Ideas about what is funny.
28. Ideas about what is sad.
29. How much friendliness and hospitality people express.
30. The amount of reserve people show in their relationships with others.
31. Eating practices such as amount of food, time of eating, and ways of eating.
32. Type of transportation used.
33. The way people take care of material possessions.

Source: J. P. Spradley and M. Phillips (1972). Culture and stress: A quantitative analysis. *American Anthropologist*, *74*, 518–529. Reproduced by permission of the American Anthropological Association from *American Anthropologist* 74: June 1972. Not for further reproduction.

the United States and American students with no experience abroad. Mean readjustment scores for each life event in each of the three groups were calculated, paralleling the SRRS's Life Change Units, and the rank ordering of these means was compared across groups. The analysis indicated that there were only moderate relationships among the readjustment rankings, highlighting the importance of culture-appropriate norms for the study of groups in transition.

Although a number of researchers have acknowledged the conceptual significance of life changes for immigrants, refugees and sojourners (Furnham and Bochner, 1986; Guthrie, 1981), relatively few have actually attempted to measure these changes directly. Masuda, Lin and Tazuma (1982) studied

Vietnamese refugees in the United States on their arrival and one year later. Scores on a Vietnamese normed version of the SRRS were related to psychological and psychosomatic symptoms as measured by the Cornell Medical Index (CMI). The authors reported that there was a significant relationship between life changes and psychological and psychosomatic distress at both periods (0.27 and 0.15, respectively); however, life changes accounted for only a small portion of the variance in CMI scores. Comparable correlations were found in studies by Ward and colleagues in Malaysian, Singaporean, and New Zealand students abroad. Using Malaysian student norms for the SRRS, Searle and Ward (1990) reported a correlation of 0.25 between life changes and depression in Malaysian and Singaporean students in New Zealand. In a later study Ward and Kennedy (1993b) found a similar relationship between life changes and total mood disturbance – 0.27 for Malaysian and Singaporean students in New Zealand and 0.19 for Malaysian students in Singapore. Finally, in a sample of New Zealand AFS students posted abroad Ward and Kennedy (1993a) reported a correlation of 0.28 between life changes, based on a shortened New Zealand normed SRRS, and global mood disturbance.

In Furnham and Bochner's (1986) earlier critique of the literature on negative life events they noted that although there is a rather consistent relationship between life events and physical and psychological distress, the significance of life events is most likely exaggerated. They estimated that correlations range, in general, from 0.2 to 0.4, accounting for only between 4–16 per cent of the variance in outcome measures. This is in line with Cochrane and Sobol's (1980) analysis of the psychological consequences of life stressors which gauged the average correlation between life changes and psychological disorder to be 0.35. So while it is apparent that there is a reliable, moderate positive correlation between life changes and psychological symptoms, these changes account for only a small proportion (generally less than 10 per cent) of the variance in the psychological well-being of sojourners and refugees. Other factors, such as personality and social support, as well as appraisal and coping styles, also affect psychological outcomes.

Appraisal and coping styles

One reason why standard life change measurements account for such a small proportion of the variance in psychological outcomes is that there are obvious and important individual differences in the cognitive appraisal of these changes. Individuals process stress-related information in a variety of ways. In one instance a potential stressor may be evaluated as threatening; in another instance it may be perceived as challenging. Beyond these individual differences there are cultural factors which are likely to affect the cognitive appraisal of stress. Indeed, Masuda *et al.* (1982), who reviewed cross-cultural research on the Social Readjustment Rating Scale, found that although there was a high correlation in the rank ordering of SRRS events, there were significant cross-cultural differences in the magnitude estimations.

The cognitive appraisal of potentially stressful demands by acculturating individuals is also likely to be influenced by broad social and situational factors, including aspects of the acculturative experience. For example, Zheng and Berry (1991) looked at the evaluation of a range of potential stressors by Chinese sojourners in Canada and by Chinese and non-Chinese Canadians. Chinese sojourners tended to view language and communication, discrimination, homesickness and loneliness as more problematic than either Chinese or non-Chinese Canadians. A similar pattern was observed in Chataway and Berry's (1989) research with Hong Kong Chinese and French and Anglo-Canadians. With reference to the cognitive appraisal of stressors, communication difficulties and prejudice were reported to be more problematic for the Chinese compared with the Canadian students.

Cognitive appraisals of stressors as well as subsequent coping strategies and adjustive outcomes may also vary due to differences in migrants' expectations. Expectations form the basis of cognitive appraisals of stressful situations. They also provide the yardstick against which experiences and behaviours can be measured. Some researchers have argued that realistic expectations, i.e. those that match actual experiences, facilitate adjustment. Indeed this is consistent with the stress and coping literature which has highlighted the negative consequences of unexpected stress (Averill, 1973) as well as the positive effects of providing realistic and accurate information prior to the occurrence of stress-provoking experiences (MacDonald and Kuiper, 1983). Expectation–experience matches attest to the psychological preparation required to cope with potentially stressful life changes, and expectation accuracy may positively affect subsequent appraisals of stressful situations, build confidence and alleviate anxiety.

It is no surprise, then, that some research has documented a simple and straightforward relationship between expectations and experiences in acculturating individuals. For example, Hawes and Kealey (1980) reported an association between expectations of a rewarding sojourn and self-rated satisfaction in Canadian technical assistants engaged in international development projects. Weissman and Furnham (1987) similarly reported that expectations were remarkably similar to experiences in a sample of Americans who had relocated to the United Kingdom. These findings are in line with the accuracy hypothesis.

A second more refined approach considers not only the (in)accuracy of expectations but also the direction and extent of expectation–experience mismatches. In this analysis a basic distinction is made between overmet and undermet expectations. The former refers to situations in which experiences are more positive than expected while the latter refers to situations in which experiences are more negative than anticipated. Along these lines Black and Gregersen (1990) found that overmet general expectations of American managers about life in Japan were associated with increased life satisfaction and decreased likelihood of premature departure. Although this study was limited by the retrospective nature of the expectation measurements, three longitudinal studies on sojourner adjustment have reported similar results. Rogers and Ward (1993) surveyed New Zealand AFS students before and after returning to their home country and found that when re-entry was more difficult than expected, greater discrepancies between expectations and experiences were associated with elevated levels of depression. The same pattern was reported by Kennedy (1999) in his predeparture and postarrival survey of Singaporean students pursuing overseas education. Similarly, Martin, Bradford and Rohrlich (1995) surveyed American students before their overseas departure and then again after return to their home country. The researchers found that when overseas experiences were less difficult than expected, students reported greater satisfaction with their cross-cultural sojourns.

Despite the general interest in stress and coping and related research on cognitive appraisals and expectations, relatively few published studies have actually examined coping strategies in relation to adaptive outcomes in sojourners, immigrants or refugees. Shisana and Celentano (1987) suggested that coping styles of Namibian refugees moderated the relationship between length of stay in exile and period of hospitalisation, and Kennedy (1994) reported a positive relationship between coping via the use of humour and diminished mood disturbance in a sample of international students in New Zealand. A more comprehensive study was conducted by Chataway and Berry (1989) who investigated coping styles, satisfaction and psychological distress in Chinese students in Canada. They employed Folkman and Lazarus' (1985) Ways of Coping Scale which includes the assessment of eight distinct coping strategies: problem solving, wishful thinking, detachment, social support, positive thinking, self-blame, tension reduction and withdrawal responses. Results revealed a significant relationship between coping styles and satisfaction in dealing with salient problems. More specifically, Chinese students who engaged in positive thinking were more satisfied with their ability to cope; however, those who relied upon withdrawal and wishful thinking were less content with the management of their problems. Despite the link between coping styles and coping satisfaction, there was little association between coping styles and psychological distress. Only detachment was significantly related to an increase in psychological and psychosomatic symptoms.

In further investigations Ward and Kennedy (in press) examined the coping styles and psychological adjustment of British expatriates in Singapore. They employed Martin and Lefcourt's (1983) Coping Humour scale and a shortened version of Carver, Scheier and Weintraub's (1989) COPE which includes twelve subscales: active coping, planning, seeking instrumental support, seeking emotional support, suppression of competing activities, positive reinterpretation, restraint coping, acceptance, venting, denial, mental disengagement, and behavioural disengagement. A second order factor analysis revealed a four factor structure of COPE: approach (planning, suppression of competing activities, and active coping), avoidance (behavioural disengagement, denial, venting, and positive reinterpretation, which loaded negatively), acceptance (acceptance and restraint coping) and social support (seeking emotional and instrumental support). The research further revealed that approach coping and coping humour were associated with lower levels of depression while avoidance coping predicted higher levels of depression; however, these variables accounted for only 28 per cent of the variance in the outcome measure. Avoidant styles were also associated with greater psychological adjustment problems in Berno and Ward's (1998) study of international students in New Zealand and Kennedy's (1998) research with Singaporean students abroad. The latter investigation additionally reported that direct, approach-oriented coping strategies predicted psychological well-being.

For the most part the findings from studies on coping with cross-cultural transition parallel the general stress and coping literature. Carver *et al.* (1989), for example, highlighted the functional aspects of direct, action-oriented coping mechanisms while questioning the long term effectiveness of disengagement strategies. Similarly, Folkman and Lazarus (1985) have drawn distinctions between problem-focused and emotion-focused coping styles, emphasising the obvious adaptive consequences of more task-oriented reactions. This is not to suggest, however, that specific coping strategies would be uniformly effective or that cultural factors have no bearing on adjustment outcomes. Indeed, Cross (1995) has speculated that there may be cross-cultural variations in coping effectiveness.

This line of theory and research begins with the distinction between primary and secondary coping strategies. Primary strategies are direct actions; they are overt task-oriented behaviours aimed at changing noxious features of a stress-provoking environment. Secondary strategies, by contrast, are more cognitive than behavioural; they most commonly involve changing perceptions and appraisals of stressful events and situations. In the simplest terms the primary strategies imply changing the environment to suit the self while the secondary strategies reflect changing the self to suit the environment. Building on earlier research by Weisz, Rothbaum and Blackburn (1984), Cross (1995) speculated that primary or direct coping strategies are highly valued by idiocentrics (that is, people with independent self-construals) and in individualist cultures, while indirect or secondary mechanisms may be more adaptive for allocentrics (that is, people with inter-dependent self-construals) and in collectivist cultures (also see Chang, Chua and Toh, 1997). In her examination of stress and coping in East Asian and American students in the United States, Cross hypothesised and found that independent self-construals predicted direct coping which was associated with decrements in perceived stress in the Asian students. Although these findings were consistent with her cultural hypothesis, the same results were not observed in American students.

Cross's study, though thought provoking on a number of counts, is none the less limited in scope. First, as the findings are confined to Asian sojourners in the United States, it is difficult to establish if the advantages of direct coping are apparent because these strategies are intrinsically more effective or because they are consistent with dominant cultural values. Second, although Cross refers to her work as a study of cross-cultural adaptation, only comparisons between sojourners and host nationals are reported. Support for her speculation about cross-cultural variation in the preferences for and effectiveness of direct and indirect coping styles, would require a comparison between international student sojourners from collectivist and individualist societies. Finally, Cross reported findings only on primary coping; secondary coping styles were not assessed in the research.

Ward and colleagues chose to explore these issues in greater depth in a more collectivist setting in their research on self-construals, stress, coping and psychological adjustment in international students in Singapore (Ward, Leong and Kennedy, 1998). After comparing independent and interdependent self-construals in the two groups, path analysis was used for the causal modelling of psychological adjustment. The analysis confirmed that East Asian students possessed more interdependent self-construals than Euro-American students while the reverse was true for independent self-construals. It also revealed that both independent and interdependent self-construals predicted the use of primary coping strategies. More significantly, results indicated that secondary coping mechanisms (i.e. acceptance and positive reinterpretation and growth) predicted lower levels of perceived stress, which, in turn, predicted fewer symptoms of depression. Primary strategies (i.e. active coping and planning), in contrast, did not exert a direct effect on perceived stress. These findings were observed in both the East Asian and Euro-American groups in Singapore.

While these data seem to converge with Cross's study and suggest that there are cultural variations in coping effectiveness, it is premature to draw such a conclusion. The hypothesis requires more systematic investigation, and comparative data from East Asian and Euro-American students who have sojourned to more individualist countries (e.g. the United States, Australia) are needed. It is also important to acknowledge that, in contrast to Cross's study which examined coping styles in response to academic pressures and problems, the study by Ward *et al.* specifically linked coping strategies to the difficulties associated with cross-cultural transition. Less information is available about secondary coping styles compared with the primary strategies; however, it may be the case that indirect tactics are intrinsically more suitable and efficacious for coping with at least some aspects of cross-cultural transition. In short, sojourners are powerless to change entire cultures, and in many cases they have limited resources for modifying the troublesome features of their new cultural milieux. In these instances, cognitive reframing strategies may be more effective in reducing stress. In any event, further research is required to clarify the relationship between culture, coping and psychological adjustment during cross-cultural transitions.

Stress, coping and psychological adjustment over time

Early writings on international relocation, particularly the popular literature on this topic, were often anecdotal and frequently limited to descriptive accounts of the stages of cross-cultural transition and adaptation (e.g. Adler, 1975; Garza-Guerrero, 1974; Jacobson, 1963). Best known among these works is Oberg's (1960) discussion of 'culture shock' which detailed four phases of emotional reactions associated with cross-cultural sojourns:

1   the 'honeymoon', with emphasis on the initial reactions of euphoria, enchantment, fascination, and enthusiasm;
2   the crisis, characterised by feelings of inadequacy, frustration, anxiety and anger;
3   the recovery, including crisis resolution and culture learning; and finally,
4   adjustment, reflecting enjoyment of and functional competence in the new environment.

Beyond this descriptive account early empirical investigations also suggested that entry to a new cultural milieu commenced in a positive manner. In a frequently cited cross-sectional study Lysgaard (1955) proposed a U-curve of adjustment during cross-cultural relocation based on his empirical investigation of Scandinavian Fulbright grantees in the United States. He reported that students who had resided in the United States for 6–18 months were significantly less adjusted than those who had been there either less than 6 months or more than 18 months. The U-curve hypothesis was further extended by Gullahorn and Gullahorn (1963) who maintained that the adjustment curve is repeated on re-entry to the home environment.

While popular and intuitively appealing, the evidence for the U-curve has been 'weak, inconclusive and overgeneralised' (Church, 1982; p. 542). A major problem has been that primarily cross-sectional research has been used to evaluate the U-curve proposition (e.g. Davis, 1971; Klineberg and Hull, 1979; Selby and Woods, 1966; Sewell and Davidsen, 1961). Given the nature of the proposed changes in sojourner adaptation over time, a longitudinal design would be more appropriate. A second and compelling shortcoming is the questionable theoretical underpinnings of the purported U-curve phenomenon. In fact, the U-curve hypothesis appears to be largely atheoretical, deriving from a combination of post hoc explanation and armchair speculation. This may be contrasted with hypotheses arising from the stress and coping literature which predict that, in contrast to 'entry euphoria', sojourners and immigrants suffer the most severe adjustment problems at the initial stages of transition when the number of life changes is the highest and coping resources are likely to be at the lowest.

To examine this proposition Ward and colleagues conducted a series of longitudinal investigations of sojourner adaptation. Their first study followed a group of Malaysian and Singaporean students who were initially interviewed and tested within a month of arrival in New Zealand and then again after 6 and 12 month periods (Ward and Kennedy, 1996a). Psychological adjustment followed a U-curve, but in the opposite direction to that described by Lysgaard (1955). That is, the overall level of depression was significantly greater at 1 month and at 1 year of residence than at the intermediate 6 month period. In addition, qualitative data indicated that the emotions experienced upon entry were even more negative. When interviewed 1 month after arrival and asked to comment retrospectively on their feelings, 68 per cent of the students described the initial entry period in exclusively negative terms; this compared with only 5 per cent of the students who used exclusively negative descriptors about their current (1 month) experiences.

Similar findings emerged in a study of Japanese students in New Zealand. In an attempt identify the 'entry euphoria' proposed by Oberg (1960), students were tested within 24 hours of arrival to New Zealand and then again at 4, 6 and 12 month periods (Ward *et al.*, 1998). The level of depression was highest during the entry period with a significant drop and only minor variations over the subsequent three time periods.

What do these two studies suggest? In contrast to beginning cross-cultural transition in a state of euphoria as proposed by Oberg (1960), it is more probable that the transition commences in a state of at least moderate distress. Psychological adjustment difficulties appear to be greatest in the early stages of transition (also see Westermeyer, Neider and Callies, 1989), drop in the first 4 to 6 months, and are then somewhat variable over time. This leads to the speculation that after the first 6 months, 'non-cultural' issues (e.g. exams, work pressures, relationship difficulties) may exert stronger influences on sojourners' psychological well-being. It is also possible that sojourners have become more effective cultural learners during this period (see Chapters 3, 7 and 8). These propositions, however, remain to be explored further in future research.

Longitudinal studies that have examined the predeparture and postarrival well-being of sojourners have also corroborated a relatively high level of psychological distress during the early months of transition. Ward and Kennedy's (1996b) study, for example, monitored the psychological adjustment of New Zealand overseas volunteers before and after being posted abroad; depression was significantly greater at 2 months into their field assignments than before departure from New Zealand. The same pattern was observed in Zheng and Berry's (1991) longitudinal research with Chinese scholars in Canada. The sojourners evidenced significantly higher levels of psychological symptoms within the first 4 months of arrival than prior to departure from the People's Republic of China. Likewise, Furukawa and Shibayama (1993, 1994) found that symptoms of anxiety and depression were more pronounced in Japanese students 6 months after the commencement of an international exchange than before departure from Japan. Along similar lines, Ying and Liese (1991) reported that 55 per cent of their foreign student sample experienced an increase in depressive symptoms after arrival in the

United States, and Kealey's (1989) study of Canadian development workers revealed that about 50 per cent of his sample commenced their overseas postings at a lower level of satisfaction.

Although stage theories have declined in favour over recent years, and carefully conducted longitudinal research has cast doubt on the utility of the U-curve proposition, this model of adjustment has retained a strong following. Why does the U-curve still feature prominently in both popular books on culture shock and academic texts on cross-cultural psychology and intercultural adaptation (e.g. Fisher, 1995; Moghaddam, Taylor and Wright, 1993)? How has the model survived conceptual criticisms and empirical arguments? And why does the U-curve continue to attract the attention of contemporary researchers? One reason is that the U-curve proposition is intuitively appealing. Many of us know what it is like to be a tourist in a foreign land and to be excited by the novelty and challenge of unfamiliar cultural surroundings. It seems logical, even expected, that this excitement and euphoria would wear thin when it becomes obvious that this new and challenging environment must be dealt with on a more permanent, and possibly inescapable, basis. It should be remembered, however, that sojourners are not tourists, and it is questionable as to whether they commence their sojourns with the same attitudes and expectations as short term holiday makers.

While the U-curve may offer a convenient, common sense heuristic for understanding cross-cultural adaptation, it is not an altogether accurate one. Are we then suggesting that the U-curve pattern of adjustment is a sheer fantasy, a mere illusion? The answer is clearly no. Some people, some of the time, demonstrate a U-curve pattern of adaptation. In Kealey's (1989) longitudinal research on 277 Canadian development workers, he observed the U-curve pattern of psychological adjustment in about 10 per cent of his sample. Herein lies a second reason that the U-curve has survived. There are longitudinal data, limited though they are, that do occasionally support this U-curve pattern of psychological adjustment in sojourners.

The third, and perhaps the most significant, reason why the U-curve proposition has continued to exert strong influence on the field, has been the lack of a credible successor; that is, a new model to explain sojourner adjustment over time. Simply put, the field has not produced a critical and credible mass of research findings that consistently support an alternative theory. The stress and coping approach to psychological adjustment seems promising, but more work is required, particularly in terms of longitudinal research. However, identifying cooperative research participants, testing them before cross-cultural relocation, and following them through at least the first year of a sojourn are difficult undertakings. Participant attrition is a major problem, and it is not uncommon to lose half of the research sample at each testing (Kennedy, 1998; Weissman and Furnham, 1987). In addition, variations in who, when and how often to test make what few studies there are difficult to integrate or synthesise.

The problems due to these methodological limitations and variations are further exacerbated by multiple measures of cross-cultural adjustment. Although originally discussed with reference to sojourners' psychological well-being and satisfaction, the U-curve has been also investigated in relationship to attitudes (e.g. Selltiz *et al.*, 1963), academic adaptation, sociocultural adjustment (Zaidi, 1975), and knowledge of the host culture (Torbiorn, 1982). It is not surprising that affective, cognitive and behavioural components of intercultural adaptation would follow different paths over time. Indeed, as mentioned in the previous chapter, the acquisition of culturally appropriate skills typically follows a learning curve. However, the indiscriminate use of multiple outcome measures has added to conceptual and empirical confusion in the field. We believe that researchers should look more critically at the area, seriously consider the merits of longitudinal research, carefully select research participants (e.g. sojourners, immigrants, refugees) and outcome measures (e.g. psychological and sociocultural adaptation), and be aware of the theoretical implications of these decisions when pursuing investigations of sojourner adjustment over time. Only then will we be able to amass a significant empirical base of theoretically grounded research to resolve this controversy.

Personality

The cross-cultural literature contains much anecdotal evidence and armchair theorising about adaptive personality qualities and the acculturative experience. Authoritarianism, rigidity and ethnocentrism, for example, have been assumed to impede psychological adjustment during cross-cultural transition (Locke and Feinsod, 1982) while extraversion and sensitivity, the embodiment of the 'universal communicator', are thought to facilitate adaptation (Gardner, 1962). Despite extensive theorising, however, relatively few investigations have empirically documented the influence of personality traits on the psychological well-being of immigrants, refugees or sojourners. Two possible exceptions to this are studies of locus of control and extraversion.

Locus of control has received considerable attention in the cross-cultural transition literature. In the main, studies have linked an external locus of control with psychological and emotional disturbances (Dyal, 1984; Kuo and Tsai, 1986; Lu, 1990). For instance, Kuo, Gray and Lin (1976) found that an external locus of control was a more powerful predictor of psychiatric symptoms in Chinese immigrants to the United States than demographic, socioeconomic or life change variables. Dyal, Rybensky and Somers (1988), who investigated locus of control in Indo- and Euro-Canadian women, reported an association between external responses, depression, and psychosomatic complaints. Seipel's (1988) study demonstrated that lower levels of life satisfaction were related to an external locus of control in Korean immigrants in the United States as did Neto's (1995) research with second generation Portuguese migrants to France. Studies of foreign students have proven likewise. Hung (1974) verified the link between an external locus of control and anxiety in Taiwanese students in the United States, and Ward and Kennedy (1993b) reported an association between external locus of control and mood disturbance in Southeast Asian students in New Zealand. The latter finding was corroborated by Kennedy (1994) in his study of multinational foreign students in New Zealand.

Although these findings are consistent with general theory and research on personality and mental health (Lefcourt, 1984), there has been speculation that an external locus of control may be adaptive for sojourners under some circumstances. For example, Partridge (1987), in her discussion of North Americans' adjustment to Japan, described the adaptive features of a fatalistic orientation in situations where one has little direct control. The migration literature, however, has failed to find evidence of the adaptive features of an external locus of control, even in very deprived and relatively powerless groups. For example, Ward, Chang and Lopez-Nerney (1999) investigated internal and external locus of control in Filipina domestics in Singapore and found that an internal locus of control was associated with lower levels of depression.

Studies on extraversion have produced less consistent results. Research has generated positive, negative and non-significant relationships between extraversion and sojourner adjustment (Armes and Ward, 1989; Padilla, Wagatsuma and Lindholm, 1985; Van den Broucke, De Soete and Bohrer, 1989). For example, a study of Malaysian and Singaporean students in New Zealand indicated that extraversion was predictive of enhanced psychological well-being (Searle and Ward, 1990). However, in native English-speaking expatriates in Singapore, extraversion was associated with increased feelings of boredom, frustration, depression and poor health (Armes and Ward, 1989). In an attempt to reconcile these conflicting findings, Ward and Chang (1997) proposed the cultural fit hypothesis. They highlighted the significance of the person × situation interaction and suggested that in many cases it is not personality per se that predicts cross-cultural adjustment, but rather the 'cultural fit' between the acculturating individual and host culture norms. To test this idea a sample of Americans in Singapore were surveyed, and comparisons were made between their extraversion scores on the Eysenck Personality Questionnaire and normative Singaporean data. Although extraversion per se did not relate to psychological well-being, those Americans whose scores were less discrepant from Singaporean norms experienced lower levels of depression, giving tentative support to the cultural fit proposition.

In more recent research Leong, Ward and Low (2000) investigated the Big Five Personality dimensions – Neuroticism, Extraversion, Openness, Agreeableness and Conscientiousness – in relation to the psychological adjustment of Australian sojourners in Singapore. As expected, neuroticism was strongly related to adjustment problems ($r = 0.6$), i.e. depression, anxiety and psychosomatic complaints. In addition, extraversion, agreeableness and conscientiousness were weakly ($rs = 0.2$), but significantly, related to psychological and emotional adjustment. Openness, however, was unrelated to sojourner well-being.

Other personality factors that have been associated with general adjustment, psychological well-being or life satisfaction have been personal flexibility (Berno and Ward, 1998; Gullahorn and Gullahorn, 1962; Ruben and Kealey, 1979), tolerance of ambiguity (Cort and King, 1979), hardiness (Ataca, 1996), mastery (Sam, 1998), self-efficacy and self-monitoring (Harrison, Chadwick and Scales, 1996). In contrast, psychological adjustment problems have been associated with authoritarianism; decrements in overall satisfaction have been related to dogmatism (Taft and Steinkalk, 1985); and high anxiety has been linked to attributional complexity (Stephan and Stephan, 1992). Attempts to investigate Eysenck's personality dimensions of neuroticism and psychoticism have demonstrated, as expected, that both are associated with psychological adjustment problems during cross-cultural transition (Ditchburn, 1996; Furukawa and Shibayama, 1993). Despite the relatively poor showing of personality in the prediction of cross-cultural adaptation, many observers believe that it is premature to dismiss its influence on the adjustment process. Along these lines it has been argued that greater attention should be paid to the person × situation interaction and the notion of cultural fit (Church, 1982; Furnham and Bochner, 1986).

Social support

Social support has been viewed as a major resource in the stress and coping literature and as a significant factor in predicting both psychological adjustment (Adelman, 1988; Fontaine, 1986) and physical health (Schwarzer, Jerusalem and Hahn, 1994) during cross-cultural transitions. The presence of social support is negatively correlated with the emergence of psychiatric symptomatology in immigrants and refugees (e.g. Biegel, Naparstek and Khan, 1980; Lin, Tazuma and Masuda, 1979); its absence is associated with the increased probability of physical and mental illness during cross-cultural sojourns (Hammer, 1987).

Social support may arise from a variety of sources, including family, friends, and acquaintances. Some researchers have emphasised the significance of the family and have concentrated on marital relations as the primary source of social support. Naidoo (1985), for example, reported that immigrant Asian women in Canada experienced substantially less stress when they had supportive husbands, and Stone Feinstein and Ward (1990) found that the quality of spousal relationship was one of the most significant predictors of psychological well-being of American women sojourning in Singapore. On the other hand, marital difficulties can increase psychological distress. Ataca (1996) observed that marital stressors were significantly related to psychological adaptation problems, including anxiety, depression, psychosomatic complaints and general dissatisfaction, in Turkish migrants to Canada. Similarly, Dyal, Rybensky and Somers (1988) found that marital strain was the strongest predictor of depressive and psychosomatic symptoms in Indo-Canadian women. These findings are not surprising as marital harmony/distress contributes to psychological well-being/malaise in intracultural settings as well. Although good marital relationships can undoubtedly offer a source of social support and buffer the effects of transitional stress, and poor relations can exacerbate problems, it should be noted that marital satisfaction/dissatisfaction and adaptive/maladaptive coping may be associated in other ways. For example, individuals who are distressed in a new cultural milieu are likely to put pressure on existing relationships; this may, in turn, contribute to increased marital difficulties.

When friends and acquaintances are considered as sources of social support, the relative merit of co-national versus host national support emerges as a controversial topic (see Chapter 7 for further discussion). Some studies have suggested that co-national relations are the most salient and powerful source of support for both sojourners and immigrants (Sykes and Eden, 1987). Ward and Kennedy (1993b), for example, found that satisfaction with co-national relations was a strong predictor of psychological adjustment in Malaysian and Singaporean students in New Zealand. Berry *et al.* (1987) reported that Korean immigrants with close Korean friends experienced less acculturative stress during their relocation to Canada, and Ying and Liese (1991) noted that postarrival mood improvement in Taiwanese students in the United States was associated with having more Chinese friends.

Adelman (1988) has also commented upon the benefits provided by co-national support systems in terms of both informational and emotional support. In her analysis of cross-cultural transition and adjustment she emphasises the significance of 'comparable others', i.e. those undergoing similar experiences who may offer knowledge-based resources and share information about coping with a new environment. She also notes that comparable others may provide emotional benefits, permitting, or even encouraging, emotional catharsis and the release of frustrations concerning life in a new environment. A similar argument was presented by Church (1982) in his earlier review of sojourner adjustment. He recognised that subcultural enclaves or 'expatriate bubbles' may serve protective functions whereby psychological security, self-esteem and sense of belonging are enhanced, and stress, anxiety, and feelings of powerlessness and alienation are attenuated. However, such enclaves can also impede culture learning and willingness to engage with the host society. Thus, Adelman cautions against a 'contagion effect' whereby highly interdependent, stressed and threatened individuals who remain insulated from the host culture milieu may be prevented from acquiring functional problem-solving skills. She further warns that continual commiseration among those experiencing stress under unstable conditions may place the members of the support group at risk by engendering a 'sinking ship' morale. There may be some evidence of this in Pruitt's (1978) study of African students in the United States which found that overall adjustment was poorer for those students who had greater contact with compatriots and spent more leisure time with Africans. Similarly, Richardson's (1974) research with British immigrants in Australia revealed that it was the dissatisfied immigrants who had more compatriot and fewer host national friends.

Apparently, co-national relationships can be harmful or helpful, depending on the nature of individual supporters and their group's dynamics. However, it should be borne in mind that the relationship between cross-cultural adaptation and co-national interaction may unfold in either direction. In some instances negative co-national contact may stifle expatriate morale, leading to greater adjustment problems; in others, distressed immigrants and sojourners may be more likely to seek support from empathetic compatriots. Alternatively, good co-national relations may function as a stress buffer, diminishing symptoms of distress; however, psychological well-being may also contribute to enhanced interpersonal relations with the co-national group.

While expatriate enclaves can provide positive or negative support opportunities, relationships with other groups, particularly members of the dominant or host culture, also affect adjustment outcomes. Some researchers have concentrated on the quality of these relationships. Having host national friends has been associated with a decrease in psychological problems in immigrants (Furnham and Li, 1993), and satisfaction with host national relationships has been positively related to psychological well-being in sojourners (Searle and Ward, 1990; Stone Feinstein and Ward, 1990; Ward and Kennedy, 1993a). Comfort and satisfaction with local contact have also been associated with greater general satisfaction in foreign students, including both academic and non-academic aspects of their overseas transfers (Klineberg and Hull, 1979). These findings are consistent with the notion that links with host nationals provide informational as well as material social support.

Other researchers have emphasised the frequency of interaction with members of the host culture, in some cases even suggesting that extensive contact is a prerequisite for sojourner adjustment. Several studies have confirmed a relationship between the amount of social contact with host nationals and general adjustment or satisfaction in immigrants and sojourners (Berry *et al.*, 1987; Gullahorn and Gullahorn, 1966; Lysgaard, 1955; Pruitt, 1978; Selltiz *et al.*, 1963; Sewell and Davidsen, 1961), and it is widely recognised that host national contact facilitates the learning of culture-specific skills for life in a new cultural milieu (see the previous chapter). However, other investigations have pointed to a link between more extensive host national contact and increased psychological distress (Ward and Kennedy, 1992, 1993b).

One way of resolving this seeming contradiction may be through the examination of the discrepancies between actual and desired contact as suggested by Chance (1965). Along these lines Minde (1985) reported that contact discrepancy was significantly correlated with stress in a sample of international students in Canada, and Zheng and Berry (1991) observed that contact incongruity was negatively related to the subjective adaptation of Chinese sojourners in Canada. However, empirical investigations of this phenomenon have yielded mixed results. Berry and Kostovcik (1990) found no support for the purported relationship between actual, desired and discrepant contact and acculturative stress.

All in all it is likely that both home and host national support affects sojourner well-being. This was confirmed by Furnham and Alibhai (1985) in their study of foreign students in the United Kingdom and by Ward and Rana-Deuba (2000) in their work with multinational aid workers in Nepal. As these results demonstrate that support may be effectively provided by both host and co-national networks, some researchers have concerned themselves with the adequacy, rather than the source, of social support and its influence on cross-cultural adaptation. Loneliness, for example, has been commonly mentioned as a negative consequence of cross-cultural relocation (Pruitt, 1978; Sam and Eide, 1991; Zheng and Berry, 1991) and has been linked to various forms of psychological distress, including global mood disturbance (Stone Feinstein and Ward, 1990; Ward and Searle, 1991), decrements in life satisfaction (Neto, 1995), and decreased satisfaction with coping ability (Chataway and Berry, 1989).

Although it is widely accepted that social support positively affects psychological well-being in immigrants, sojourners and refugees, the assessment of social support has attracted surprisingly little comment in the acculturation literature. Researchers have seldom relied upon standard measures (e.g. scales by Sarason *et al.*, 1983; Vaux, Riedel and Stewart, 1987), and in many cases investigations have been limited to the use of single rating scales to assess the quality and quantity of intercultural and intracultural contact. An exception to this trend is work by Yang and Clum (1995) which described the development of the Index of Social Support (ISS) scale. The 40-item instrument, constructed to assess the perceptions and use of social support by Asian students in the United States, incorporated themes of contact, trust, satisfaction, availability, and the meaning of social support in reference to family, friends (in old and new countries), institutions (e.g. church, school) and the larger community. The ISS emerged as a reliable and valid instrument, and the research findings demonstrated that social support was associated with lower levels of depression, suicidal ideation and hopelessness in the international students; however, Yang and Clum did not present a fine-grained analysis of the data which might have shed light on the differential influences of quantity versus quality measures of social support.

More recently, Ong (2000) has developed a social support scale for sojourners based on research with both international students and business people in Singapore. The scale highlights the availability of social support and asks respondents to indicate if there are persons (no one, someone, a few, several, many) who would perform a variety of supportive behaviours (Table 4.2). Ong was able to identify two distinct factors – socioemotional and instrumental support – in his psychometric analyses. In addition, availability of social support was related to sojourners' satisfaction with social support,

Table 4.2 The Index of Sojourner Social Support

1. Listen and talk with you whenever you feel lonely or depressed.
2. Give you tangible assistance in dealing with any communication or language problems that you might face.
3. Explain things to make your situation clearer and easier to understand.
4. Spend some quiet time with you whenever you do not feel like going out.
5. Explain and help you understand the local culture and language.
6. Accompany you somewhere even if he/she doesn't have to.
7. Share your good times and bad times.
8. Help you deal with some local institutions' official rules and regulations.
9. Accompany you to do things whenever you need someone for company.
10. Provide necessary information to help orient you to your new surroundings.
11. Comfort you when you feel homesick.
12. Help you interpret things that you don't really understand.
13. Tell you what can and cannot be done in _____ (the country's name).
14. Visit you to see how you are doing.
15. Tell you about available choices and options.
16. Spend time chatting with you whenever you are bored.
17. Reassure you that you are loved, supported and cared for.
18. Show you how to do something that you didn't know how to do.

Source: A. Ong (2000). *The construction and validation of a social support scale for sojouners: The Index of Sojourner Social Support* (ISSS). Unpublished masters thesis, National University of Singapore.

an increased sense of mastery, less social isolation and lower levels of depression. The correlates of social support, along with the sources of social support, the stress-buffering influences of the structural versus the functional components of social support, and the significance of the perceived availability versus the actual use of social support, merit more systematic attention in future research.

Coping resources: Knowledge and skills

Culture-specific knowledge and skills, as discussed in the previous chapter, provide the foundation for effective intercultural interactions; they can also facilitate psychological adaptation to new sociocultural environments. One route to knowledge and skills acquisition is through prior experience. Klineberg and Hull (1979), for example, found that foreign students who had previously resided abroad were significantly better adjusted during their subsequent cross-cultural sojourns. Another avenue for culture learning is through training and educational programmes (see Chapter 11). Along these lines, Deshpande and Viswesvaran's (1992) review and meta-analysis documented the positive effects of cross-cultural training on self-development (psychological well-being, increased self-confidence), interpersonal skills (in interaction with host nationals), cognitive skills (better understanding of host social systems and values), adjustability (the development of expected behaviours in a new culture), and work performance.

Adequate communication has been regarded by many as the key component of intercultural effectiveness (Gudykunst and Hammer, 1988; McGuire and McDermott, 1988); in fact, it has often been used as a measure of intercultural competence as was mentioned in the previous chapter. However, the relationship between communication skills and psychological adjustment is not always straightforward. Certainly a number of studies have linked language fluency to psychological well-being, adjustment and general satisfaction (e.g. Gullahorn and Gullahorn, 1966; Sewell and Davidsen, 1961). Ying and Liese (1991) found lower levels of depression in US-based Taiwanese students who had good English language skills. Decreased psychological and psychosomatic symptoms in Laotian refugees and Indian immigrants in the United States (Krishnan and Berry, 1992; Nicassio *et al.*, 1986) and in Greek Cypriot immigrants to the United Kingdom (Mavreas and Bebbington, 1990) have also been observed in those more fluent in English. However, in some instances researchers have failed to find a significant relationship between language skills and psychological adjustment (e.g. Ward and Kennedy, 1993a). In other cases an inverse relationship between linguistic ability and psychological satisfaction or well-being has been observed. For example, Takai (1989) reported that increased fluency in Japanese was associated with decreased satisfaction in foreign students in Japan. He suggested that this was related to the higher expectations of bilingual foreigners for friendship and the perceived rejection by their Japanese hosts. This interpretation highlights the significance of personal and situational factors and considers the interaction of at least three variables: language fluency, expectations, and hosts' reactions. It also acknowledges the difficulty in identifying and confirming the direct influence of single variables on psychological adjustment during cross-cultural transition.

Despite the occasional exception, the acquisition and maintenance of culture-specific skills facilitate cross-cultural adaptation and are positively related to psychological well-being (e.g. Scott and Scott, 1991). Indeed, the mainstream psychological literature has long recognised the complementarity of the stress and coping and social skills analyses of human behaviour. From the former perspective Folkman, Schaeffer and Lazarus (1979) emphasised that the management of stressful circumstances includes instrumental control of the situation and maintenance of personal integrity and morale. From the latter viewpoint Trower, Bryant and Argyle (1978) linked the social skills domain with the psychology of adjustment by noting that certain forms of adaptation difficulties can be caused or exacerbated by the lack of social competence. They also commented on the reciprocal relationship between the two domains, with social inadequacy leading to isolation and psychological disturbance as well as psychological distress affecting behaviour, including an array of social skills and interactions.

The relationship between stress and coping and social skills is prominently featured in Ward's systematic investigations of psychological and sociocultural adaptation which were introduced in Chapter 2. Across a range of studies involving diverse groups such as foreign students, diplomats, aid workers, and business people, Ward and colleagues have consistently found a positive relationship (0.20 to 0.62 with a median correlation of 0.32) between social difficulty and depression (see the review by Ward and Kennedy, 1999). They have also noted that the magnitude of the relationship varies. Evidence suggests that the association is stronger under conditions involving a greater level of social and cultural integration. For example, the relationship between psychological and sociocultural adaptation is stronger in sojourners who are culturally similar, rather than dissimilar, to hosts; it is greater in sedentary groups, compared with groups involved in cross-cultural relocation; it increases over time; and it is stronger in those adopting integrationist and assimilationist strategies of acculturation, compared with the separated and the marginalised (Kennedy, 1999; Ward and Kennedy, 1996a; Ward *et al.*, 1998; Ward and Rana-Deuba, 1999).

Modes of acculturation

Many studies have considered the relationship between acculturation status and mental health or illness; however, the results of this research have not been entirely consistent. Studies have shown that acculturation is related both to *more* (Singh, 1989) and to *less* stress (Padilla, Wagatsuma and Lindholm, 1985); similarly, acculturation has been related both to *more* (Kaplan and Marks, 1990) and *less* depression (Ghaffarian, 1987; Torres-Rivera, 1985). To explain these inconsistencies some researchers have argued that the intermediate or bicultural mode of acculturation is most adaptive (Buriel, Calzada and Vasquez, 1982) while others have maintained that the effects of acculturation are moderated by variables such as age (Kaplan and Marks, 1990), gender (Mavreas and Bebbington, 1990), and religion (Neffe and Hoppe, 1993). It is likely that these factors, in addition to acculturation measurement error, have contributed to the discrepant findings. These issues, with emphasis on the measurement of acculturation, are discussed in greater detail in the following chapter.

A smaller, but substantial, number of investigations have relied primarily on Berry's (1974, 1984a, 1994b) model to consider the relationship between acculturation and acculturative stress (see Chapter 2 for an elaboration of the model). Correlational research based on early studies of native peoples and immigrants in Canada documented positive relationships between integration and assimilation and adjustment. In contrast, separation and marginalisation were found to be related to psychological maladjustment and psychosomatic problems (Berry and Annis, 1974; Berry *et al.*, 1987; Berry *et al.*, 1982). More recent research has extended the external validity of these findings. These studies have had the advantage of employing a wider variety of adjustment indicators, including measurements of self-esteem, anxiety, depression, acculturative stress, clinical psychopathology, general contentment, and life satisfaction. They have also included a more diverse set of migratory samples (e.g. sojourners and refugees) and a broader range of cultural settings with widely varying levels of cultural pluralism (Ataca, 1996; Donà and Berry, 1994; Partridge, 1988; Pawliuk *et al.*, 1996; Phinney, Chavira and Williamson, 1992; Sam, 2000; Sam and Berry, 1995; Sands and Berry, 1993). A particularly interesting example of this research was undertaken by Schmitz (1992) who reported that integration is associated with reduced levels of both neuroticism and psychoticism and that separation is associated with higher levels of neuroticism, psychoticism and anxiety in his study of East German migrants to West Germany. He also argued that assimilation is linked to impairment of the immune system and that separation is related to cardiovascular problems and drug and alcohol addiction.

Extending research on acculturation and adaptation Ward and Kennedy (1994) set out to combine Berry's theorising on the two dimensions (host and co-national identity and relations) and four modes (integration, separation, assimilation, and marginalisation) of acculturation with their own research on the psychological adjustment of sojourners. Using the Acculturation Index in their study of New Zealanders on overseas assignments, they found that those who strongly identified with their culture of origin displayed fewer symptoms of depression. This appears to be conceptually consistent with Berry and Blondel's (1982) contention that links to one's ethnic community are crucial for mental health. It is also in accordance with Muhlin's (1979) findings that demonstrated a strong inverse relationship between density of an ethnic group and mental illness, and with Mena, Padilla and Maldonado's (1987) research which documented a negative correlation between stress levels and ethnic loyalty. Ward and Kennedy's (1994) study also found that although host national identification did not directly affect the psychological adjustment of the sojourners, it did interact with co-national identification. More specifically, psychological adjustment was adversely influenced by host national identification only when co-national identification was weak, i.e. assimilation was associated with more psychological adjustment problems than was integration. There were no other significant differences in psychological adjustment across the four acculturation modes. Although using a different methodology to test the same model, work by Ward and Kennedy was consistent with Berry's (1997) proposition that integration is the most successful and adaptive strategy.

Acculturation status and demographic factors

While research has frequently demonstrated that sojourners, immigrants and refugees have more psychological and sociocultural adaptation problems than host nationals (Chataway and Berry, 1989; Furnham and Bochner, 1982; Furnham and Tresize, 1981; Sam, 1994; Zheng and Berry, 1991), there have been few systematic studies of psychological adjustment across different types of migrant groups. A major exception to this is Berry *et al.*'s (1987) research which compared the level of acculturative stress, i.e. psychological and psychosomatic symptoms, in refugees, sojourners, immigrants, native peoples and ethnocultural groups within a multicultural society. Their results indicated that native peoples and refugees experienced the greatest level of acculturative stress, immigrants and ethnic groups the lowest level, and sojourners an intermediate level of stress. As the experiences of refugees and native peoples often involve involuntary displacement and resettlement which are dictated by others, it is not surprising that their levels of acculturative stress are considerably higher than those of immigrants, sojourners and ethnic groups who voluntarily choose to relocate and/or to pursue intercultural contact.

The finding that refugees display more psychological distress and dysfunction than other acculturating groups appears consistent across cultures. Pernice and Brook (1994) reported that refugees, compared with immigrants, in New Zealand demonstrated poorer mental health, and Wong-Rieger and Quintana (1987) documented lowered levels of life satisfaction in refugee populations compared with immigrants and sojourners in the United States. These findings are in accordance with the 'push–pull' analysis of geographical movement. Kim (1988), for example, found that relocating persons with greater 'push' motivation experienced more psychological adaptation problems. It is also worth noting that refugees experience high levels of premigration stress, often of a traumatic nature, which may affect later adaptation (Tran, 1993). This is discussed in greater depth in Chapter 10.

A variety of demographic factors have also been examined in relation to migration stress and coping. Gender, age, generational status, income and education are common examples. Although it is often reported that migrant women run a greater risk of psychological symptomatology (e.g. Beiser *et al.*, 1988; Furnham and Shiekh, 1993), the research on gender differences in stress and coping has produced mixed results. It has been noted that women are more often socially isolated than men, partly because they are less likely to be employed and less likely to possess the requisite language skills for integration into the broader community. Despite these handicaps, many studies have failed to establish greater psychological dysfunction in women (e.g. Furnham and Tresize, 1981; Nwadiora and McAdoo, 1996), and some studies have, in fact, reported poorer adjustment in men (Boski, 1990, 1994). It should be acknowledged that the findings arising from research on gender differences in stress, coping and adjustment are strongly influenced by the choice of outcome measures. For example, in his study of adolescent immigrants to Norway, Sam (1994) observed that girls experienced more depressive symptoms while boys were more likely to report antisocial behaviours – findings which are consistent with commonly reported intracultural gender differences in psychopathology. As in other instances, it is likely that the influence of gender on psychological adjustment is moderated by a range of personal and situational factors.

Research findings pertaining to age and adaptation are also somewhat ambiguous. Some studies have reported that younger persons cope better with transition while others have concluded that older people have fewer problems (Church, 1982). These seemingly contradictory results are undoubtedly influenced by imprecise and variable definitions of 'young' and 'old' within and across samples. It is likely, however, that a curvilinear relationship exists between age and adaptation. Beiser *et al.* (1988) have suggested that adolescence and old age are the high risk periods. In the first instance the stress of migration may be intertwined with the stress of adolescent identity and development. In the latter instance, it may be that culture learning is more difficult for older people who have fewer psychological resources to manage a successful transition. In either case, there is reliable evidence that migration at an older age is associated with greater risk (Beiser *et al.*, 1988). One example of this is found in Padilla's (1986) research with Japanese and Mexican Americans which indicated that older migrants have lower levels of self-esteem and experience higher levels of acculturative stress.

There are also mixed findings on adaptation across generations. It is often reported that earlier generations of migrants experience more psychological adjustment problems. For example, Furnham and Li (1993) found that a greater proportion of first, compared with second, generation Chinese migrants to Britain exhibited psychological and psychosomatic symptoms. Padilla (1986) similarly found that acculturative stress was greater in first, compared with second, generation Mexican-Americans. Other studies have suggested that the later generation migrants experience more psychological disturbances. Heras and Revilla (1994) reported that second generation Filipino Americans had poorer self-concepts and lower levels of self-esteem than did first generation migrants, and Padilla (1986) noted that self-esteem was lower in second, compared with first, generation Japanese-Americans.

In light of these conflicting results, some researchers have speculated that it is the nature of the stress that changes over generations. First generation migrants may experience more life changes and have fewer coping resources. Second generation migrants, in contrast, may experience greater pressure to reconcile competing demands from traditional families with those from the new, more modern society (Mumford, Whitehouse and Platts, 1990). Along these lines, Furnham and Shiekh (1993) confirmed that having parents living at home was associated with increased psychological distress in second generation migrants. In contrast, first generation migrants experienced more psychological malaise in connection with limited language ability.

Education, occupation and income have also been considered as influential factors in the stress and coping process. Education is conventionally associated with better adaptation and lower levels of stress (Jayasuriya, Sang and Fielding, 1992). This is not surprising as it is linked to other resources such as culture-specific knowledge and skills and to socioeconomic assets such as higher status occupations and greater income. Although both occupation and income may function as stress-buffering influences, more attention has been directed towards the relational analysis of status mobility. Downward social mobility has been associated with an increase in psychological problems in the general stress and coping literature (Dohrenward and Dohrenward, 1974), and investigations of migration and status mobility have corroborated a higher risk of psychological dysfunction, particularly depression, when upward mobility is blocked (Aycan and Berry, 1996; Beiser, Johnson and Turner, 1993).

Cultural distance and modernisation

Babiker, Cox and Miller (1980) first introduced the concept of cultural distance to account for the distress experienced by sojourners during the process of acculturation. They initially argued that the degree of psychological adjustment problems is a function of the dissimilarities between culture of origin and culture of contact. To examine this proposition they constructed a Cultural Distance Index, an individual difference measure of the perceived discrepancies between social and physical aspects of home and host culture environments. Babiker *et al.*'s hypothesis about the link between cultural distance and psychological well-being was borne out in their original research which demonstrated that cultural distance was related to symptoms of anxiety and medical consultations in foreign students in Scotland.

In more recent sojourner research the link between cultural distance and psychological disturbance has been further substantiated (Ward and Searle, 1991). These findings are not surprising and may be easily interpreted within the stress and coping framework. More specifically, those who experience greater cultural distance likewise experience a greater intensity of life changes during cross-cultural transition and, consequently, more acculturative stress. Cultural distance also influences sociocultural adaptation and the acquisition of culture-specific skills (Searle and Ward, 1990). This was mentioned in Chapter 3 and will be discussed in greater detail in Chapter 11.

Social, political and economic characteristics of the society of settlement may also affect psychological well-being. Torbiorn (1982), for example, found that expatriates are generally more content in industrialised, economically developed countries. Along similar lines Korn-Ferry International (1981) noted that American expatriates were most satisfied with assignments within Europe. Yoshida *et al.* (1997) recently reported that Japanese expatriates experienced more positive mood and higher levels of life satisfaction in American, compared with Egyptian, postings. These findings, however, are limited to a specific type of sojourner, i.e. those found in the employment of multinational companies. In contrast to this trend, there has been some earlier research which indicated that morale and satisfaction of Peace Corps volunteers are higher in rural locales where traditional patterns of indigenous culture are more consistently observed (Guskin, 1966). Again, it is likely that there is an interaction between the characteristics of the individual in transition, the acculturating group, the culture of origin and the culture of settlement that affects the adjustment process.

Prejudice and discrimination

The probable effects of racial prejudice on acculturation strategies and psychological and social adjustment of immigrants and refugees have been widely discussed in the acculturation literature (e.g. Abbott, 1989; Berry *et al.*, 1989; Moghaddam, Ditto and Taylor, 1990). A number of researchers have speculated that attitudes held by members of the dominant culture strongly influence patterns of immigrant, sojourner, and refugee adaptation (e.g. Tanaka *et al.*, 1994; Ward and Searle, 1991). Indeed, Fernando (1993) argued that racism is the most serious risk factor for immigrants. Unfortunately, there have been few investigations that have empirically examined both host culture attitudes toward and the psychological responses of acculturating groups.

A small number of studies, however, have considered the correlates of *perceived* discrimination or prejudice, and findings have revealed a uniformly negative association between perceptions of racism and psychological well-being. Ataca (1996) found that perceived discrimination by Turkish immigrants in Canada was related to poorer psychological adaptation. Furnham and Shiekh (1993) observed that the self-reported experience of racial prejudice was linked to psychological distress in their sample of Asian migrants to the United Kingdom. Vega *et al.* (1993) confirmed that perceived discrimination was associated with a variety of antisocial behaviours including drug use and delinquency in Cuban adolescents in the United States, and in an unpublished study of American sojourners in Singapore, Ward and Chang (1994) noted that psychological adjustment problems increased in relation to Americans' perceptions of negative Singaporean attitudes toward resident expatriates. A more comprehensive discussion of intergroup perceptions and relations will be presented in the following chapter.

CHAPTER SUMMARY

The chapter has described current theory and research on cross-cultural transition and adjustment. As recent trends suggest, researchers have largely adopted a broad-based stress and coping perspective on the study of immigration, acculturation and adaptation. Acknowledging that life changes, whether within or across cultures, tax adjustive resources and necessitate coping responses, this framework allows 'culture shock' to be explained and interpreted in much the same way as other stressing experiences. Both macro and micro level variables affect transition and adjustment, and characteristics of both the individual and the situation mediate and moderate the appraisal of stress, coping responses, and long and short term outcomes. As in other situations involving extensive life changes, cognitive appraisal, personality and social support exert significant influences on stress and coping during cross-cultural transitions. Beyond these general attributes and processes, there are other important factors, such as cultural distance and acculturation strategies, that relate specifically to immigration and adaptation. The stress and coping framework encompasses both these general and specific features of coping with cross-cultural transition in the analysis and interpretation of the adaptation process.

The stress and coping perspective on migration and mental health represents a significant improvement over the older clinical approaches. It is more dynamic and process-oriented. It goes beyond medical models of psychopathology and offers a broader view of cross-cultural transition and adaptation. The framework incorporates and builds on some of the more traditional descriptions of 'culture shock' such as fatalism and locus of control as well as more recent explanations such as negative life events and social support (Furnham and Bochner, 1986). It acknowledges the significance of culture learning, noting that cultural knowledge and skills provide valuable resources for cross-cultural adaptation. It also highlights the contribution of cultural identity and acculturation strategies, which are described more fully in the next chapter, to adjustive outcomes. In these terms the stress and coping framework has offered an integrated approach to theory and research on intercultural contact and cross-cultural adaptation.

5 Social identification theories

So far we have described culture contact in terms of learning and coping processes; that is, people exposed to unfamiliar cultural settings must learn culturally relevant social skills in order to survive and thrive in their new milieux. More recent formulations on the culture learning approach have recognised that culture contact is stressful and that the acquisition of inter-cultural skills depends to some extent on culture travellers developing coping strategies to deal with stress. The terms adjustment and adaptation have been used in connection with this approach which emphasises the psychological and emotional outcomes of intercultural interactions. As described in Chapter 2, both the culture learning and stress and coping perspectives can be incorporated into the broader acculturation literature which provides a major theoretical framework for contemporary research on tourists, sojourners, immigrants and refugees.

The main thrust of the acculturation literature has been to describe and account for the process of change. In this chapter we look at specific dimensions of acculturative changes, in particular issues pertaining to cultural identity and intergroup relations. Here the emergent literature from contemporary social, ethnic and cross-cultural psychology is applied to the study of sojourners, immigrants and refugees. Its conceptual base is largely drawn from theories of social cognition which deal with the ways in which people perceive and think about themselves and others, including how they process information about their own group (in-groups) and about other groups (out-groups). Ethnic and cultural identity forms the core of the conceptual frameworks, directly linking self-definition to group member-ship; however, intergroup processes and dynamics are also considered. Broadly speaking, these conceptual approaches may be referred to as social identification theories (Abrams and Hogg, 1990; Deaux, 1996).

Social identification theories have been shaped and guided by the strong cognitive influence in contemporary psychology. Consequently, the theories are largely concerned with internal mental processes rather than external, observable behaviours. They focus on how groups see each other; how preju-dice arises; why some people choose to leave certain groups and not others; and most importantly, how group membership affects self-esteem. Both identification and intergroup relations feature prominently in social identification theories, and special attention is given to perceptions, attributions, expectations, attitudes and values held and expressed at the group level.

THEORETICAL PERSPECTIVES

Immigrants, refugees and sojourners must consider two salient questions in connection with culture contact and change: 'Who am I?' which includes reference to shifting ethnic, cultural and/or national identities, and 'How do members of my group relate to other groups?' which concerns emergent intergroup attitudes and perceptions. Two major conceptual and empirical approaches have been used to examine these questions and to explore the complex issues associated with social identification. These are: (1) acculturation models and measurements and (2) Social Identity Theory (Phinney, 1990). The first approach, arising from empirical studies about social identity and intercultural contact, has been strongly influenced by personality theory and research and emphasises the structure and content of cognitions about self (Deaux, 1996). Basic research has been concerned with the measurement of acculturation and the correlates of home and host culture identification (Ward, 1996). While this approach has been frequently adopted by ethnic and cross-cultural psychologists, some aspects of the work are also popular with anthropologists and sociologists (Phinney, 1990). The second conceptual framework, Social Identity Theory (SIT), proposed by Tajfel (1978, 1981) and elaborated by Tajfel and Turner (1979, 1986), has emerged from contemporary social psychology. Social Identity Theory highlights the significance of group membership for individual identity and discusses the role of social categorisation and social comparison in relation to self-esteem. SIT has been applied to both naturally occurring groups, such as racial and religious communities, as well as minimal groups artificially created in laboratory conditions.

Acculturation and identity

As previously discussed, acculturation refers to changes that take place as a result of continuous first-hand contact between individuals of different cultural origins (Redfield, Linton and Herskovits, 1936). While such contact may produce changes in attitudes, values, and behaviours, one important component of acculturation relates to changes in cultural identity. On the most basic level, ethnic or cultural identification involves the recognition, categorisation or self-identification of oneself as a member of an ethnocultural group.[1] Identification, however, is also seen as including a sense of affirmation, pride and a positive evaluation of one's group, as well as an involvement dimension, relating to ethnocultural behaviours, values and traditions (Phinney, 1992). For example, ethnic and cultural identity scales frequently incorporate items pertaining to belongingness (how much one feels part of a particular group), centrality (how important one's group membership is for personal identity), evaluation (positive and negative perceptions of one's group), and tradition (the practice of cultural customs and the acceptance of the group's long-standing traditional norms and values). The acculturation literature has employed a broad concept of identification, encompassing the study of attitudes, values and even behaviours. Sometimes the terms identity and acculturation have been used interchangeably as if they were synonymous. At other times identity has been used to describe attachment to various groups and employed in reference to ethnic orientation, cultural familiarity and group commitment. In still other circumstances identity has been viewed at a general level in relation to subjective culture, the characteristic way in which members of a cultural group experience their surrounding environment, including beliefs, evaluations, expectations, norms, roles, self-definitions, stereotypes, and values (Triandis, 1994a).

Although influenced by personality, developmental and social psychological studies of identity in ethnic minority groups within culturally plural societies, acculturation research focuses more specifically on identity changes that occur as a result of intercultural contact between individuals from different societies. Consequently, those who have engaged in cross-cultural transition and relocation, e.g. sojourners, recent immigrants and refugees, receive special attention. Intercultural contact is likely to be experienced by these groups in a different way than it is experienced by members of established ethnic minorities. Immigrants, refugees and sojourners enter a new society embedded with long-standing, distinctive cultural norms and values. The newcomers may have originated from relatively homogeneous countries where cultural identity is rarely, if ever, challenged, and in many cases they may have had no previous exposure to the new host culture. Under these conditions the pressures for cultural change are often perceived as intense, immediate and enduring. It is likely, however, that these intercultural demands become more familiar and less acute for successive generations of immigrants as their groups evolve into established ethnocultural communities within plural societies.

While it is widely agreed that identification with both culture of origin and culture of contact is an important component of identity in immigrant groups, there is little agreement about the nature of the relationship between these two referent identifications. Most of the early studies of immigrants relied upon a rather simplistic, unidimensional and unidirectional model of acculturation and identity (Figure 5.1). Immigrants were seen as

Figure 5.1 A unidirectional model of acculturation

relinquishing identification with the culture of origin and 'progressing' towards identification with the culture of contact by adopting the cultural traits, values, attitudes and behaviours of the host society (Olmeda, 1979); in short, acculturation was equated with assimilation. The assimilation model, still popular with a number of contemporary researchers, is embodied in a range of self-report measurements designed for the assessment of acculturation. These include the Acculturation Rating Scale for Mexican Americans-I (ARMSA; Cuéllar, Harris and Jasso, 1980), the Greek Immigrant Acculturation Scale (Madianos, cited in Mavreas, Bebbington and Der, 1989), and the acculturation scale devised by Ghuman (1994) for Asian adolescents in Canada and the United Kingdom.

The unidimensional, bipolar conceptualisation of acculturation, where members of immigrant and refugee groups are regarded as having to choose between identification with either heritage or contact cultures, came under increasing scrutiny as theory and research on bicultural identity developed throughout the 1980s (Mendoza, 1984; Ramirez, 1984; Szapocznik and Kurtines, 1980). Identification with home and host culture came to be seen as counterbalancing, rather than opposing, forces in shaping the social identification of members of immigrant groups. The first wave of bicultural theory and research reflected a balance model of acculturation and identity. Biculturalism was viewed as the middle ground between assimilation and separatism; however, because measurement scales situated biculturalism at the midpoint between identification with heritage and contact cultures, the two referent identities were still viewed as interdependent, rather than orthogonal, domains (Figure 5.2).

Although an improvement on the assimilation model, the balance model posed obvious measurement problems. The assessment instruments largely failed to distinguish between bicultural individuals who weakly identify with two cultures and those who strongly identify with two reference groups. Despite this limitation, the model still underpins the most popular psychometric approach to the assessment of acculturation. Measurements that rely upon this approach include: the Multicultural Acculturation Scale (Wong-Rieger and Quintana, 1987), the ARMSA-II (Cuéllar, Arnold and Maldonado, 1995), the adult and youth versions of the Short Acculturation Scale for Hispanics (Barona and Miller, 1994; Marín *et al.*, 1987); the Behavioural Acculturation Scale for Hispanics (Szapocznik *et al.*, 1978), the Suinn–Lew Asian Self-Identity Acculturation Scale (Suinn *et al.*, 1987), the Acculturation Scale for Southeast Asians (Anderson *et al.*, 1993), the Acculturation Scale for Asian Americans (Lai and Linden, 1993), and the

Figure 5.2 A balance model of acculturation

International Relations Scale for International Students (Sodowsky and Plake 1991).

More sophisticated models have conceptualised home and host culture identity as independent or orthogonal domains (e.g. Cortés, Rogler and Malgady, 1994; Szapocznik, Kurtines and Fernandez, 1980), and some have also considered these referent identities in conjunction with the categorisation of acculturation strategies. Although the latter approach has been adopted by a number of researchers (Bochner, 1982; Hutnik, 1986; Lasry and Sayegh, 1992), Berry (1974, 1984a, 1994b) is perhaps the best known proponent of the categorical approach. His model, guided by questions concerning the maintenance of heritage culture ('Is it of value to maintain my cultural heritage?') and relations with other ethnocultural groups ('Is it of value to maintain relations with other groups?'), was introduced in Chapter 2. Four acculturation attitudes or strategies – integration, separation, assimilation and marginalisation – arise in connection with these questions, and these are graphically presented in Figure 5.3.

Categorical models are not without their critics (Boski, 1998; Weinreich, 1998). Some have argued, for example, that the categorical approach is too

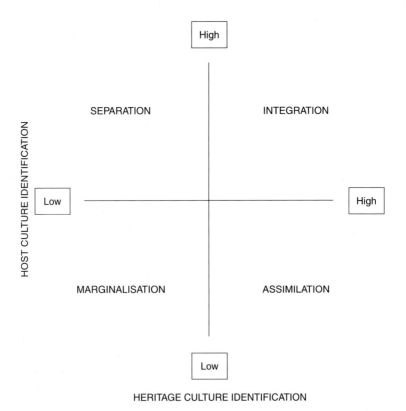

Figure 5.3 A categorical model of acculturation

simplistic as the acculturation strategies used by immigrants, sojourners and refugees change depending upon the specific issues in question. Others have suggested that the two dimensions of cultural identity – culture of origin and culture of contact – are more effective in predicting cross-cultural outcomes than the four acculturation modes (Ward, 1999). Still, the use of categorical approaches, particularly Berry's framework, has increased over the last decade, and a variety of measurement techniques have been developed in connection with these models of acculturation. Some instruments allow the independent assessment of both home and host culture identity and the combination of the two scales for categorical assignment. Ward and Kennedy's (1994) Acculturation Index, Felix-Ortiz, Newcomb and Meyers' (1994) Cultural Identity Scale, and Nguyen, Messé and Stollak's (1999) Acculturation Scale for Vietnamese Adolescents are structured along those lines. Berry and colleagues, however, have generally preferred the independent assessment of marginalisation, assimilation, separation and integration with parallel scales as found in their work with Portuguese, Hungarian, and Korean immigrants to Canada (Berry *et al.*, 1989).

As will be further discussed in this chapter, the core of research on identity and acculturation relates to the components of identity, how identity is modified over time, and the conditions associated with identity and identity change. Investigators have considered characteristics of the individual such as age, gender, and education; characteristics of the migrant group, such as cultural similarity and 'push' versus 'pull' motivations; and characteristics of the receiving society, such as monoculturalism versus multiculturalism and loose versus tight systems of sociocultural organisation. Generally speaking, these variables are viewed as antecedents or correlates of acculturation and identity change. Identity and acculturation, in turn, have also been con-ceptualised as predictors of migrant adaptation to new environments. While psychological and sociocultural dimensions of adjustment have been most frequently examined, identity and acculturation have been related to a wide range of cognitive and behavioural outcomes, including achievement styles (Gomez and Fassinger, 1994), compliance with medical therapy (Lai and Linden, 1993) and even responses to advertising (Lee, 1993).

Social identity theory

Social psychological theories of identity provide a somewhat different per-spective on changing perceptions of self and others during cross-cultural transition and intercultural contact. Among the social psychological theories identity is most frequently discussed and analysed within the context of Tajfel's (1978, 1981) Social Identity Theory. Tajfel pointed to three major defining features of social identity: (1) it is part of the self concept; (2) it requires awareness of membership in a group; and (3) it has evaluative and emotional significance. On the process level, social identification rests on social categorisation and social comparison; that is, the recognition that various in-groups and out-groups exist, that they may be compared, and that favourable and unfavourable comparisons have consequences for self-esteem.

Although Tajfel imbued self-esteem with motivational properties and discussed its enhancement through favourable social comparisons of positive distinctiveness and status, some researchers have argued that a sense of belongingness may be sufficient to enhance self-esteem in members of naturally occurring groups. Bat-Chava and Steen (cited in Deaux, 1996), for example, found moderately strong correlations between ethnic identification and self-esteem across a range of age, gender and ethnic groups in their meta-analytic review. It has been pointed out, however, that any relationship between the components of ethnic identity and self-esteem is likely to be moderated by the overall contribution of ethnicity to self-identity (Phinney, 1991). That is, a relationship between ethnic or cultural identity and self-esteem only occurs in cases when an individual consciously perceives ethnicity or culture as a central, salient feature of identity. Such a relationship would not be likely to emerge, for example, in the case of a third generation Polish-New Zealander who has largely or completely assimilated and does not refer to him- or herself as Polish.

Tajfel has also argued that intergroup bias is an inevitable consequence of social identification, and, indeed, social psychological research has routinely demonstrated that in-group favouritism is common, even in those groups artificially created under laboratory conditions (Tajfel and Turner, 1986). In minimal group experiments in-group favouritism has been frequently investigated in terms of reward allocations. In natural groups, where this line of research has been more commonly pursued in connection with stereotypes and attributions, the results are much the same. For example, individuals are more likely to make internal attributions for positive behaviours displayed by members of their ethnic, cultural or religious in-groups while they are inclined to make external attributions for the same behaviours displayed by out-group members (Hewstone and Ward, 1985; Lynskey, Ward and Fletcher, 1991; Taylor and Jaggi, 1974). That is, they explain their own group's positive behaviours as due to personality characteristics (e.g. kindness, honesty, and intelligence) whereas the out-group's behaviours are attributed to circumstances. It has also been recognised that out-group derogation increases when identity is under threat. Branscombe and Wann (1994) found that American students, particularly those with strong social identities, were more likely to disparage national groups, including Soviets, South Africans, French and Chinese, when their own identities were threatened. Out-group derogation during intercultural contact is likely to occur in members of both the migrant and the host communities, and this will be explored further in later sections of this chapter.

Social Identity Theory considers not only the tendency for groups to exhibit in-group favouritism and out-group derogation, it also explores the responses to out-group devaluation. The theory is particularly concerned with the strategies that individuals use to maintain self-esteem in the face of an unfavourable group identity. Migrant groups, like other minorities, are often subjected to negative stereotyping and prejudicial attitudes by members of the majority. If this is perceived as threatening, individuals may adopt a variety of responses to change their social identities and to restore self-esteem (see Table 5.1). According to Tajfel, these strategies may include 'passing' or changing in-groups, a range of cognitive processes to redefine or enhance social comparisons, and collective social action for the betterment of the group (Tajfel and Turner, 1986).

Much of Tajfel's social identity theorising has been based on groups that experience perceived threats to identity (also see Breakwell, 1986). This aspect of his work makes the theory particularly relevant to immigrants and refugees. Research has suggested that both cognitive and affective components of identity are more strongly aroused in minority groups and that members of these groups may experience a stronger need for in-group identification than members of a privileged majority. It has also been suggested that transition points in the life cycle, which could include significant life events such as cross-cultural relocation, evoke more emotional aspects of the identity process (Deaux, 1996). Given the generally less privileged status endured by migrant groups and the magnitude of change involved in cross-cultural transition, it is not surprising that Tajfel's Social Identity Theory has been one of the most frequently used conceptual frameworks for exploring identity and intergroup relations in immigrants, refugees and sojourners (see Moghaddam, 1998; Phinney, 1990).

While the proponents of Social Identity Theory have emphasised the

Table 5.1 Reactions to threatened social identity (adapted from Tajfel and Turner, 1986)

Reaction	Description	Example
1. Individual mobility	Individual tries to leave low status group; attempt at upward social mobility; group boundaries must be permeable	'Passing'
2. Social creativity	In-group members seek positive distinctiveness by redefining elements of comparison	Comparing in-group and out-group on new dimensions; reevaluating attributes assigned to the group; changing target group for comparison
3. Social competition	Group members seek positive distinctiveness through direct competition with out-groups	Reversing the relative positions of in-groups and out-groups on salient dimensions; social change results

relationship between group identity and self-esteem, the theory is more frequently used in the investigation of intergroup perceptions and relations. Ethnocentric attributions and intergroup stereotyping are primarily interpreted within this theoretical framework. Social Identity Theory is also commonly evoked in studies of perceived discrimination, including the strategic responses used by immigrants, sojourners and refugees in pursuit of favourable social comparisons and the achievement of higher status within their new societies.

IDENTITY, ACCULTURATION AND INTERCULTURAL CONTACT

Social identification theories acknowledge that identity entails a set of dynamic, complex processes by which individuals define, redefine and construct their own and others' ethnicity. As identity changes in response to temporal, cultural and situational contexts, the predictors, antecedents and correlates of cultural identity have attracted considerable attention. Empirical research on acculturation has examined a range of intrapersonal, interpersonal, and intergroup variables that affect the patterns of and changes in social identities in immigrant and refugee groups.

Although few have explored these changes from an explicitly developmental perspective (for exceptions see work by Aboud, 1987; Phinney, 1989; Schönpflug, 1997), many have investigated identity issues cross-sectionally to explore age and generational differences. In general, younger migrants appear to be more malleable than older ones, and they tend to take on more readily host culture norms and values (Marín *et al.*, 1987; Mavreas *et al.*, 1989). When acculturation starts early, particularly before admission to primary school, it appears to proceed more smoothly (Beiser *et al.*, 1988). One possible reason is that younger migrants tend to have better language skills and are more easily accepted into the receiving country (Liebkind, 1996). Despite this advantage, adolescent migrants are known to be at risk (Ghuman, 1994; Sam and Berry, 1995). As they reach a stage in which they experiment with their identities, they may be simultaneously influenced by peer pressure and familial conflict over changing attitudes and behaviours. Cross-cultural transitions made in later life present different challenges. A strong sense of identity with heritage culture may be well established, and attachments to both home and host cultures are often more resistant to change.

Although the results of research on gender differences in identification and acculturation have not been completely consistent, there is moderately strong evidence that assimilation proceeds more rapidly in boys than girls and that men assimilate more quickly than women (Ghaffarian, 1987). There is also evidence that women have more negative attitudes toward assimilation and are more likely to retain a stronger sense of identity with culture of origin (Harris and Verven, 1996; Liebkind, 1996; Ting-Toomey, 1981). The traditional roles that women play have been cited as a reason for this difference. In many cases women are more isolated from members of the receiving culture, particularly if they are unemployed or lack requisite language skills. In addition, women are often perceived as cultural gatekeepers, teaching their children about ethnic customs and traditions and nurturing identification with heritage culture norms and values (Yee, 1990, 1992).

Cultural transmission exerts a strong influence on the development and maintenance of cultural identity in successive generations. Parents' immersion in their own ethnic community as well as perceptions of parental attitudes toward cultural change significantly influence adolescent ethnic identity and acculturation strategies (Rosenthal and Chicello, 1986; Sam, 1995). Research suggests that immigrants typically display an increasingly strong orientation toward the host culture over generations (Montgomery, 1992). This does not mean, however, that they necessarily relinquish identity with their culture of origin. For example, Mavreas *et al.* (1989) described second generation Greek migrants to the United Kingdom as balancing both Greek and British identities, unlike their parents who were more strongly and exclusively Greek. The interplay between home and host culture identities may be affected by a number of factors, and their development does not always follow a linear or unidirectional path. A variety of identity changes may be observed as recently arrived immigrant groups evolve into more firmly established minorities in multicultural societies. Keefe and Padilla (1987), for example, found that cultural awareness decreased substantially from first to second generation Mexican-Americans and continued to decline gradually; however, ethnic loyalty showed only a slight decrement over the first two generations and then remained fairly stable. In contrast, Atkinson, Morten and Sue (1983) described changing patterns over three generations of immigrants, noting that the first generation is often separatist, retaining a strong identity with the heritage culture; the second generation more closely approximates the host culture; and the third generation often emerges as reaffirmationists with a renewed interest in ethnic customs, values and behaviours.

While generational studies have provided information about the patterns of shifting identity in immigrants and refugees, a separate line of innovative research has compared migrant groups with nonmigrant groups in both their country of origin and their country of settlement. Altrocchi and Altrocchi (1995) examined identity, attitudes and behaviours in four groups of Cook Islanders, comparing them with a group of non-Cook Island New Zealanders. Their sample included two sedentary Cook Island groups, one from Mitiaro, a small outer island with a population of 247 and one from Rarotonga, the capital island and centre of tourism; and two migratory groups, one which had relocated to New Zealand and another which included people born in New Zealand. The research revealed that identification as a Cook Islander was strongest in the Mitiaro group and steadily declined across the Rarotonga group, the migrant group and the New Zealand-born group, respectively. Group-referent or collective identification was strongest in the Mitiaro sample and weakest in the New Zealand group, with New Zealand-born Cook Islanders between these two extremes. In addition, the New Zealand-born Cook Islanders more closely resembled New Zealanders in terms of their attitudes and behaviours than they did the other Cook Islanders. Despite this general pattern of acculturative change, which suggested movement toward New Zealand norms and values with increasing contact, the researchers also found that a subsample of Cook Island migrants, specifically those who were heavily involved in Cook Island community activities, retained more traditional Cook Island attitudes and behaviours than those resident in Rarotonga. This was interpreted as a sign of ethnocultural affirmation.

At this point in the discussion it seems appropriate to consider the distinction between cognitive and behavioural aspects of acculturation. Although research has demonstrated that the two are inter-related (Der-Karabetian, 1980; Ullah, 1987), they exhibit different patterns of change over time (Cuéllar, Arnold and González, 1995; Szapocznik *et al.*, 1978). Immigrants and refugees are usually willing to learn new behaviours and skills, but their attitudes and values are generally more resistant to change (Triandis *et al.*, 1986; Wong-Rieger and Quintana, 1987). One example of this can be found in a study by Rosenthal and colleagues (1989) who compared Greek Australians with Anglo-Australians and with Greeks. Although Greek Australians were more similar to Anglo-Australians in terms of behaviours, they more closely resembled native Greeks in terms of values. Returning to our earlier discussion of culture learning, findings such as these suggest that successful immigrants will acquire the functional skills that enable them to succeed in their new social environments but that this may be independent of any changes in their self-concepts. (For further discussion see Chapter 3 on skills acquisition and Chapter 11 on changing behaviours and cognitions.)

This has also been discussed by Camilleri and Malewska-Peyre (1997), albeit from a slightly different perspective. They observed that North African migrants in France often assume a pragmatic approach to adapting to life in their new environment. Children may maintain a more traditional style of interacting with parents but use a modern style when interacting with peers. Business people may drink wine with colleagues at social functions, but refrain from doing so at home. Despite these pragmatic behavioural responses, core values remain largely unchanged. In short, neither changing behaviours nor the acquisition of new cultural skills is necessarily indications of cultural identification (LaFromboise, Coleman and Gerton, 1993). These attitude–behaviour discrepancies deserve further attention, particularly in light of findings that suggest members of receiving communities are largely supportive of immigrant groups retaining their cultural traditions relating to food, music or dress, but have stronger reservations about the maintenance of traditional, potentially conflicting, values (Lambert *et al.*, 1990).

In addition to demographic factors such as age and generational status, quality and quantity of intercultural contact also exert strong influences on ethnic and cultural identity. Greater overall exposure to the host culture is associated with stronger assimilative responses (Mendoza, 1989). Increased length of residence in a new culture seems to strengthen host, but weaken home, culture identity, and those born within the contact culture assimilate more quickly than those born overseas (Cortés *et al.*, 1994). Education and socioeconomic status also affect the experience of acculturation. Higher levels of education predict stronger host culture identification (Mavreas *et al.*, 1989; Suinn, Ahuna and Khoo, 1992), and higher socioeconomic status is associated with more rapid assimilation (Barona and Miller, 1994; Nicassio, 1983), at least in instances of cross-cultural movement towards Western industrialised countries such as the United States and the United Kingdom.

The conditions under which intercultural contact occurs may also affect the likelihood of cultural assimilation. What are the national policies regarding race, ethnicity and culture? Multicultural societies that advocate policies of cultural pluralism offer a wider range of acculturation opportunities than do assimilationist societies (Berry, 1997; Sam, 1995). Loose societies (i.e. those that tolerate a range of views about what constitutes correct action and maintain flexibility about the extent to which individuals are expected to conform to conventional norms and values), compared with tight societies, also place fewer constraints on social identity and the acculturation options available for immigrant groups (Triandis, 1997). How similar or dissimilar is the migrant group to members of the receiving culture? Cultural differences, like perceived discrimination, discourage assimilation, particularly in members of visible minorities (Lalonde and Cameron, 1993; Richman *et al.*, 1987). Is there a match or mismatch between immigrant and host expectations about acculturation? Immigrants sometimes perceive host culture expectations for them to assimilate as much stronger than their own willingness to do so, and this may affect identity with both original and contact cultures (Horenczyk, 1996).

Patterns of intracultural contact and communication similarly influence social identity. Assimilation proceeds more slowly when immigrants reside in intra-ethnic enclaves (Cuéllar and Arnold, 1988), and intra-ethnic interactions, including membership in ethnocultural organisations, foster maintenance of heritage identity (Altrocchi and Altrocchi, 1995). Native language usage and preference are generally associated with weaker assimilative responses (Berry *et al.*, 1989; Lanca *et al.*, 1994; Montgomery, 1992). This is not surprising as language choice has both cultural and political dimensions (see work by Giles, Bourhis and Taylor (1977) on ethnolinguistic vitality). Language may serve as a symbol of identity and a route to positive distinctiveness and status. Indeed, there is considerable evidence to suggest that members of ethnocultural groups emphasise indigenous languages when identity is under threat (Bourhis and Giles, 1977) and that motivation to learn a second language in minority group members is lower when there is fear of assimilation (Clément, 1986; Clément and Bourhis, 1996). Young and Gardner's (1990) study of Chinese immigrants in Canada, for example, found that those who were proficient in Chinese and feared assimilation were reluctant to learn English, while those who identified strongly with Canadian culture perceived their Chinese language skills to be weak. These findings are also consistent with Lambert's (1974, 1978) theory of subtractive bilingualism, i.e. the loss of first language and culture by a minority group when a second (dominant) language is mastered.

Finally, the characteristics and conditions of migration are also important, particularly the duration of the cross-cultural transition and the voluntariness of the move. Those who view their stay in a new culture as temporary, such as sojourners or short-term migrants, retain a stronger identity with their culture of origin and a weaker identity with the culture of contact, compared with those who plan for their residence to be more permanent (Mendoza, 1989; Ward and Kennedy, 1993c). Even among more long term immigrants and refugees, however, assimilation is less likely to occur among those who were 'pushed' into relocation compared with those who were motivated by 'pull' factors (Wong-Rieger and Quintana, 1987).

The bulk of the work on identity and acculturation, as reviewed in this section, has examined the antecedents and correlates of identity and identity change. A separate line of research on immigrants, refugees, and sojourners, however, has considered identity and acculturation as predictors of cross-cultural adaptation. Although a range of psychological and social outcomes has been explored, self-esteem has received particular attention. The most comprehensive review of this topic has been provided by Moyerman and Forman's (1992) meta-analytic study which reported a positive relationship between acculturation and self-esteem in immigrants and native peoples in North America. The greatest esteem gains were found in older, non-Hispanic and lower SES migrants as they more closely approximated members of the host culture. These findings, however, appear at odds with Phinney's (1992) research which reported a significant relationship between ethnic identity and self-esteem in established black, Hispanic, and Asian minority groups in the United States. They are also discrepant with studies on identity and self-esteem in Turkish adolescents in The Netherlands (Verkuyten, 1990) and Vietnamese migrants in Australia (Nesdale, Rooney and Smith, 1997).

These apparently conflicting results present a challenge to Social Identity Theory and serve to reinforce the importance of considering aspects of both heritage and contact cultures in studies of ethnicity, acculturation and intergroup relations. Indeed, this was explored in some depth by Heine and Lehman (1997) in their cross-cultural work on acculturation and self-esteem. Their study involved the administration of self-esteem measures to Japanese and Canadian sojourners on two separate occasions. The Canadian group was tested before departure from Canada and then again after 7 months in Japan. The Japanese group was tested within 2 days of arrival in Canada and then again after 7 months of residence. Findings revealed that the Canadian sojourners demonstrated a significant decrease in self-esteem over the 7 month period while Japanese sojourners showed a significant increase in self-esteem. Heine and Lehman interpreted these findings in terms of cross-cultural differences in self-concept and self-esteem (i.e. the well-documented finding that North Americans report higher levels of self-esteem than Japanese) and sojourners' tendencies to become more similar to members of the host culture over time.[2] Although this study had a number of limitations, e.g. the Canadian sojourners were English teachers while the Japanese sojourners were students, and the former group was tested before departure while the latter was tested soon after arrival overseas, it raises some interesting issues regarding acculturation and cultural influences on self-esteem.

There is also evidence to suggest that as sojourners, refugees and immigrants more closely approximate the host culture over time, they incorporate a range of negative, undesirable qualities found in the receiving society. Moyerman and Forman's (1992) meta-analytic study, based primarily on North American research, demonstrated that cultural assimilation was weakly associated with addiction, affective and impulse control disorders, anxiety, stress and health problems. The relationship between acculturation and adaptation is a complex one and is likely to be moderated by both intra-personal and interpersonal factors. Rogler, Cortés and Malgady's (1991) review of research indicated that 12 studies supported a positive relationship between acculturation and mental health, 13 supported a negative relationship, three supported a curvilinear relationship, and two produced both positive and negative results. Different models and measurements of identity and acculturation no doubt contribute to the inconsistent findings as do the wide variety of outcome measures. For example, Ward and Kennedy (1994) and Ward and Rana-Deuba (1999) have demonstrated that home culture identification and host culture identification make independent contributions to cross-cultural adjustment and that they influence different adjustment domains. Identification with culture of origin is associated with better psychological adjustment while identification with contact culture is linked to better sociocultural adaptation. Further research is no doubt required to clarify the relationship between identity and cross-cultural adaptation.

INTERGROUP PERCEPTIONS AND RELATIONS

Immigrants, sojourners and refugees are required to deal with issues concerning both maintenance of cultural heritage and contact with members of the receiving society. Berry's (1974, 1984a) model recognises these issues as the two fundamental components of acculturation. Accordingly, it forms a theoretical bridge between the social identification theories that concentrate on self-definition and ethnic identity and those that highlight the significance of intergroup perceptions and relations. Prominently featured in this model, as previously mentioned, are four basic acculturation attitudes or strategies:

integration, separation, assimilation and marginalisation. The selection, acceptance and adoption of these attitudes and strategies vary across individuals and groups and are shaped by multiple influences including sociocultural and political factors.

Berry and his colleagues have clearly demonstrated that integration is the strategy most favoured by newcomers in multicultural societies. Hungarian, Korean, Portuguese and Lebanese immigrants, as well as Central American refugees, in Canada display a significant preference for integration (Berry *et al.*, 1989; Donà and Berry, 1994; Sayegh and Lasry, 1993). There is also evidence, though less consistent, that integration is preferred in culturally homogeneous settings, even by members of visible minorities. Sam (1995) reported that it is favoured by immigrants from developing countries who relocated to Norway, and Partridge (1988) found it popular in Japan with the expatriate wives of Japanese men. It appears that integration is also the preferred strategy of returning migrants, as reported in Georgas and Papastylianou's (1996) study of Greek remigration from the former Soviet Union, Albania, Australia, Canada, and the United States.

Although Social Identity Theory proposes that individuals strive for positive social identity through social categorisation, comparison and in-group favouritism, empirical evidence on acculturation does not consistently support this view. Instead, it suggests that migrant groups prefer integrationist strategies; that is, they have strong preferences for retaining their cultural identities while sustaining good relationships with members of the dominant culture. The question may then be asked, is this a viable option? From an acculturation perspective integration can only be achieved if migrant groups are permitted to retain cultural distinctiveness and if they are accepted by members of the receiving community. Social Identity Theory, however, emphasises the importance of social categorisation, comparison and in-group favouritism. This suggests that the integrative efforts of migrant groups may be blocked by members of the receiving culture and that the emerging social identities of the newcomers may be negatively affected by out-group stereotyping, prejudice and discrimination.

Attributions and stereotypes

Attributions refer to judgements or causal explanations about human behaviour. While individuals use attributions to make sense of their surrounding environments, their causal accounts are often influenced by motivational biases. One of these biases is related to the need to maintain and enhance self-esteem. Social psychological research has demonstrated that in most cases individuals attribute their successes to internal or dispositional factors and their failures to external or situational factors. This tendency to accept credit for success and deny responsibility for failure has been termed the self-serving bias.

Social identity theory suggests that people are likewise motivated to make group-serving attributions; that is, to generate behavioural explanations that favour members of their in-groups. Taylor and Jaggi (1974) first uncovered this tendency in their Indian study which compared the attributions given for socially desirable and undesirable Hindu and Muslim behaviours. Members of the majority Hindu community gave internal attributions for desirable acts when those behaviours were performed by in-group members; however, they relied upon external attributions when the same behaviours were performed by out-group Muslims. In cases of undesirable behaviours the pattern of in-group and out-group attributions was reversed. In a similar vein Rosenberg and Wolsfeld (1977) investigated attributions for Arab and Israeli actions during the Middle Eastern conflict. Israeli students in the United States gave more internal attributions for Israeli moral acts and fewer internal attributions for Israeli immoral acts than did Arab students. In contrast, Arab students gave fewer internal attributions for Arab immoral behaviours than did Israeli students.

In-group favouritism is also found in intergroup stereotypes. Wibulswadi (1989) studied the intergroup perceptions of Thais, Chinese, Hmong and Americans in Northern Thailand. Overall the majority Thai group was rated most positively; however, there was also a strong tendency to attribute desirable characteristics to one's own group and less desirable traits to other groups. Lambert, Mermigis and Taylor (1986) also found some evidence of in-group favouritism in their study of ethnic stereotyping in Canada. Greek-Canadians, for example, described their own group as more helpful, hardworking, honest and trustworthy than English-, French-, Jewish-, Portuguese-, Italian- and black Canadians. Likewise, Georgas (1998) reported that Greeks perceived themselves as more industrious, reliable, and honest than non-Greeks, but more interestingly, the perceptions of repatriating Greeks fell between the Greek and non-Greek stereotypes. Negative out-group stereotypes have significant implications for prejudice and discrimination in receiving societies. Stephan and associates identified these stereotypes as one of the four basic threats (along with realistic and symbolic threats and intergroup anxiety) that lead to prejudice. This was confirmed in their studies of prejudicial attitudes toward Moroccan immigrants in Spain, Russian immigrants in Israel, and Mexican immigrants in the United States (Stephan *et al.*, 1998; Ybarra and Stephan, 1994).

Given the widespread biases in stereotypes and attributions, are there strategies that could be used to reduce in-group favouritism and enhance intergroup perceptions and relations? Social psychological theory has suggested that increased contact – at least under certain conditions – may improve intergroup perceptions and relations. Harry Triandis and Vasso Vassiliou (1967) were the first to examine this with international groups of sojourners in the United States and Greece. Greeks and Americans with low, medium and high amounts of intercultural contact completed questionnaires about perceptions of their own group and perceptions of the other group. Both groups agreed that Greeks had somewhat more negative features (e.g. lazy, rigid, suspicious) than did Americans. More significantly, however, increased contact with Americans resulted in more favourable stereotypes for Greeks, but increased contact with Greeks resulted in more negative stereotypes for Americans. Triandis and Vassiliou suggested that stereotypes usually contain a 'kernel of truth' and that increased contact provides first hand knowledge that sharpens or crystallises intergroup perceptions. Amir and Ben-Ari (1985) provided further evidence of the 'crystallisation' hypothesis in their study of Israeli tourists in Egypt. Positive perceptions of Egyptians improved with contact while negative perceptions became more firmly entrenched.

A more recent investigation of this phenomenon was undertaken by Kosmitzki (1996) in her study of German- and American-born nationals living in either their own country or overseas. Germans and Americans described themselves in addition to German and American in-group and out-group members on a number of characteristics. They also rated the overall desirability of these traits. Level of contact failed to predict out-group evaluations; there was no significant difference in the favourability of out-group stereotypes of German and American nationals who lived at home compared with those who lived abroad. There were, however, differences in in-group evaluations. Consistent with Social Identity Theory and reflecting the need for positive distinctiveness in intercultural comparisons, German and American sojourners rated their own group more favourably than German and American home nationals. The sojourner groups also saw the German and American cultures as less similar than did the home-based samples. Furthermore, those living abroad saw themselves as more similar to their native cultural group than those residing at home.

Despite supporting evidence for the contact hypothesis (Clément, Gardner and Smythe, 1977), the influence of contact on stereotyping is likely to be affected by a range of personal, social and situational variables. Amir and Ben-Ari (1988) argue that contact may furnish an opportunity for mutual acquaintance and understanding; however, the prerequisites for positive perceptions and interactions are: equal status, pursuit of common goals, contact of an intimate, rather than casual, nature, and a broader social climate supporting intergroup contact. Some of these factors can be observed in Kim, Cho and Harajiri's (1997) study of Koreans in Seoul and in Tokyo and their perceptions of the Japanese. Direct contact proved to be important but its effects were moderated by linguistic and social skills. Overall, sojourners emphasised the more positive characteristics of the Japanese (e.g. orderly, safe, secure, advanced) and were less likely to endorse traditional negative stereotypes (e.g. colonialist, superior). Positive perceptions, however, were associated with effective participation in the culture; negative, more critical evaluations were linked to dissatisfying experiences, including perceived discrimination. Nevertheless, it is also interesting to note that those who had lived in Japan longer viewed the Japanese as more ethnocentric.

Perceived discrimination

While social identity may facilitate a sense of belonging and contribute to positive self-perceptions and self-esteem, negative consequences can ensue if members of an immigrant community are held in low regard by the dominant ethnocultural group. Perceived discrimination has been associated with less willingness to adopt host culture identity (Mainous, 1989). It has also been related to a variety of negative outcomes including increased stress (Vega *et al.*, 1991), identity conflict (Leong and Ward, 2000), depression and social skills deficits (Berno and Ward, 1998). However, the psychological, social and cultural outcomes of perceived discrimination are moderated by other factors. For example, a study of international students in Australia revealed that those who believe that their cultural group is held in low regard by members of the host culture adapt better when the intercultural boundaries between sojourners and hosts are perceived as permeable (Pelly, 1997).

Perceptions of discrimination vary considerably across individuals and groups. Malewska-Peyre (1982) found that seven out of ten second generation adolescent migrants in France reported feeling deeply affected by prejudice and discrimination. Girls perceived greater discrimination than boys, and Arabs perceived greater discrimination than Spanish or Portuguese. While cultural differences are associated with such perceptions, even migrant groups that are linguistically, ethnically and culturally similar to majority members of the host culture may feel socially disadvantaged. Leong (1997), for example, found that sojourners from the People's Republic of China perceived at least a moderate level of prejudice and discrimination in Singapore. Furthermore, their perceptions of discrimination grew stronger with an increasing amount of contact with Singaporeans.

In addition to intergroup differences, there are also differences in perceptions of individual versus group discrimination. It is typically the case that members of disadvantaged groups view more discrimination as directed toward other members of their group than towards themselves as individuals (Taylor, Moghaddam and Bellerose, 1989; Taylor *et al.*, 1990). This bears some resemblance to the social psychological third person effect where others are seen as more vulnerable to adverse occurrences than oneself (Adams, Bochner and Bilik, 1998). The phenomenon is robust, but the mechanisms are not completely understood. Taylor and colleagues have suggested that both denial of individual discrimination and exaggeration of group discrimination play a role in these self–other discrepancies. The functional advantages of these perceptions are apparent in terms of preserving self-esteem and well-being (Taylor and Brown, 1988); nevertheless, further research is required to shed more light on these perceptual processes.

Which strategies are most likely to be used by members of an immigrant group in response to perceptions of discrimination? Social Identity Theory suggests that members of disadvantaged groups may adopt assimilationist responses, attempting to pass as members of the dominant, positively regarded culture; or they may resort to certain cognitive strategies such as selecting alternative groups for social comparison or reevaluating the in-group stereotypes; or they may opt for more collective solutions, such as social action for the betterment of the group. Choice of strategy is influenced by individual, group and societal factors (Camilleri and Malewska-Peyre, 1997). In their study of Iranians in Montreal Moghaddam, Taylor and Lalonde (1987) found that immigrants pursued one of two acculturative responses. An individualistic approach, concerned primarily with personal social mobility rather than maintenance of cultural heritage, was adopted by one group. Collectivist strategies, including reliance upon the support of Iranian cultural organisations and the larger Iranian community to help with social advancement, were engaged by the others. These groups differed on a number of salient characteristics, including willingness to remain in Canada and perceived necessity of liaisons with the Iranian community. Most importantly, however, those who adopted collectivist strategies had a stronger belief in the justice and fairness of the Canadian system. Moghaddam *et al.* acknowledge that there are likely to be marked differences in the accultur-ation beliefs and strategies employed by other immigrant groups. They point out, for example, that integration may be a realistic alternative for Iranians, who, unlike many other immigrant groups, tend to be well-educated, come from middle and upper middle class backgrounds, and are not members of obviously visible minorities.

With these issues in mind, their research was extended to other immigrant groups in Canada, with particular attention given to women and members of visible minorities (Lalonde, Taylor and Moghaddam, 1988). One of their early studies compared the perceptions of discrimination and the use of acculturation strategies by Haitian and Indian women in Montreal. The Haitians, who were more recent migrants to Canada and outnumbered their Indian counterparts, reported more perceived discrimination and showed a stronger preference for collectivist strategies.

More recently, Lalonde and Cameron (1993) studied Chinese, black Caribbean, Italian and Greek immigrants to Canada. They suggested three reasons why social identity would be more problematic for the Caribbean and Chinese immigrants than for the Greeks and Italians. First, fewer immigrants came to Canada from Asia, Africa, and the Caribbean compared with the more familiar migrants from Europe. Second, early immigration policies dis-criminated against blacks and Asians, and third, persons of colour in Canada are viewed less favourably than whites (Berry, Kalin and Taylor, 1977). Indeed, Lalonde and Cameron's findings indicated that perceived disadvan-tage was greatest in the Caribbean migrants, followed by the Chinese, and that both of these groups perceived greater disadvantage than the Greeks and Italians. In addition, Caribbean immigrants preferred collective strategies more than the two European groups, and the Chinese preferred those strategies significantly more than the Italians. The strongest predictor of the preference for collective acculturation strategies was perceived disadvantage.

In line with Social Identity Theory, those who appear disadvantaged by negative social identities are motivated to redress the inequities. If ethnocultural boundaries are perceived as impermeable, as is more likely the case for visible minorities, immigrants demonstrate a stronger tendency to adopt collective strategies in an effort to enhance group status.

SOCIAL IDENTIFICATION THEORIES AND MULTICULTURAL IDEOLOGY

In an age of expanding intercultural contact and growing international migration, questions pertaining to cultural identity and intergroup relations have become increasingly important. Is it possible for ethnic groups to retain their language, customs and traditional values and at the same time maintain harmonious relationships with other groups? Do positive in-group perceptions necessitate negative out-group evaluations? Is self-esteem dependent upon in-group favouritism and out-group denigration?

Acculturation models and Social Identity Theory have rather negative implications for multicultural societies. Much of the acculturation literature, for example, sees assimilation as a natural, desirable and inevitable consequence of migration. This limits options for the maintenance of cultural identity in sojourners, immigrants and refugees. Social Identity Theory, on the other hand, argues that positive social comparisons, involving both in-group favouritism and out-group devaluation, are a primary source of self-esteem enhancement, suggesting that conflict, prejudice and discrimination are inevitable outcomes of intercultural contact.

In contrast, multicultural ideologies assume that the development and maintenance of a secure in-group identity can lead to greater intergroup acceptance and tolerance. This has been discussed as the 'multicultural assumption' by Berry (1984a,b) in relation to studies of ethnic relations in Canada, where national policy seeks to improve intergroup harmony by simultaneously encouraging the development of vital ethnic communities and promoting mutual interaction and sharing. Here we consider three questions about identity and intergroup relations and how the multicultural assumption challenges aspects of Social Identity Theory and features of the popular models of acculturation.

• *Question 1. Are positive in-group perceptions uniformly related to negative out-group perceptions?* On this, the Canadian evidence appears mixed. National survey data have revealed that, on the whole, more positive in-group evaluations are associated with increasingly negative out-group evaluations. This trend does not hold, however, for British and French Canadians. For these 'charter' groups, who together constitute the numerical majority in Canada, in-group and out-group evaluations are positively related (Berry *et al.*, 1977). Even with in-group biases,

Canadians are somewhat discerning in their patterns of ethnic stereotyping. Lambert *et al.*'s (1986) study of Greek Canadians revealed that while the in-group was generally perceived more positively than out-groups, evaluations varied across trait-specific domains. For example, English-Canadians were perceived as more law-abiding while Jewish-Canadians were seen as more intelligent than Greek-Canadians.

- *Question 2. Does a positive sense of cultural identity predict out-group denigration?* The answer seems to be, 'it depends'. If in-group and out-group stereotyping is considered, as described in the previous section, there is some evidence of in-group favouritism and out-group devaluation. Berry and colleagues, however, have approached this question from a slightly different angle by considering identity in relation to perceptions of cultural and economic security. Their findings have shown that an increasing sense of security is associated with more positive attitudes toward other ethnic groups (Berry *et al.*, 1977; Lambert *et al.*, 1986). The same pattern has been observed in the analysis of self-esteem; those with higher levels of self-esteem are more tolerant of ethnic out-groups (Aboud and Skerry, 1984). Consequently, Berry maintains that there is clear support for the multicultural assumption if positive identity is understood in terms of a sense of security or self-esteem; under these conditions, a more positive sense of identity is linked to more favourable out-group perceptions.

- *Question 3. Does increased contact augment the need for in-group distinctiveness and favourable social comparison?* The answer here is clearly 'no'. When groups interact within a social and political context of racial tolerance and cultural pluralism, it appears that increased contact fosters positive intergroup relations. National surveys of the Canadian population reveal that greater geographical mobility and exposure to diverse environments are associated with more positive perceptions of out-groups (Kalin and Berry, 1979). Familiarity with ethnic out-groups has been related to their more favourable evaluation (Berry, 1984a,b), and there is evidence that higher proportions of ethnocultural groups in a geographical area are associated with more positive evaluations of these groups by their out-group neighbours (Kalin and Berry, 1982). Overall, there is converging evidence that increased contact is associated with more positive intergroup perceptions in the Canadian setting.

The 'multicultural assumption' does not provide a comprehensive theory of ethnic identity and intergroup relations. Nor is there compelling evidence for the external validity of these findings which are largely limited to the Canadian context and to studies undertaken in the 1970s and 1980s. More contemporary research in other multicultural settings would be useful for further theory development in this area. Nevertheless, the 'multicultural assumption' points to limitations of acculturation models and Social Identity Theory. Minimally, it draws attention to the significance of the sociopolitical context in which intercultural relations occur. It also highlights the ethno-centric biases in theoretical models that feature assimilation and absorption as natural outcomes of acculturation.

None of the existing theories has been able to offer a comprehensive account of the dimensions of identity, the complexities of identity change, and the processes and patterns of intergroup relations in immigrant and refugee communities. Although Social Identity Theory and acculturation models have guided empirical research in this area, these are not the only theories available to explore identity and intergroup relations in a cross-cultural context. Turner's (1982) Self-Categorisation Theory and Weinreich's (1989) Identity Structure Analysis provide two alternatives. Both have attracted attention recently in social psychological studies of changing European identities (Breakwell and Lyons, 1996). Brewer's (1996) Optimal Distinctiveness theory and Gaertner, Dovidio and Bachman's (1996) model of Common In-group Identity are also gaining popularity. The former has been recently used to explore changing identities in Hong Kong during the political transition to China (Brewer, 1999). It is probable that these theories along with others will come to exert an increasing influence on the study of identity and intergroup relations in coming years.

CHAPTER SUMMARY

This chapter has described theoretical perspectives on social identity and intergroup relations. These theories complement the culture learning and stress and coping frameworks and provide the third major conceptual approach to the study of intercultural contact and change. Contemporary work on social identification processes in immigrants, sojourners and refugees has its origins in two related bodies of theory and research. The first is the expanding literature on identity and acculturation found primarily in the cross-cultural and ethnic psychology literature. The second is Tajfel's (1978) classic Social Identity Theory (SIT), drawn from mainstream social psychology and applied to the study of intercultural interactions. Both approaches are grounded in theory and research from social cognition and are primarily concerned with the way in which people view themselves and their perceptions of in-group and out-group members.

The acculturation and identity literature is considerably more diverse than the writings on SIT. Theory and research are more difficult to synthesise, due to different, sometimes incompatible, conceptualisations of acculturation. These include unidimensional, bidimensional and categorical models. Nevertheless, it is clear from the empirical literature that identity is affected by a wide range of factors, including individual characteristics, such as age, gender, class and education; group characteristics, such as permanence of cross-cultural relocation and motivation for migration; and the broader social context, including cultural pluralism and the extent of prejudice and discrimination apparent in a society. It is also evident that acculturation and identity changes have consequences for cross-cultural adaptation, including self-esteem, psychological well-being and social skills acquisition. The precise nature of these relationships, however, is difficult to summarise, as the models and measurements of acculturation and the range of adjustment indicators have varied considerably across studies.

Although Social Identity Theory has a long-standing history in the psychology of intergroup relations, only relatively recently has it attracted much attention in the study of intercultural interactions between immigrant and host communities. There have been some attempts in social identity research to incorporate specific dimensions of cross-cultural diversity (e.g. individualism–collectivism) and to consider their varied effects on perceptions and interactions (e.g. Brown *et al.*, 1992); however, in the main, SIT offers a rather pessimistic perspective on harmonious intergroup relations, highlighting the significance of social categorisation and social comparison and the widespread existence of in-group favouritism and out-group derogation. However, as we shall see in Chapter 11 on culture training, there are ways of overcoming some of these barriers to intergroup harmony. One technique consists of making participants mindful of the intrusive nature of these processes. Another strategy involves increasing the inclusiveness of the basis on which social categorisations are made by emphasising intergroup similarities rather than differences, e.g. 'act locally, think globally'. Getting people to place themselves in the role of the other person is a third way of reducing the negative consequences of group distinctiveness.

Social Identity Theory proposes that increased intergroup contact motivates greater status striving and augments the need for positive group distinctiveness. In this regard, special attention has been given to members of disadvantaged groups, particularly visible minorities in immigrant communities. Research has suggested that there is a range of strategies that members of these groups may use to enhance self-esteem. Some are directed towards the migrant's individual social mobility while others are aimed at improving the status of the immigrant community as a whole.

Multicultural ideologies have contributed a more optimistic perspective on social identity and intergroup relations. Although a systematic theoretical framework on immigration and multiculturalism has not been developed, the significance of multiculturalism is becoming widely recognised in social and counselling psychology (Pedersen, 1999). Bochner (1999) has suggested that there is evidence of multicultural processes and structures within particular culturally heterogeneous societies, and empirical research from Canada supports the notion that cultural maintenance and harmonious intergroup relations can be achieved in plural societies. This, however, requires an assurance of cultural and economic security for diverse ethnocultural communities and the promotion of intercultural interactions under non-threatening, mutually rewarding circumstances. In these instances, increased intergroup contact and interaction are associated with more positive intergroup perceptions.

In conclusion, social identity frameworks have offered a cognitive perspective on theory and research on intercultural contact and change. The cognitive perspective complements the behavioural analysis provided by the culture learning approach and the affective emphasis in the stress and coping framework. Together, these three perspectives provide the ABC basis for the comprehensive analysis of cross-cultural transition and adaptation and will be elaborated in greater detail in the following chapters.

NOTES

1 Although ethnicity and culture may be distinguished on the conceptual level, ethnic and cultural identity are used interchangeably in this chapter. This is done because the chapter synthesises empirical investigations from two distinct research traditions: ethnic psychology that has primarily investigated identity and identity change across various established ethnic groups in plural societies and cross-cultural psychology that has considered identity and cultural maintenance in recent migrants, sojourners and refugees.

2 While studies demonstrate that North Americans score higher on conventional measurements of self-esteem, there is a larger debate as to whether these measurements are culturally appropriate to tap esteem in cultures where self-effacing, rather than self-enhancing, strategies are preferred (e.g. Leong and Ward, 1999; Markus and Kitayama, 1991).

Part III

Varieties of culture travellers

In Chapter 2 we introduced the topic of intercultural contact and briefly listed the main groups which featured in the empirical and theoretical literature. These include tourists, international students, international business persons, immigrants, and refugees. In this section we will review the literature in more detail and interpret and present the main findings in terms of the ABC model of acculturation. We will also draw attention to contemporary developments by contrasting current approaches with those that informed the first edition of this book, in turn, linking these to the sociopolitical changes that have occurred in the last two decades.

Throughout this book we have maintained a distinction between two categories of culture contact: contact which occurs between societies, or more precisely, between members of different societies, and contact between ethnically different individuals or groups which occurs within culturally heterogeneous societies. Tourists, international students, and expatriate business persons are examples of contact which is predominantly of the between-society kind. Immigrants and refugees, in their interaction with established ethnocultural groups in the recipient nation, provide examples of within-society culture contact.

We have also found it useful to classify culture-in-contact persons in terms of several key categories, in particular, the purpose of the contact and its intended duration. Thus, tourists, international students and expatriate executives embark on their culture travels primarily in order to play, study, and work, respectively, although in practice most such individuals will pursue a mixture of these goals. The primary intention of immigrants and refugees is to achieve a better life for themselves and their families.

The distinction between short and long term time frames is also important because it has implications for the acculturation process. Tourists are an example of short term second-culture exposure. Students and business people usually, although not necessarily, experience medium length culture contact. For immigrants and refugees, culture contact is a life long experience.

An associated issue is the extent to which culture travellers make a commitment to their new society. This is often expressed in terms of whether there is an explicit intention to return to the culture of origin after the purpose of the visit has been achieved. In the literature, the term 'sojourner' has been used to describe culture travellers who regard their stay as temporary and intend to return home in due course. Tourists, students, and business people are usually referred to as sojourners, and immigrants and refugees tend to be classified as permanent settlers. Empirically, many students remain in the country where they were educated, tourists become illegal immigrants, and expatriates 'go native'. Similarly, immigrants and refugees may return to their countries of origin if circumstances change. But by and large, the distinction between sojourners and permanent settlers is a good approximation of real life events, and we have used it to organise our review of the literature.

In this book we have described the outcomes of culture contact with reference to the acculturation framework described in detail in Chapter 2. Specific effects have been classified in terms of their ABC characteristics (Affect, Behaviour, Cognitions) with cognitions also covering self-construals. For instance, we have assumed that the acculturation of an overseas student will involve feelings and emotions which may be positive or negative; that it will include the acquisition of culturally relevant skills and habits; and that it may result in changes in self and other perceptions, ethnic identification, and values. In the first edition of this book, these separate outcome categories were not explicitly distinguished although they were implied in much of the treatment. Thus Oberg's description of culture shock as 'buzzing confusion' emphasised some of the affective consequences of contact, as did the large section on mental health and migration; the culture learning extension of Argyle's social skills model clearly referred to behavioural changes that successful acculturation requires; and the assimilation/integration analysis in terms of a progression from a monocultural self to a bicultural and ultimately mediating identity is a precursor of the cognitive, social categorisation strand made explicit in the ABC model. In the following chapters we will interpret the literature more deliberately in terms of the ABC conceptual framework.

Much has changed in the world since the appearance of the first edition of this book. In particular, international education, business, and leisure travel now have different functions and structures than they did 20 or 30 years ago. Likewise, the movement of immigrants and refugees and their impact on receiving societies are substantially different from those that were evident during the immediate post-war period. These changes are reflected in the way in which the topics have been studied.

During the post-war period and virtually up to the time when Furnham and Bochner were reviewing the overseas student literature for their 1986 edition of *Culture Shock*, study abroad was still primarily a form of aid or technology transfer from developed to developing countries. It should be remembered that this period also coincided with the Cold War. In practice this meant that students from Asian and African countries, many emerging from Western colonial influence, undertook higher education in the United States, Britain, Canada, Australia, and later in European countries such as

France and Germany. Students from China, Cuba, and other communist countries went to universities in Russia. Cold War rivalries also provided the political justification for allocating public funds to support the various programmes. The best known Western schemes were the Fulbright programme in the United States, the East–West Centre in Hawaii, and the Colombo Plan funded by Australia. British and Canadian governments also funded what were basically programmes with foreign-policy objectives. Western countries openly acknowledged that the aims were to boost the economies of the recipient countries, create markets for their own export industries, stem the tide of communism by improving the standard of living in Third World regions, win the hearts and minds of future leaders, and make influential friends who would support the donor countries in world forums such as the United Nations (Furnham and Bochner, 1986).

The world today at the beginning of the new century presents a different picture. Most of the countries that were the recipients of technical and educational aid are now highly industrialised and have thriving economies. They are also developing an indigenous tertiary system that is increasingly capable of providing high quality education for many of its citizens. Nevertheless, there is still a large demand for overseas education in non-Western countries. This is in part due to a growing middle class resulting in demand for higher education exceeding the local supply of places. As well, there are several countries that still practise discrimination against particular ethnic groups by restricting their entry to university. Such students are then forced to go abroad to pursue higher education. There is also a certain amount of prestige attached to being a graduate of one of the better known overseas universities.

The upshot of all of these changes is that the psychological status of overseas students has undergone a radical transformation from that of a 'grantee' to that of a customer. The other significant change is in the economics of international education. Whereas in the past the sojourn of most overseas students was being subsidised financially by the taxpayers of the host countries, the situation is now almost completely reversed. The majority of overseas students are charged fees that are usually higher than those paid by local students. International students also have to support themselves, further boosting local economic activity.

Cross-cultural goodwill and mutual understanding are no longer the primary aims of either the programmes or the research that they stimulate. These objectives have been largely replaced by identifying and capturing the international market and improving customer service. International education is now a major export industry, and many institutions have become highly dependent on the income so derived. Current contact research reflects this change in the status of the international student, and some of this will be reviewed in this section of the book.

Major changes have also occurred in the tourist industry. In the 1970s and 1980s many of the studies were concerned with assessing the effects of tourist presence on poorer, less complex societies, and the extent to which their cultures would suffer tourist-related adverse consequences. That is a much less visible area of research nowadays, mainly because there exist very few tourist destinations in the world which have not been irrevocably altered by the uncontrolled influx of relatively wealthy and often insensitive visitors. Tourism also has become a major industry with the economic viability of many places, even entire countries, being dependent on short-term visitors. Research has followed suit, and there is an increasing number of studies which concentrate on training host nationals in tourist-related customer-service skills. Other studies look at the stresses associated with being a tourist and how these might be reduced, again with a view to maximising economic returns.

There have also been changes in the structure and function of international business. In the post-war period most business sojourners were expatriates managing the local branches of their firms on behalf of head offices in London, New York, Sydney, or Zurich. Gradually, with the growth in indigenous wealth and a corresponding move towards independence and self-determination, the emphasis has shifted toward joint ventures. Persons managing these types of organisations need different skills and encounter different problems from those experienced by the earlier breed of neo-colonial executives.

In the field of immigration and refugee movement there have also been some major, significant developments in the last 20 or 30 years. The main changes have occurred in the receiving societies. Until around the 1970s, most receiving countries maintained fairly tight control over the number and type of persons admitted as immigrants. Many countries supported restrictive immigration policies that were highly discriminatory with respect to the ethnicity of the prospective settlers. Australia had an overt White-Australia policy that was not dismantled until the early 1970s, which effectively pre-vented Asian immigration. Britain, Canada, and the United States also made it difficult for certain ethnic groups to enter as permanent settlers.

All that has now changed, with significant implications for the ethnic mix of what were once relatively homogeneous societies. There are cities in the United States and Canada where the original 'charter' groups are rapidly becoming minorities, and the same applies to specific suburbs in cosmo-politan cities such as Sydney. Once again, research has followed suit, moving away from such topics as the mental health of migrants and refugees to issues of multicultural living.

In the chapters to follow we will describe each of the major categories of culture travellers (tourists, international students, international business per-sons, immigrants, and refugees). We will briefly review the pertinent literature in historical context and then move on to consider the current approaches, issues and findings using the ABC model as a means of organising this material.

6   Tourists

In absolute terms, international tourists undoubtedly constitute the largest group of persons exposed to between-culture experiences, and their numbers are steadily increasing. World Tourism Organisation (WTO) figures cited in Vellas and Becherel (1995) indicate that the number of international journeys more than doubled in the 18 years between 1975 and 1993 from 222 million arrivals to 500 million. Projections suggest that this will increase by an average of 3.6 per cent annually until the year 2010 to a total of 940 million international tourists per year. These figures do not include domestic tourism, which accounts for over 80 per cent of all tourism movements (cited in Baldacchino, 1997). The rapid growth in recreational travel is attributed to the advent of mass tourism in the 1970s, a consequence of the availability of easier and cheaper travel, increased wealth, more leisure time, longer paid holidays, earlier retirement, and longer life expectancy in the industrialised countries of the world (Law, 1994).

International tourism is big business, the WTO estimating it to be a US five trillion dollar economic activity. It employs 125 million people directly, and it accounts for 7 per cent of the total of world exports and 18 per cent of the total world trade in services (Alzua, O'Leary and Morrison, 1998; Baldacchino, 1997). The economies of many regions in the world have become highly dependent on the income from visitors. For instance, in Costa Rica, foreign exchange receipts from tourism exceed those earned from traditional export products such as coffee and bananas, and tourism has become the country's major economic activity (Campbell, 1999; Evans-Pritchard, 1993).

The bulk of the tourism literature consists of demographic, economic, and geographic analyses. However, there is an increasing interest in the psychological aspects of tourism, such as the motives for travel, the perceptions that tourists have of their destinations, and the extent to which they are satisfied with their experiences. There has also been emerging work on the intercultural interactions between tourists and hosts and the psychological impact of tourism on local residents. In the last 15 years a number of specialised journals have been established to publish research findings in these areas.

Another development has been the increasing use and sophistication of psychological procedures and techniques to describe tourist characteristics and the effects of their presence on both sociocultural and economic aspects of the communities visited. Examples include: the construction of elaborate customer and employee satisfaction instruments (Bojanic and Rosen, 1994; Lawton, Weaver and Faulkner, 1998; Testa, Williams and Pietrzak, 1998), the application of the culture-assimilator technique in training hospitality industry workers (Bochner and Coulon, 1997), the use of personal construct theory in developing repertory grids (Fransella and Bannister, 1977) to measure how tourists evaluate the places they visit (Walmsley and Jenkins, 1993; Walmsley and Young, 1998), the development of a multinomial logit model to measure tourists' decisions about which destination to visit (Luzar *et al.*, 1998), and the use of inferential rather than just descriptive statistics in the analysis of survey data (Morrison *et al.*, 1996).

Our approach in this chapter has been to concentrate on those aspects of tourism that are directly relevant to the central theme of this book. Of particular interest are issues relating to whether contact between tourists and hosts is a pleasant or stressful experience; whether the motives for travel include culture learning; what determines the nature of the affect, behaviours and cognitions which such contact evokes; and what systematic interventions are available to reduce stress and increase positive outcomes. At a broader level, the questions underlying the more thoughtful research in international education can also be posed with respect to tourists, in particular whether the industry contributes to intergroup harmony and world peace. What follows is a brief review of recent developments in these areas.

The effect of the travel experience on tourists has been the subject of extensive debate. The optimists have maintained that international travel promotes tolerance and understanding of other cultures. Mahatma Gandhi, cited in Theobald (1994), called travel the language of peace. Robert F. Kennedy (1963) asserted that travel has become one of the great forces for peace and understanding in our time. More recently, Ronald Reagan (1985) wrote that travel for pleasure between countries helps to achieve understanding and cooperation. Some academics, also, have argued that tourism contributes to world peace and harmony (e.g. D'Amore, 1988; Khamouna and Zeiger, 1995; Zeiger and Caneday, 1991).

Other observers are not so sanguine. Barthes (1973), Huxley (1925), and Turner and Ash (1975) have all described the tourist experience as shallow and unlikely to leave any lasting impressions on the traveller. And a recent review of the research literature has found very little evidence for the proposition that tourism promotes peace (Litvin, 1998). Although the resolution of this argument ultimately depends on empirical evidence, there is an underlying issue that has to be dealt with, namely the conditions under which tourists can be regarded as experiencing culture contact in the first place. In other words, two separate questions tend to be confounded, creating confusion and inconsistency in the literature: (1) whether or not a particular category of tourists is exposed to genuine second-culture influences; and (2) what tourist-related contact variables enhance or diminish mutual understanding and international harmony.

The WTO defines an international tourist as a visitor whose length of stay reaches or exceeds 24 hours, thus spending at least one night in the visited country, and whose main purpose is other than to exercise an activity for which they are remunerated (cited in Vellas and Becherel, 1995). Clearly, under this definition, there would be many visitors classified as tourists whose contact with members of the host culture would be minimal. Add to that all of the tourists who travel in groups as part of packaged tours, effectively cocooning themselves from any meaningful contact with the local culture, and the emerging picture suggests that a sizeable minority of those categorised as tourists cannot be regarded as having been exposed to significant second-culture influences.

However, from the perspective of members of the visited society, all interactions with tourists, irrespective of their motives, length of stay, and culture-of-origin, constitute culture-contact episodes. The shopkeeper, bus driver, restaurant owner, or just the local person on a casual stroll in a street, beach or park, will categorise those who are visibly foreign as tourists and will respond accordingly. Consequently, it is vital to include research on the affective and behavioural responses of hosts to the tourists in their midst, and there is a growing literature that deals with this issue.

Finally, an introduction to this topic would not be complete without referring to the distinction often made between tourists and travellers (Dann, 1999). A further distinction is also sometimes made between visitors and guests, particularly in the Pacific Islands (Berno, 1999). Before the advent of mass tourism, recreational travel abroad took the form of the 'Grand Tour' with wealthy individuals spending months and sometimes years in foreign places (Pratt, 1992; Sitwell, 1925; Starke, 1802). In particular, the British and Americans had extended sojourns in destinations that they regarded as the centres of culture and the arts in Europe. Exotic regions of the world such as Africa and Asia also attracted western travellers, many of them explorers or amateur archaeologists. There is no doubt that these travellers were directly exposed to contemporary second-culture influences and were personally changed by the experience.

The modern equivalent of the Grand Tour phenomenon can be found in best selling travel narratives by Michael Palin, Paul Theroux and others, who make a good living out of recording their first hand experiences at the cultural coal-face of the countries they visit (e.g. Palin, 1997; Theroux, 1988). Some observers have attributed the success of this genre to its ability to provide vicarious cultural experiences to persons unable or unwilling to gain these first hand (Urry, 1990). The popularity of guidebooks such as *The Lonely Planet* series may also in part be due to their emphasis on everyday cultural manifestations.

THE TOURIST EXPERIENCE

The psychological effects of unfamiliar cultural environments on tourists

Tourism is often represented as being an enjoyable, desirable and pleasurable experience, and most people look forward to and expect their visit abroad to be interesting, relaxing and worthwhile. In fact, the annual holiday has been stated as a major reason for saving money (Furnham, 1985). Research on tourism, however, has found the reality to be somewhat different. Boredom, bewilderment, rage, disgust, physical and mental illness, excessive alcohol consumption, depression, and antisocial behaviour are as much in evidence as delight and recreation (Cort and King, 1979; Furnham, 1984; Pearce, 1981; Prokop, 1970). The early studies on the tourist experience, guided by Pearce's (1982a,b) pioneering work, were reviewed in the first edition of this book. There it can be observed that the investigations concentrated mainly on the signs and symptoms of 'culture shock'.

Recent research has also confirmed that being a tourist can be a stressful experience, but it has additionally considered the consequences of 'culture shock' for intercultural relations, including the attitudes and perceptions of tourists and members of the host society. For example, a useful current conceptualisation of tourist stress is in terms of risk perception, which includes the psychosocial costs of travelling in general as well as to particular destinations. Along these lines, researchers have recognised that tourism can involve various degrees of risk ranging from simple disappointment to serious injury, even death, due to such calamities as sickness, accidents, or crime (Evans and Berman, 1992; Mansfeld, 1992).

Crime, in particular, affects tourists' perceptions of safety. A considerable literature now exists showing that tourists' intentions to visit a destination are influenced by their perceptions of risk and feelings of personal safety and that they will avoid regions where they feel threatened (Pizam, 1999; Pizam and Mansfeld, 1996). A good example is New Orleans, a city which has become a major urban tourist destination, due to its French Quarter, river boats, antebellum homes, and Mardi Gras. But underneath the glossy brochures the real New Orleans is a city with major social problems, including poverty, urban decay, poor education and inadequate public health, all contributing to rising crime (Dimanche and Lepetic, 1999). New Orleans is a violent city, and even though in absolute terms very few tourists are killed, many have been subjected to robberies and muggings, and this has affected visitor numbers.

Tourists are also increasingly becoming direct and indirect targets of international terrorism. Sonmez and Graefe (1998) list 28 terrorist incidents involving tourists between 1993 and 1996, and there is evidence that these exacerbate public perceptions of danger associated with travel, particularly to politically unstable destinations that have become notorious for terrorist activity (Hall and O'Sullivan, 1996). For instance, nearly two million Americans changed their overseas travel plans in 1986, following attacks in 1985 on Americans in the Middle East (Edgell, 1990).

As a significant portion of the contemporary literature tends to conceptualise tourist stress in terms of the 'culture shock' that travellers experience, it is important to identify the typical or frequent emotions, cognitions, and behavioural responses that tourists manifest. However, our preferred way of dealing with this topic is a systems approach that places the reactions of tourists in the context of an interacting encounter between the visitors and their hosts. This will be done in the section on tourism and intercultural contact. To foreshadow that discussion, the amount of 'shock' that tourists convey depends on the relative proportion of tourists to locals, technically referred to as the 'Tourist Ratio' (Faulkner and Tideswell, 1997), the relative wealth, sophistication and economic development of the respective cultures (Dogan, 1989), and the ethnic composition and prejudices of the groups in contact (de Kadt, 1979; Farrell, 1979). Tourists tend to be particularly disliked in poor, small, simple and isolated communities. At the other end of the scale, residents in popular tourist destinations including large cities such as London and Paris become less than welcoming during the height of the tourist season (Rothman, 1978).

Tourist motives and behaviours

As we indicated earlier, our aim in this chapter is to look at those tourists whose sojourn is at least in part motivated by a desire to learn something about the culture of the visited country. Tourist motives, however, are sometimes difficult to define. Assessment techniques have traditionally included self-report questionnaires, focus groups, and interviews (Ballantyne, Packer and Beckmann, 1998); however, these procedures yield mixed results that are often difficult to interpret. In addition, some of the categories employed in taxonomies of tourist motives may be misleading, as we shall suggest later in this chapter.

A more direct method to investigate tourist motives is in terms of specific 'niche' travel markets that have emerged during the last decade. Whereas in the past the tourist industry sold its wares in terms of general attractions such as climate, shopping, beaches and exotic food, current marketing strategies are now concentrating on promoting specific attractions and tourist destinations to travellers with special interests. The tourists can then be defined or labelled by their main purpose or activity. This approach provides a much more direct index of whether the tourists have any leanings toward culture learning experiences, or at least, the data can be used to identify those tourists who have little or no interest in the cultures they are visiting.

To illustrate, visitor categories where culture learning is minimal include sex tourism (Oppermann, 1999); scenic spots such as waterfalls (Hudson, 1998); movie-induced tourism to film locations (Riley, Baker and Van Doren,

1998); visits to specific overseas sporting events such as the Olympic Games, World Cup soccer, and other international championships (Green and Chalip, 1998); bicycle tourism (Cope, Doxford and Hill, 1998); and wildlife attractions including salt-water crocodiles (Ryan, 1998), trophy hunting (Baker, 1997), and captive animals in zoos (Broad and Weiler, 1998). The quite extensive literature in each of these areas hardly ever makes reference to the sociocultural context of the physical attractions that draw tourists to these sites.

In contrast, the growing 'heritage tour' industry is an example of a tourist category in which culture plays at least a modest role in attracting visitors. However, the cultures that such tourists seek to experience are not the present societies where these attractions are located, but their historical representations. For instance, a major subset of heritage tourism is what Seaton (1996, 1999) calls thanatourism, or travel to sites associated with death and disaster, such as Auschwitz, Pompei, the book depository in Dallas where Kennedy was assassinated, battlefields, graveyards, catacombs, and war memorials. According to Seaton, the site of the Battle of Waterloo is Belgium's second most important tourist site.

Singapore attracts approximately seven million visitors a year (Singapore Tourist Promotion Board, 1996) with shopping probably the most popular activity. However, more recently the Tourist Board has been making efforts to diversify Singapore's tourist attractions based on its wartime heritage. The fall of Singapore in 1942 has become a major part of this campaign and includes several museums featuring artefacts from 1942–45, displays at Fort Silosa, Sentosa Island, the Changi Prison, and a number of War Memorials such as Kranji. These displays attract visitors mainly from the former colonial powers. As Henderson (1997) notes, the surrender is presented as a disaster for Britain and its allies, the role of the local population having been largely ignored.

In Britain, what Robb (1998) calls 'mythical' heritage forms a large part of the heritage industry, based on archaeological sites such as Stonehenge, Tintagel, which is associated with the Arthurian legend, and other places linked to ancient events in Britain's history. Visitors to these sites are not interested in current British culture. What attracts them is Britain's 'mythical' past.

Heritage tourism's emphasis on the past is reflected in the growing literature on the role of authenticity in determining the attractiveness of a tourist destination. Here a distinction is sometimes made between authentic experiences and the authenticity of toured objects (Wang, 1999). This may relate to whether one is in search of the 'real' Spain, Italy or Greece (Waller and Lea, 1999); the meaning and significance of visits to period theme parks (McIntosh and Prentice, 1999); or the issue of contrived or staged authenticity (Cohen, 1995; MacCannell, 1973), including the quest for 'genuine fakes' (Brown, 1996) and sanitised versions of authentic but uncomfortable, dirty, and unpredictable bona fide experiences. The point is that these contrived experiences are unlikely to put the tourist into contact with the contemporary mainstream cultural manifestations of the visited society.

Nevertheless, at least these tourists are interested in attractions that provide them with information about the lifestyle, values and cultural practices of people from whom they differ significantly, even if this culture learning is often a historical exercise. Heritage tourism shades into what has been called cultural tourism. This is operationally defined in the literature by the following activities: 'ethnic' events, including festivals, music and food; cultural attractions such as the theatre, concerts, dance, opera, ballet; visiting museums and galleries; observations of unique people such as Australian Aborigines, Amish communities and Native Americans in the United States; visits to places of historical or archaeological interest; and visits to sites commemorating important people (Alzua O'Leary and Morrison, 1998; Moscardo and Pearce, 1999).

It should be noted that this list clearly overlaps with the attractions and motivations that characterise an interest in historical heritage sites. Its usefulness in the present context is to contrast it with the motives of those tourists who are primarily interested in beaches and warm weather, outdoor and nature destinations, resorts, entertainment, and visiting friends and family, i.e. those who form the majority of contemporary tourists. Our review of this literature has also shown that from the point of view of culture learning, so called heritage and cultural tourism does not refer to a homogeneous population. As we have seen, the exposure to contemporary, second culture influences varies according to a range of circumstances, and labelling a particular group of visitors as cultural tourists may in some circumstances be misleading.

A tourist category that makes explicit reference to culture learning is ecotourism, said to be the fastest growing tourist segment in recent years (Buckley, 1994; Ecotourism Society, 1998). There is some debate in the literature as to exactly what the term refers. Blamey's (1997) review of this controversy lists several definitions that would seem to satisfy the criterion of culture contact. Examples include 'travel to enjoy the world's amazing diversity of natural life and human culture without causing damage to either'; 'travelling to relatively undisturbed areas with the specific objective of studying ... the scenery, wild plants and animals, as well as any ... cultural manifestations, both past and present'; and 'ecologically sustainable tourism that fosters environmental and cultural understanding' (p. 110). Some of these attributes overlap with the nature and heritage characteristics listed earlier and point to the difficulties of trying to achieve precise definitions in this area. And yet, a reasonably accurate definition is necessary if we wish to estimate the proportion of all tourists who are ecotourists, and, in turn, identify the subset who might have a genuine interest in cultural manifestations. A further problem is that the term 'ecotourism' is sometimes misused as a catch-cry and marketing ploy by developers, politicians and tourist operators to justify commercialising wilderness areas (Chirgwin and Hughes, 1997).

Probably the group most likely to come into genuine contact with ordinary members of the societies they visit are the so-called 'backpackers', broadly defined as people who travel with backpacks (Hampton, 1998; Loker-Murphy and Pearce, 1995; Wilson, 1997). In many ways, the backpacker phenomenon seems to be a modern version of the 'Grand Tour'. The travellers are young and idealistic, not in regular employment and therefore not under the time pressures of conventional holiday-makers. This gives them the leisure to explore the visited places in depth and to immerse themselves in the local scene. They tend to gravitate to locations off the beaten track, and because they are usually on a tight budget, they use local transport, eat indigenous food, and live in cheap accommodation. This means that they are in a much better position to gain first hand experience of the local culture than the traditional tourists staying in international hotels and attending sanitised cultural displays. It should also follow that backpackers are the group most likely to be personally changed by their tourist experiences. However, evidence on this latter assumption is hard to come by.

The 'niche' market approach to identifying tourists and categorising them in terms of their implicit motives and type of culture contact offers a valuable perspective on tourist–host interactions. There are, however, other taxonomies that can shed light on the nature and type of intercultural encounters between tourists and hosts. One example is provided by Smith (1989) who considered the type, frequency and adaptational patterns of tourists (Table 6.1).

According to Smith, explorers are not conventional tourists and are more comparable to anthropologists who live as active participants among members of the visited culture. They are few in numbers but adapt almost completely to the local norms concerning accommodation, food and lifestyle. Elite tourists are also uncommon. They prefer to travel 'off the beaten track' for holiday experiences. Although they adapt easily and enjoy 'living native', they differ from the explorers in that they are engaged in recreational travel. Off-beat tourists are those who either seek to get away from the tourist crowds or to do something out of the ordinary for their holiday experience. They adapt well to the host culture norms although more in the form of 'putting up' with the local conventions for the duration of their stay. The

Table 6.1 Frequency, type and cultural adaptation of tourists (Smith, 1989)

Type of tourist	Number of tourists	Adaptation to local norms
Explorer	Very limited	Accepts fully
Elite	Rarely seen	Adapts fully
Off-beat	Uncommon but seen	Adapts well
Unusual	Occasional	Adapts somewhat
Incipient mass	Steady flow	Seeks familiar amenities
Mass	Continuous influx	Expects familiar amenities
Charter	Massive arrivals	Demands familiar amenities

Source: *Hosts and Guests* 2nd edition, edited by Valene L. Smith. Copyright © 1989 University of Pennsylvania Press. Reprinted with permission.

unusual tourists are interested in local culture but prefer to view it at a distance. They adapt to a certain extent, but may prefer to engage in activities such as organised tours for their cultural experiences. Mass tourists may arrive in a steady flow or a continuous deluge; they seek familiar 'Western' amenities and are often cocooned from the local culture. The mass tourists described by Smith as incipient may travel as individuals or in small groups and may visit out of the way places. Other mass travellers generally travel to popular destinations and isolate themselves in tourist 'bubbles'. The final category of tourists, the charter travellers, arrive en masse, stay in popular, well-established tourist destinations and expect familiar and comfortable amenities. Their contact with the host population is almost exclusively confined to service related situations. What is striking about Smith's (1989) taxonomy is that as the number of tourists increase in a particular category, their contact with the local culture appears to decrease. This converges with the 'niche' market data to suggest that the proportion of tourists who have significant intercultural contact with members of the host community is relatively small.

Section summary

In this section we tried to answer two questions: how much real contact do tourists have with their hosts, and, in terms of the ABC model of culture contact, in what way are the tourists' feelings, behaviours, and cognitions changed as a consequence of their contact experiences. In other words, the issue boils down to specifying the quantity and quality of contact from the perspective of the tourists. The answer to the first question is relatively straightforward: the amount of contact can vary from practically zero to a great deal, depending on which tourist category is under scrutiny. However, the more interesting question, the effect of contact on the psychology of the tourists, is much more difficult to pin down, mainly because of the lack of hard evidence in this regard. The literature contains a number of assertions, but with varying degrees of empirical support.

There is little doubt that being a tourist is not necessarily enjoyable and that it can under certain conditions be quite stressful, leading to medical and even psychiatric problems. There is also some evidence that tourists can develop feelings of hostility towards the culture they are visiting. The corollary of that reaction has similarly been noted, namely a re-evaluation of the attitudes of the tourists towards their own country. Tourists from the wealthier parts of the world sometimes conclude that things are much better in their own countries. In these cases international travel can unfortunately contribute to increasing ethnocentrism. Finally, there is evidence that many tourists return home absolutely unchanged in their psychology, this group probably forming a majority.

There is also evidence that in some instances tourists develop favourable images of the visited country. This is particularly the case with respect to tourists whose goals are to enjoy the scenery, historical sites, museums, art, and food. There have also been assertions that tourism is a vehicle for increasing international understanding and promoting world peace, but there is very little evidence to support such a contention.

One reason for the lack of evidence on the effect of culture contact on tourists is that most researchers are not interested in the question. It is also the case that such research is extremely difficult to conduct, mainly because conclusive studies would require longitudinal, before–after designs, an almost impossible requirement to meet with such a transient population.

TOURISM AND INTERCULTURAL CONTACT

Tourist–host perceptions and interactions

Contact between tourists and host nationals can be regarded as a unique form of intercultural interaction. First, tourists have different motives for travel than other cross-cultural voyagers such as sojourners, immigrants and refugees. Second, they stay for a very short time in an overseas location. Third, they tend to be relatively affluent compared with the local residents. Because of these distinguishing features, tourists are placed in an unusual position within the resident population that allows them to observe and examine the host culture without necessarily adapting to it (Berno, 1995; Pearce, 1982b).

Although tourist–host interactions can unfold in a variety of contexts, the most common encounters occur when tourists purchase goods or services from members of the host community (Nettekoven, 1979). These interactions do not generally involve equal status contact as tourists usually have economic and material advantages. The interactions are also uneven with regard to knowledge, as hosts generally possess greater information about local customs, culture and resources. Contact theory, which emphasises the positive consequences of equal status, cooperative interactions, suggests that the asymmetrical nature of host–tourist encounters does not bode well for harmonious intergroup relations (Amir and Ben-Ari, 1988).

In addition to economic and informational imbalances, tourist–host interactions are also characterised by brevity and superficiality. Although tourists often consider their intercultural encounters interesting, novel, and unique, hosts frequently view them as fleeting, shallow, and mundane. It has been suggested that this results in an orientation towards immediate gratification on the part of both hosts and tourists and that intercultural interactions which could be natural and spontaneous have become more commercial, contrived and even exploitative (English, 1986; Mathieson and Wall, 1982; Noronha, 1979). This suggestion has led some researchers to interpret tourist–host relations in terms of social exchange theory (e.g. Ap, 1992).

The application of social psychological theory on intergroup relations to tourist–host interactions has also included the use of conflict theory to account for residents' attitudes toward the social impact of tourism (Bystrzanowski, 1989) and the similarity-attraction and selective perception hypotheses to explain tourists' attitudes toward hosts (Amir and Ben-Ari, 1985). Motivational biases in causal attributions have likewise received attention. In line with self- and group-serving attributions, Jackson, White and Schmierer (1996) found that tourists rely upon internal explanations for their positive travel experiences and external explanations, including poor relations with the host population, for negative events.

A number of studies have shown that increased visitor frequencies lead to more negative attitudes toward tourism by the residents so affected (Allen *et al.*, 1988; Ap, 1990). In a recent study, Smith and Krannich (1998) used the concept of 'tourism dependence' to hypothesise that increasing levels of tourism development will generate more negative attitudes among local residents. They measured 'tourist dependence' with an economic index based on the ratio of tourist-related receipts to per capita personal income. They also administered a questionnaire regarding the importance that residents attached to the economic well-being of their community. Residents were then asked whether they would prefer more or less tourism in their communities, whether higher levels of tourism would lead to friction between local residents and tourists, whether the quality of life would decline, and whether crime would increase. The study was carried out in four rural Rocky Mountain communities that differed in their degree of tourist dependence. The data largely confirmed the hypothesis that residents in the two communities with higher levels of visitors expressed more negative attitudes and perceptions towards tourism than residents in the two communities with lower tourist concentrations.

The effects of tourism on host cultures

One can be fairly definite about the effects of tourism on the cultures, communities, cities, regions and individuals of the visited countries. There is an extensive literature indicating that tourists have a profound impact in all of these domains. Their presence changes the economy of the receiving societies by affecting the extent and nature of employment; encouraging investment in commercial and residential buildings; stimulating infrastructure development such as airports, shipping terminals and highways (Smith and Eadington, 1992); broadening the economic base and replacing declining industries such as the coconut trade in Thailand (Kontogeorgopoulos, 1998) and extractive industries in rural communities in the United States (Long, Perdue and Allen, 1990); subsidising the visual and performing arts, including the building of theatres, museums, and art galleries; helping to restore and run the Great Houses and feudal castles that a disappearing aristocracy can no longer afford to maintain; and providing finance for nature and conservation projects.

However, such economic changes have an inevitable impact on the culture, physical surroundings and way of life of the local population, and these influences are not always for the better (for a recent review of this literature see Brunt and Courtney, 1999). Every one of the examples cited above can have potential adverse consequences. The jobs that are created tend to be menial, particularly in the hospitality industry (Farver, 1984; Lea, 1988; Wilkinson and Pratiwi, 1995). Many of the hotels and resorts in under-developed countries tend to be owned by multinational chains and operated by expatriate managers. Much of the profit is also creamed off and ends up in the hands of shareholders in New York, London or Tokyo. Low wages may not compensate for the subsistence or barter economies they destroyed and supplanted, so that in some cases the local people, although in employment, experience worse living conditions than before the advent of tourism. There are also some of the less salubrious commercial activities that tourism generates, such as prostitution (Harrison, 1994; Leheny, 1995) and alcohol and substance abuse, which can have profound negative consequences for the host community. In addition, tourism may lead to the erosion of traditional value systems, family relationships and collective lifestyles (e.g. Milman and Pizam, 1988).

The tourist-related building boom can have adverse effects on the built environment by stimulating highly inappropriate construction and destroying local amenities such as open spaces, free access to the beach, and traditional fishing and hunting grounds (Hester, 1990). Airports and golf courses utilise scarce agricultural land. In some popular tourist destinations, the number of visitors may exceed the size of the local population, putting pressure on the water supply and sewage disposal, creating aircraft noise, increasing traffic congestion, and reducing air quality.

Tourist demands on the arts can distort the production and display of indigenous art forms and increase the fake, mass reproduction of souvenirs and objects of religious significance (Ryan, 1997). The sacred rituals of many traditional peoples are routinely staged in a sanitised form to cater to the tastes of international visitors, who often merely want a superficial, quick demonstration and a photo opportunity of ceremonies that might take hours or days to present authentically.

The great churches and cathedrals of the world have become thoroughfares for large groups of non-believing tourists who tramp through these sacred places without much regard for their spiritual significance. For instance, Notre Dame receives about 12 million visitors a year (Pearce, 1997) with 30,000 entering the cathedral on peak days. Pearce notes that exhortations to silence and respectful behaviour are not universally followed, guides raise their voices to make themselves heard, and tourists continue to use their flashes to film the interior despite this practice being explicitly prohibited.

Heritage sites, whether outdoor places such as Stonehenge in Britain and Uluru (Ayers Rock) in Australia or the great houses and castles in Europe, are under threat of destruction from the vast tourist hordes that descend upon them during the season. And the very crush of visitors in high volume tourist destinations makes life inconvenient, to say the least, for the local population. For instance, Paris attracts 20 million visitors a year (Pearce, 1999).

A recent review of the literature dealing with these issues by Moscardo and Pearce (1999) refers to a substantial number of studies which conclude 'that ethnic tourism is in danger of consuming the commodity on which it is based' (p. 417). The authors also cite studies which note that tourism can restore indigenous arts, revitalise local skills, foster creativity, and provide a means for communities to present themselves in a positive light to the outside world. In sum, modern mass tourism is very much a mixed blessing.

As indicated at the outset of this section, our interest in culture-contact is to draw conclusions about the effects of the tourist presence on the psychology of the local people and their broader sociocultural consequences. Although there is a substantial literature on tourist impacts, much of it deals with economic effects, and it is only indirectly concerned with the attitudes, behavioural responses and self-perceptions of members of the host society. There is also a discernible pro-development bias in many of the writings in this area. An exception to this trend is Berno's (1995) study on the psychological and sociocultural impact of tourism in the Cook Islands.

Berno (1995) surveyed and interviewed 100 residents of the Cook Islands. Participants came from four locations, each reflecting a different level of population density and tourist development: Raratonga (population: 9678; tourist–host ratio: 3.6:1), Aitutaki (2391; 2.7:1), Atiu (955; 0.03:1) and Mitiaro (272; 0.2:1). The survey data indicated that residents of the high contact islands were less likely to retain traditional Cook Island practices such as speaking Cook Island Maori and regularly attending church. They also expressed more concern that tourism would have negative effects on Cook Island culture. Although there was no significant difference in the level of acculturative stress reported by the residents of the four islands, young Cook Islanders experienced more psychological symptoms than older ones.

More in-depth interviews with Cook Islanders uncovered mixed attitudes toward tourism. On the positive side, the opportunities for mutual learning and educational exchange were emphasised. On the negative side, imitating tourists (the demonstration effect), potential loss of language and culture, and changing values were highlighted. This was particularly the case with reference to a perceived decrease in collectivism.

> If more tourists, the culture could easily be affected, traditional things, our way of sharing, our closeness. The closeness of people I knew as a boy is becoming more individual, especially here. It's no good . . . Before we accepted others into our homes, now we are more individual. You do your own thing and not help others.
>
> (Berno, 1995: 160)

Overall, hosts' responses to tourists are a function of situational factors including the maturity of the tourism industry, the degree of dependence on tourism, and the nature, frequency and duration of the interactions between tourists and residents (Husbands, 1986). Tourist characteristics, including cultural similarity and degree of integration and adaptability, likewise influence hosts' perceptions (Smith, 1989). Individual differences across members of the local population such as age, occupation, location and socioeconomic status are also important. Shopkeepers whose livelihood depends on serving mass tourists during the relatively short season in a coastal town, or for that matter commercial operators in Oxford or Cambridge, will take a different view from local surfers unable to catch a wave at their usual spot because it is crammed with day trippers, or the College don whose local pub has been taken over by loud foreigners demanding exotic drinks.

There is some evidence to support this contention. For instance, Campbell (1999) interviewed 19 Ostional (Costa Rican) residents about their attitudes to tourism. Nine respondents believed tourism was good, five said it was good and bad, and five believed it was bad. The author concluded that these opinions reflected the respondents' perceptions of the economic advantages of tourism versus the social and environmental repercussions. In a recent review of this issue, Faulkner and Tideswell (1997) cite a number of studies reporting that those residents whose livelihood depends on tourism will emphasise the positive impacts of tourism on their community, or at least accept more readily any negative effects. The authors also suggest that even those individuals who do not benefit directly from tourism may be willing to trade off some of their personal costs in the interests of broader community benefits. A study by the Hawaiian Department of Business and Economic Development (1989) likewise proposes that direct employment in the tourism industry is seen as less of a benefit than earning a good income in a tourism-driven economy.

CHAPTER SUMMARY

In keeping with the theme of this book, the tourist literature was reviewed in terms of the effect of contact between tourists and their hosts on their respective attitudes, behaviours and cognitions. The literature is quite clear on the finding that tourism, although promoted as an enjoyable and carefree experience, can in fact be quite stressful. It is also clear that although tourists constitute by far the largest number of sojourners, or persons who travel to other cultures for a temporary visit, the extent to which they actually experience genuine culture contact varies according to their motives for travel, the cultures of origin and destination, and the length of the visit. Travellers in many of the tourist categories have very few non-trivial encounters with host nationals. As a result, any consequences, adverse or otherwise, cannot be attributed primarily to contact with unfamiliar cultures. However, it is likely that any 'culture shock' that tourists experience in these circumstances is due to the absence of familiar cues, persons and activities.

In the case of those tourists who do make contact with the culture they are visiting, the evidence indicates that the psychological effects on the traveller vary from contributing to a broadening of the mind, as presumed by the optimists, to an increase in inward-looking ethnocentrism. With reference to the specific claim that tourism can serve to promote world peace and harmony, there is very little evidence for this assertion.

There is a large literature on the effects of tourists on the societies they visit. The majority of the studies have looked at the economic impact of tourism. There is no doubt that tourism makes a huge financial contribution to the economies of the receiving locations, but this does not always translate into genuine improvements in the quality of life for members of the visited societies. Often, there are adverse effects on the natural and built environment, as well as on indigenous cultural practices such as artistic and spiritual manifestations, family patterns and collective social arrangements. The attitudes of host society members towards tourists have been found to vary from mildly positive to hostile reactions, depending on self-interest, tourist densities, and the socioeconomic status of the tourists relative to their hosts. Our reading of this literature leads us to the view that from the perspective of the visited societies, mass tourism is at best neutral with respect to increasing mutual understanding and intergroup harmony and, more than likely in some circumstances, it has adverse psychological consequences.

As in the case of other sojourner categories such as overseas students and expatriates, there is a potential for improving the contact experience for both tourists and those hosts who are directly involved in the hospitality industry. Such systematic intervention would entail more careful management of the whole tourist enterprise, from identifying suitable locations to controlling the numbers and types of tourists and how the attractions are presented and made available. One consequence of such an approach would be an increased likelihood that tourist–host contact might lead to positive psychological outcomes for both parties. There are indications in the literature that at least some commentators are aware of this issue and are willing to debate it. However, because of the economic imperatives that have become dominant in this industry, it is doubtful whether mass tourism is capable of making a significant positive contribution to intergroup relations.

7 Sojourners: International students

A sojourn is defined as a temporary stay in a new place. It occurs voluntarily for an unspecified, though relatively short, period of time. Although there are no fixed criteria for defining a sojourn in terms of its duration, 6 months to 5 years are commonly cited parameters. Consequently, student and business sojourners are usually more committed than tourists to their new location, but less involved than immigrants and resettled refugees. Like immigrants, they voluntarily relocate abroad; however, 'returning home' is anticipated and planned.

There are many types of sojourners: expatriate business people, diplomats, members of the armed forces, students, volunteers, aid workers, and missionaries. They do business; represent their country; protect civilians or instruct other armed forces; study; teach or advise locals; convert and proselytise, respectively. It is important that these sojourners adapt to the new culture rapidly in order that they may operate effectively in whatever they are doing. Consequently, the process and predictors of sojourner adaptation are discussed in this chapter and the following one.

Despite the fact that people have sojourned since time immemorial, it is not until the last 50 years that systematic research has been done with this group of cultural travellers. Although there have been some studies of diplomats and volunteers (particularly studies of the Peace Corps in the 1960s), most sojourn research has concentrated on two types of sojourners: international students and international business people. There are similarities and differences between these two groups. Both, for example, are likely to be relatively well educated and highly motivated. However, whereas students mostly originate from less developed countries and sojourn in the industrialised world, the opposite is usually true of business people. This, of course, is not uniformly the trend. American students undertake exchanges with European countries, British managers may relocate to the continent, and Japanese managers sojourn to Canada. Nevertheless, the general flow of student and business sojourners is typically in opposite directions. Because of the enormous research literature on both students and expatriate business people, and because there are some salient differences between these groups of sojourners, they will be reviewed separately in Chapters 7 and 8.

Most of the research on student sojourners has considered the affective, behavioural and cognitive consequences of cross-cultural transition and has attempted to establish which individual, interpersonal, social, structural and economic factors reliably predict adjustment (Kagan and Cohen, 1990). The best research is difficult and expensive to undertake because it is done longitudinally and with a good matched control sample of host nationals (Gerdes and Mallinckrodt, 1994). Equally, it is important to take into account the countries/cultures from which the sojourners come and to which they go, both to replicate findings supporting culture-general effects and to examine the highly specific effects that occur in unique cultural circumstances.

Hammer (1992) has noted that the literature on international students broadly appears to cover four areas: the problems of sojourners, the psychological reactions of sojourners to encountering a new cultural environment, the influence of social interaction and communication on sojourner adaptation, and the culture learning process apparent in the cross-cultural sojourn. This chapter will review some of this work, paying particular attention to the ABCs of acculturation for those who study abroad.

HISTORICAL PERSPECTIVES

In historical perspective, overseas students are probably the most intensely studied group in the culture contact literature. Early biblical references provide accounts of travelling scholars, and intercultural education can be traced to the 272–22 BC reign of Asoka the Great of India and the establishment of the University of Taxila in Asia Minor. Over the next thousand years international centres of scholarship arose in Egypt, Greece, Persia, China, and Japan. By the late Middle Ages universities in Western Europe, such as Seville, Paris, Rome and Bologna, flourished, and during the Reformation and the Counter-Reformation of the sixteenth and seventeenth centuries, there was a steady increase in international education, encouraged by the governments of England, France, Germany and Russia. During the nineteenth century, interest in international education continued to expand and included increasing participation by institutions in the United States (Brickman, 1965; Fraser and Brickman, 1968).

Underlying the development of international education were the social, economic, and political motives and objectives of the early rulers, public figures, and governments who initiated the programmes and provided financial and civic support to justify them. The first goal can be described as geo-political. International education, from the earliest times, was regarded as a tool of foreign policy and as a means of extending the political and commercial influence of the states that established centres of intellectual excellence. The second purpose can be described as moral, or more precisely, as a missionary zeal to proselytise the values of the dominant culture. Later this shaded into more secular goals, such as the spread of democratic values, the diffusion of particular educational practices, and the promotion of international harmony. Both of these strands are still very evident in recent and contemporary international education.

Despite a long history of intercultural education, systematic research into the concomitants and outcomes of overseas study, both at the personal and societal level, began to appear only after the Second World War. It coincided with a large and growing number of students going abroad to undertake higher education. The intercultural educational programmes were driven mainly by the modern version of the two pragmatic considerations referred to above. The first was to assist in the reconstruction and economic development of countries that had been adversely affected by the war or whose educational infrastructure was at a rudimentary stage. Although the explicit aim was to train scientists, technologists, teachers and other professionals for employment in their home countries, the sub-text of these programmes was to create receptive markets for the industrialised sponsor countries and to extend their spheres of sociopolitical influence abroad. The second aim of the educational exchange programmes was to foster international good will and harmony. A subset of this commendable approach was national self-interest, the assumption being that overseas students, who would rise to positions of responsibility in industry or government on returning home, would develop and retain positive attitudes towards the host country which had provided them with an education.

Early investigations, such as studies supported by UNESCO and the Social Science Research Council in the United States, reflected these twin objectives. This was similarly the case for studies conducted in Great Britain (e.g. Carey, 1956; Singh, 1963) and Australia (Bochner and Wicks, 1972). The research, however, was largely atheoretical, its main aim being to survey the outcomes as they related to pragmatic social and political considerations. Most of the evaluation studies were not particularly rigorous in their designs or the manner in which they drew their conclusions; however, as their aims were undoubtedly worthy, there was some reluctance to probe too closely into their effectiveness. The few studies which did sound a sour note during this period, e.g. Tajfel and Dawson's (1965) *Disappointed Guests*, were largely ignored.

Despite the optimistic perspective of most intercultural investigators, demographic and social trends suggested that the economic-development aims of international educational exchanges were infrequently realised. As the programmes unfolded, it became obvious that a sizeable proportion of students either did not return home, or if they did, emigrated at the first opportunity, usually to the country where they had obtained their education. This phenomenon was given the label of 'brain drain' (Rao, 1979), and although it had a positive effect on the economies of the societies where the graduates settled, it failed in its aim to raise the technical expertise of developing countries. Indeed, even in those instances where international students resettled in their homelands, it became apparent that there was frequently a problem of incorporating overseas-based technological innovations into the sociopolitical systems of under-resourced and under-developed countries (Alatas, 1972, 1975). Often, the returning students tried to introduce changes that were not sensitive to local customs and traditions or which required a degree of infrastructure support that was not readily available (Kumar, 1979; Seidel, 1981). These problems are evident to this day although not to the same extent as during the height of the reconstruction phase.

The early literature on overseas students was comprehensively reviewed in the first edition of this book, and readers wishing to acquaint themselves with the historical context will find the relevant information in Furnham and Bochner (1986). In the intervening years, as Cold War and technical reconstruction considerations receded, social scientists began to use overseas student populations as a valuable resource for testing theoretical propositions about the nature, determinants and outcomes of culture contact. Most of these theoretical principles have already been identified and critically discussed in earlier sections of this book. They include the degree of cultural distance between the participants, leading to the conclusion that the greater the distance, the more difficult the interaction; whether culture learning (or acculturation) follows a systematic developmental sequence, the ongoing debate as to whether adjustment follows a U-curve, W-curve, a learning curve, or takes some other shape; changes in self-construal as a function of exposure to second-culture influences; the nature and determinants of stress and coping responses in persons exposed to unfamiliar cultures; the determinants of prejudice and ethnocentrism; and possible remedial action to prevent or at least reduce intergroup friction. All of these phenomena and their associated theoretical formulations could (and have been) investigated with other contact populations (such as migrants or expatriate executives) but have featured prominently in the empirical literature on students because of their greater accessibility as potential research participants.

We continue this chapter with a selected review of recent studies to indicate the direction this literature is taking. As was suggested earlier, in the contemporary world overseas students are no longer participating in economic aid or technical reconstruction, nor are they the targets of political influence. Ironically, overseas students have become part of the export industry of the very countries that in earlier times footed their bills. There are now more than 1.3 million international students world-wide, and in the United States alone they contribute $7.5 billion annually to the national economy (Hayes, 1998; Koretz, 1998). It is not surprising that fierce competition exists for these fee-paying overseas students, and Britain, Canada, Australia, and New Zealand also devote considerable resources to attracting international 'consumers' from key 'markets'. Although there is some resistance by traditional academics to the notion that they are now part of a commercial industry and that functionally students have become clients, there is no turning back. Many institutions have now become utterly dependent on the income generated in this way.

Current research on academic exchanges reflects this concern with students as sources of income. Although it would be unfair to say that the research has degenerated into customer satisfaction surveys, many of the studies nevertheless look at the adjustment of these students from the perspective of how to reduce their stress and enhance the positive aspects of their sojourn experience. The unspoken assumption is that word of mouth accounts for successful market penetration and that the students who feel that their study abroad has been worthwhile will provide favourable publicity for the country and the institution where they obtained their education.

Despite the pragmatic nature of much of the current work, many of the studies also reflect the increasing sophistication of the research strategies gradually being adopted in this field. The better studies are now explicitly driven by theory, and some of this research will be reviewed in the next section. There is also a growing literature reporting the results of longitudinal studies, a very welcome development.

EMPIRICAL RESEARCH ON STUDENT SOJOURNERS

The psychological and educational literature on student sojourners is massive, and it would be impossible to present a comprehensive review of this rapidly expanding body of empirical research in a single chapter. Investigations in this area, however, are largely consistent with other studies of 'culture shock' and have been guided by the three theoretical frameworks that were reviewed in the first half of this book. To complement the studies previously described in Chapters 2–5, this section additionally identifies and elaborates salient themes in research specific to student sojourners. These include interpersonal and intergroup interactions; the difficulties faced by international students; academic issues in the intercultural classroom; temporal variations in psychological, sociocultural and academic adaptation; and the re-entry experience.

Each of the major theoretical perspectives on acculturation has been concerned with the development of interpersonal relationships and the associated patterns of intra- and intercultural interactions. Bochner's functional model of the friendship networks, arising in the 1970s from culture learning theory, remains influential, and researchers have continued to examine the patterns and outcomes of monocultural, bicultural and multicultural relationships in overseas students. Stress and coping theories have also considered sojourner interactions but have focused more specifically on the quality and quantity of interpersonal encounters rather than the cultural backgrounds of the persons involved in these interactions. These theories have additionally placed emphasis on social support and its consequences for the psychological well-being of student sojourners. Finally, social identification theories, though relatively less developed in the international student literature, have concentrated on the intergroup perceptions of foreign students and their hosts, as well as issues relating to perceived discrimination.

These topics are considered in the first section on interpersonal and intergroup relations.

A second matter that has concerned contemporary researchers is the problems typically experienced by overseas students. As these students have become a major source of revenue for many secondary and tertiary institutions, 'customer' service and satisfaction have become important considerations. Feedback about student problems is useful for university administrators to ensure adequate service provision. It also can assist with the development of orientation and training programmes to facilitate students' academic and cultural adaptation. In addition to addressing these pressing practical concerns, research on student problems has assumed a central position in the broader literature on cross-cultural transition and adaptation. Culture learning theory has concerned itself with the description, explanation, and prediction of social difficulties while the stress and coping approach has focused on the identification of factors that function as significant stressors and impair adaptation to a new cultural milieu. Student problems are discussed in the second section of this review.

Academic objectives and goals distinguish students from other intercultural sojourners, such as business people and volunteers. Because students sojourn for the purpose of obtaining a degree, academic performance is a significant component of cross-cultural adaptation. In addition to research that has examined the antecedents and correlates of academic performance, there is a developing literature on the intercultural classroom. This literature explores factors such as the definitions and perceptions of intelligence, student and teacher expectations, and classroom communication, as well as their influences on academic performance and satisfaction. This literature will be briefly described in the third section.

The empirical research on student sojourners can be further distinguished from studies of other cross-cultural travellers by its methodological approaches. Compared with tourists, immigrants and refugees, sojourners, particularly student sojourners, are more likely to have participated in longitudinal studies. These longitudinal investigations have concentrated on two basic themes: the prediction of successful adaptation by pre-departure variables and the changing patterns of adaptation over time. These will be reviewed in the fourth section. Finally, sojourner research, particularly studies of international students, has included investigations of the re-entry process. This will be reviewed in the last section.

Interpersonal and intergroup relations

Bochner's functional model of friendship networks

Studies of the friendship patterns of foreign students show that they tend to belong to three distinct social networks, each serving a particular psychological function (Bochner, McLeod and Lin, 1977). The primary network consists of bonds with fellow compatriots, its function being to rehearse, express, and affirm culture-of-origin values. Another network consists of links with host nationals, its function being largely instrumental, to facilitate the academic and professional aims of the students. Typically, the persons in this network will be other students, teachers, counsellors, university bureaucrats, and government officials, and the relationships will tend to be formal rather than personal in nature. The third network consists of friendships with other non-compatriot foreign students. The function of this network is largely recreational, as well as providing mutual social support based on a shared foreignness.

Consistently, studies conducted in the United States, Britain, Australia, Israel, and Europe have found that despite the benefits of host national contact, this is the least salient of the three networks (Bochner, Buker and McLeod, 1976; Bochner, Hutnik and Furnham, 1985; Bochner, McLeod and Lin, 1977; Bochner and Orr, 1979; Furnham and Bochner, 1982; Klineberg, 1982; Klineberg and Hull, 1979; Nowack and Weiland, 1998; Wiseman, 1997). In general, overseas students are most likely to report that their best friend is from the same culture (Bochner *et al.*, 1976). In Bochner, McLeod and Lin's (1977) study, for example, 44 per cent of overseas students indicated that their best friends were co-nationals compared with 29 per cent of those with host national friends. Furnham and Bochner (1982) found that close links with British people accounted for only 18 per cent of the friendships of foreign students in the United Kingdom compared with 39 per cent co-nationals and 38 per cent other overseas students. In Bochner, Hutnik and Furnham's (1985) later study only 17 per cent of the international students in their Oxford sample had host national friends, and 70 per cent had no close foreign friends after one year in the United Kingdom. International students, on the whole, have significantly more difficulties establishing friendships than do locals (Barker *et al.*, 1991; Zheng and Berry, 1991); they also tend to find their relationships less satisfying (Furnham and Tresize, 1981).

Although overseas students generally want and need intercultural contact, the ability and willingness to interact meaningfully with host culture peers are largely dependent upon cultural distance (e.g. Bochner *et al.*, 1977; Furnham and Alibhai, 1985). This was apparent in Redmond and Bunyi's (1993) research which examined social integration in 644 international students in a mid-Western American university. Assessing social integration in terms of the ability to initiate interactions and maintain interpersonal relations with host nationals, they found that British, European, and South American students were best integrated while Korean, Taiwanese, and Southeast Asian students were least integrated. There are, however, ways to increase sojourner–host interactions. Peer-pairing programmes are particularly effective, and international students who participate in these schemes are more likely to prefer local companions than those who do not (Westwood and Barker, 1990). Pre-departure contact with the target culture also increases the likelihood of sojourner–host friendships and spending leisure time with host nationals (Pruitt, 1978).

Bochner's functional model specifies that international students use networks in different ways. Local students are preferred for informational support, such as providing help with language and academic difficulties, while co-nationals are preferred for companionship and emotional support (Bochner *et al.*, 1977; Furnham and Alibhai, 1985). The culture learning advantages of host national contact are obvious. A greater amount of interaction with host nationals has been associated with fewer academic problems (Pruitt, 1978) and fewer social difficulties (Ward and Kennedy, 1993b) as has satisfaction with host national contact (Ward and Kennedy, 1993a). Interacting with local students has also been found to improve communication competency and to facilitate general adaptation to life overseas (Ward and Kennedy, 1993b; Zimmerman, 1995). Sojourner–host interactions may provide functional benefits whether they occur in formal or informal circumstances. For example, international students who participate in structured peer-pairing programmes demonstrate better social adjustment than those who do not (Abe, Talbot and Geelhoed, 1998). This is also true for international students who spend more informal leisure time with their local peers (Pruitt, 1978).

Although Bochner emphasised the culture learning benefits of host national encounters in his early work, more recent researchers have also noted the emotional benefits of these interactions. Frequent contact with host students has been associated with greater sojourn satisfaction (Rohrlich and Martin, 1991); social integration and having local friends have been linked to lower levels of stress (Berry and Kostovcik, 1990; Redmond and Bunyi, 1993); spending more time with host national students is related to fewer psychological adjustment problems (Pruitt, 1978); and satisfaction with host national relations predicts better psychological adjustment among international students (Searle and Ward, 1990). In addition, favourable attitudes toward socialising with host nationals are related to more positive mood states (Furnham and Erdmann, 1995).

Bochner's model also highlights the significance of compatriot relations, particularly their function in enhancing self-esteem and cultural identity. This has been borne out in research by Ward and colleagues with foreign students in both Singapore and New Zealand where studies revealed that greater co-national interaction is associated with stronger cultural identity (Ward and Kennedy, 1993b; Ward and Searle, 1991). This was also reported in Kennedy's (1999) work with Singaporean students in the United States, United Kingdom, Australia, New Zealand, and China. In addition, the amount of co-national interaction and the satisfaction with co-national contact are related to students' psychological well-being (Searle and Ward, 1990; Ward and Searle, 1991).

Bochner has further suggested that interactions with other foreign students are important. These occur largely for recreational purposes and may additionally function to provide social support. This suggestion is consistent with Kennedy's (1999) recent study which found that the quantity of interactions with non-compatriot foreign students was associated with the perceived quality of social support; however, the amount of interaction with these students was unrelated to psychological and sociocultural adjustment. The latter finding was also reported by Ward and Searle (1991) in their study of international students in New Zealand, but in an earlier investigation by Pruitt (1978) in the United States, the frequency of interactions between African students and their non-compatriot African peers was weakly, but significantly, related to greater psychological adjustment problems. On the whole, there has been less empirical work on the patterns and outcomes of this type of multicultural interaction, and there is room for further research in this area.

The importance of social support

Bochner's functional model of student friendships reflects a culture learning perspective on intercultural contact with its emphasis on the maintenance of original cultural behaviours and values, the acquisition of new culture-specific information to facilitate academic and professional success abroad, and the functions of social–recreational activities in a new cultural milieu. This may be contrasted with recent work on social support, which derives more from a stress and coping approach to student adjustment. The social support hypothesis places greater emphasis on the quality and quantity of support than the actual support network, and research has demonstrated that both host and co-nationals can provide assistance and contribute to the enhancement of psychological well-being.

Research findings on social support in the international student community mirror those in the broader stress and coping literature. The number and perceived adequacy of friendship networks are associated with decreased psychiatric morbidity (Furukawa, 1997). Social support alleviates homesickness (Hannigan, 1997). Greater support is linked to psychological satisfaction and well-being (Tanaka *et al.*, 1997; Yang and Clum, 1995). Social support buffers the relationship between stress and depression (Jou and Fukada, 1997), and poor social support accounts for a significant proportion of the variance in depressive symptoms, over and above that explained by neuroticism (Ong, 2000).

Not surprisingly, international students frequently report needing more social support than local students. Jou's (1993) study of Chinese students in Japan suggests that overseas students perceive a greater need for support but that local students secure more. In addition, smaller discrepancies between needed and actual support are associated with greater satisfaction and psychological well-being. Although the actual sources of social support have conventionally received less attention in the international student literature, they do exert influence on psychological outcomes. This was observed in

Chataway and Berry's (1989) study of domestic and international students in Canada. They found that social support from friends was related to better psychological adjustment for the overseas students but that support from family predicted psychological well-being in the local students. Given the availability of various support networks, the structural aspects of social support should be given further consideration in the international student literature.

Intergroup perceptions and relations

Student exchange programmes have been generally assumed to foster positive intergroup perceptions and congenial relations. Research findings, however, have been mixed, and the contact hypothesis has received only qualified support in the empirical literature. A good example of this can be found in work by Bond (1986) which focused on the constructive aspects of stereotyping and their role in maintaining harmonious intercultural contact between host and sojourning students. Bond examined auto-stereotypes (in-group perceptions), hetero-stereotypes (out-group perceptions) and reflected stereotypes (how the out-group is perceived to view the in-group) in local Chinese and American exchange students in Hong Kong. The outcome of the auto- and hetero-stereotype analysis is presented in Table 7.1.

In addition to this item level analysis, the trait data were subjected to a factor analysis resulting in four factors: extraversion, openness, emotional control and beneficence. Both the local and the sojourning groups agreed that the Chinese were less extrovert, more emotionally controlled and less open than the Americans; however, both groups also perceived the other to be

Table 7.1 Auto- and hetero-stereotypes of Chinese and American students in Hong Kong (from Bond, 1986)

Chinese (hetero-) stereotypes of Americans	*American (hetero-) stereotypes of Chinese*
Questioning, casual, wide range of interests, group-oriented, independent, flexible, considerate, optimistic, active, energetic, frank, spiritual, objective, helpful, open, talkative, sincere, assertive, trusting	Diligent, group-oriented, responsible, prudent, composed, spiritual, helpful, gentle, emotionally controlled, conservative, humble, obedient
American auto-stereotypes	*Chinese auto-stereotypes*
Questioning, casual, wide range of interests, independent, flexible, active, frank, open, talkative, assertive, trusting	Composed, gentle, emotionally controlled, conservative, obedient

Note: Identification of a trait as stereotypically 'Chinese' or 'American' is based on significant differences between the auto- and hetero-stereotype ratings.

more beneficent. Overall the analyses revealed that the stereotypes held by the Americans and Chinese are strong, comprehensive and generally in agreement. Bond argued that the stereotypes also reflect a 'kernel of truth' in that they accurately mirror significant differences in the behavioural characteristics of the two groups.

Although the Chinese and Americans largely agreed upon their mutual characteristics, there were some significant differences between auto- and reflected stereotypes. The Americans believed that the Chinese saw them as even more emotionally expressive than they saw themselves, but less beneficent than they believed themselves to be. The Chinese, on the other hand, believed that the Americans saw them as more beneficent, controlled and introvert than they saw themselves.

Bond argued that the nature of these stereotypes contributes to harmonious intergroup relations among university students in Hong Kong. First, the auto- and hetero-stereotypes share a large overlap that accurately reflects intergroup differences. Second, the nature of the stereotypes, which casts the Americans as more open, extrovert and emotionally expressive, appropriately suggests that the burden for the initiation of relationship-building should be borne by the overseas students. Despite the asymmetry of the responsibility for relationship-building, both groups perceive the other to be more beneficent than their own, and this further encourages positive intercultural interactions.

Bond concludes that: 'These groups co-exist happily in the same geographical space and interact across a wide range of student activities. There is no overt conflict. Clearly, it is possible to have intergroup harmony despite the presence of broad and clear stereotypes about one's in-group and the relevant out-group' (p. 270). When he further considers how this might occur, he notes that students largely engage in voluntary, equal status contact. He also suggests that there are strong motivations for intercultural interactions, with the Chinese eager to improve their English and the Americans keen to learn about Chinese life first hand. In addition, the relatively small number of American exchange students in Hong Kong precludes the presence of a powerful threat. Indeed, all of these factors have been examined in connection with the contact theory and have been empirically related to a reduction in intergroup conflict (Bochner, 1982).

Unfortunately, not all intercultural contact between overseas and local students is equal status, voluntary, and cooperative. Sodowsky and Plake (1992) reported that although 41 per cent of the foreign students in an American university said that Americans treated them well, 15 per cent indicated that their treatment was superficial, and another 17 per cent described their treatment as negative. Similarly, 41 per cent of the overseas students said that they treated American students in a friendly fashion, but 10 per cent were reserved and cautious, 9 per cent said the interactions were superficial, and 6 per cent indicated that they did not try to make friends with American students. In addition, not all sojourns result in largely favourable intergroup perceptions. Stroebe, Lenkert and Jonas (1988), for example, reported that student exchanges led to the sharpening of negative stereotypes in their study of American undergraduates in France.

It is not uncommon for international students to perceive prejudice and discrimination, and these perceptions are often stronger in students who are more culturally dissimilar from members of the host population. Perceptions of discrimination are also stronger in sojourners compared with immigrant students (Sodowsky and Plake, 1992). The correlates of perceived discrimination are almost exclusively negative and include increased stress, more identity conflict and greater psychological and sociocultural adjustment problems (Berno and Ward, 1998; Leong and Ward, 2000; Pak, Dion and Dion, 1991).

The problems of international students

Furnham and Bochner (1986) have argued that overseas students face four types of problems, only two of which are exclusive to their international status. As student sojourners they experience a range of difficulties that are common to other cross-cultural travellers, such as insufficient linguistic and cultural skills, prejudice, discrimination, homesickness and loneliness. They also face pressures associated with the role of 'foreign ambassador' in their interactions with host culture students. Beyond these difficulties, however, they experience problems similar to those of local students, including identity conflict related to personal development in late adolescence and early adulthood, academic challenges, and the stressors associated with transition to a new school or university.

The empirical literature broadly supports Furnham and Bochner's contention. Overseas students report more social difficulty than do host students (Furnham and Bochner, 1982); they also experience more sociocultural adaptation problems than their compatriots who remain at home (Kennedy, 1999; Ward and Kennedy, 1993a). Uehara's study (cited in Jou and Fukada, 1996) of foreign students in Japan found that the differences in host–sojourner difficulties were greatest for language fluency and interpersonal relations. This was also observed in Chataway and Berry's (1989) research with overseas students in Canada which indicated that international pupils experienced more problems with communication and prejudice than did their Canadian peers. Loneliness is a significant problem among overseas students and was reported as such in almost one quarter of the international sample surveyed by Sam and Eide (1991) in Norway. Homesickness is also frequently observed (Lu, 1990; Sandhu and Asrabadi, 1994), and it has been found to be more problematic for international students than their domestic counterparts (Zheng and Berry, 1991).

On the other hand, overseas and domestic students share a number of common problems. Eng and Manthei (1984) reported that local and foreign undergraduates in a New Zealand university experienced similar difficulties, the most prominent ones being study-related, such as establishing priorities between academic and non-academic concerns and developing appropriate study techniques. Academic difficulties were also ranked as some of the most salient problems by overseas and local students in a Canadian study (Chataway and Berry, 1989). There has been less comparative research that has concentrated on the developmental issues discussed by Furnham and Bochner (1986) although investigations have shown that concerns about interpersonal maturity are apparent in the overseas student community. For example, problems pertaining to dating, male–female relations, and morals were highlighted in Crano and Crano's (1993) research on adjustment strain, and difficulties in these areas were related to poorer self-concept in South American students in the United States.

The problems experienced by overseas students are likely to vary depending upon the type of sojourning sample (e.g. secondary school students vs post-graduates) and their cultural origins and destinations (e.g. the extent of cultural and linguistic similarity with the host population). Rohrlich and Martin's (1991) research with American undergraduates in Europe reported that housing, money, coursework, and language were their most significant concerns. Similar results were cited by Henderson, Milhouse and Cao (1993) in their research with Asian students in the United States. They found that the absence of adequate language skills, apparent in 97 per cent of their sample, was the most serious and frequently identified difficulty, and this was followed by financial problems. Matsubara and Ishikuma (1993) similarly noted that foreign students in Japan sought assistance for language and financial problems, rather than help for psychological complications, when using their university's counselling services. In contrast, Schreier and Abramovitch's (1996) research with overseas students in Israeli medical schools distinguished initial from ongoing problems and stressors. In this instance they found that the most frequent sources of stress at the initial period were adapting to life in Israel (28.2 per cent), difficulty in finding accommodation (17.5 per cent), study problems (16.5 per cent), and homesickness (15.5 per cent); however, the greatest persistent and ongoing stressor was financial (59 per cent).

In addition to sample differences, variations in methodologies (e.g. interview, survey), data gathering techniques (e.g. open or closed ended prompts), research content and emphasis (e.g. academic, cultural, interpersonal), and statistical analyses (ratings, rankings, frequency counts) understandably lead to diverse and sometimes discrepant outcomes. One example of problem-oriented research is presented below. The data have been taken from Opper, Teichler and Carlson's (1990) study on the impacts of study abroad programmes. Table 7.2 presents the 10 most commonly experienced problems of 'living and learning abroad' as reported by 439 students from the United States, United Kingdom, France, Germany, and Sweden.

In this instance the potential difficulties were identified by the research team, and the students responded by rating the intensity of the problem. We

Table 7.2 Problems faced by international students (from Opper *et al.*, 1990)

Type of problem	%
Too much contact with people from the other country	28.6
Differences in teaching/learning methods	23.4
Administrative matters	20.9
Readiness of teaching staff to help foreign students	15.2
Guidance concerning academic programme	15.0
Not enough time for travel	15.0
Accommodation	13.6
Financial matters	12.9
Finding a place to concentrate on studies	12.1
Interaction with host country students	11.6

Note: Percentage includes responses of 1 and 2 on a 5-point rating scale, where 1 = very great difficulties.

have no way of knowing if the same types of problems would have been spontaneously generated by the student sample. In any event, what is clearly apparent in this research is that only a minority of the students report significant difficulties. However, it should be noted that this sample was characterised by a number of pre-departure resources, including previous international exposure, a structured educational exchange programme, a predominantly middle class family background, and a pre-departure preparation programme with language training. If contrasted, for example, with students who undertake independent study abroad, possess more modest financial resources, and have limited experience with international travel, the results may be significantly different.

Fortunately, a small number of researchers have attempted to develop standardised measures of the problems experienced by international students (e.g. Sandhu and Asrabadi, 1994). One noteworthy example is the Inventory of Student Adjustment Strain by Crano and Crano (1993). The instrument requires respondents to consider if a particular item represents a personal strain for them and, if so, the extent to which they are affected by the problem. Crano and Crano's factor analysis of the 60-item inventory yielded six subscales: education (e.g. concern with grades, inability to concentrate on studies); host family (e.g. relating with host family brothers or sisters, not feeling like a member of the family); language (e.g. difficulties in speaking English, being unable to understand slang), problems (conventional 'culture shock' issues, e.g. dietary concerns, differences in food, health matters); personal (e.g. inability to maintain good relations, homesickness); and social (e.g. dating, relationships between men and women). When the instrument was administered to South American students 4 and 10 months after arrival in the United States, the problems associated with language and 'culture shock' were reported as precipitating significantly more strain than difficulties in other areas. Increasingly frequent use of standardised instruments such as this one would allow researchers to establish a more comprehensive understanding of student problems, which are influenced by a number of factors, including cultural distance (Furnham and Bochner, 1982; Redmond, 2000; Searle and Ward, 1990).

The intercultural classroom

Although international students perceive limited language skills as the most significant source of their academic problems, and language proficiency is related to academic performance (Jochems *et al.*, 1997), there are a number of other factors that impinge on academic success and satisfaction. Individual differences exert influences on learning styles and academic achievement, and factors that are known to vary cross-culturally, such as the relative importance of intrinsic and extrinsic motivation, the level of field dependence and independence, the preference for cooperative, competitive and individualistic learning styles, and even perceptions of intelligence, have been discussed in the intercultural educational literature (Chen, 1994; Irvine and York, 1995; Shade and New, 1993; Thomas, 1994). Of primary concern in this section, however, are cross-cultural differences in educational expectations and practices, including communication in the classroom (Powell and Andersen, 1994).

The educational environment is a microcosm of the larger society and reflects its values, traditions and practices. Just as sojourners must learn the general rules, regulations and skills for adapting to life in a new culture, they must also develop the ability to apply these to their specific operational domains. For student sojourners, this requires special attention to the educational setting. Although there is an expanding literature on intercultural education and increasing development of training materials to enhance sensitivity among intercultural educators, in practice, the responsibility for adapting to and succeeding in a new educational system falls on the overseas student (Banks and Banks, 1995).

Educational practices and procedures reflect considerable cross-cultural diversity, and Hofstede's (1980) research on work-related values and Triandis' (1990) critical analysis of cultural variability provide interpretive frameworks for these differences. Two dimensions that exert strong influence on classroom communication and interactions are individualism–collectivism (I–C) and power distance (PD). In the broadest terms students from individualist cultures are more likely to want to 'stand out' in class, to ask questions, give answers and engage in debate. They are often seen as competitive. Students from collectivist cultures, in contrast, are more strongly motivated to 'fit in'. They are less likely to be verbally interactive in classes and are usually unwilling to draw attention to themselves. Collectivism is strongly related to power distance, and those students who are from high PD cultures are also less likely to question and debate. This is generally seen as an inappropriate challenge to the teacher, which may result in loss of face.

Students from high power distance cultures are more strongly motivated to show respect to teachers and to maintain formal and distant relationships with them. It is not difficult to see that these differences in cultural values can lead to misperceptions across cultural groups. From one perspective, quiet but attentive collectivist students may be perceived as uninterested or withdrawn by individualist teachers. From another viewpoint, the relatively frequent interruptions to lectures by individualist students may be seen as rude and unmannered by their collectivist classmates.

The empirical literature on intercultural education illustrates these differences. McCargar's (1993) research with Indonesian, Chinese, Korean, Japanese, Persian, Arabic, Hispanic and Thai ESL (English as a second language) students demonstrated that there are significant discrepancies between their expectations and those of their American teachers. The differences were most pronounced in connection with classroom participation and student–teacher relationships. For example, compared with the teachers, overseas students generally wanted more error correction, believed that they should agree with the lecturer, and more strongly favoured acceptance of authority. On the other hand, the educators were more likely to believe that students should have an internal locus of academic control. There were also noticeable differences across the student groups. For example, the Indonesian and Chinese students most strongly opposed the idea that students should be encouraged to disagree with the teacher. The Arab and Persian students were less willing to work in small groups than were the Hispanic, Chinese and Japanese, and the Arab and Hispanic students were most likely to agree that students should write down everything that the teacher says.

Liberman's (1994) qualitative research with Asian students in the United States is largely in agreement with McCargar's (1993) quantitative findings. His interviews revealed that international students were often critical of informality in the classroom, perceived lack of respect for professors, and insufficient focus in classroom interactions. They were also occasionally disparaging of their American peers, particularly with respect to egotism. As stated by a Japanese undergraduate: 'American students seem to want to show off their knowledge and intelligence in class and are often overconfident and egotistical; discussions seem to be like competitions' (p. 184). On the other hand, interviews revealed that many students responded positively to a decreased emphasis on memory skills and a closer relationship with teaching staff. They came to be especially enthusiastic about the active learning environment and the ability to express themselves. As noted by a Singaporean student: 'They encourage learning. They try to get you interested in the process of learning. In Singapore they don't care if you are interested or not, you just learn it' (p. 181). Overall, the vast majority of Asian students in Liberman's study approved of the critical thinking skills facilitated in the American system.

A number of researchers have concentrated specifically on comparisons between British or American and Chinese educational systems and values, and it has been common to interpret these differences explicitly in relationship to individualism–collectivism and power distance. Cortazzi and Jin (1997) described the expectations of British and Chinese academics in their recent discussion of culture and communication in the classroom (see Table 7.3).

Because of these underlying value differences, Chinese and British students have different assumptions about student and teacher roles (Cortazzi and Jin, 1997). Chinese students are more likely to view the teacher as a model, an authority and a 'parent', compared with the British view of the teacher as a facilitator, organiser and friendly critic. Chinese students are also more likely to see their own roles as result-focused, learning by listening and reflection. British teachers, however, expect their students to develop independence, engage in dialogue and develop critical thinking. These differing views are likely to result in dissatisfying and unproductive classroom encounters.

From an American perspective Pratt (1991) similarly noted that teachers are regarded as facilitators who promote learner autonomy. The educational system is adaptive and accommodates the learner who is the centre of the educational process. To the Chinese, however, the teacher is a transmitter of knowledge, a role model and the focus of educational practice. Consequently, if students are unsuccessful in academic pursuits, this is widely perceived as a matter of motivation, effort and ability, not the fault of the teacher. In China it is deemed important to master academic material without questioning; indeed, questioning is often seen as disruptive and disrespectful. Furthermore, emphasis is placed on additive learning, the acquisition of skills and information that complement previously attained knowledge. It is assumed that this type of learning results in greater proficiency and that questioning core beliefs often results in unnecessary difficulties.

Similar contrasts have been drawn between the North American and the

Table 7.3 Expectations of British and Chinese academics (Cortazzi and Jin, 1997)

British	Chinese
Individual orientation	Collective consciousness
Horizontal relations	Hierarchical relations
Active involvement	Passive participation
Verbal explicitness	Contextualised communication
Speaker/writer responsibility	Reader/listener responsibility
Independence of mind	Dependence on authority
Creativity	Originality
Discussion, argument, challenge	Agreement, harmony, face
Seeking alternatives	Single solution
Critical evaluation	Assumed acceptance

Source: M. Cortazzi and L. Jin (1997). Communication for learning across cultures. In D. McNamara & R. Harris (Eds), *Overseas students in higher education*. Reprinted with permission of Routledge.

Japanese systems of education where there is greater social distance between students and teachers, more vertical student–teacher relationships and a one way flow of information, greater formality in the classroom, and more emphasis on rote memory (Becker, 1990). While it is clear that there are a number of cross-cultural differences in educational expectations and practices, these differences have not always been accurately interpreted by educators and academics. Cultural differences are often viewed in a stereo-typic and negative fashion, not only with respect to the educational traditions of Oriental cultures but also in connection with the academic practices of Asian students attending universities in Western, English-speaking countries (e.g. Ballard and Clanchy, 1984; Samuelowicz, 1987). Volet and Renshaw (1995) have described the situation as follows:

> A major problem with this literature is the application of a deficit model which has provided a negative, stereotyped and static view of Asian students' learning. It has failed to consider these students' cognitions and behaviours in interaction with the context in which they are embedded, it has neglected to examine students' adjustments to the new educational context over a period of time, it has underestimated the magnitude of individual differences amongst the international student population, and it has seldom systematically compared international students' cognitions with that of their local counterparts.
>
> (Volet and Renshaw, 1995: 409)

This limited perspective needs to be re-evaluated, particularly as Australian studies have shown that Asian students are more strongly motivated than locals and that they set higher academic goals (Niles, 1995; Volet and Renshaw, 1995). Research has also demonstrated that Asian students adapt successfully over time and that even after one semester their learning goals, evaluations of study techniques, and appreciation of the learning process begin to converge with those of local students (Liberman, 1994; Volet and Renshaw, 1995).

Longitudinal studies of international student adaptation

As international students are generally more accessible to investigators than other groups of cross-cultural travellers, they have more frequently been the focus of longitudinal research. These studies have concentrated on two basic themes: predicting cross-cultural and educational adaptation by pre-departure variables and monitoring changes in the levels of psychological and sociocultural adaptation over time. Although there has also been a strong interest in the outcomes of intercultural education, these studies have not generally been conducted as longitudinal investigations, and a number of them are limited by their retrospective design (e.g. Bachner, Zeutschel and Shannon, 1993).

Ying and Liese's (1990, 1991) study which examined the impact of pre-departure variables on the post-arrival adaptation of 172 Taiwanese students in the United States is an example of the first type of longitudinal investigation. In addition to demographic factors, predictive variables included pre-departure adaptation (depression), personality (internality, norm adherence, self-actualisation and femininity), expectations and self-assessed language ability. A hierarchical regression analysis revealed that the pre-departure level of depression was the strongest predictor of post-arrival adaptation, and this accounted for 16 per cent of the variance in the depressive symptoms of student sojourners. However, psychological femininity, poor self-assessed language ability, and anticipating more interpersonal problems were also significant predictors of post-arrival adaptation problems. Furukawa and Shibayama's (1993, 1994) work with Japanese sojourning students also revealed that pre-departure individual differences affect post-arrival adaptation. In their research pre-departure neuroticism and inadequacy of interpersonal attachments predicted greater psychological disturbance as assessed by the General Health Questionnaire.

Kennedy (1999) undertook a more comprehensive investigation of cross-cultural transition in his study of the academic, psychological and socio-cultural adaptation of Singaporean students abroad. Students were surveyed before departure from Singapore and then again 1 and 6 months after their arrival overseas. Results revealed that pre-departure need for achievement, language ability and overmet expectations (the comparison of pre-departure expectations with post-arrival experiences) predicted academic performance. In the case of sociocultural adaptation, pre-departure language ability and previous cross-cultural experience emerged as significant predictors. Although language ability also influenced subsequent psychological well-being, pre-departure stress and undermet expectations were stronger predictors of post-arrival adjustment problems. Early experiences abroad also predicted later adjustment. For example, greater identification with host nationals within the first month of the overseas sojourn resulted in fewer sociocultural problems at 6 months, and avoidant coping styles used soon after arrival increased psychological distress later in the sojourn.

In contrast to the predictive studies of adaptation, a second strand of longitudinal research has monitored student adjustment over time. These studies have been generally designed to test the U-curve hypothesis, but they have largely failed to produce supportive evidence. Although some researchers have reported no significant differences in psychological adjustment over time (e.g. Nash, 1991), it is more common to find a decrement in adjustment between departure and arrival (Ying and Liese, 1991) and a rapid improvement in psychological adjustment in the early stages of the sojourn (Lu, 1990; Ward and Kennedy, 1996a). Sociocultural adaptation, likewise, decreases on entering a new environment, improves markedly in the initial stages, continues to increase over time and eventually stabilises (Kennedy, 1999; Ward and Kennedy, 1996a).

These patterns were observed in Ward *et al.*'s (1998) longitudinal investigation of the adaptation of Japanese students in New Zealand. Figures 7.1 and 7.2 show the pattern of psychological and sociocultural adaptation in overseas students upon entry (within the first 24 hours), at 4 months, at 6 months and at 12 months (after returning home for school holidays). In both cases only the changes between entry and 4 months were significant. Although psychological adjustment was variable in the later stages, the pattern of sociocultural adaptation approximated a learning curve. Additional analyses suggested that students' integration into the host society increased over time as the relationship between psychological and sociocultural adaptation strengthened significantly over the one-year period.

Re-entry

In her 1984 discussion and review of re-entry Martin remarked that despite the probability that readjusting to one's home culture may be more difficult than an overseas sojourn, there was relatively little research on the re-entry process. She argued that we should view re-entry as one form of cultural adjustment and that we need to understand how this process is similar to and different from adjusting to life in a foreign culture. It is interesting to note that Martin foreshadowed developments in the field, suggesting that both culture learning models and coping styles offered suitable frameworks for the

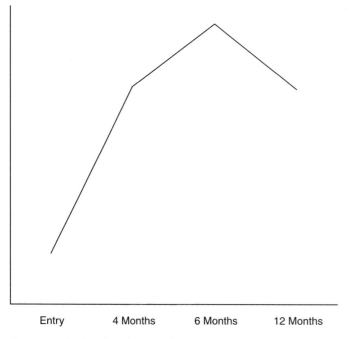

Figure 7.1 Sociocultural adaptation over time

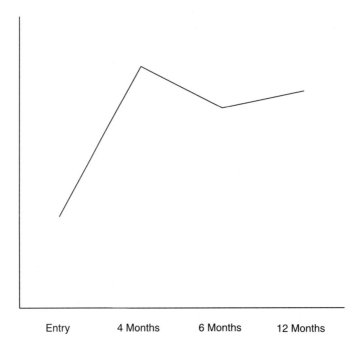

Entry   4 Months   6 Months   12 Months

Figure 7.2 Psychological adaptation over time

study of re-entry. Over the intervening 15 years, these conceptual frameworks have indeed been used for the examination and interpretation of the re-entry experience. So have many of the critical variables that Martin recommended for exploration, including demographic factors, such as age, gender and nationality, interpersonal relations and interactions, and readiness and willingness to return home. Of particular significance, however, are expectations. Here Martin specifically suggested that the major reason re-entry is so difficult is that few problems are actually anticipated.

This was borne out in a later study by Rogers and Ward (1993) that examined the re-entry expectations and experiences of AFS (American Field Service) students from New Zealand. While still residing overseas, students were queried about their expectations of re-entry (e.g. social difficulties such as maintaining friendships, adapting to the pace of life), and then within 4–10 weeks of return, they completed a second questionnaire on their actual experiences. The research revealed that students had largely inaccurate expectations; there was no significant correlation between expectancies and experiences. More importantly, when re-entry was more difficult than anticipated, students reported greater depression and anxiety.

While returning students expect few re-entry problems in general, there is some evidence that they do specifically anticipate interpersonal difficulties. Bochner, Lin and McLeod (1980) examined expectancies of Asian students in the United States prior to re-entry, and although the majority were eager to return home, interpersonal concerns were clearly apparent. In particular, there was a high degree of ambivalence expressed about peer and professional contacts. This was less true for family relations, which engendered largely positive expectations. More recent research has suggested that expectations such as these may be fairly accurate (Martin, 1986b). For example, American AFS returnees reported that changes in parental relations were generally for the better, but that changes in relations with friends were more mixed. Interestingly, the changes, whether positive or negative, were most frequently attributed to their intercultural experiences.

The difficulties encountered during the re-entry transition often take their toll on the psychological well-being of student sojourners. Returnees present more symptoms of psychological distress than those students who have remained at home (Uehara, 1986). Rohrlich and Martin (1991) reported that American students were generally less satisfied with their lives at home than abroad. Sahin (1990) found that one in three of the Turkish adolescents in his investigation regretted returning home, and Sorimachi (1994) concluded that the Japanese students in his study uniformly experienced re-entry shock. Wilson's (1993) investigation found that most American high school exchange students felt it difficult to return home although they generally agreed that they did not experience major problems.

What difficulties are typically experienced? Communicating with friends, dealing with stereotypes, uncertainty over cultural identity, social withdrawal, and decreased relationship satisfaction have been commonly reported outcomes (Enloe and Lewin, 1987; Martin, 1984, 1986b; Raschio, 1987; Sahin, 1990; Seiter and Waddell, 1989; Wilson, 1993; Zapf, 1991). In addition to social difficulties, psychological problems are also apparent. Uehara (1986) described the manifestation of 're-entry shock' in terms of physical distress, anxiety, apathy, loneliness, and feelings of loss. In a minority of cases psychological symptoms reach clinical proportions. Sahin's (1990) study of 785 Turkish returnees found that 18 per cent of the sample was classified as clinically depressed, and 45 per cent had significant problems with anxiety. However, studies also suggest that the extent of serious re-entry difficulties is not great. The results of a recent study by Gaw (2000) with American students are summarised below.

There have also been a small number of studies on the determinants of re-entry adaptation, and these have frequently incorporated perceptions of satisfaction and adjustment while abroad. The outcomes of these studies are mixed. Ward, Berno and Main (2000) found that individual difference measures, such as emotional resilience, perceptual acuity, autonomy and flexibility, were associated with psychological and sociocultural adaptation of Singaporean students in Australia but were unrelated to their subsequent re-entry adaptation. Students who were better adjusted psychologically in Australia experienced less psychological distress on return; however, sociocultural adaptation in the two countries was unrelated. Brabant, Palmer and

Table 7.4 Problems of student returnees (adapted from Gaw, 2000)

Loneliness	30.3	Roommates	15.2
Adjustment to college	27.3	Dating problems	15.2
Career choice	25.8	Inferiority feelings	13.7
Alienation	24.2	Making friends	10.6
Depression	22.7	Sexual relations	7.6
Trouble studying	22.7	Conflicts with parents	6.1
Financial concerns	19.7	Speech anxiety	4.6
Test anxiety	19.7	Insomnia	4.6
Shyness	16.7	Alcohol problems	4.5
Personal/ethnic identity	16.7	Sexual functioning	4.5
General anxiety	15.2	Drug addiction	0
Academic performance	15.2		

Note: The Personal Problems Inventory was used in this reasearch. The table reports the percentage of students who rated the item as a significant or severe problem.

Gramling (1990) found that international students who reported adapting well to life in the United States were less likely to experience severe psychosocial problems on re-entry, but Uehara (1986) was unable to substantiate a relationship between overseas and re-entry adjustment in American returnees.

Demographic factors may also predict post-return adaptation. Although length of stay abroad appears unrelated to re-entry adaptation in student sojourners (e.g. Uehara, 1986), age may be an important factor. Sorimachi (1994) suggested that Japanese students who lived overseas during a critical period, i.e. 9–15 years old, were most likely to experience re-adjustment problems. This may be related to broader issues in identity development, known to be problematic in early adolescence. There is also evidence to suggest that there are gender differences in re-entry adaptation. Rorhlich and Martin (1991), for example, found that women expressed more life satisfaction after returning than did men.

Cultural factors almost certainly exert an influence on re-entry adaptation, and Kidder (1992) has argued that re-entry into a 'tight' society is more difficult than returning to 'loose' countries. This is likely to be the case for the 12–13,000 students who return annually to Japan (Ministry of Education, 1999). Returning students are noticed for looking physically different, having different interpersonal styles, and behaving with different manners. Interactions with teachers, peers and even family members imply that that there are requirements for being a 'proper Japanese', and that if the returnees do not conform to expectations, they will be treated as outsiders. This may be a significant source of distress for returning students.

> I cried a lot when I had to come home . . . The first thing my mother said, before saying 'welcome home,' she checked my face for makeup and my ears (not pierced) and said 'good.' And that really hurt.
>
> Kidder (1992: 385–386)

In many cases the strong expectations for re-entry conformity lead return-ing students to hide their international experiences.

> When school started, I heard when *kikokushijo* (returnees) came to school they get *ijime* (bullied). So I didn't do anything, was just quiet and calm and didn't talk.
>
> (Kidder, 1992: 389)

In either instance the returning student often feels that the 'self' he or she has become is not acceptable in Japanese society.

> My mother says that when I first came back I was trying too hard to conform to be Japanese, that I couldn't be myself, express myself.
>
> (Kidder, 1992: 387)

The re-entry transition may be difficult and distressing in a number of ways, but social and psychological problems can be alleviated by preparation. Westwood, Lawrence and Paul (1986) have recognised the need for re-entry programmes and have argued that the primary responsibility for assistance lies with the host culture educational institutions. They also recommend that international student advisers be used to establish and facilitate re-entry workshops and group support networks. Their guidelines for programmes include: alerting students to the need to prepare for returning home; providing students with the opportunity to receive first hand information about re-entry through dialogue, reading or other media; enabling students to maintain better contact with home during their overseas sojourn; and providing students with feedback about acculturation and personal growth and development that may affect their re-entry experiences.

CHAPTER SUMMARY

This chapter has selectively reviewed contemporary research on student sojourners. As is the case for other cross-cultural travellers, the literature concentrates on the ABCs of transition and adaptation. Studies of the affect-ive component of culture contact have been concerned with the description and prediction of the psychological adjustment of student sojourners. The behavioural aspects of culture contact have been featured in research on the patterns of intercultural interaction, including the friendship networks of overseas students; they have also emerged in the discussion of culture learning in the classroom. Cognitive facets of the student sojourn have been highlighted in work on intergroup perceptions and relations, particularly studies of stereotypes and perceived discrimination.

Research on intercultural interactions indicates that although overseas students would like contact with host nationals and that they benefit socially and psychologically from these encounters, the extent of host–sojourner interactions is limited. Overseas students are more likely to have co-national friends, and on the whole, they find establishing friendships more difficult than their local counterparts. Although host nationals, co-nationals and other non-compatriot international students can provide both informational and social support, research suggests that host nationals are preferred for tangible, instrumental assistance while other students, particularly co-nationals, are more heavily relied upon for socio-emotional support.

There are a number of factors that affect the structural components and functional outcomes of intercultural contact, and stereotypes, in particular, are known to exert a strong influence on the interactions between local and overseas students. In some situations, such as equal status contact under conditions of low threat, stereotypes may foster positive intergroup relations. However, this is not uniformly the case for interactions between domestic and international students. Research has suggested that a significant proportion of overseas students feel ambivalent about their relations with host nationals and that many perceive discrimination. There is also evidence that increased contact can lead to a sharpening of negative intergroup stereotypes in international students over time. These research findings remind us that the contact theory can only account for an improvement in intergroup relations under very specific circumstances.

A considerable amount of research on overseas students has concerned itself with the assessment of student problems. These investigations are useful for applied objectives, such as improving the satisfaction of (and increasing the revenue generated by) overseas students; they are also useful for theory testing, especially hypotheses arising from the culture learning and the stress and coping approaches to sojourner adaptation. Studies show that international students experience a wide range of problems, particularly those relating to academic pressures, financial resources, friendship development and culture-specific aspects of sojourning. They also suggest that serious difficulties are not widespread and that many of the problems experienced by overseas students are shared by their local counterparts. However, because research samples and methodologies differ so widely across studies, it is difficult to draw firm conclusions about the prevalence, seriousness and consequences of student sojourner problems and their relationship to the difficulties encountered by their host national peers.

It is clear, nevertheless, that some of the most significant problems arise from the academic environment and that overseas students must engage in 'culture-learning' as well as intellectual endeavours to achieve academic success. Student and teacher expectations, the patterns of classroom interaction, and even perceptions and definitions of intelligence, vary across cultures. Although there is increasing sensitivity to the challenges of intercultural education, the burden for successful adaptation to the new educational milieu is placed largely on the international students.

One distinctive aspect of research on student sojourning is the increasing prevalence of longitudinal studies. These have been conducted primarily on the relationship between pre-departure factors and post-arrival adaptation and the temporal fluctuations in sojourner adjustment. The first line of studies has shown that certain personality factors (e.g. neuroticism, need for achievement), language ability, previous cross-cultural experience and expectations exert influences on academic, psychological and sociocultural aspects of post-arrival adaptation. The second line of investigations has demonstrated that both psychological and sociocultural adjustment problems are greatest during the early stages of transition and that they decrease over time. The longitudinal approach has also been adopted in recent studies of re-entry. In an analogous fashion, these investigations have highlighted the significance of pre-return expectations and dispositional factors (e.g. emotional resilience) for post-return adaptation.

Although there has been relatively less research on re-entry compared with sojourning abroad, investigations in this area are increasing. Re-entry has been shown to create a range of difficulties, and many returning students clearly experience psychological distress. Interpersonal relationships, particularly those with friends, appear to suffer, and loneliness is one of the most commonly reported problems of returnees. While there are aspects of the re-entry process that can be unsettling to anyone (e.g. concerns over changing identity), it is likely that return to a 'tight' culture is even more difficult than return to a 'loose' society (Triandis, 1989). Interviews with students returning to Japan bear this out and, as will be seen in the next chapter on international business people, this appears to be the case for adults as well as children and adolescents.

8 Sojourners: International business people

In the last chapter we selectively reviewed research on international students, one of the most frequently studied groups of sojourners. Persons going abroad for commercial and business reasons constitute another major group of short-term cross-cultural travellers. These are individuals who have usually been sent by their employers to work and live temporarily in countries where the organisation is conducting business through a branch, a subsidiary, or a joint venture structure. Although each of these arrangements differs in various significant ways, from the perspective of the sojourner the psychological problems are very similar. Their time abroad will have a finite limit, after which they will return home; they will have clear work-related assignments that they are expected to accomplish; they will have to be able to interact successfully with their local counterparts to achieve their goals; they and their families, if they have any, will experience the dislocation associated with exposure to unfamiliar cultural settings; and their career path may be affected, positively or negatively, by choosing or agreeing to undertake service abroad.

Although work-related cross-cultural travel in the broadest sense includes all occupational levels from factory and domestic staff to highly skilled technicians, professionals and managers, the present chapter will only deal with those at the executive end of the spectrum. There are two reasons for this. First, the literature on the so-called guest *arbeiter* group is rather sketchy. Furthermore, many of the persons in that category are often in reality immigrants or intending immigrants, and in that sense do not fit our definition of sojourners, that is, unambiguously temporary culture travellers. Second, there is a large and growing literature on what we will call the expatriate experience, with most of the studies having been conducted with workers in managerial and professional roles.

There are several reasons why there is considerable research interest in the expatriate experience: there are large numbers of expatriates; they provide the human link in international trade; and their effectiveness has a direct impact on the profitability and often the viability of international commerce. That is why business travellers are also the sojourner group most likely to receive at least some pre-departure culture orientation and training and to undergo psychological and other assessment procedures as part of their selection for overseas assignments. The general training and selection literature will be reviewed in Chapter 11 and will not be explicitly referred to here, with the one or two exceptions that are particularly germane to the expatriate experience.

Our aim in this chapter is to describe the expatriate experience and to identify those features that are unique to this group of sojourners. In keeping with the ABC (affect, behaviour, cognitions) approach adopted throughout this book, we will review studies that deal with the general adaptation of expatriates to their unfamiliar sociocultural environments as well as identify specific work-related adaptation processes. In the case of business travellers, unlike immigrants and most students, objective performance criteria are easily accessible. These are not confined to economic indicators, but also include traditional industrial/organisational indices such as job satisfaction, organisational commitment and labour turnover. In other words, there are measurable outcome variables that can be used to quantify sociocultural adaptation. And we will again attempt to identify the personal and social conditions that serve as barriers to successful adaptation and those that enhance it.

Topics specific to the expatriate experience include the acquisition, or at least the expression, of appropriate work-related cognitive styles and responses. Much of an executive's day-to-day activities involve negotiating with business partners and influencing and leading subordinates, all processes which may have idiosyncratic culture-specific forms. This consideration also relates to the more general finding that managerial practices in most cases do not transfer easily across cultural boundaries. The role of the spouse in influencing both the affective adjustment of the expatriate, as well as the person's job related performance, is also a major issue. Another key subject is the re-entry process. On returning home, expatriates not only have to readjust to the general cultural milieu of a country from which they might have been absent for several years, but they also have to reintegrate themselves with their employing organisation. Another topic on which there is a nascent literature relates to the growing number of business sojourners who are women and the special problems that female expatriates encounter. Finally, we will also briefly review the literature on inpatriation, where multinationals bring indigenous managers from their local branches to the head office for training and then send them back to manage the subsidiary operation.

CULTURAL DISTANCE, WORK PERFORMANCE AND ADAPTATION OF BUSINESS SOJOURNERS

A robust finding in the culture-contact literature is that the adjustment and coping difficulties of sojourners increase with the distance between their culture of origin and that of the host society. As this literature was reviewed previously, only studies specifically relevant to business travellers will be cited in the present discussion. The role of cultural distance in expatriate adjustment is evident in all three of the components of our ABC model. It affects how people feel about their life and work abroad; how adept they are in achieving their personal as well as work-related goals; and the veracity and utility of their general as well as work-related perceptions and decisions. All of these factors are related to effective strategic thinking and are important ingredients for business success.

The key underlying practical problem is that human resource management and business practices do not easily migrate across cultural boundaries (Abo, 1994; Bochner, 1992; Graen and Wakabayashi, 1994; Kenny and Florida, 1993; Martin and Beaumont, 1998; Oliver and Wilkinson, 1992; Shadur *et al.*, 1995). What succeeds in New York may not work in Sydney and will probably fail in Beijing or Tokyo. In a recent review of the literature Tayeb (1999) concluded that some management practices, such as flexible working hours, have been easier to transfer than others. Some have had to be modified, such as quality circles and teamwork (an issue we will deal with in more detail later). And some, like morning ceremonies that are a feature of many Japanese companies, have steadfastly resisted transfer.

More technically, none of the following, largely North-American-derived assumptions about work-related human nature are universal: preferences for a consultative leadership style (versus a structured, directive command system); egalitarian interpersonal relationships between employees occupying different levels in the hierarchy (versus being highly conscious of and emphasising differences in status, salary and seniority); an emphasis on task achievement (versus maintaining harmonious interpersonal relations); the use of direct and immediate performance feedback (versus avoiding giving frank feedback because it might damage the employee's face and lower the worker's loyalty to the organisation); reliance on written and unwritten rules (versus a more informal regulatory system); the treatment and reward of employees based on individual performance (versus being integrated into a team); the practice of negotiation based on rational, factual grounds (versus emotional appeals associated with interpersonal considerations and subjective feelings); the selection, recruitment and promotion of employees on the basis of merit (versus taking into account the personal relationship between the worker and the employer); the acceptance of a psychological contract setting out an explicit formal relationship between the worker and the organisation, as captured by the phrase 'a fair day's work for a fair day's pay', together with the right of the worker and the employer to sever the connection when expedient (versus an association that is modelled on the concept of family, emphasising mutual obligations and long term relationships through good times and bad (Adler, 1997; Brewster *et al.*, 1996; Budhwar and Sparrow, 1998; Earley, 1993; Guzzo, Noonan and Elron, 1994; Hofstede, 1991; Kashima and Callan, 1994; Redding, Norman and Schlander, 1994; Triandis, 1994b; Weiss, 1996).

Because these assumptions determine many management practices, it is important to know whether they hold in particular circumstances. The practical consequences of cross-cultural diversity in values are captured by Hofstede's (1998) assertion that 'Nobody can think globally . . . Management in general, and personnel management in particular, are culturally constrained' (p. 7). This poses a dilemma for expatriate managers employed by multinational corporations. On the one hand, they are expected to put into effect uniform corporate-wide policies and practices whose functional benefits may be lost in certain subsidiaries. On the other hand, if they do take into account cultural differences and change their practices accordingly, this may result in an unacceptable dilution of the corporate culture and the centralised control systems which drive their particular multinational organisation (e.g. Martinez and Jarillo, 1991; Muralidharan, 1998; Snell, 1992). This issue is never far below the surface in the international management literature.

Another problem facing expatriates is that significant changes in workforce demographics have occurred as a result of globalisation. Increasingly, work groups are becoming culturally diverse (Erez, 1994; Milliken and Martins, 1996; Triandis, Kurowski and Gelfand, 1994). This is true not only for those that the expatriates manage but also the teams to which they belong. In many cases co-workers will also be expatriates who hail from other parts of the world.

Research has shown that the greater the cultural heterogeneity of a work group, defined as the greater the relative cultural distance among group members, the greater the likelihood that this will have adverse consequences on group performance. At the very least, such groups will be more difficult to manage. Heterogeneity, however, does have some advantages. In particular, heterogeneous groups tend to be more creative, largely because they bring a variety of perspectives to the task in hand. But research has also shown that cultural diversity may lead to lower levels of interpersonal harmony, more stress and greater turnover (Adler, 1997; Bochner and Hesketh, 1994; Jackson, 1992; O'Reilly, Caldwell and Barnett, 1989; Storey, 1991; Thomas, 1999; Triandis, Kurowski and Gelfand, 1994). The costs and benefits of diversity have led commentators such as Cox and Blake (1991) and Cox, Lobel and McLeod (1991) to suggest that if companies can learn how to manage such variety, they would gain a competitive advantage by being able to harness the positive aspects of heterogeneity.

To illustrate some of the problems of cultural heterogeneity in the work place, as the pace of globalisation intensifies, an increasing number of middle managers are reporting to superiors from dissimilar cultures. In an article provocatively titled 'Would you trust your foreign manager?' Banai and Reisel (1999) compared the attitudes of British managers working in a British bank in London with expatriate managers in banks in Britain, the United States, The Netherlands, and Israel. They found that trust between managers and their supervisors was greater in homogeneous than heterogeneous work settings. The authors interpret their findings in terms of the degree of cultural similarity among the individuals surveyed. These findings are significant for the culture-distance hypothesis in that from a global perspective, the distance between the participants was only moderate, suggesting that the effect would be greater in more heterogeneous work settings.

Leadership style

The major functions of expatriate personnel are to manage, coordinate, motivate and generally direct the activities of local subordinates and colleagues. The explicit behaviours that are assumed to serve these functions, however, may vary considerably across cultures. Unfortunately, as in the case of intercultural education, management practices that diverge significantly from Euro-centric norms and standards are often perceived as poor replacements. Although more recent research has incorporated an emic perspective on these issues, some of the old 'colonial' attitudes still remain in the investigation of organisational processes.

Leadership is a case in point. From its first appearance in the literature, it was conceived as a process that involves a power relationship between persons designated as leaders and their followers (McGregor, 1944). Effective leadership was defined in terms of the amount of compliance or acquiescence leaders could elicit from their subordinates. A great deal of subsequent research compared and contrasted the effects of various types of leadership behaviours (for a review see Hollander, 1985).

The main contrast was and largely still is between the authoritarian/ autocratic versus participative/democratic approach, based on whether leaders make all of the decisions themselves or whether they share power with their subordinates. Another major distinction is between task-oriented versus people-oriented styles, also sometimes described as initiating structure versus consideration. These terms refer to whether leaders concentrate on getting the job done irrespective of any adverse human relations consequences or whether they regard it as important to foster job satisfaction and achieve a cohesive, stable and committed work force. There is wide agreement that effective leaders, as measured by followers' job satisfaction and productivity, will be high on both consideration and structure; however, almost all of the research has been conducted in Western cultural contexts.

The models described have been called contingency theories because they define the leadership process in terms of the contingencies that shape the relationship between leaders and followers. Contingency models tend to ignore, or at least greatly de-emphasise, the personality traits and characteristics of the leader, a position that is inconsistent with lay notions of charismatic leadership. Recently, however, Bernard Bass has proposed a model which makes explicit reference to both the characteristics of the leader and the leader–follower relationship (e.g. Bass, 1997).

Bass makes a distinction between transactional and transformational leadership. Transactional leadership is based on the exchange principle; that is, material or symbolic rewards and resources under the control of the leader are offered to followers in return for compliance (Hollander and Offermann,

1990). Transformational leadership is based on the ability of a leader to motivate followers to work for goals which go beyond immediate self-interest for the good of the group, organisation or country. Unlike transactional leaders, transformational leaders inspire their followers in the sharing of vision, symbolism and sacrifice.

According to Bass (Bass and Avolio, 1994), transformational leaders are more effective than leaders who follow a contingent reward strategy. Furthermore, Bass proposes that this advantage is common across all cultures and that transformational leadership is superior in both autocratic and participative systems. It is also supposed to transcend organisational boundaries. Clearly, if this conclusion were warranted, it would have huge practical implications for the day-to-day behaviour of expatriate executives. It gives a clear 'No' to the question as to whether one should lead differently in different cultural settings.

However, to some cultural observers the emphasis on vision and sacrifice smacks of hypocrisy and manipulation. Bass (1997) reviews an impressive amount of empirical support for his thesis, but most of the studies cited are by workers using his Multifactor Leadership Questionnaire. Still, in the final analysis the issue will be decided by empirical research, and there is a considerable amount of theory and some evidence in favour of an emic, culturally specific approach to leadership.

In particular, there is strong support for the view that collectivist values (see Chapter 1 for a discussion of the individualistic/collectivist distinction) are congruent with transformational leadership, whereas an individualistic outlook would be more congruent with a transactional approach. That is because individualists are more driven by self-interest and short term personal goals, whereas collectivists value their long term association with their reference groups. Collectivists tend to inhibit their personal aspirations if these conflict with the goals of their group, precisely what transformational leaders require of their subordinates.

Collectivist cultures are also characterised by high power distance, which would make them more willing to accept their leader's beliefs and vision. And a recent study co-authored by one of Bass's major collaborators supported at least some of these implications (Jung and Avolio, 1999). The study compared the performance of individualists with collectivists who were either led by a transactional or a transformational leader. The dependent variables were the number of ideas generated to solve a management problem and the practicality of these solutions. The study found that individualists generated more recommendations in the transactional than in the transformational leadership condition whereas the performance of the collectivists was superior in the transformational leadership condition. The study clearly demonstrated that individuals will respond to the way they are led as a function of the congruence of their cultural orientation with the leadership style they are experiencing. This conclusion echoes previous findings in the literature (e.g. Earley, 1989; Erez and Somech, 1996; Wagner,

1995) and has important implications for managing cultural diversity in the work place.

In a recent study by Eylon and Au (1999), East Asian (high power distance) and Canadian and Northern European (low power distance) MBA students were randomly assigned to an in-basket management simulation (Hakstian, Woolsey and Schroeder, 1986) that varied in the extent to which the participants were 'empowered', that is, the extent to which they were given information, responsibility and trust. The dependent variables were job satisfaction and work performance. Results showed that all participants, irrespective of their culture of origin, were more satisfied when working under empowered circumstances. However, work performance did vary as a function of the interaction between the participants' culture and the extent to which they were empowered. High power distance, empowered participants performed less well than empowered workers from low power distance cultures, thus confirming that high power distance workers operate more effectively under a benevolent autocratic leadership style whereas low power distance workers respond better to a more decentralised and consultative system.

Self-managing teams

A related issue is the increasing reliance in Western organisations on self-managing work teams. These changes in work practice are based on the belief that if workers are given greater freedom to make decisions affecting the way in which they do their jobs, this will promote feelings of ownership about the tasks they are performing and should lead to higher productivity and greater job satisfaction. There is also the assumption that decisions which are made closer to the coal-face are better able to deal with any issues and problems as they arise, rather than deliberations which occur at more remote board-room levels.

The rise in self-managing groups is consistent with another modern management trend, the move towards organisational structures with flattened hierarchies. The term 'semi-autonomous work groups' is also sometimes used in this context and is a key element in the Tavistock Institute's Sociotechnical Systems (STS) model of organisational functioning. The strength of STS is that it is explicitly derived from a systematic set of theoretical principles, namely open systems theory. STS was developed soon after the end of the Second World War by some of the great pioneers of the human relations movement in industrial psychology, including Fred Emery, Philip Herbst, A. K. Rice, Einar Thorsrud, and Eric Trist. In particular, they used STS as the theoretical basis for their applied interventions to introduce organisational change and development (for a recent review see Fox, 1995; Pasmore, 1995; Scarbrough, 1995).

There is no doubt that replacing hierarchical structures with semi-autonomous interlocking work groups is a highly effective strategy in the right circumstances. It increased productivity, job satisfaction, quality, safety, customer service and organisational commitment in many of the projects in which it was introduced (Pasmore, 1988; Wall *et al.*, 1986). In an article titled 'Whither industrial psychology . . . in a changing world of work?' Cascio (1995) explicitly refers to the 'empowered worker' (p. 930) in the context of workplace democracy as a defining feature of the industrial landscape of the future. Although he is referring to the United States, it is clear that he regards this as a global trend.

The issue in relation to the present discussion is that most Western-trained expatriate managers would have been exposed to this literature. This may incline them to install self-managing work team (SMWT) structures into their overseas assignments without taking into account the possibility that such an approach could be inappropriate in some cultural settings. SMWTs include a number of characteristics: the team deciding who will do which task and in what sequence; the team having its own identifiable 'whole' task; the team doing its own quality control, imposing internal discipline on its members, and setting its own production goals; and workers being paid and their performance evaluated on the basis of their membership of a team rather than as individuals (Wellins *et al.*, 1990). An inspection of these attributes suggests that at least some of these SMWT features could be culture-specific.

As was the case with leadership style, there may be cultures where introducing SMWTs could be incompatible with its core values and hence counterproductive. Kirkman and Shapiro (1997) used Hofstede's individualism–collectivism model to derive such predictions. They define self-management in the work place in terms of the degree of workers' discretionary decision making powers and suggest that resistance to the introduction of self-managing groups will occur in high power distance cultures, that is, societies which accept that power is distributed unequally (Hofstede, 1980). However, the evidence they present for this contention is only circumstantial and largely based on Adler's (1997) statement that employees in high power distance countries, such as the Philippines, Venezuela, and India, regard bypassing their supervisors as insubordination. Similarly, the Japanese reliance on authority and deference to superiors (Kato and Kato, 1992) is interpreted as indicating that Japanese workers would resist SMWTs, but no direct evidence is cited to support this claim.

Kirkman and Shapiro (1997) also invoke the individualism–collectivism (I–C) continuum to predict that workers in collectivist cultures will be more inclined to accept SMWT structures than individualists. The argument is based on the proposition that collectivists prefer cooperating rather than competing, will give precedence to achieving group over individual goals, and have the social skills needed to work harmoniously in a group. However, empirically it is the case that power distance and collectivism are highly correlated (Bochner and Hesketh, 1994). Consequently, the hypothesis predicting a preference for SMWTs in collectivists is discrepant with the earlier prediction that high power distance workers will resist this managerial structure. These discrepancies highlight the problems associated with content-free theorising.

Ross (1999) provides another example of this tendency. He extends the person–environment fit model (Pervin, 1968), widely used in industrial psychology, to make the quite sensible point that the business strategy of a multinational should match the cultures of the countries in which it operates. He then uses Hofstede's (1980) framework to deduce a set of guidelines for expatriate managers to use in their Chinese operations. For instance, because China is high on power distance and medium on uncertainty avoidance, Ross says that the Chinese would prefer a centralised authority system. However, no evidence is presented for this contention.

We do know that the incidence of social loafing is greater in individualistic cultures (Earley, 1989), but that by itself is insufficient to draw conclusions about any culturally-determined preference or resistance to SMWTs. It would be highly advisable to base any decisions about SMWTs on the specific composition of the work force as revealed by empirical investigation rather than relying on general, abstract theorising. In a study that does provide some support for the power distance hypothesis, Ralston *et al.*, (1992) compared the value orientations of managers from the United States, Hong Kong and the People's Republic of China (PRC), using the Chinese Value Survey developed by Michael Bond and colleagues (Chinese Culture Connection, 1987). As predicted, they found that the PRC managers scored significantly higher on the Confucian Work Dynamism scale than the Hong Kong managers, who in turn scored higher than the American managers. Confucian teachings emphasise maintaining a social hierarchy and protecting the status quo, which are important features of high power distance cultures.

The literature on the fit between management practices and national culture is currently in its infancy. Studies employing this framework are now beginning to appear that do have some empirical content, such Aycan, Kanungo and Sinha's (1999) comparison of Canadian and Indian human resource management practices and Hoffman's (1999) survey of managers in three European cultures (Germanic, Latin, and Nordic). However, the empirical findings tend to be equivocal at best, and the genre is limited by its reliance on Hofstede's somewhat dated work to define the cultural categories. No doubt all this will change as the field develops further.

Joint ventures in China: A case study

Joint ventures between overseas companies and domestic enterprises in the People's Republic of China provide a window to some of the difficulties of conducting international business. The Chinese market is huge, with over one billion potential consumers, and the growth in its Gross National Product (GNP) has averaged 10 per cent over the last 15 years. The business opportunities inherent in such a setting have not gone unnoticed, causing foreign companies to be seized by what some commentators have called 'China fever'. To illustrate, the investments of Canadian companies in China increased by 700 per cent between 1991 and 1995. Foreign investment in 1995 was US$38 billion, and in the first 6 months of 1997, China attracted US$23 in direct foreign investment (Abramson and Ai, 1999; Milman, 1999; O'Connor and Chalos, 1999).

One of the reasons why the term 'China fever' is appropriate is that the history of joint ventures shows that many of these undertakings have been failures in financial terms (Child, 1994; Rondinelli, 1993). For instance, a survey by Andersen Consulting (1995) found that only 44 per cent of joint venture companies reported meeting their profit targets. Despite statistics such as these, investment in China shows no signs of abating.

In the business literature, failed joint ventures in China and elsewhere tend to be attributed to commercial factors such as cost control, product quality and pricing, inflation, and poor strategic planning (Fry and Killing, 1989; O'Connor and Chalos, 1999). The uncertainty caused by the gradual transformation from a planned to a socialist market economy is also cited as a factor (Leung, 1995). However, there is a growing realisation that cultural differences play a major role in exacerbating market-related difficulties (Abramson and Ai, 1999; Boyacigiller and Adler, 1991; Schrage *et al.* 1999). One factor in particular is often cited, i.e. the emphasis on personal relationships known as *guanxi* which distinguishes Chinese from Western business practices (Shenkar and Ronen, 1993).

Guanxi relationships are characterized by mutual trust and a willingness to enter into commercial arrangements that produce mutual benefits over a long period of time (Davies, 1995). *Guanxi* has been an integral aspect of traditional Chinese business practices since these were codified by Tao Chu Kung in the fifth century BC and is a key element for successful commercial transactions in China. In contrast, Westerners regard a business relationship as a short term transaction in which each party attempts to maximise its benefits, if necessary at the expense of the other. In a survey of 76 Canadian companies doing business in China, Abramson and Ai (1999) found that firms where each party pursued their own goals either in competition with each other or without reference to each other performed less well than joint ventures based on shared goals and trust. Still, even if Western companies are willing to take *guanxi* into account, their outsider status may preclude them from doing so.

Selecting international managers

In Chapter 11 on cross-cultural training, we will review the literature on the selection of employees for overseas assignment. We will do this in the context of the conventional approach widely used in personnel selection, namely the empirical identification of the knowledge, skills, attitudes and abilities (KSAAs) underlying successful performance in particular jobs. These are then used as the basis for deciding whether a candidate would make a suitable

adjustment empirically and not just rationally. As we indicated earlier, it is generally accepted that expatriate adjustment will be facilitated by low distance between the sojourner and host cultures. This conclusion is based on a widely cited and influential article by Church (1982) which reviewed numerous studies conducted in a variety of contexts. One would therefore expect that Hong Kong executives would have minimal difficulties in adjusting to life and work on the mainland, two regions with different recent histories but a shared Chinese heritage (Bond, 1996).

But that is not what Selmer and Shiu (1999) found in their study of the adjustment of Hong Kong expatriate business managers in the PRC. They conducted on-site, semi-structured personal interviews lasting up to two hours with ten such expatriates. Although most of the participants regarded themselves as successful in their jobs, many reported that they were lonely, frustrated with their staff, and that their PRC subordinates did not like them. The expatriates complained about communication problems with their headquarters in Hong Kong. They also referred to serious difficulties with local subordinates who resisted the introduction of changes in work practices and tried to isolate them as newcomers. Most expatriates said that they did not participate in local social functions and that they kept their distance in order to maintain fairness at work. Their wives also did not belong to local social networks, instead preferring the company of other expatriate families.

The authors comment that paradoxically, the common cultural heritage of the Hong Kong expatriates and their hosts seems to aggravate adjustment difficulties instead of facilitating integration. They explain this counter-intuitive finding by suggesting that when expatriates are assigned to an entirely different host culture, they are consciously aware of and expect dissimilarity, and factor it into their coping approaches. However, managers posted to a similar culture are less sensitive to the differences that do exist and may attribute any difficulties they encounter to deficiencies in themselves, their subordinates and their organisations. It may not occur to them that they are caught up in a culture clash and that this could account for their problems.

Personality

Studies that attempt to verify a direct empirical link between particular personality characteristics and expatriate adjustment are scarce. Personality does get a mention in the adjustment literature, but usually as a predictor variable, rather than in terms of any systematic evaluation of its effects. This is not surprising because of the daunting, methodological requirements of such research. For instance, in a study with a great deal of heterogeneity both in their sample and in what they measured, Parker and McEvoy (1993) administered a large battery of tests to 169 American expatriates in 12 countries. Included in the measures was the Myers–Briggs Type Indicator (MBTI;

Carlyn, 1977), a self-report inventory that includes an Extraversion–Introversion scale. Parker and McEvoy found that extroversion was significantly correlated with interaction adjustment but not work or general adjustment. In a later study of American expatriates in Europe, Harrison, Chadwick and Scales (1996) found that self-efficacy was associated with greater general, interaction and work adjustment (Black, Gregersen and Mendenhall, 1992). Self-monitoring was similarly related to adjustment in the general and interaction domains. Although studies as these may prove useful for employee selection, there is not a sufficient amount of data currently available to draw firm conclusions about personality and expatriate adjustment.

Host attitudes and interactions

A number of studies have investigated whether the psychological adaptation of international business people is affected by how host members treat them, or more precisely, the perceived attitudes of the indigenous population toward expatriate personnel. Hostility from the local community can have several sources: opposition from local managers who feel that their career advancement is being blocked by foreign outsiders (Hailey, 1996); local suppliers who see foreign control as a threat to their business (Zeira and Banai, 1981); hostility towards particular expatriate national groups (Stewart and DeLisle, 1994); and a more generalised xenophobic reaction to multinationals which prevails in some countries (Kopp, 1994).

In a direct test of the hypothesis that expatriates' work attitudes would be adversely affected by perceptions of host ethnocentrism, Florkowski and Fogel (1999) conducted a survey of expatriates employed by 22 multinational firms. Host ethnocentrism was measured by items reflecting perceived cultural superiority and intolerance (e.g. 'the extent to which local managers felt that much could be learned from individuals in other countries'). Participants also responded to work adjustment, general adjustment and organisational commitment scales. Results showed that, as predicted, perceived ethnocentrism was negatively associated with work adjustment and commitment to the local branch of the organisation.

Motivation to undertake an expatriate assignment

According to Spiess and Wittmann (1999), the decision by companies to send executives abroad is often made on an ad hoc basis dictated by market forces rather than as part of a deliberate strategy of staff career development. The motives of the sojourners tend to be ignored, and their willingness to go abroad is often taken for granted. This neglect of personal aspirations may contribute significantly to the expatriate attrition rate. As will be discussed in Chapter 11, the early repatriation of inadequately performing executives and their families is a fiscal burden on companies, including, but not limited to, the costs of lost business deals. It is estimated that between 20 and 50 per cent of expatriate executives return prematurely (Black and Gregersen, 1990; Harris and Moran, 1991; Tung, 1988a).

In mainstream industrial psychology, the 'realistic job interview' (sometimes called a 'preview') has been used to alert applicants to both the negative as well as the positive aspects of the job they are seeking (e.g. Katzell and Thompson, 1990). The rationale for this procedure is to give candidates information to allow them to decide if they really want the job they are applying for, thus avoiding a lot of grief for themselves and expense for the employer. No such procedure seems to be in regular use with respect to international assignments.

Candidates for expatriate assignments should be asked (or be encouraged to ask themselves) questions such as: Why would they want a job abroad? What personal goals do they wish to achieve? Under what conditions would they remain committed to the expatriate decision, and what would induce them to reverse the decision (Gollwitzer, Heckhausen and Ratajczak, 1990)? There is some tentative evidence that candidates who are encouraged to explore these questions will be more likely to last the distance (Spiess and Wittmann, 1999).

Mentoring as a special case of social support

Mentors have been defined as seasoned individuals who support, guide, and provide counsel to less experienced colleagues in order to facilitate their careers (Kram, 1985). There is a growing interest in studying the role of mentoring in the adjustment of expatriates during the three stages of the sojourn: the pre-departure phase, while they are overseas on assignment, and after they have returned home.

The three phases involve somewhat different forms of mentoring. Pre-departure mentoring provides the prospective sojourner with a 'mental map' to interpret both the personal as well as the organisational aspects of the forthcoming assignment (Harvey *et al.*, 1999). Mentors can foreshadow some of the problems that expatriates will encounter and ensure that they entertain realistic expectations about their foreign assignments.

On-site mentoring, including advice about potential pitfalls, is related to the faster learning of new jobs, higher commitment to the organisation, and greater expatriate adjustment to the new culture (Chao, Walz and Gardner, 1992). On-site mentoring contributes to both work-related and sociocultural adjustment (Black, 1992; Oddou, 1991; Tung, 1988a). Theoretically, the effectiveness of on-site mentoring has been attributed to the reduction of uncertainty about the new environment (Ostroff and Kozlowski, 1993). Four types of on-site mentoring have been distinguished: task assistance, career assistance, social support, and role modelling (Dreher and Ash, 1990; Turban and Dougherty, 1994). Although these labels suggest that mentoring is a systematic process, in fact very few companies have formal mentoring policies or practices. In most instances mentoring occurs on an informal, ad hoc basis.

Feldman and Bolino (1999) investigated the benefits of mentoring in their research with the expatriate employees of Fortune 100 multinational corporations. Participants were asked about the extent to which a mentor in the host country provided them with the four types of assistance mentioned above. The expatriates were then given questionnaires that included measures of job satisfaction, intention to complete the expatriate assignment and knowledge about the determinants of success in international business. The results confirmed that on-site mentoring was positively related to each of the three outcome variables.

Back-home mentors have been found to be crucial in facilitating the reintegration of returning expatriates in two important areas: to adjust to the changes in the corporate culture which occurred while they were overseas and to find appropriate and career-enhancing positions (Feldman and Thomas, 1992; Feldman and Tompson, 1993; Napier and Peterson, 1991). This issue will be discussed further in the section on repatriation.

WOMEN IN INTERNATIONAL MANAGEMENT

Expatriate women

Women are under-represented in global assignments. For example, 6.5 per cent of Australian expatriates are women compared with 22 per cent in local management (Hede and O'Brien, 1996). In North America (the United States and Canada), the respective numbers are 14 and 45 per cent, and world wide only 11 per cent of expatriates are female (Caligiuri, Joshi and Lazarova, 1999). These figures have raised several questions, such as whether there exists a gender bias in sending expatriates on global assignments; whether there is a difference between male and female expatriates in how effective they are; and what are the determinants that affect female expatriates' success. There is some evidence with respect to each of these issues.

According to Adler (1997), women are under-represented because of what she calls myths that inhibit women from being offered global assignments. These include assumptions by management that women do not wish to work overseas. In a large scale study of MBA students, Adler found no differences between males and females in their intentions to accept international assignments. However, Lowe, Downes and Kroeck (1999) criticised that study on the grounds that the questions were poorly worded. In Adler's study the students were asked whether they would be interested in an expatriate position in a foreign country without specifying the location of the assignment. This, according to Lowe *et al.*, allowed the respondents to conjecture an international posting that would be ideal for them, rendering the results meaningless.

To correct for this limitation they surveyed 217 American business students, who were given an alphabetical list of 41 overseas locations. They were asked to rate each of these places in terms of their willingness to work there for three years. A culture-distance index (from the United States) was calculated for each of the countries based on Hofstede's work and the method developed by Kogut and Singh (1988). The countries were also given scores on a level of development scale and their degree of political instability. Results showed that there was a decrease in the willingness of both men and women to work in countries high on cultural distance and political risk. Economic development, however, increased their willingness to accept an overseas assignment. Males and females differed in their willingness to work in 36 of the 41 locations. The greatest differences were found in the reluctance of women to accept assignments in Vietnam, Saudi Arabia, and Indonesia. No gender differences were found for Canada, France, Britain, Italy, and Venezuela. Country attractiveness ratings also distinguished the sexes, the women rating Korea, Sweden, and Brazil as low in attractiveness. The study indicates that women's (as well as men's) willingness to work in particular locations depends on economic factors, such as the level of development, and on sociocultural factors, such as cultural distance, political stability, and host attitudes to gender issues. These findings have implications for selecting and training expatriates and the type of on-site mentoring that would be most beneficial for them.

According to Adler (1997), another myth is the assumption that males in some host countries will refuse to do business with women (Caligiuri and Cascio, 1998). In a study of expatriate women regarding their perceptions of how they were treated by host-national men, Adler found that only 20 per cent of the respondents reported any negative attitudes, whereas 42 per cent said that being female was an asset. However, other studies have found that Western foreign women do experience discrimination while overseas, particularly in countries such as Japan and Korea (Stone, 1991). In a recent study of the effect of host nationals' cultural values on the acceptance of expatriate women, Caligiuri and Tung (1999) used cultural distance as the reference variable in predicting responses to American female executives. They surveyed 98 expatriates who were located in 25 different countries, providing a wide spread in cultural distance. Seventy-eight males and 20 females participated in the study. The participants' degree of adjustment to living and working in their host country and their desire to seek early termination were measured on 4-item scales. Their performance was assessed by asking their immediate supervisors to rate the managers on 15 work-related items such as 'establishing interpersonal bonds with host nationals'.

The results showed that women were less adjusted than men in masculine countries as identified by Hofstede's (1980) country index. Women also reported lower adjustment in countries with fewer females in the workforce, usually also countries that were higher on Hofstede's power distance dimension. Overall, there were no differences between men and women in either supervisor-rated performance or their desire to terminate the assignments. The authors draw the conclusion that men and women are equally successful in expatriate assignments but that adjustment is to some extent affected by the work values that characterise the host culture. These findings are interesting and supported by theory, but due to the small number of women participants in this study, caution should be exercised in the interpretation of the results.

Nevertheless, these findings are consistent with other studies recently reviewed by Caligiuri, Joshi and Lazarova (1999). To explore further the topic of female expatriate adjustment, these authors conducted a study of American women executives on assignments in Europe, Australia and Asia. They found that marital status, company support, position power, and perceptions of host national attitudes all contributed to sociocultural adjustment. Married female expatriates were better adjusted than single females; company support such as cross-cultural training and relocation assistance had a large and significant effect; expatriates who reported positive perceptions of host national attitudes toward their gender were better adjusted; and women in higher-level positions had more positive experiences overall than women in lower positions. The bulk of the empirical research clearly shows that the adjustment of expatriate women is greatly affected by the amount of broad social support that they receive.

Dual-career expatriates

With an increase in female participation in the workforce, there has also been a significant rise in the number of what are sometimes called dual-career expatriated families. These are households where both partners are pursuing active careers with one or both as expatriates (Harvey, 1995, 1996, 1997a, 1998; Harvey *et al.*, 1999). Dual-career families are susceptible to a variety of potentially adverse influences that could lead to marital discord. These may include physical separation and career sacrifice. In the first instance it is typically the case that both partners cannot be given, or do not wish to take up, jobs in the same location overseas. In the second situation it is usually the wife who will interrupt her career to accompany her husband overseas and play the role of the 'trailing spouse'. Although many of these problems are basically insoluble, Harvey and colleagues propose that companies should put in place explicit support policies to deal with these issues as they arise during each of the three temporal phases of the sojourn.

REPATRIATION AND INPATRIATION

Repatriation

Despite the potential cost to both the returning employee and the organisation, Black, Gregersen and Mendenhall (1992) believe that repatriation has been given the least attention among the various aspects of global assignments. Their own research shows that up to 80 per cent of expatriates suffer what they call 'culture shock' during repatriation. A review of the literature by Adler (1997) found that one in five employees want to leave the company when they return; less than half of expatriate managers receive promotion upon return; two-thirds feel that their overseas sojourn had an adverse effect on their careers; and about half felt that their re-entry position was less satisfying than their overseas assignment.

The early literature interpreted these findings in terms of the W-curve of adjustment, described in Chapter 2. There is no doubt that this stage in an expatriate's life can be stressful, but there is a great deal of debate about the actual determinants of the stress and how to deal with it. A partial list includes attributing the difficulties to: unexpected re-entry and adjustment problems; changes that have occurred in the sojourner's organisation, country and social networks during his or her absence overseas; a lower standard of living on the part of those sojourners whose assignments took place in low cost countries; and the acquisition and retention of new cultural values and behaviours by long term expatriates (Smith, 1991).

In a recent empirical study of some of these hypothesised antecedents of 're-entry shock', Hammer, Hart and Rogan (1998) found support for only one of the proposed variables. They reported a significant relationship between re-entry expectations and repatriation outcomes, such that the more positive their expectations, the greater their level of satisfaction and the fewer their re-entry difficulties. This study, like so many in the field, shows once again the importance of going beyond theorising to actual empirical evidence.

Re-entry for Japanese expatriates is a special case in point. Because of Japan's economic growth during the past 20 years, there are a substantial number of Japanese who live and work in various parts of the world. The phenomenon is so common that the term *kaigai seicho nihonjin* has been coined to describe Japanese who have spent some time abroad or grew up overseas (Isogai, Hayashi and Uno, 1999). A review of the literature by Isogai *et al.* (1999) found the majority of returnees experience difficulties in readjusting to Japan. They often feel rejected by Japanese society, particularly after returning from a lengthy sojourn abroad, and they frequently struggle with core issues pertaining to identity. Friction is caused by being perceived as having adopted 'foreign characteristics' which are incompatible with Japanese cultural manifestations. These may include increased assertiveness on the part of the returned person, a more individualistic orientation, less conformity to group norms, and for women, a new found resistance to male dominated social practices. Similar themes emerged in the Japanese studies of student re-entry that were described in the previous chapter. Although the issue of sojourners acquiring the cultural mores of their host country is a general and not a peculiarly Japanese re-entry problem, as mentioned earlier, it takes on added significance in traditional 'tight' societies such as Japan (Pelto, 1968).

Inpatriation

With the expansion of multinational companies (MNCs) there has developed a growing shortage of competent, qualified international managers who can operate effectively across cultures (Harvey, 1997b). A complementary source of managerial talent for the MNCs is local, host-country managers who may be sent to the Head Office for technical training as well as exposure (or more accurately, indoctrination) to the corporate culture of their MNC employer. After returning to the field they will then be expected to serve as a link between the domestic headquarters and the markets that the foreign subsidiary is attempting to penetrate (Harvey, Speier and Novicevic, 1999).

Other advantages claimed for employing inpatriate managers is their culturally-based knowledge of how local business is conducted; they can serve as informal mentors for expatriate managers; they can provide a local perspective on developing strategic business plans; they are in a better position to maintain channels of communications with local suppliers and government officials; and they are less expensive to employ than expatriates, particularly when the cost of expatriate failures is factored into the equation.

Although all this makes a great deal of intuitive sense, to date there is very little empirical evidence in support of these contentions. It should also be noted that there has been a reluctance by some MNCs to employ 'foreign managers' stemming from a desire to maintain tight control over their subsidiaries overseas. There is also the view that expatriates would be in a better position to install the MNC's headquarters-based corporate culture in the local branch (Truss *et al.*, 1997). Nevertheless, it is likely that the future will see a steady growth in the incidence of inpatriation, particularly through the increased participation of bicultural executives holding dual citizenship in their host and home cultures.

CHAPTER SUMMARY

Expatriate business personnel constitute a large segment of the world-wide sojourner community. In this chapter we described the various categories of expatriate executives, the problems they face, and the ways in which they cope with and adapt to their role as the human link in international commerce.

Two general principles provide some coherence to the rather diverse literature in this area.

The first is that work-related values and practices reflect the broader cultural beliefs that regulate a society's institutions. And because there exist major cross-cultural differences across countries in their core human values, these also govern their commercial and industrial systems (Bond, 1988; Schwartz and Bilsky, 1990). This constitutes a major problem for international corporations because of the implication that many of the human resource and management policies they espouse are not universal, but characterised by culture-specific manifestations. In other words, the way in which business is conducted may differ significantly from location to location. This means that multinationals cannot simply transfer all of their head office practices to their subsidiaries. Many of the procedures will have to be modified to take into account local customs and cultural values. Two major human resource practices that have a significant emic or culturally specific component are leadership style and team based production strategies.

Making allowances for the cultural specificity of work-related values creates a new set of problems; if local variations in human resource management are allowed to become too extreme, a head office may lose an unacceptable amount of control over its subsidiaries. One consequence of this is that the company may have to sacrifice some global uniformity of its image and product. This may be problematic in that corporation-wide standardisation is regarded by many MNCs as a desirable characteristic that will give them a competitive market edge. Expatriate executives are the persons usually charged with accomplishing this difficult balancing act.

The bulk of the executive sojourn research has been concerned with identifying the determinants of successful expatriate performance. In keeping with the central theme of this book, we have approached this issue by looking at the coping, adjustment and culture learning responses of the expatriates. The adjustment literature can be unified by referring to the second general principle underlying the expatriate experience, namely, the effects of cultural distance on the difficulties that expatriates experience. A robust finding is, broadly speaking, that as the dissimilarity between the expatriates' home and host cultures increases, so will their adjustment difficulties.

To be able to make useful statements about expatriate coping behaviour it is necessary to establish empirically verifiable criteria of successful performance. Consequently, specific, quantifiable aspects of expatriate adjustment were identified in this chapter. We treated the expatriate experience in terms of the life history of the executive, in keeping with our approach to other categories of sojourners such as overseas students. Accordingly, we distinguished between the pre-departure, on-site and re-entry phases of expatriation, and we reviewed the key determinants of success in each stage.

Pre-departure processes that improve on-site performance include recruiting persons for expatriate assignments on the basis of systematic selection procedures that take into account the candidates' technical competence as well as their personal characteristics, family circumstances, motives and career aspirations. Assisting the recruits to arrive at a set of realistic expectations about the negative as well as the positive aspects of the assignment is also desirable, as is the provision of culture awareness and training.

Work-related problems during the on-site phase of the sojourn stem from the complications associated with managing a culturally diverse workforce and the requirement to manage in a culturally appropriate manner. Particular difficulties relate to establishing good interpersonal relations and trust with local subordinates and colleagues. It is not uncommon to find domestic resentment towards expatriates, often because of the apprehension that they will have an adverse effect on the career prospects of indigenous employees. In some countries there may also exist a general climate of ethnocentric hostility toward particular classes of outsiders.

Non-work problems include the need to acquire the social skills required to survive and thrive in the local community and to be accepted by its members. With respect to the latter issue, many expatriates have difficulties in crossing the barriers preventing them from interacting with local individuals and groups, and during their sojourn they tend to associate mainly with other expatriates. As we reported earlier in our discussion of overseas students, this is a predicament common to most groups of sojourners. In the case of business travellers, however, this kind of social isolation has a special significance because it can affect the expatriate's ability to succeed commercially. The special case of joint ventures in China was used to illustrate this problem and the difficulties that emerge for expatriate managers who function in a business culture that so strongly values personal relations.

On-site procedures to enhance both work-related coping and culture learning mainly depend on the provision of social, technical and informational support. There is evidence that a formal mentoring system is an effective technique although in practice most mentoring occurs on an ad hoc basis.

Re-entry problems of adjustment largely stem from the rapid social change that characterises contemporary life worldwide. Both the sojourner's society and company are likely to have changed significantly during the executive's absence overseas, particularly if the sojourn was a relatively lengthy one. Some societies such as Japan also have a culturally determined negative attitude to persons perceived as having lost some of their core ethnic traits and practices due to corrupting foreign influences. Problems such as these can be reduced by means of a systematic mentoring programme which aims to reintegrate the returned executives not just into their home culture but also into the culture of their organisation.

The growing female participation rate in the work force is reflected in an increase in the number of women expatriates, although in relative terms females are under-represented in comparison with males in foreign assignments. Special gender-related topics that have attracted attention in the literature include questions about whether management discriminates against recruiting women and if so, why; whether women are less motivated than men to undertake overseas assignments; whether it is objectively more difficult for women to work effectively in some cultural and organisational settings; and whether women find it more difficult to adjust to some cultural environments. The evidence on all of these issues is rather mixed, partly because this is a relatively new field of inquiry.

9 Immigrants

Migrants may be broadly distinguished from other groups of cross-cultural travellers in terms of their motivation for relocation and their level of commitment to the country of resettlement. Unlike refugees (see Chapter 10), who are forcibly 'pushed' into an alien environment, migrants are 'pulled' towards a new country in pursuit of personal, familial, social, financial and political goals. The most significant 'pull' is economic opportunity. Although family reunification and political pressures may act as motivating forces, economic factors exert the strongest influence over the decision to emigrate (Winter-Ebmer, 1994). As a group, migrants are more likely to be dissatisfied with their employment and come from the lower socioeconomic spectrum than non-migrants (Neto, 1988; Winchie and Carment, 1988). These characteristics are also likely to distinguish them from many of their sojourning counterparts, the international business people, who are typically better educated and employed in professional occupations.

Immigrants generally relocate with the intention of long term, if not permanent, resettlement. This differs from the intentions of tourists and sojourners who were described in Chapters 6–8. However, the temporary–permanent or short term–long term distinction made earlier in this book and conventionally relied upon in the acculturation literature sometimes fails to capture the dynamic nature of the immigrant experience. Research on immigration to Australia illustrates the difficulties of these static classification schemes. Icduygu's (1994) study of Turkish emigration, for example, noted that a significant proportion of the migrants who entered Australia had the intention to be 'guest workers', but that they never returned to Turkey and eventually became permanent settlers. On the other hand, Kee and Skeldon (1994) estimated a 30 per cent return rate of recent migrants from Hong Kong to Australia. Clearly, postmigration factors may alter migrants' original intentions regarding resettlement.

When do immigrants become members of established ethnocultural groups in culturally plural societies? Technically, overseas born, first generation settlers should be described as migrants; second or later generation descendents of these settlers are more appropriately referred to as members of ethnocultural groups (Berry, 1990). Hurtado et al. (1993) adhere to this

1   Pluralism ideology. This ideological perspective reflects the expectation that immigrants will adopt the public values of the country of settlement, e.g. civil and criminal codes, but that the private values of citizens, e.g. their community involvement related to linguistic and cultural activities, are not regulated by the state. Although 'private' activities are free from state intervention, ideological pluralism permits the government to offer financial and social support, when requested, to indigenous and immigrant groups. A distinctive feature of pluralist ideologies is that it is considered to be of value to the larger society for members of immigrant communities to maintain their cultural and linguistic heritage. An example of an immigration policy inspired by the pluralism ideology is Canada's Multiculturalism Act adopted in 1988.

2   Civic ideology. The civic ideology shares common assumptions with cultural pluralism in its distinction of public and private values, demanding adherence to the former and regarding the latter as a matter of private choice. However, state policies reflecting civic ideology are explicitly non-interventionist with respect to private values; state funds are not used for these purposes although the rights of individuals or collectives to organise activities promoting cultural maintenance are recognised. Bourhis and colleagues suggest that civic ideology is most readily legitimised in ethnically and culturally homogeneous states but cite a range of immigration policies in Great Britain as exemplifying this position.

3   Assimilation ideology. Although the assimilation ideology is largely consistent with the first two perspectives with respect to public and private values, it accepts that there are some areas of private values in which the state is entitled to intervene. It also implicitly assumes that immigrants should abandon their cultural and linguistic distinctiveness and adopt core values of the host community. In some instances it is anticipated that assimilation will occur voluntarily while in others specific policies are enforced to ensure compliance. The United States in the first half of the twentieth century strongly endorsed the assimilationist ideology, but according to the authors, the nation has recently moved more towards civic ideology. The Republican ideology, a variation of assimilationism, is found in France. Here 'the notion of the equality of the "universal man" as a legitimizing tool for the suppression of ethnocultural differences deemed to be backward or divisive for the unity of the state' is relied upon for the justification of national policy (Bourhis *et al.*, 1997, p. 374).

4   Ethnist ideology. The ethnist ideology not only holds that immigrants must adopt the public values of their hosts, but also that the state has the right to regulate certain aspects of private values. The adoption of public values and the rejection of cultural maintenance by immigrants, however, need not be related to assimilation. Although a reduction in cultural distinctiveness usually occurs, in some instances assimilation is impossible because members of the receiving society have no intentions of

accepting immigrants as equal partners in national development. Immigration policies found in countries that rely upon the ethnist ideology generally define who can and cannot be citizens in ethnic or religious terms (e.g. the policies of Germany, Israel, and Japan).

After identifying the four positions Bourhis *et al.* describe the pattern of relationships between immigration ideologies and the acculturation orientations of members of the receiving society. According to the authors, support for the integration of immigrants is associated with cultural pluralism, and advocacy for exclusionism is linked to ethnist ideologies. Preferences for assimilation may be related to both civic and assimilationist ideologies while endorsement of segregation is associated with assimilationist and ethnist ideologies.

How do these ideologies relate to immigrant acculturation? Although a considerable body of research has indicated that immigrants prefer integration as an acculturation strategy, there is also evidence that this preference and the ease with which it is achieved varies across social and cultural conditions. Bourhis and colleagues have noted, for example, that immigrant attitudes toward integration and choice of acculturation strategies differ in Québec and Anglo-Canada (also see Berry, 1984a; Berry and Kalin, 1995; Dompierre and Lavallée, 1990). In addition, research has indicated that anglophones in Anglo-Canada are more supportive of the state's multiculturalism policy than are francophones in Québec. It is likely, then, that acculturation preferences and strategies of immigrants are strongly influenced by the acculturation orientations of members of the host culture. To examine these immigrant–host interactions in more detail Bourhis *et al.* (1997) have provided a framework that incorporates the acculturation orientations of migrants and members of the receiving society and the interpersonal and intergroup outcomes that are the products of these orientations (Table 9.1). It should be noted, however, that host community attitudes may vary in relation to the target group and that immigrants from the same ethnocultural background may not be uniform in their acculturation preferences.

Relying upon the IAM Bourhis *et al.* (1997) argue that positive relational outcomes are likely to result when immigrants and members of the receiving community share similar attitudes toward acculturation. Dissimilar attitudes, however, result in problematic or conflictual outcomes. Problematic outcomes are the product of partial agreement on acculturation options. More extreme conflictual outcomes eventuate when there is no substantial overlap between the acculturation preferences of hosts and immigrants. The greatest intergroup conflict is predicted to occur when the members of the host community are exclusionist and the immigrants prefer the separation option. Bourhis and colleagues emphasise that the conflict arising from immigrant–host mismatches may be attenuated or accentuated by state policies. State ideologies at the pluralism end of the continuum diminish antagonism while ethnist ideologies tend to increase hostility.

Table 9.1 The Interactive Acculturation Model (IAM; Bourhis *et al.*, 1997)

Host community: low, medium, high vitality groups	Immigrant community: low, medium vitality groups				
	Integration	Assimilation	Separation	Anomie	Individualism
Integration	Consensual	Problematic	Conflictual	Problematic	Problematic
Assimilation	Problematic	Consensual	Conflictual	Problematic	Problematic
Segregation	Conflictual	Conflictual	Conflictual	Conflictual	Conflictual
Exclusion	Conflictual	Conflictual	Conflictual	Conflictual	Conflictual
Individualism	Problematic	Problematic	Problematic	Problematic	Consensual

Source: R. Bourhis, L. Moïse, S. Perrault, and S. Senécal (1997). Towards an Interactive Acculturation Model: A social psychological approach. *International Journal of Psychology*, 32, 369–386. Reprinted by permission of the International Union of Psychological Science.

Note: The IAM equates Anomie with Berry's (1980, 1990) notion of marginalisation; however, it also recognises that there are immigrants who dissociate themselves from both their ethnocultural origins and the host majority cultures because they prefer to identify themselves as individualists. From the host culture perspective, exclusionists are intolerant of cultural maintenance in immigrants but are also unaccepting of immigrant assimilation. Individualists define themselves and others as individuals rather than members of group categories.

Attitudes toward immigration and immigrants

Although Bourhis and associates have suggested a link between national ideologies, acculturation orientations and attitudes toward migrants, members of the host community are likely to endorse official policies to varying degrees. They are also likely to have their own interpretations of national policy and ideology. This was clearly demonstrated in an Australian study by Ho *et al.* (1994). More than half of the native-born respondents agreed that Australia benefits from its multicultural policy. Nevertheless, the support for government programmes that integrated immigrant groups, e.g. English language courses, was much stronger than for those that dealt with issues of cultural maintenance, e.g. native language broadcasts. Many social commentators, such as Betts (1991), believe that while there is strong support for immigrants in terms of access and equity issues in Australia, there is little endorsement of cultural pluralism more generally. Along these lines, Goot's (1993) analysis of multicultural data confirmed that equity issues enjoy strong support; however, he also pointed out that more than half of Australians agree that 'multiculturalism means that migrants get too much assistance from the government', and 44 per cent believe that 'immigration deprives Australians of jobs'. In summary, Goot argued that the multiculturalists in Australia outnumber the monoculturalists but that many, perhaps most, Australians are caught between the two positions.

Issues relating to employment are perhaps the most contentious in debates about the need for and the value of immigration. Despite Canada's multicultural policy, a recent poll revealed that 49 per cent believe immigration increases unemployment among people already in the country (Angus Reid poll, cited in Esses, Jackson and Armstrong, 1998). Similarly in the United States, the majority of Americans are more likely to agree that immigrants burden the country because they take jobs, than they are to acknowledge that immigrants strengthen the country because of hard work and talent (Adler and Waldman, 1995). Realistic threat theory has been used to account for negative attitudes toward immigrants and immigration with threat of job loss and increased social assistance to immigrants being strong predictors of negative attitudes toward migrants in the United States (Stephan, Ybarra and Bachman, 1999), Canada (Esses, Jackson and Armstrong, 1998), and Spain (Stephan *et al.*, 1998). In addition, unemployment figures are strongly related to opposition to immigration. Reviewing demographic data over a 20-year period Palmer (1996) noted a significant correlation between higher unemployment rates and agreement with the proposition that immigration should be decreased in Canada. The same trend was reported in the United States by Espenshade and Hempstead (1996) who found that unemployment was the strongest predictor of anti-immigration attitudes. See Figure 9.1.

A similar trend may be emerging in less traditional immigration destinations such as Singapore where the government's initiative to attract 'foreign talent' into the country's labour force and to entice highly skilled workers to

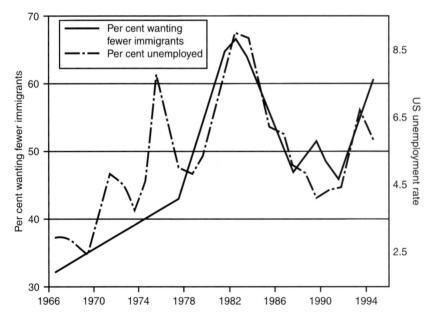

Figure 9.1 Unemployment and attitudes towards immigration (adapted from Espenshade and Hempstead, 1996). Reproduced with permission of the Center for Migration Studies, New York.

become permanent residents was recently announced. In 1997 there were half a million foreign workers in Singapore, making up one quarter of the country's work force ('Are foreign workers', 1998). The ensuing Asian economic crisis, however, shifted the labour market from one where there were too few people to fill available positions to one with unemployment figures of about 4 per cent ('Lay-offs soar,' 1999). These changes appeared to generate some opposition to the government's new economic policy. Surveys conducted by Forbes Research indicated that about one third of Singaporeans polled agree that there are too many foreign workers in the country and one in four believe that foreign workers take away jobs from locals ('Most neutral', 1998).

Responses to general questions about increases and decreases of the number of foreign-born settlers provide only a partial understanding of attitudes toward immigrants and immigration. Perceptions, evaluations and 'acceptability' indices vary across different migrant groups. There is some evidence that in Singapore more favourable appraisals are given to foreign professionals from the United States than from China (Lim and Ward, in press). In the United States it has been suggested that light skinned immigrants encounter more favourable receptions than dark skinned migrants (Espin, 1987). In many cases these evaluations are based upon perceptions of cultural distance. When asked if more, less, or about the same number of persons should be accepted for immigration, Australian respondents were more likely to recommend the acceptance of fewer migrants from Asia (43 per cent) and the Middle East (50 per cent) than from Britain (19 per cent) and Southern Europe (22 per cent; Ho *et al.*, 1994). This trend parallels an earlier study that indicated Australian-borns view Asian (e.g. Vietnamese, Japanese, Indians) and Middle Eastern (e.g. Turkish, Lebanese) groups as more socially distant than Southern European (e.g. Greek, Italian) or British ones (McAllister and Moore, 1991).

Are different attitudes toward immigration and immigrants held by native-borns and settlers? There is some evidence that native-borns and members of dominant ethnocultural groups are less likely to favour cultural diversity than others. For example, native-borns and British migrants in Australia are less likely to embrace multiculturalism than migrants from Europe and Asia (Goot, 1993; Ho *et al.*, 1994). This is not to imply that immigrant groups are uniformly multicultural in their outlook. McAllister and Moore's (1991) study which compared native-born Australians with Maltese, Lebanese, and Vietnamese migrants found that the Maltese were the most ethnocentric of the four groups. Migrants' attitudes toward culture and ethnicity are likely to be influenced by a number of factors, including both premigration beliefs and postmigration experiences. In some cases it has been suggested that the negative out-group perceptions held by immigrants are shaped by prevailing attitudes in the receiving culture, particularly the attitudes of the politically and socially dominant ethnic groups. A study by Goldenberg and Saxe (1996), for example, reported that 72 per cent of Russian immigrants to the United States indicated that their opinions toward blacks changed in a negative direction after migration. The same pattern of attitude change was observed in British migrants to South Africa in an earlier study by Tyson and Duckitt (1989).

Relations between migrants and members of the receiving community are influenced by a number of factors, and one that has been discussed extensively is social contact. The contact hypothesis, described in Chapter 5, assumes that intergroup perceptions and relations can be improved by equal status contact and mutual cooperation in working towards a common goal. However, research has shown that, for the most part, members of non-dominant groups, including both established ethnocultural minorities and recent immigrants, are more willing to engage in such contact. This has been demonstrated in studies of whites, blacks and Hispanics in the United States (Dyer, Vedlitz and Worchel, 1989), and Jews, Arabs and Russian immigrants in Israel (Hofman, 1982; Sagiv and Schwartz, 1995, 1998). It has been suggested more recently, however, that the readiness for social contact in non-dominant groups is moderated by social identity. Sagiv and Schwartz (1998) found that Russian immigrants to Israel were more willing to interact with Israeli Jews only if they were motivated to identify with the dominant cultural group. Immigrants who preferred to preserve their original cultural identity, in contrast, were no more likely to demonstrate a readiness for intergroup interaction than were Israelis.

Contact, perceptions, identity and acculturation strategies are all inter-twined in dynamic intergroup processes as exemplified by Horenczyk's (1996) research with immigrants to Israel. In this study Russian adolescents were asked about their own acculturation attitudes and their perceptions of the attitudes held by their Israeli peers. Israelis were questioned about their acculturation orientations concerning the Russian immigrant group as well as their perceptions of the immigrant group's acculturation preferences. Integration was clearly preferred by both immigrants and members of the receiving society and recognised as such by the former who acknowledged Israeli support for their linguistic and cultural maintenance. Despite the shared preference for integration, there were some tensions that arose in connection with assimilationist pressures. Migrants were less willing to assimilate than they believed their hosts would like, and this was an accurate perception. Members of the receiving community had a stronger preference for assimilation than did the migrants; however, they also believed that migrants were more willing to assimilate than in fact they were. This misperception allowed the Israelis to view themselves as liberals with respect to immigration policies and issues.

As Horenczyk's study suggests, mutual perceptions are a key feature of intergroup relations; however, it is often the case that there are perceptual mismatches between immigrants and members of the receiving society. While it is widely agreed that perceptions of prejudice may be inaccurate and differ from actual prejudice (Keefe, 1992), these perceptions are nevertheless related to the formation of migrant identity and the selection of acculturation orientations. Perceived discrimination has been associated with an increase in ethnic loyalty (Padilla, 1986), resistance to assimilation (Mainous, 1989) and conflicts about acculturation (Vega *et al.*, 1993). It is also felt more strongly by those who adopt separatist compared with assimilationist strategies (LaFromboise, Coleman and Gerton, 1993).

MIGRANT ADAPTATION

Psychological adaptation

In view of the long history of research on migration and mental illness, it is not surprising that medical models and clinical perspectives continue to exert some influence in the field. Studies that focus on the incidence and prevalence of psychiatric diagnoses and the differential hospital admission rates for migrants and non-migrants retain prominence in the psychiatric literature. A number of recent investigations have supported earlier research findings linking migration to physical and mental health problems. For example, Jews from the former Soviet Union report more symptoms of demoralisation (low self-esteem, hopelessness, dread, sadness, anxiety, and psychosomatic symptoms) than Israeli-born settlers of European descent (Zilber and Lerner, 1996). The incidence of chronic illness is greater in foreign-born settlers than the native-born population in Sweden (Sundquist and Johansson, 1997). In the United Kingdom Irish immigrants have a higher rate of suicide, and Afro-Caribbeans are more frequently diagnosed as schizophrenic, than native Britons (Balarayan, 1995; Harrison, 1990; Wesseley *et al.*, 1991). However, not all studies conclude that immigrants suffer more physical and psychological distress (Noh *et al.*, 1992; Roebers and Schneider, 1999; Sam and Berry, 1995). In fact, some investigations have shown that immigrant groups display fewer symptoms of psychopathology. Southeast Asian migrants in the United Kingdom, for example, have lower levels of depression compared with the white majority (Berthoud and Nazroo, 1997), and adolescent migrants in Norway who have come from Third World countries have fewer behavioural problems than their native-born peers (Sam, 1998).

Despite the value of clinical and epidemiological studies, there are a number of methodological and conceptual difficulties with this type of research. These include problems with the cross-cultural equivalence of assessment instruments, potential cultural biases in diagnoses, and differential access to or use of medical and psychiatric facilities across migrant and non-migrant groups, all of which undermine the validity of these investigations (Tanaka-Matsumi and Draguns, 1997; Westermeyer, 1987). Some observers, like Patel and Mann (1997) and Lonner (1990), have recommended strategies for improving research designs and quantitative methods, including modifications of the diagnostic procedures for cross-cultural comparisons. Others have argued for a shift in research emphasis, suggesting that it is time we move beyond the question of 'how' do immigrants and native-borns differ to 'why' these differences occur. As a consequence of these and other issues, static group comparisons have been largely replaced with studies of adaptation processes in the psychological literature, and longitudinal, comparative research has revealed that the patterns and predictors of psychological adaptation are very similar between natives and immigrants (Scott and Scott, 1991).

The process of psychological adjustment in immigrants parallels the general patterns of cross-cultural adaptation described in the first half of the book. It may be analysed within the broad acculturation framework elaborated in Chapter 2 or in terms of Berry's (1997) model of immigration and adaptation presented in Chapter 4. In either case the process involves the exposure to significant life changes, the evaluation of stressors and the implementation of coping responses to facilitate psychological adjustment (Thomas, 1995). As previously discussed, the stress and coping process is influenced by macro and micro factors as well as the characteristics of the individual and the situation.

Although immigrants experience a range of stressors, Zheng and Berry's (1991) study of Chinese Canadian university students suggested that some of their most significant difficulties relate to love, marriage and scholastic concerns, problems not noticeably different from those experienced by non-Chinese Canadians. The researchers also reported that the most common coping strategies adopted by the migrant group were wishful thinking, active problem solving, self-blame and withdrawal; however, these strategies were not significant predictors of acculturative stress or subjective adaptation. Huang, Leong and Wagner (1994) took a somewhat different approach to stress and coping in their study of Chinese American children and suggested that the effectiveness of coping styles would vary by level of acculturation. Their hypotheses received partial support. Situational stressors were more likely to precipitate depression in highly acculturated children who used suppression, problem-solving and diversion as coping strategies. In less acculturated children who were exposed to stressors, however, suppression decreased the probability that depression would occur.

Which personal and situational factors predict psychological adaptation in immigrants? Length of settlement appears to influence the physical and psychological well-being of immigrants. Bagley (1993) reported that recent Chinese migrants to Canada experienced more depression and anxiety than long term, established ones and that the physical and mental health profiles of immigrants who had been settled for 20 years or more were similar to those of Euro-Canadians. This may in part be due to increasing language fluency which has been associated with psychological adjustment in migrants (e.g. Krishnan and Berry, 1992; Mavreas and Bebbington, 1990). Personality factors also make a significant contribution to psychological well-being, particularly mastery (Sam, 1998), an internal locus of control (Neto, 1995), hardiness (Ataca, 1996), a sense of coherence (Aycan and Berry, 1994), and low levels of dogmatism (Taft and Steinkalk, 1985).

Loneliness is a major problem for new migrants, and it has been linked to decrements in life satisfaction (Neto, 1995). Social support, in contrast, has been associated with increased psychological well-being (Biegel, Naparstek and Khan, 1980; Golding and Burnam, 1990). Evidence suggests that it may also affect migrants' commitment to settlement. Elich and Blauw's (1981) study of Dutch returnees found that although economic aspirations provided the primary incentives for emigration, return to the Netherlands was more frequently motivated by relational problems. The network of supportive relationships that facilitates intercultural adaptation need not be large but may be diverse as both co-ethnics and host nationals can assist immigrants with their emotional and informational needs (Berry, 1997; Neto, 1995). In addition, spousal support is important and exerts a strong influence on migrant satisfaction and well-being (Ataca, 1996; Naidoo, 1985).

There has been some attention to the mixed outcomes of co-ethnic support, and its positive and negative consequences have been discussed in depth by Barker (1991) in her analysis of kinship dynamics and Samoan migration to the United States. In this instance kin-linked extended migration is generally determined by the '*aiga* who select, sponsor and sometimes pay for migrants to relocate. The '*aiga* provides housing, support and assistance with employment; its members also help the migrant to integrate into the local Samoan community. This supportive process, however, has both advantages and disadvantages. Although it rapidly establishes the newcomer as a productive member in a familiar social environment, it may shelter the migrant from the necessity of learning how to cope directly with the new cultural environment. Barker (1991: 180) has suggested that migrants 'build a cocoon of Samoan-ness' (p. 180) which is unsustainable over a period of time and that the allegiance to kin which is initially stress-buffering eventually becomes time consuming and burdensome. After a time the allegiance creates considerable stress. Mamak (1990) estimated the critical stress-inducing period is about five years, at which point the conflict between the communal nature of the '*aiga* and the competitive individualism of the new culture takes its physical and psychological toll. An increased prevalence of obesity, hypertension, diabetes, cardiovascular disease and psychiatric disorders is seen by Mamak as an outcome of this conflict, and there is reliable evidence that Western Samoan migrants in Hawaii suffer more psychological distress, including anger, loneliness, confusion, eating disorders and psychosomatic problems, than those who remain in Samoa (Hanna and Fitzgerald, 1993).

Intergroup interactions are also related to migrant adaptation, and not surprisingly, perceived discrimination is associated with increased psychological distress (Furnham and Shiekh, 1993; Ying, 1996). Acculturation orientations, which encompass both heritage and host cultural identities, likewise affect psychological adjustment. Research based on unidimensional models of acculturation shows that biculturalism is related to psychological well-being and satisfaction (e.g. LaFromboise *et al.*, 1993).[1] Investigations employing categorical models have demonstrated that integration is associated with the lowest levels of psychological distress; marginalisation has been linked to the highest level of distress, and separation and assimilation fall between these two extremes (Berry *et al.*, 1989). This pattern has been found in adult migrants to Canada and has been replicated, at least in part, in the United States (Krishnan and Berry, 1992; Phinney, Chavira and Williamson, 1992), Japan (Partridge, 1988), Germany (Schmitz, 1992), and Norway (Sam, 2000). It has also been partially replicated in studies of immigrant children (e.g. Pawliuk *et al.*, 1996; Sam, 1994).

Altogether the stress and coping model of adaptation has been widely applied to predict and explain the psychological adaptation of immigrants to life in their new countries. A particularly impressive and thorough example of this approach is found in Noh and Avison's (1996) study of Korean immigrants in Canada. The research included the longitudinal assessment of 860 immigrants, the majority of whom were between 36 and 55 years old and had on average been resident in Canada for 12 years. The follow-up study 1 year later retained 71 per cent of the original sample (609 respondents). In addition to demographic variables, the research included the measurement of undesirable life events (e.g. loss of job, death of family member), chronic strains (adaptation strains pertaining to language, homesickness, social isolation, discrimination, marginality, opportunities for financial and occupational mobility, and family problems), psychological resources (mastery and self-esteem), and social resources (social support from Koreans and non-Koreans). The results revealed that symptoms of depression were stable over a 1-year period (see Figure 9.2). Chronic strain, self-esteem and mastery had significant and direct effects on depression as did support from Korean sources. The longitudinal path analysis indicated that psychological resources reinforce subsequent levels of both psychological and social resources. Self-esteem enhanced mastery and co-ethnic social support; similarly, mastery enhanced self-esteem and co-ethnic social support. Levels of co-ethnic social support also had a stress suppression effect, demonstrating an indirect influence on depression through life events. Finally, life events exerted a direct effect on depression as well as an indirect effect through self-esteem. In this case exposure to stressful events increased self-esteem, suggesting a counteractive model of coping (Ensel and Lin, 1991). In addition to the path analysis, Noh and Avison (1996) also examined interactions among variables and found that the effects of stressful life events were moderated by the psychological resources of mastery and self-esteem.

Sociocultural adaptation

There has been less work explicitly undertaken on the sociocultural adaptation of immigrants although the significance of cultural learning for immigrant groups has been recognised and discussed (e.g. Boekestijn, 1988). The limited research that is available is consistent with findings in the sojourner literature. For example, there is evidence that the social skills of immigrants

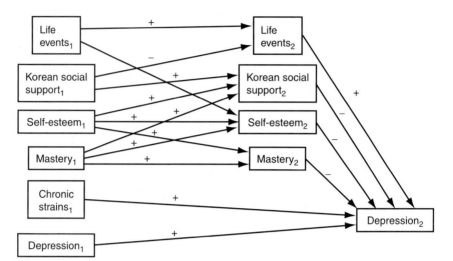

Figure 9.2 Direct and indirect associations among stressors, psychosocial coping resources and depression in Korean immigrants over a 1-year period (adapted from Noh and Avison, 1996)

are poorer than those of native-borns. Huang, Leong and Wagner's (1994) work with Chinese-American children suggested that self-perceptions of competence (social, physical, cognitive, and general) were somewhat lower in the immigrant group compared with their Caucasian counterparts. Similarly, Ataca's (1996) study of Turkish immigrants in Canada found that immigrants experienced more social difficulty than members of the host culture. As would be expected, sociocultural adaptation is a function of resources such as education, income and language fluency, as well as amount of contact with host nationals (Ataca, 1996). Furthermore, it is inversely correlated with perceived discrimination (Aycan and Berry, 1994).

Sociocultural adaptation is related to various measures of psychological well-being, including positive self concept and decreased feelings of alienation (Ataca, 1996; Aycan and Berry, 1994). In fact, Scott and Scott (1991) found that cultural skill is more strongly related to self-esteem in immigrants than in natives. They argued that not only is there a greater range of cultural skills in the immigrant population, but also that these skills are more salient for natives when appraising foreigners than members of their own group.

Economic adaptation

The majority of immigrants resettle for economic reasons. Despite their aspirations for financial security, however, migrants encounter more obstacles to economic success than natives. It is widely recognised that immigrants are more often unemployed and underemployed and that they face particular difficulties obtaining recognition of their educational qualifications and occupational experience, especially if they migrate from non-traditional or culturally distant locations (Swan *et al.*, 1991). Even when employment is secured, migrants tend to be disadvantaged compared with native-borns. Economic migrants to Austria, including those from Turkey, Yugoslavia and Eastern Europe, have lower growth in wages than natives, and they face no realistic prospects of catching up (Winter-Ebmer, 1994). The profile of the economic advancement of recent immigrants to Canada is much the same. In an analysis of economic data Borjas (1988) concluded that Third World immigrants will never match the average income levels for native-borns of the same age with similar educational qualifications and occupational experience.

Pre- and postmigration economic status was examined in detail in Aycan and Berry's (1996) study of Turkish migrants to Canada. The research revealed that relative SES dropped in newly arrived immigrants, that it rose over subsequent years, but that it did not regain its original position. The same pattern was found for occupational status, although income (defined in terms of purchasing power) eventually exceeded that in the homeland. (See Figures 9.3 and 9.4.) These figures are striking in light of the widespread economic motivation for migration and the impact of economic success on migrant adaptation more generally.

Other than education and job experience, what factors are associated with migrants' economic success? Cultural networks appear to be important in this regard. Padilla *et al.* (1988) found that employment was frequently

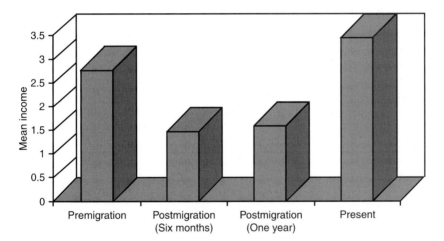

Figure 9.3 Pre- and postmigration income of Turkish migrants in Canada. (From Z. Aycan and J. W. Berry (1996). Impact of employment-related experiences on immigrants' psychological well-being and adaptation to Canada. *Canadian Journal of Behavioural Science, 28*, 240–251.) Copyright 1996 Canadian Psychological Association. Reprinted with permission.

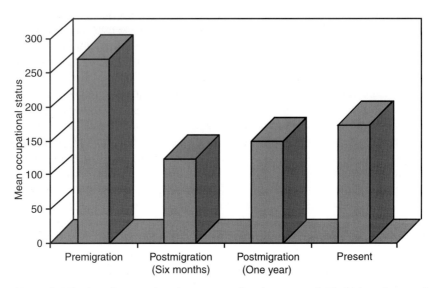

Figure 9.4 Pre- and postmigration occupational status of Turkish migrants in Canada. (From Z. Aycan and J. W. Berry (1996). Impact of employment-related experiences on immigrants' psychological well-being and adaptation to Canada. *Canadian Journal of Behavioural Science, 28*, 240–251.) Copyright 1996. Canadian Psychological Association. Reprinted with permission.

secured by Mexican and Central American migrants to the United States through contacts made through family acquaintances. Scott and Scott's (1991) research in Australia suggests that sociocultural and economic dimensions of adaptation are related as cultural skill is strongly associated with increased material well-being. However, premigration factors may also exert influence on later economic adaptation. It has been shown that those migrants who relocate for economic rather than for family or political reasons do enjoy higher incomes (Winter-Ebmer, 1994). They also appear to appraise their economic situation more favourably. Aycan and Berry's (1996) Canadian study reported that those migrants who relocated for economic reasons and who experienced less status loss, shorter periods of unemployment, and more gains in relative status reported more positive evaluations of accomplishment in the economic sphere of life. Beyond these primarily economic indicators, adaptation was also related to psychological and social factors, including more positive self-concept, better family relations, less acculturative stress, weaker feelings of alienation and lower levels of perceived discrimination.

The phenomenology of immigration and economic adaptation is likely to vary in relation to a number of cultural, social, political and historical factors. Mak (1991) has provided an interesting example of this in her discussion of economic and employment issues affecting Hong Kong migrants to Australia. Noting that many of these migrants were the elite '*jing ying fen zi*' of Hong Kong and a driving force behind the country's economic achievements, she describes their transition 'to strangers in an unfamiliar physical environment' (Mak, 1991: 146). She argues that loss of income and status, amplified by resettlement in a more egalitarian society, not only negatively affects self-esteem in these migrants, but also has implications for their broader adaptation and commitment to remain in the country. Migrants cope with these changes in a variety of ways, and Mak (1991) has proposed a typology of Hong Kong immigrants which includes contented settlers, warriors, opportunists, prisoners and astronauts.

Contented settlers are prepared to accept a reduction in income and status for the other advantages that Australian society has to offer. They recognise constraints on the recovery of their social and economic standing, but despite their more modest economic success, they retain a commitment to remain in the country. Over time they may gradually devote themselves to other activities and often look toward the next generation for educational and economic success. Warriors, by contrast, retain a strong determination to resume a successful and financially rewarding lifestyle. They are quick to seek employment, improve relevant skills and adopt a flexible view on earning money. Fundamentally, they rely upon the same strategies that proved successful in Hong Kong. Opportunists, including full-time students, are undecided about settlement. If they are unable to secure suitable employment, they may remain in Australia long enough to obtain citizenship and then return to Hong Kong. Members of this group, in the main, like to keep their options open. In contrast to the first three categories of immigrants, the prisoners and astronauts retain a clearer and stronger commitment to Hong Kong, based at least in part on economic considerations. Prisoners have no intention of settling, but see themselves as 'completing the immigration jail sentence' to retain a safe, fallback position should life in Hong Kong become difficult or impossible (Mak, 1991: 152). This group of immigrants can be divided into three categories: those who have the resources to take an extended break while gaining citizenship; those who are flexible in their choice of employment as the situation is regarded as temporary; and those who have engineered temporary overseas transfers from their Hong Kong firms. Finally, astronauts are motivated by economic concerns to remain in Hong Kong for employment purposes and to 'commute' intermittently to their adopted country to join family members. The most common pattern is that the husband remains in Hong Kong where the earning power is considerably higher while his wife and children are held 'as hostages (or *ren zhi*) in a foreign country' (Mak, 1991: 152).

PERSPECTIVES ON IMMIGRANT YOUTH

Ethnic identity

Most research on ethnic identity in minority and immigrant groups has been conducted within the social identity framework as proposed and refined by social psychologists. A smaller number of investigators has assumed a developmental perspective on these issues and proposed stage theories of ethnic identity formation. Although examples are provided by Kim's (1981) work on the development of Asian-American identity and Arce's (1981) discussion of identity development of Chicanos, the best known theory of ethnic identity formation has been advanced by Phinney (1990, 1993).

Phinney (1990, 1993) proposed a three stage progression of ethnic identity development: (1) diffusion, an initial stage at which ethnicity is not seen as a salient issue and has not been adequately explored; (2) awareness, which occurs as a result of experiences which force one to examine issues pertaining to ethnicity and identity; and (3) acceptance and internalisation, the achievement of a clear sense of ethnic identity. There is reliable evidence that these stages progress from childhood through adolescence. For example, a greater proportion of 15-year-olds than 13-year-olds are actively engaged in identity search (Phinney, 1989), and a sense of ethnic identity is more frequently internalised by university students than by high school students (Phinney, 1992).

Rosenthal and Hrynevich (1985) examined developmental trends in ethnic identity at an earlier age in their study of 9- and 11-year-old Anglo-, Italian-, and Greek-Australians. At age 9 all children clearly distinguished the three ethnic groups; however, at age 11 the Anglo children drew distinctions between their in-group and the immigrant out-group. The patterns of ethnic identity found in the Greek and Italian children reflected both similarities and differences. Children from both groups had a strong ethnic identity, and perceptions of cultural cohesiveness increased over age. The Greek children, however, strongly valued their ethnic origins, retained a positive sense of cultural distinctiveness, and were inclined towards separation. The Italians, in contrast, demonstrated less interest in cultural preservation and leaned more towards assimilation. However, as the older Anglo children perceived Greeks and Italians as one homogeneous migrant group, this suggests that majority members of the settlement society may not be sensitive to the differing needs and aspirations of the various ethnic communities.

Phinney's work focuses primarily on identification with heritage culture, and she acknowledges that the meaning of ethnic identity achievement differs across groups because of historical experiences (Phinney, 1990). She also recognises, as does social identity theory, that there may be additional issues to resolve for members of ethnic minorities, including immigrant groups. These would include possible conflicts over differences between their own group and the majority group as well as matters relating to the lower or disparaged status of migrant communities (Phinney, Lochner and Murphy, 1990). Despite these tensions, Phinney's (1991) research has demonstrated that positive psychological outcomes are associated with the achievement of ethnic identity. For both Asian and Mexican Americans more positive self-evaluations, a greater sense of mastery, and better family and social relations are associated with the later stages of ethnic identity development.

Immigrant youth must consider their relationship with both their heritage culture and with the broader (or dominant) culture of the wider society. Several studies have shown that these relationships may be considered separately and that heritage and host cultural identities are independent (e.g. Hutnik's (1986) study of Indian and British identities in South Asian adolescents in the United Kingdom). There is also evidence that identity with both referent cultures, 'native' and 'resident,' is associated with positive psychological outcomes. Oetting and Beauvais (1991) found that self-esteem in Mexican American youth increased in relation to identity with both Mexican and American reference groups. This is in line with many arguments that favour biculturalism, e.g. bicultural Hispanic youth in the United States experience less acculturative stress (Gil, Vega and Dimas, 1994); bicultural Korean-Americans have more positive educational outcomes (Golden, 1987); and the acquisition of bicultural skills through bicultural effectiveness training is associated with a decrease in family and school conflict in Cuban Americans (Szapocznik *et al.*, 1984). The findings are also in accordance with the broader literature on integration, separation, assimilation and marginalisation that was elaborated in Chapter 5.

The importance of peer influence and social-situational factors on bicultural identity was discussed by Rotheram-Borus (1993) in her study of adolescents in urban high schools in the United States. Rotherham-Borus compared students in two New York secondary schools. The first was an integrated school where the classes were ethnically balanced, the teaching staff was ethnically diverse, and students from different ethnic backgrounds had similar levels of academic achievement and came from similar socioeconomic backgrounds. The second institution also had students of similar socioeconomic standing, but the school was less ethnically balanced and experienced high racial tensions. In the integrated school almost half of the Puerto Rican and Filipino students identified themselves as bicultural, one third of the minority groups identified primarily with their ethnocultural group and the remainder with 'mainstream' (white normative) culture. Although two-thirds of the white students saw themselves as 'mainstream', the remainder was equally split between bicultural and ethnic (largely Irish and Polish) identifiers. In the racially tense school, in contrast, over 70 per cent of the students in each ethnic group reported themselves as ethnically identified. In line with social identity theory, Rotheram-Borus (1993) suggests that when people feel threatened, ethnicity becomes more salient and increasing differentiation occurs across groups.

The majority of studies mentioned so far have been concentrated on the native-born offspring of immigrant parents and members of relatively established ethnocultural communities. Identity issues may be somewhat different for children and adolescents who have themselves migrated to a new culture. Olmeda and Padilla (1978) have argued, for example, that three factors are important with respect to acculturation and identity issues in immigrant youth: (1) the developmental stage at which the cultural transition occurs; (2) the age of the individual; and (3) the length of exposure to the new culture. Identity with heritage culture has been shown to be weaker in those who have arrived at an earlier age and have lived longer in a new culture (Garcia and Lega, 1979; Rogler, Cooney and Ortiz, 1980).

Immigrant parents and children

It is widely accepted that adolescents take on the values of the host culture more rapidly than their parents (e.g. Heras and Revilla, 1994), and resultant value differences have been cited as a significant source of conflict in immigrant families (Esquivel and Keitel, 1990). Yau and Smetana (1993), who discussed conflicts between parents and children in Chinese immigrant families, highlighted the tensions between the traditional collectivist values of the parents and the emerging individualist preferences in children. Sethi (1990) is largely in agreement and has suggested that adolescence is more turbulent for Indian youth in the United States than in their native country. She has attributed this to the conflict between the emphasis on autonomy in the United States and the traditional preference for strict parental control in India. She has also argued that the second generation adolescents, who have grown up in an environment where critical thinking and questioning are encouraged, are not inclined to accept blindly traditional values and behaviours. As articulated by an Asian youth in California, 'They say that their parents expected them to follow tradition without asking questions. Our parents do not have a deep knowledge of American culture and their knowledge of Indian culture is not extensive' (Sethi, 1990, p. 13).

These tensions are clearly recognised by Indian parents in the United States where opposing value systems are a major source of conflict. Juthani (1992) suggests that this is particularly salient for Indian immigrants in North America, compared with the overseas communities in Kenya, Fiji and the United Kingdom, where the societies are less absorptive and there is less mixing with the native population. However, Patel, Power and Bhavnagri (1996) note that parental values also change, and that in many cases Indian families are selective in the retention of 'traditional' versus the acceptance of 'modern' values. In their study, for example, fathers maintained traditional values regarding interpersonal relations at home, particularly for daughters, but adopted American conventions regarding interactions in other domains, especially the workplace.

Clearly, value conflicts are not confined to immigrant families, leading a number of researchers to suggest that the extent to which parents and children disagree does not differ between immigrant and non-immigrant groups. Despite this contention, findings on intergroup variations in family conflict have been inconclusive. Sam (1998) compared immigrant and non-immigrant families in Norway on a range of family values and found that the value discrepancies between adolescents and parents were no greater for immigrants than non-immigrants. In both cases parents more strongly valued obligations while children more strongly valued rights. On the other hand, Rosenthal (1984) reported more conflict between parents and adolescents in immigrant than non-immigrant families in Australia and also found that the greatest amount of conflict was apparent in those families with assimilated children.

It is interesting to note that family conflicts appear to repeat themselves over generations. Moon and Pearl (1991) studied Korean migrants over the age of 60 who had followed their children to the United States. They found that the migrants who were older and spent less time in the US felt more alienated by the way their children and grandchildren had assimilated American attitudes. In particular, the elderly migrants expressed concern about attitudes toward the aged and respect for Korean traditions regarding the care of parents. Similar themes have been echoed in studies of the elderly in other migrant groups in the United States including Samoans, Mexicans, Cubans and Puerto Ricans (Barker, 1991; Krause and Goldenhar, 1992) as well as the Chinese in Australia (Mak and Chan, 1995).

Parents and children disagree on a range of acculturation issues and often prefer different acculturation orientations. Pawliuk *et al.* (1996) reported that 54 per cent of their sample of immigrant children in Canada could be classified as integrated and 40 per cent assimilated, compared with the parents who were more likely to be separated (47 per cent). Nevertheless, parents strongly influence their children's acculturation experiences and behaviours. Adolescents who maintain a strong sense of ethnic identity have parents who report conscious efforts to prepare their children for life in a diverse society (Phinney and Nakayama, 1991). Adolescents' perceptions of parental attitudes toward acculturation predict their own preferences (Sam, 1995). Parental attitudes and behaviours also have consequences for children's sociocultural and psychological adaptation. Parental acceptance of the majority culture has been linked to healthy functioning in children (Barankin, Konstantareas and de Bossett, 1989). Furthermore, children of assimilated parents are more socially competent (Lasry and Sayegh, 1992).

THE ACCULTURATION PROCESS

Similarities and differences across generations

Identity and intergroup relations

Ethnocultural identity is stronger in first generation migrants (Yamada, Marsella and Yamada, 1998), and in general, a move towards biculturalism occurs in the second generation (Cortés, Rogler and Malgady, 1994; Der-Karabetian, 1980; Mavreas, Bebbington and Der, 1989). It is not completely clear, however, what emerges in the third and subsequent generations. Montgomery's (1992) study of Mexican-Americans in the United States revealed an increasing Anglo orientation over five generations; however, a number of other researchers have suggested that reaffirmation of cultural identity arises in the third generation (Atkinson, Morten and Sue, 1983; Constantinou and Harvey, 1985).

Changes in identity over generations will undoubtedly be influenced by the unique social, cultural, political and historical circumstances of the migrant group and their relationship to the settlement society. Hurtado *et al.* (1993) have described this process in persons of Mexican descent in the United States.

> Ethnic identity in particular is more likely to be highly differentiated among Chicanos – the native-born, English speakers in the Mexican-descent population – because their family histories illustrate changing attitudes toward Mexico and the United States. Their great-grandparents were initially loyal to Mexico and identified as Mexican. Their grandparents gradually changed how they thought of themselves and developed more global ethnic identifications such as Latin, Latin American, Hispanic, and Spanish. These changes in thought created a wider range of identifications. They did not represent the simple transference or replacement of one identity with the next. The newer generation added new ways of thinking about the self as they refined and retained older ways as well. With time, ethnicity became equated with style and bicultural ties. Being an American of Mexican descent or an American eventually became acceptable. ... In contrast, ethnic identities of the Mexicanos – foreign-born Spanish speakers in the Mexican-descent population – are less likely to be differentiated because, as a group, they have not gone through this long history in the U.S. of cultural shifts in the construction of ethnicity.
>
> (Hurtado *et al.*, 1993: 136)

Intergenerational variations in patterns of identity change may also be due to a differential emphasis on the various components of ethnocultural identity. Hurtado *et al.* (1993) found that second and later generations of

Mexican-Americans were less concerned about issues such as exposure to Spanish media or living in Mexican neighbourhoods, but they were no less likely than first generation migrants to desire that their children retain Mexican culture. Keefe and Padilla (1987) found that cultural awareness decreased substantially between first and second generation immigrants and continued to decline over subsequent generations whereas ethnic loyalty decreased only slightly in second generation immigrants and remained fairly stable over the next two generations. In a more recent discussion of these issues Keefe (1992) argued that cultural knowledge decreases over generations but that loyalty remains more stable. She also suggested that different aspects of ethnic identity are salient for first generation migrants and members of established ethnocultural groups. Recent migrants are more concerned with 'ethnic culture', or a traditional cultural orientation. In addition, cultural awareness is a definitive feature of ethnicity. In contrast, ethnic membership is a more salient aspect of ethnicity in later generations and established ethnocultural groups.

Hurtado, Gurin and Peng (1994) have also suggested that the defining features of social identity are different for first and later generation migrants and that exposure to prejudice and discrimination over successive generations may at least partially account for these differences. In their study of first and later generations of Mexican-Americans they noted that social class was the most salient component of identity for Mexicanos while a politicised ethnic identity was more significant for Chicanos. They interpreted their findings in light of Tajfel's (1978) social identity theory, suggesting that in an effort to gain positive distinctiveness, Chicanos engage in reactive identity formation to counter discrimination, categorical treatment and stereotyping. Although these processes may begin in the first generation, they are not critical until the commitment to remain in the United States is firm and the aspirations of returning to Mexico have faded. This is in line with Portes and Rumbaut's (1990) summary of immigrant research in the United States which reveals that awareness of group-based discrimination becomes more widespread the longer persons of Mexican decent have lived in the United States. It should be acknowledged, however, that this pattern is not uniformly found across cultures (Richman *et al.*, 1987) nor is it consistently observed in all ethnic groups in the United States (e.g. Sodowsky and Plake, 1992).

Academic achievement

While identity changes over generations have received particular attention in the acculturation literature, a wider range of social and psychological variables have also been examined. One variable of interest has been the academic achievement of immigrant children and adolescents. There have been three major theories proposed to account for the patterns of achievement across generations (Kao and Tienda, 1995).

1   Straight-line assimilation. This hypothesis predicts that immigrant youth will have the lowest educational attainment but that it will increase over generations. This is supported by Matute-Bianchi's (1986) study of Mexican-American students in California high schools.
2   Accommodation without assimilation. This hypothesis predicts that recent immigrants are in the best position to perform well scholastically because they have not been 'tainted' by native peer culture. Some suggestion of this was found in Gibson's (1993) study of Punjabi youth in California.
3   Immigrant optimism. This hypothesis assumes that differences between immigrant and native parents are the key feature in the prediction of achievement. Although initially at the bottom of the socioeconomic ladder, immigrants hold high hopes for upward mobility; immigrant parents who are more optimistic about their children's future than their own may influence their children to excel academically. This may apply to first generation migrants but even more so to the second generation who have the added advantage of better language skills (also see van de Vijver, Helms-Lorenz and Feltzer, 1999). On the other hand, established minorities may have experienced bitter disillusionment and pass this on to their children.

Kao and Tienda's (1995) research investigated these three hypotheses in various migrant communities in the United States and reported mixed outcomes with acculturation effects varying across the three ethnic groups. First and second generation Asian students were more likely to get better grades and maths and English scores than third and later generation students. For Hispanics there were no intergenerational differences in grades, but first and second generation migrants expressed a stronger desire to go to university than later generations. For blacks, who originated primarily from the Caribbean, first generation immigrants achieved higher maths scores than subsequent generations, but second generation migrants had higher reading scores.

The Asian data were interpreted by Kao and Tienda in support of either the accommodation without assimilation or the immigrant optimism hypothesis. The black data were seen as somewhat compatible with the immigrant optimism hypothesis but could also illustrate the negative assimilation of black youth. In no case was there evidence to support the straight-line assimilation hypothesis. Hispanic, black and white students with immigrant parents performed as well as their peers whose parents were US-born, and Asian students who had foreign-born parents performed better than those with native-born parents.

Cross-cultural comparisons

Acculturation processes may also be examined by comparing the identity, values and attitudes of migrant groups with members of both their heritage and settlement cultures. Along these lines, an impressive series of studies has been undertaken by Rosenthal and colleagues in her work with immigrants in Australia. In one of her earlier studies Greek Australians were compared with both non-migrant Greeks and Anglo-Australians (Rosenthal *et al.*, 1989). Findings indicated that the Greek Australians were more similar to Anglo-Australians in their behaviours but more closely resembled native Greeks in their values. This is in line with Bochner's (1972, 1986) contention that the instrumental benefits of culture learning do not require changes in core cultural values.

Research with Greek immigrants has also been undertaken by Siefen, Kirkcaldy and Athanasou (1996) who compared Greeks, Germans and Greeks in Germany. Adolescents were asked about parental attitudes on a range of topics including achievement, family conflict and parental control. As might be expected, the attitudes of migrant Greeks were generally situated between Greek and German attitudes.

Feldman and Rosenthal's (1990) study of family values in Anglo-Australians, Chinese Australians and Hong Kong Chinese demonstrated the same pattern with the immigrant group assuming an intermediate position. Additional analyses were reported in a more recent paper on personal and family values by Feldman, Mont-Reynaud and Rosenthal (1992) which included data from the United States. In this study first and second generation Chinese adolescent migrants from Hong Kong or Canton who were resident in Australia and the United States were compared with Anglo-Australians and Euro-Americans in their country of settlement and with Hong Kong Chinese who had not emigrated. The Chinese living in Australia and the United States placed less value on traditions (e.g. rites and rituals, repayment of favours) and the extended family but more value on outward success (e.g. wealth, power) than the Hong Kong Chinese. However, there were only modest differences between first and second generation immigrants, and second generation migrants could still be distinguished from the Western youth. For example, Chinese migrants placed more importance on the extended family than did Euro-Americans and Anglo-Australians. While the overall pattern of acculturation of Chinese migrants was the same in Australia and the United States, there was some evidence that the movement away from heritage culture and towards contact culture was more pronounced in the Australian setting.

CHAPTER SUMMARY

This chapter has extended the theoretical perspectives presented in the first half of the book to interpret recent research on immigrants and immigration. Issues pertaining to identity and acculturation have been discussed, and migrant adjustment has been considered with specific reference to psychological, sociocultural and economic adaptation. Attitudes to immigrants and immigration received special attention, and the Interactive Model of Acculturation was offered as an integrative framework for the analysis of immigration ideologies and national policies.

In response to an increase in international migration, receiving nations have formulated a range of policies to regulate and control the entrance and settlement of migrants. These policies are linked to broader ideologies (i.e. plural, civic, assimilationist and ethnist), and these ideologies, in turn, influence the acculturation orientations of members of the receiving society. These orientations may complement those of immigrants and lead to intergroup tolerance and acceptance, or they may conflict with immigrant preferences and contribute to increased interethnic hostilities. The Interactive Model of Acculturation by Bourhis *et al.* (1997) has provided a useful framework for describing and explaining the patterns and consequences of host–migrant orientations on both the group and individual levels of analysis.

Social identity theory has also played an important role in interpreting the mutual patterns and processes of intergroup perceptions, attitudes and interactions. Research has demonstrated that the cultural identity of immigrants is affected by ethnic, social, political and historical factors. It has also shown that identity influences the readiness for intergroup contact, with those immigrants who prefer to maintain their cultural distinctiveness being less willing to interact with members of the receiving society. Although many factors, including perceived threat, may impede intercultural interactions, cross-cultural research converges to highlight the adaptive outcomes of integrative acculturation responses. Biculturalism has been associated with a range of social and psychological advantages as has integration, when compared with assimilation, separation and marginalisation.

In addition to social psychological theory on intergroup relations, developmental perspectives on acculturation and identity were considered in this chapter. Developmental theorists such as Phinney were discussed, and evidence of peer, parental and institutional influences on identity formation was presented. Research demonstrated that the internalisation of ethnic identity increases over age, that it is largely accomplished by young adulthood, and that it is related to a range of positive psychological outcomes, including enhanced self-esteem. The achievement of ethnic identity generally entails some consideration of norms and values, and these were examined in intergenerational and cross-cultural studies. Research revealed that adolescents are quicker to absorb the values of the new culture than are their parents, and the differential rate of acculturation has been cited as a significant source of conflict in immigrant families. Cross-cultural comparisons, which have examined values and behaviours in immigrants and non-immigrants in both the native and settlement countries, reveal that although immigrants demonstrate a significant shift toward acceptance of their new culture's practices and preferences, they remain distinguishable from members of the receiving country.

Finally, immigrant adaptation was discussed. Clinical and epidemiological studies comparing the physical and mental health of migrants and non-migrants produced mixed results; however, recent psychological investigations have suggested that the predictors of general adaptation are much the same for both groups and can be interpreted within a stress and coping framework. Research has shown that for immigrants, as for other cross-cultural travellers, psychological adaptation is facilitated by social support, integrative acculturation strategies and personal resources including mastery, a sense of coherence and an internal locus of control. Sociocultural adaptation, viewed from a culture learning perspective, has been associated with higher levels of education and income, language fluency and contact with members of the receiving society. Economic adaptation may be predicted by premigration factors such as motivation for relocation; it is also related to weaker perceptions of discrimination, better family relations and lower levels of acculturative stress.

This chapter has provided only the briefest glimpse of the massive body of literature on immigrant acculturation. We acknowledge that it is difficult to identify the boundaries of immigrant research since between-culture contact merges into within-culture contact over time and as subsequent generations evolve into established ethnocultural communities. It is also difficult to synthesise the results of hundreds of investigations that reflect significant between and within group differences. In the end cross-cultural research reminds us that the ABCs of acculturation do not occur in a social vacuum, but that they are influenced by a broad range of micro and macro factors.

NOTE

1 Unidimensional models of acculturation conceptualise heritage and host culture identities as polar opposites with biculturalism as the midpoint between the two extremes. Categorical models of acculturation conceptualise heritage and host culture identities as orthogonal domains. These two dimensions may be used in conjunction to identify four acculturation options. The integration option is similar to biculturalism in that it entails identification with both heritage and host cultures. See Chapter 5 for a more in-depth discussion.

10 Refugees

Like tourists, sojourners, and immigrants, refugees have significantly contributed to the global expansion of international migration. The number of
world-wide refugees has steadily increased over the last three decades with
estimates climbing from the 1970 figures of 2.5 million, to 8.2 million in 1980
and an estimated 19 million in the early 1990s (Leopold and Harrell-Bond,
1994). The United Nations High Commission for Refugees (UNHCR) has
acknowledged that reliable statistical data on refugees are very difficult
to produce but has reported that the 1996 estimate for people under the
UNHCR's mandate was 26 million or 1 in every 220 people on the planet!
More recently, Beiser (1999) has put this number at 27 million. This reflects
massive global relocation and an enormous range and variety of intercultural
interactions.

Table 10.1 describes the geographical distribution of the world's recent
refugee population. Afghanistan, Iraq, Burundi, Somalia, Bosnia-
Herzegovina, and Sierra Leone are the largest sources of displaced persons
and refugees (UNHCR, 1998). The burden for hosting refugee populations
has largely fallen on economically disadvantaged countries, particularly those
in Asia and Africa which shelter more than two thirds of the world's displaced persons. Although Europe and North America have seen an increase
in asylum-seekers over the last decade, countries in those regions accept a
relatively small proportion of the growing refugee population. Previously
Europe and North America accepted less than 5 per cent of the refugee
population (Leopold and Harrell-Bond, 1994; Salt, 1995); however, the number of refugees in Europe has risen slightly but steadily since 1996 (UNHCR,
1998).

Who are refugees? The 1951 Geneva Convention of the United Nations
defined a refugee as a person who

> owing to well founded fear of being persecuted for reasons of race,
> religion, nationality, membership of a particular social group or political
> opinion, is outside the country of his nationality and is unable or owing to
> such fear, is unwilling, to avail himself of the protection of that country.
>
> (United Nations, 1951, cited in Beiser, 1999, p. 37)

Table 10.1 Regional distribution of persons under UNHCR mandate (end 1998)

	Refugees	*Total population of concern*
Africa	3,270,860	6,284,950
Asia	4,744,730	7,474,740
Europe	2,667,830	6,212,620
Latin America	74,180	102,400
North America	659,800	1,305,400
Oceania	74,310	79,510
Total	11,491,710	21,459,620

Note: The total figures include refugees, returned refugees, asylum-seekers, internally displaced persons, returned internally displaced persons and others. The global refugee population fell by 4% between 1997 and 1998.

Social science and medical researchers have generally taken a broad view of 'refugees', one that encompasses a range of threatened and displaced persons, including asylum-seekers, who have been forced to leave their countries of origin. The causes of displacement may be attributed to a variety of political, social, economic and environmental factors and conditions, including war, revolution, ethnic conflict, religious persecution, genocide, political upheaval and the formation of new states, widespread human rights violations, economic crises and collapse, drought, famine and other natural disasters (Richmond, 1993).[1] But the pattern of displacement is the same; it involves forced migration to accessible geographical locations that provide safer havens and more adequate resources.

Refugees share many of the same characteristics and concerns of other groups that experience intercultural contact and change. Like sojourners and immigrants they have crossed cultures and are confronted with demands of adapting to life in new and often unfamiliar settings. Unlike immigrants, sojourners or tourists, however, the relocation of refugees is involuntary. Rather than being 'pulled' by the attractiveness of a new host culture, refugees are 'pushed' into an alien environment. They are more strongly motivated to escape from threatening circumstances in their countries of origin. Because of these conditions, two distinctive features of refugee research are apparent when compared with studies of tourists, sojourners or immigrants. First, greater attention has been paid to premigration factors, including threat, loss, destruction, torture, imprisonment and witness to genocide, and their influences on the adaptation process. Second, greater emphasis has been placed on mental health outcomes. Despite these emphases, contemporary researchers have recognised that refugees face many of the same intercultural issues as immigrants and sojourners. Consequently, identity, acculturation, values, intergenerational similarities and differences, and social interaction have also been studied in refugee populations. These topics, along with migration and mental health; stress, coping and adjustment; and refugee adaptation over time will be examined in this chapter.

REFUGEE STATUS AND MENTAL HEALTH

Although all groups in transition have distinctive assets and liabilities, it has often been suggested that refugees are the most disadvantaged of the relocating groups. First, they have been exposed to overwhelmingly stressful premigration experiences in their countries of origin which may strongly affect their subsequent adjustment (Farias, 1991). Second, their migration is involuntary and largely motivated by 'push' rather than 'pull' factors, which increases the risk of psychological and social adjustment problems (Kim, 1988; Mayada, 1983). Third, their displacement is usually permanent; compared with immigrants and sojourners, refugees are far less likely to be able to return home (Beiser *et al.*, 1995; Majodina, 1989). Fourth, they often come poorly prepared for the cross-cultural transition and are frequently under equipped with tangible resources to deal with life in a new culture. In many cases refugees relocate without the benefits of language proficiency, without financial resources, and in some cases without practical skills (Boman and Edwards, 1984). Fifth, they are likely to originate from cultural backgrounds that are extremely different from those of the receiving countries (Stein, 1986).[2] It is no wonder that the refugee experience has been described as a 'social earthquake' (Mollica, 1990).

With this background it is not surprising that comparative studies have frequently found that refugees exhibit more symptoms of psychological distress than members of the receiving society (Smither and Rodriguez-Giegling, 1979; Sundquist, 1993). Chu's (1972) community-based study in Taiwan, for example, revealed that the rate of neuroses was three times higher in a group of newly arrived Chinese, composed predominantly of those who had experienced refugee trauma, than in the native population. Majodina (1989) similarly reported that exiled Namibians exhibited higher levels of anxiety than a matched sample of host Ghanaians. Furthermore, refugee children have been found to be at greater risk for subsequent alcohol abuse (Morgan, Wingard and Felice, 1984), drug addiction (Amaral Dias *et al.*, 1981), depression (Skhiri, Annabi and Allani, 1982) and posttraumatic stress disorder (PTSD; Sack, 1985) when compared with children in the receiving nation.

One limitation of this type of comparative study is that differences between refugees and members of the receiving community are merely described; they are not adequately explained. Indeed, refugee–host differences are difficult to interpret; the discrepancies could be attributed to being foreign-born versus being native-born or to migrating versus remaining sedentary. To consider these issues in greater depth Young and Evans (1997) undertook a carefully designed comparative investigation of relocation and adaptation with Salvadoran refugees and Anglo-Canadians. Both groups had relocated to London, Ontario, and either had arrived within the past two years or had been settled for more than five years. The Salvadorans and Canadians were compared on measures of psychological distress, quality of life and life satisfaction. There were no significant differences in severity of psychological distress between the two groups. The refugees appeared extremely robust and did not differ from the Anglo-Canadians in global symptom severity; however, both the refugee groups had lower quality of life scores than their Canadian counterparts. In addition, recent refugees were less satisfied with their lives than recently relocated Canadians. This research serves to illustrate the inadequacies of descriptive refugee–host comparisons that fail to consider the influences of broader psychosocial factors on adaptation.

Comparisons have also been undertaken between refugees and other acculturating groups. These studies have typically reported more adjustment problems in refugee communities (Jensen *et al.*, 1989; Hicks, Lalonde and Pepler, 1993). For example, Indochinese refugees in New Zealand demonstrated a higher incidence of clinical depression than immigrants from either the United Kingdom or the Pacific Islands (Pernice and Brook, 1994). Vietnamese boat people in Canada reported elevated levels of acculturative stress (anxiety, depression and psychosomatic symptoms) compared with immigrants from Korea and sojourners from Malaysia (Berry *et al.*, 1987). Similarly, Latin American refugees in Sweden manifested more symptoms of psychological distress (anxiety, psychosomatic complaints, drug consumption and long term mental illness) than Southern European and Finnish labour migrants, although in this case it should be acknowledged that the percentages of psychological dysfunction were generally low: 18.3 per cent, 6.1 per cent, and 4.3 per cent, respectively (Sundquist, 1994).

While these data are suggestive, it should be noted that the refugee groups included in these studies tended to be more culturally dissimilar to host nationals than the other migrants. The refugees were also more likely to originate from countries lacking linguistic and historical ties to the receiving nations and to come from more distant geographical areas. It is possible, then, that the elevated levels of psychological distress observed in these investigations could be accounted for, at least in part, by cultural distance (Babiker, Cox and Miller, 1980). These potentially confounding factors of historical ties and cultural distance were eliminated in a study by Dube (1968) who compared Punjabi and Sindhi migrants to Agra, Uttar Pradesh. Members of both communities originated from nearby northern parts of the Indian subcontinent and shared some common cultural characteristics with the population of Agra. The Punjabis, according to Dube, were forced to emigrate from Pakistan 'much against their inclination and had suffered more privation, bloodshed and terrifying experiences' compared with the Sindhis who 'migrated more peacefully' and 'settled more readily' (p. 142). Under these conditions Dube found that the refugee Punjabi population experienced a greater incidence of psychological disorders than the Sindhi migrants. These findings support previous arguments that premigration factors associated with forced migration affect psychological adjustment during resettlement.

A number of researchers have specifically concentrated on the prevalence and diagnoses of psychiatric problems in refugee populations. Mghir *et al.*'s

(1995) study of Afghan adolescents and young adults in the United States reported that 29 per cent of the sample met the criteria for major depression and 11 per cent for PTSD. Indeed, these tend to be the most commonly diagnosed conditions in refugees. Kinzie *et al.*'s (1986) research with 40 Cambodian high school students in the United States found that 50 per cent of the sample developed PTSD, and 55 per cent met the criteria for major, minor or intermittent depressive disorders. These rates, however, are rather high compared to larger community-based samples. Westermeyer, Vang and Neider (1984) found that 15 per cent of their community sample of Hmong refugees in the United States could be diagnosed as clinically depressed while Hauff and Vaglum (1995) reported an incidence of 17.7 per cent for depressive disorders in Vietnamese refugees in Norway.

Other studies have examined broader categories of distress in community samples. Ebata and Miyake's (1989) study of Vietnamese refugees in Japan found that 65 per cent of the females and 32 per cent of the males displayed emotional disturbances. Arieli (1992) noted that 27 per cent of Ethiopian Jews who were refugees to Israel reported moderate to severe anxiety, depression and psychosomatic disorders. A range of psychological and behavioural disorders has also been observed in studies of refugee children. Ekblad (1993) interviewed children from Bosnia-Herzegovina, Serbia, and Croatia who had been placed in interim camps in Sweden and found that 68 per cent experienced depression, 62 per cent somatic symptoms, 59 per cent nightmares and 42 per cent fears. Behavioural difficulties such as aggressiveness (35 per cent), reduced interest in school (17 per cent) and repetition of trauma in play (9 per cent) were also reported. Along similar lines, Ajdukovic and Ajdukovic (1993) observed a range of behavioural, emotional, and cognitive problems in a group of internally displaced children in Zagreb, particularly separation fears (17 per cent), eating disorders (16 per cent) and sleep disturbances (10 per cent).

Diagnostic studies that have been confined to clinical populations are summarised in Table 10.2. These data show that depressive conditions and PTSD are the most common diagnoses, although studies have also found neurotic and personality disorders, psychoses and organic impairments. While the most frequently diagnosed conditions such as depression and PTSD are probably outcomes of refugee experiences, other conditions such as psychoses and personality disorders are more likely to have preceded flight and resettlement.

As can be seen in the discussion of refugee status and mental health, a significant portion of research on refugees has been conducted by psychiatrists and undertaken from a medical perspective. This body of research paints a 'doom and gloom' picture of refugee status and resettlement, views psychopathology as an inevitable consequence of the refugee experience, and emphasises symptoms, diagnoses and the need for psychiatric intervention. There are, however, conceptual and empirical criticisms of this medically-based approach. It has been argued, for example, that the refugee experience

Table 10.2 Psychiatric diagnoses in clinical studies of refugees

Name	Sample group	N	Age	Gender	Country	Criteria	Disorder
Kinzie and Manson (1983)	Indochinese	263	17–88	153 males 110 females	USA	DSM III	• Major depressive disorder (48%) • Schizophrenia (19%) • Neurosis and personality disorders (14%) • Organic disorders (8%) • Adjustment disorder (4%) • Alcohol and drug abuse (1%) • Other (6%)
Williams and Westermeyer (1983)	Southeast Asian	28	12–20	15 males 13 females	USA	DSM III	• Functional psychosis (21%) • Mental retardation/OBS (21%) • Depression (14%) • Conduct disorder (14%) • Psychological effects on somatic disorder (7%) • Personality disorder (4%) • Learning disorder (4%) • No psychiatric disorder (14%)
Kinzie et al. (1984)	Cambodian	13	24–63	7 males 6 females	USA	DSM III	• Depression (69%) • Dissociative disorder (15%) • Alcohol abuse (8%) • Adjustment reaction (8%)
Mollica, Wyshak and Lavelle (1987)	Southeast Asian	52	—	25 males 27 females	USA	DSM III	• Major affective disorder (71%) • PTSD (50%) • Psychoneurosis (13%) • Schizophrenia (10%) • Organic brain syndrome (8%) • Drug and/or alcohol addiction (2%)[1]

Table 10.2 (continued)

Name	Sample group	N	Age	Gender	Country	Criteria	Disorder
Jensen et al. (1989)	Middle Eastern (61%) European (22%) African (9%) Latin American (4%) Asian (4%)	49	17–47	45 males 4 females	Denmark	DSM III	• PTSD (retrospective classification) (69%) • Crisis reactions (43%) • Affective reactions (39%) • Dysphoria/depression (25%) • Psychosomatic complaints (20%) • Psychosis (16%) • Drugs/alcohol abuse (10%) [1]
Kroll et al. (1989)	Southeast Asian	404	—	162 males 242 females	USA	DSM III	• Major depressive episode (73.3%) • PTSD (13.9%) • Anxiety and somatoform disorders (5.7%) • Schizophrenia (3%) • Organic disorder (2.2%) • Psychoactive substance use disorder (2%) • Personality disorder (0.7%) • No psychiatric diagnosis (13.9%) [1]
Kinzie et al. (1990)	Southeast Asian	322	—	109 males 213 females	USA	DSM III R	• Depression (81%) • PTSD (75%) • Schizophrenia (16%) [1]
Moore and Boehnlein (1991)	Mien	84	18–64	25 males 59 females	USA	—	• Depression (89%) • PTSD (88%) • Paranoid schizophrenia (5%) • Postencephalitic dementia with delusions (1%) • Atypical psychosis with alcohol dependence (1%) • Mental retardation with deafness and muteness (1%) • Conduct disorder (1%) [1]

Dadfar (1994)	Afghan	58,200	0–18 (13%) 19–40 (57%) >40 (30%)	Pakistan	DSM III R	• Anxiety disorder/PTSD/depressive disorders (51%) • Somatoform disorders (16%) • Psychosis (8%) • Organic disorders (8%) • Neurotic disorders (7.5%) • Torture victims (4%) • Psychoactive substance abuse (3%) • Postconcussion syndrome (2.5%)
Lavik et al. (1996)	African (12%) Far Eastern (19%) Middle Eastern (52%) Latin American (8%) European (9%)	231	<20->44 —	Norway	DSM III R	• PTSD (48%) • Dysthymic and depressive (16%) • Adjustment disorders (10%) • Anxiety disorders (6%) • Other diagnoses (20%)

Note: [1] Percentages exceed 100 as some patients have multiple diagnoses.

should be viewed in terms of process, rather than in terms of symptomatic outcomes. In addition, research findings have cast doubt on the assumptions that refugees routinely encounter psychological adjustment problems and that they necessarily manifest more psychological symptoms than members of the receiving community.

Do refugees consistently suffer psychological and social adjustment problems as suggested by clinical and epidemiological studies? A number of psychosocial investigations have shown that, in at least some instances, refugees fare very well. Gelfand (1989), for example, found little evidence of depression in older illegal Salvadoran refugees who had been settled for at least five years in the United States. Daly and Carpenter (1985) described a sample of Vietnamese refugee youth as adapting well to life in the United States, and Cochrane and Stopes-Roe (1977) found that Asian refugees in the United Kingdom were better adjusted than their native-born neighbours. In addition to these findings, there is also recent evidence concerning the academic and economic achievements of refugees. Southeast Asian refugees in the United States, for example, surpass white and most ethnic minority groups in terms of academic performance (Ima and Rumbaut, 1989; Wehrly, 1990). Similarly, Asian refugees from Uganda who migrated to the United Kingdom have made rapid economic progress in the last 25 years, obtaining, and in some cases exceeding, economic parity with the majority white population, and becoming one of the most prosperous groups in Britain's South Asian community (Mattausch, 1998). No doubt, the pessimistic picture painted by clinical studies can be significantly altered when a broader psychosocial perspective is taken.

The limitations of a clinical approach and the concentration on psychiatric taxonomy have also been pointed out by Eisenbruch (1991) who offered an alternative theoretical perspective on the refugee experience. He proposed that cultural bereavement may be a more appropriate framework for understanding and explaining the distress and difficulties of refugee resettlement. Cultural bereavement refers to a constellation of experiences, including, but not limited to, persistent intrusion of past images into daily life, feelings of guilt over abandonment of culture and homeland, and mourning over the loss of social structures, identity and values. While the taxonomy from the *Diagnostic and Statistical Manual of Mental Disorders* (DSM) provides symptom-based diagnostic criteria and a convenient classification scheme, Eisenbruch argues that cultural bereavement gives meaning to the refugee experience. It represents a normal, constructive response to traumatic life events and the obstacles to maintaining cultural identity.

Nicassio (1985) similarly commented on the limitations of descriptive clinical studies of refugee mental health. He argued that the clinical approach concentrates on symptomatic outcomes and neglects the more important process dimension of refugee adaptation. In an effort to explore this dimension in greater depth Nicassio proposed three theoretical frameworks to understand and interpret the refugee experience: stress and coping, acculturation and learned helplessness. The first two models have attracted considerable attention over the last decade and are elaborated in the remainder of this chapter. Although briefly mentioned in the earlier edition of *Culture Shock*, the learned helplessness model (Seligman, 1975) has remained somewhat under-developed in refugee studies. Nevertheless, a good case can be made for its usefulness. Nicassio argued that refugees are thrust into 'passive, victimized roles' during flight, displacement and resettlement; that they are frequently forced to surrender control to various organisations and bureaucracies; and that unpredictability and lack of control become a way of life (p. 165). In such circumstances refugees may come to believe that efforts on their part to regain control and to improve the quality of their lives are largely futile. This could account for the passivity sometimes observed in resettled refugees and explain the prevalence of depressive disorders in refugee communities.

All in all, studies of refugee mental health have provided valuable descriptive information on the psychological adjustment problems of this group of involuntary migrants. The studies have been somewhat limited, however, in that they have been primarily confined to psychiatric diagnoses. In addition to the issues raised earlier, the psychiatric approach can be criticised on the following grounds. First, there is considerable debate about the adequacy of conventional diagnostic criteria for the assessment of people from non-Western cultures (Mollica, 1989). Second, awareness of culture-specific beliefs and traditions and their influences on clinical encounters are often ignored. Third, psychiatric studies largely fail to incorporate broader, non-clinical measures of psychological and social adaptation. As the studies have been largely descriptive, they have provided little explanation of the patterns of refugee adjustment, and they have neglected the process of adaptation in favour of the analysis of static, symptomatic outcomes. Fourth, most clinical studies have lacked a sound theoretical base for understanding and interpreting refugee displacement and resettlement. The absence of sound theory is particularly apparent in the consideration of refugee adjustment over time and in the dynamics of stress and coping. These issues are discussed in the following sections.

PRE- AND POSTMIGRATION EXPERIENCES AND ADJUSTMENT OVER TIME

Despite the widespread recognition of the significance of both pre- and postmigration events for cross-cultural transition and adaptation, there is some debate as to which events are responsible for the more powerful influences on psychological adjustment in refugees (Clarke, Sack and Goff, 1993; Westermeyer, Vang and Neider, 1983). This was examined in detail by Nicassio *et al.* (1986) who investigated both pre- and postmigration stressors as predictors of depression in Southeast Asian refugees in the United States.

Premigration (emigration) stressors included traumatic experiences such as death of family members, threat, internment and separation from friends and homeland. Postarrival (acculturation) stressors, in contrast, entailed difficulties with jobs, housing, discrimination and climate changes. Both emigration and acculturation stressors were associated with psychological malaise; however, postarrival stressors did not significantly contribute to the prediction of depression above and beyond premigration stressors and language proficiency. This is broadly consistent with Chung and Kagawa-Singer's (1993) later study of Southeast Asian refugees in the United States.

While premigration stressors such as persecution and war are responsible for strong and lasting effects, it is generally agreed that these experiences exert a greater influence on psychological distress in the earlier stages of resettlement. Postmigration circumstances, particularly economic and cultural pressures, become increasingly important over time (Beiser, Turner and Ganesan, 1989; Rumbaut, 1991). It is also recognised that some premigration stressors exert more permanent influence over subsequent adjustment than others. Beiser *et al.* (1989), for example, found that although the impact of camp experiences diminished four to five years after refugee resettlement, other premigration events, such as bereavement, had more enduring consequences.

The variety and type of premigration circumstances to which refugees have been exposed are both shocking and horrific. Mghir *et al.* (1995) described the traumatic experiences of Afghan refugees which included near death incidents (60 per cent), forced separation from family (30 per cent), the witness of murder (of strangers, 23 per cent, and of family or friends, 16 per cent), lack of food and water (23 per cent), lack of shelter (21 per cent) and imprisonment (16 per cent). Bowen's *et al.* (1992) study of refugee women from El Salvador found that 55 per cent had been victims of assault, 32 per cent victims of rape and 19 per cent victims of torture. Violence has a particularly profound effect on both victims and observers; witnesses to wounding, mutilation and murder are more likely to suffer psychological distress, particularly PTSD (Hauff and Vaglum, 1993). Altogether, exposure to violent premigration trauma is associated with significantly less successful postmigration health and adaptation (Fox, Cowell and Montgomery, 1994). But other factors may also influence subsequent adaptation; those who become separated from their families during evacuation, for example, are at greater risk for mental health problems (Majodina, 1989; see Bowlby, 1969, on the psychology of loss).

Refugees may also be forced to endure great hardship in interim camps where conditions are not always conducive to effective coping with pre- and post-relocation stressors. Overcrowding and health problems are common, and excessive levels of psychological dysfunction, e.g. depression, anxiety and attempted suicide, along with social problems such as domestic violence and sexual abuse, are often observed in refugee camps (Mollica *et al.*, 1989). Studies have also demonstrated that camp experiences are related to subsequent indices of psychological distress in Indochinese refugees (Chung and

Kagawa-Singer, 1993); that those who were interned in camps are more likely to suffer emotional and psychological disturbances than those who were not (Ebata and Miyake, 1989); and that the number of years spent in refugee camps predicts subsequent depression (Nguyen, 1982).

The pattern of refugee adjustment over time remains controversial. Tyhurst (1977), who studied both Eastern European (Hungarian and Czechoslovakian) and Ugandan (Asian) refugees in Canada, contrasted the first months of resettlement, characterised by energetic, even euphoric feelings, with a later period of distress and disequilibrium. Based on clinical observations he described the six month onset of a 'displaced persons syndrome', a constellation of symptoms including paranoid behaviour, psychosomatic complaints, anxiety, depression, social skills deficits and identity conflict. In some cases Tyhurst reported spontaneous improvement; however, in most instances therapeutic intervention was recommended during the symptomatic phase. While optimistic about refugee recovery with therapeutic assistance, Tyhurst did not suggest that displaced persons return to the previous level of euphoria purportedly experienced in the early months of resettlement.

Nguyen (1982) similarly proposed three stages of refugee adaptation. The first month of resettlement is supposedly experienced in positive terms with emphasis on excitement and euphoria; the second phase, occurring within two to six months after resettlement is dominated by the pressures of culture learning and the fulfilment of basic needs, and the third, more long term phase from 6 to 36 months entails a period of reflection and coming to grips with the realities of life in a foreign country. Due to ensuing conflicts, Nguyen suggested that the final period presents the greatest risk for psychological dysfunction; however, his model fails to consider the simultaneous decrements in the negative impact of pre-existing trauma on subsequent refugee adaptation.

Can the U-curve theory of adjustment – initial feelings of euphoria, followed by psychological distress and eventual recovery – be applied to refugees? In many ways the U-curve model seems more plausible for refugee populations, compared with sojourning groups, given the relief from threatening and debilitating conditions experienced in the homeland and in interim camps and the decrease in the number and intensity of life changes between the evacuation stage and the first year of resettlement (Masuda, Lin and Tazuma, 1982). As with the sojourner literature, however, there is simply not enough well designed research to support the U-curve proposition. Studies have reported increases (Ekblad, 1993), decreases (Rumbaut, 1991) and no changes over time (Lin, Masuda and Tazuma, 1982). And in some instances the relationship between length of residence and psychological adjustment has been moderated by the period of resettlement in the receiving country. Chung and Kagawa-Singer (1993), for example, reported a linear relationship between length of residence and psychological outcomes in those refugees who had been resettled in the United States for more than five years; a longer period of resettlement was associated with significantly more depression and anxiety. In contrast, for those who had more recently arrived, length of residence was unrelated to psychological outcomes.

Many of the investigations that have examined the temporal patterns of refugee adjustment have been limited to cross-sectional data (e.g. Lerner, Mirsky and Barasch, 1994). Others, which have adopted a longitudinal approach, often omit the most critical time periods from their analyses. Beiser (1987), for example, reported data that indicated depression peaks at 10–12 months in Southeast Asian refugees in Canada. Rumbaut (1985) was less precise but suggested the greatest risk period occurs between 6–18 months. Few studies, however, have incorporated these time frames in their multiple sampling procedures.

One of the most comprehensive longitudinal investigations on refugee adaptation was undertaken by Westermeyer, Neider and Callies (1989) who surveyed Hmong refugees in the United States at three points in time over a 6 year period. The research was conducted with an adequate sample size and a moderately low level of attrition. Despite these methodological advantages, the research findings were mixed. Psychological and psychosomatic symptoms, assessed by the Symptom Check List, increased in the normal cases but decreased in clinical cases over the first two testings; there were no significant changes between the second and third testings. Depression, as measured by the Zung Self-rating Depression Scale, decreased between the first and second testings, but then increased at the third time period. These equivocal results are, in all probability, at least somewhat dependent upon the inadequate sampling frame. At the time of the first testing Hmong refugees had been resident in the United States for an average of 1.5 years. Under these conditions it is unlikely that the study could provide sufficient information about the earliest, and perhaps most variable, stages of cross-cultural transition and adaptation.

While the relative influences of pre- and postmigration factors on subsequent refugee adjustment appear fairly clear, the pattern of adjustment over time is equivocal. For obvious reasons there are no studies that have examined psychological well-being before displacement, so the actual extent of psychological recovery after resettlement remains unknown. After resettlement, however, there is the realistic probability that more sophisticated research could be designed and conducted. More systematic studies are required that incorporate adequate longitudinal sampling across appropriate time frames and include the careful selection of predictor and outcome measures to assess refugee adaptation for the duration of the resettlement process. This will enable the identification of high risk periods in changing patterns of adjustment over time.

STRESS, COPING AND ADJUSTMENT

As we have seen, clinically-oriented studies of refugees highlight the incidence, prevalence and diagnoses of psychopathology. Stress and coping research, in contrast, is more concerned with the process of adaptation. Pre- and postmigration experiences form the core of the stress and coping models. These experiences are typically examined in conjunction with variables such as personality, social support, and educational and occupational resources and deficits for their direct and mediating influences on acculturative stress and psychological adjustment.

Refugees experience a wide range of life changes and are subjected to a variety of stressors upon entry to a new cultural milieu. Lin (1986) has enumerated eight major pre- and postmigration sources of stress: loss and grief, social isolation, status inconsistency, premigration trauma, 'culture shock,' acculturation pressures, accelerated modernisation and minority status. Many of these stressors are also shared by immigrants and sojourners. Some, such as 'culture shock' and acculturation pressures, are routinely experienced, and others, such as social isolation, minority status, accelerated modernisation and status inconsistency, are often encountered. In most cases, however, loss and grief and previous traumatic experiences are more specific to refugee populations.

What are the adjustment problems most typically experienced by refugees? Duke's (1996) study of 263 asylum-seekers in Britain highlighted the significance of language, housing, employment and health problems. Table 10.3 summarises the findings of Nicassio and Pate's (1984) more comprehensive study of over 1600 Cambodian, Laotian, and Vietnamese refugees in the United States. As can be seen, premigration factors such as separation from family and painful memories of war appear the most widely reported problems; however, language ability, homesickness and financial worries also rank high on the list. In addition to documenting the frequency of various adjustment problems, Nicassio and Pate employed factor analysis to identify broader adjustment domains. Six factors emerged in this analysis. The first was related to employment and income, including problems pertaining to finances, job skills, job placement and job dissatisfaction. The second was related to family concerns, such as conflict and child-rearing, while the third covered issues associated with the homeland, including separation from family, homesickness and communication with the home country. The fourth factor concerned food, nutrition and medical care. Factors five and six were both associated with acculturation and integration pressures and included adjustment difficulties relating to prejudice, American institutions, language ability and socioeconomic status.

Understandably, attachment to homeland plays a significant role in postmigration adaptation in a group of people who were forced to relocate quickly and involuntarily through the pressures of war, famine and political upheaval. It has been reported, for example, that up to 85 per cent of

receives public assistance, and welfare status has been linked to elevated levels of psychiatric symptoms, including PTSD (Abe, Zane and Chun, 1994; Chung and Kagawa-Singer, 1993; Westermeyer, Callies and Neider, 1990).

Higher education, like language fluency, functions as a resource and is associated with both employment and enhanced psychological well-being in refugee populations (Berry and Blondel, 1982; Mouanoutoua et al., 1991). There is evidence, however, that in some instances, higher levels of premigration education, particularly in connection with previous employment in professional occupations, may lead to problems in postmigration adaptation. Refugees who were involved in lucrative, high status professions in their homelands may have more difficulties coping with the low status occupations available to them after resettlement; consequently, they display more symptoms of psychological distress (Tang and O'Brien, 1990). In addition to the problem of status disjuncture, unrealistically high expectations of upward mobility can put refugees at greater psychological risk (Fraser and Pecora, 1985–6).

While most refugees share a common experience of displacement and relocation, cross-cultural transition and adaptation are experienced in different ways by younger and older migrants. The young appear more resilient and effective in coping with the transition process. Older refugees, by contrast, seem to suffer more psychological dysfunction and distress (Lin, Tazuma and Masuda, 1979) and are particularly at risk for depression (Mouanoutoua et al., 1991; Rumbaut, 1985; Sundquist, 1994). Rai (1988) has suggested that the experience of refugee transition is fundamentally different for younger and older groups. In her research with Tibetan refugees in India she argued that older refugees encountered more difficulties living outside of their native country; younger refugees, by contrast, were more preoccupied with educational changes and economic adaptation. This seems to be supported by Beiser's (1987) study that found older refugees were more nostalgic, emphasising the significance of the past, compared with younger refugees who were more future-oriented.

Transition and adaptation are also experienced differently by males and females (Yee, 1990). Liebkind's (1994, 1996) studies of acculturative stress and psychological adjustment of Vietnamese refugees in Finland have provided evidence of both similarities and differences in stress and coping among young refugees and their parents and caregivers. Overall, adult women reported the greatest stress symptoms across the four groups. Women were most strongly affected by traumatic premigration experiences, particularly witnessing violence and killing, but their psychological adjustment was also influenced by satisfaction with resettlement and acculturation attitudes and experiences. Men's psychological well-being was similarly affected by premigration and acculturation experiences, but they were even more strongly influenced by perceived prejudice and discrimination. Acculturation experiences related to psychological adjustment in both boys and girls. For girls, however, the presence and density of co-ethnic supports were strongly associated with decrements in anxiety while for boys it was adherence to traditional family values that predicted a reduction in anxiety.

Social support features prominently in the stress and coping approach to understanding and explaining cross-cultural transition and adaptation in refugees. There is strong evidence that refugees who are satisfied with social support suffer less psychological distress than those who are dissatisfied (Mouanoutoua *et al.*, 1991). It is also widely agreed that social support affects the relationship between stress and refugees' physical and mental health (Schwarzer *et al.*, 1994; Shisana and Celentano, 1987). Social support can come from a variety of sources; from spouse, family, sponsors and the larger community. However, interpersonal encounters with support givers may result in both positive and negative outcomes, depending on the nature and extent of the interactions. Consequently, social support is best examined in conjunction with moderating variables.

The chronic stress of family separation is related to emotional dysfunction, and those who arrive in the country of resettlement with a spouse seem to fare better during cross-cultural relocation. Marriage is positively associated with coping, reduces the risk of developing depressive symptoms, and is associated with lower levels of acculturative stress in refugees (Beiser *et al.*, 1989; Berry and Blondel, 1982; Hauff and Vaglum, 1993). Living in family units is also related to better adjustment. Elderly refugees who reside in nuclear or extended families manifest better social adjustment than those living outside of the family (Tran, 1991). Similarly, unaccompanied children and adolescents are at significant risk for adjustment problems (Kinzie *et al.*, 1986; Williams and Westermeyer, 1983); they display fewer psychological symptoms, however, when placed in intra-ethnic foster care, compared with placement in either interethnic families or group homes (Porte and Torney-Purta, 1987).

While living in family groups can function as a significant resource, the quality of intrafamilial relationships, particularly parent–child relations, is also important. Intrafamilial distress can affect the psychological well-being of individual family members. Maternal apathy or instability, for example, is known to put refugee children at risk (Ekblad, 1993). Parenting styles also influence adjustment in refugee children. Research has shown that children of parents whose child-rearing practices are low in authoritarianism and dogmatism are more immune to psychological dysfunction (Allodi, 1989).

In many cases the sources of social support extend beyond the immediate family. The presence of members from the refugee's ethnic community facilitates well-being in both children and adults (Beiser, 1988; Tran, 1987). Ethnic enclaves provide a familiar operating environment, assist with cultural maintenance and function to preserve cultural identity. Refugees who arrive for resettlement without the support of a receiving community may be at greater psychological risk. Berry and Blondel (1982), for example, reported that the early Vietnamese arrivals to Canada who had the ability to speak Chinese experienced less acculturative stress. They speculated that these language skills provided them with access to the resident Chinese community before there were sufficient numbers of Vietnamese resident in Canada. In a similar vein Nguyen (1982) noted that Vietnamese refugees seem to adjust better than other Southeast Asian groups in the United States. He commented that the first wave of refugees had greater economic, educational and linguistic resources, being wealthier, better educated and more likely to speak English. The second wave, though disadvantaged in socioeconomic terms, had the benefit of being received into an established community that was able to provide a range of social, cultural and emotional resources.

More formalised sources of social and economic support have been made available through sponsorship programmes designed to assist refugees in making successful cross-cultural transitions. The programmes are administered through various aid organisations, often with religious affiliations, and generally provide host family sponsors for refugees during the early stages of resettlement. Although sponsorship programmes were introduced primarily for economic assistance, they also offer opportunities for more extensive contact with members of the host culture and avenues for both culture learning and social support (Matsuoka and Ryujin, 1989–90). Despite these apparent benefits, sponsorship programmes are not uniformly effective (Montgomery, 1996). Farmer and Hafeez's (1989) study of Southeast Asian refugees in New Zealand reported that sponsorship assistance was quite variable. Sponsors were perceived to be effective in many practical activities such as assistance with finding accommodation, finding furniture and arranging medical services. Refugees were less satisfied with assistance in obtaining jobs, enrolling in language classes and learning about new cultural values. In addition, almost one in five refugees reported that during the first month of resettlement, sponsors were not helpful at all. In light of these varied responses it may not be surprising that empirical research has failed to demonstrate a positive association between sponsorship and mental health in refugees. Indeed, in some instances, sponsorship may contribute to greater psychological adjustment problems. Beiser *et al.*'s (1989) study of Southeast Asian refugees in Canada reported that religious differences between sponsors and hosts were associated with higher levels of depression.

Stress and coping perspectives on refugee resettlement have acknowledged the significant influence of a range of moderating and mediating variables on the relationship between pre- and postmigration stressors and refugee adaptation. These include personality, social support and educational, linguistic and financial resources. In an attempt to synthesise a model of refugee adjustment Tran (1987) assessed the impact of variables such as language, education, income, length of residence in the host country, self-esteem and ethnic supports on psychological well-being. Using causal modelling, he reported that four factors appeared to exert direct effects on psychological adjustment: membership in ethnic organisations, availability of ethnic confidants, self-esteem and income. As can be seen in Figure 10.1, education and length of residence predicted income, and consequently influenced

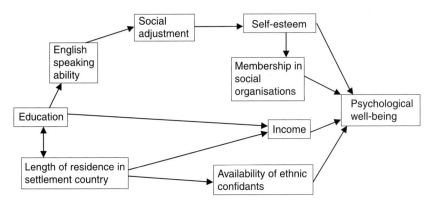

Figure 10.1 A path model for the prediction of psychological well-being in refugees (adapted from Tran, 1987)

psychological well-being in an indirect manner. These variables, along with English ability, also predicted social interaction with members of the host community, which, in turn, exerted an indirect effect on psychological well-being through self-esteem. In total these factors accounted for 57 per cent of the variance in psychological well-being as measured by an index of life satisfaction. Tran's (1987) study has provided us with one of the most comprehensive models of adjustment in refugees and is consistent with both the culture learning and coping interpretations of the transition experience.

ACCULTURATION, IDENTITY AND INTERCULTURAL RELATIONS

Although a significant proportion of refugee research has concentrated on psychological adjustment and mental health, there has also been concern with acculturation, i.e. the changes that result from sustained first hand contact between members of different ethnic and cultural groups. Along these lines, cultural identity, cultural maintenance, changes in behaviours and values, and attitudes toward the country of resettlement have been investigated in a diverse cross-section of refugee groups.

The process or stages of acculturation have also received empirical attention. A popular model has been provided by Berry and Kim (1988) who identified and elaborated four phases of acculturation: (1) the precontact stage, (2) the contact stage, (3) the conflict stage and (4) the adaptation stage. Although acculturation per se does not commence until refugees resettle in the host community, precontact characteristics of both the relocating and receiving groups influence the nature of their subsequent intercultural interactions. As has been previously discussed, refugees, perhaps more than other groups in transition, are strongly affected by traumatic premigration experiences. These include the 'push' factors that forced them to leave their homelands, the involuntariness of the movement, and the permanence of the resettlement. Furthermore, their cultural and linguistic traditions may not be compatible with those of the host community. Social, political and cultural aspects of the receiving community are also important, in particular the acceptance of refugee resettlement and general attitudes toward cultural pluralism. In addition to these macro factors, individual differences among refugees in precontact resources, including level of education, language ability and financial situation, may facilitate or impede culture learning and positively or negatively affect the acculturation experience. In short, precontact variables foreshadow later intercultural relations and affect the probability of cultural diffusion.

The second stage of contact involves intercultural interactions between refugees and members of the receiving community. Refugees, compared to host country nationals, are more likely to be affected by these interactions and to experience greater demands for acculturative changes. In many instances the changes occur slowly and gradually. Indeed, Tyhurst (1977) has argued that refugees do not make a psychological transition into the new culture until about six months after arrival. Certainly, the earlier points of contact are often dominated by culture learning, and only in later months do refugees pause to reflect more seriously about the meaning of resettlement in a new country (Nguyen, 1982). At this time the third stage, that of conflict, is likely to occur. Extensive contact often results in cultural clashes based on discrepant values, contrasting lifestyles, multiple identities and the pleasures versus the perils of modernisation. In most cases conflict is eventually managed and adequately resolved, despite some residual difficulties, and the fourth stage of adaptation ensues.

Although Berry and Kim's (1988) model specifies a conflict phase in a linear stage model of acculturation, in reality problems may occur at many points and for many reasons during the acculturation process. For example, difficulties that arise in managing the acculturative pressures exerted by the host society may result from either lack of information and knowledge about the dominant culture or from rejection of host culture norms and values after familiarisation with them. Refugees who fall into the first category are typically those who have limited opportunities for cultural learning, for example those who are less well educated, unemployed, older and have spent less time in the host community. These refugees are also likely to experience higher rates of psychiatric morbidity (Celano and Tyler, 1991; Cheung, 1995). Refugees who are typical of the second category may have ample opportunity for cultural learning, but develop and maintain more negative attitudes toward the host culture. These refugees are also less likely to identify with host nationals and often experience lower levels of life satisfaction (Nguyen and Henkin, 1982).

In either case, refugees' identification with and relationship to members of the receiving country have been recognised as important components of the acculturation process. Along these lines, a number of researchers have examined alienation, feelings of separation and social isolation. Financial and cultural deficits such as limited language ability and lower socioeconomic status predict alienation as do negative self-perceptions, lack of host culture friends and acquaintances, and greater perceived differences between self and members of the host country (Nicassio, 1983). Social interaction anxiety and lack of social support further increase the likelihood of alienation (Tran *et al.*, 1987).

In some cases refugees experience alienation because they perceive resettlement as a threat to their traditional values and way of life. Matsuoka and Ryujin (1989–90), for example, reported that most Vietnamese parents (88 per cent) would like their children to retain traditional features of Vietnamese culture, but that a substantial proportion (25 per cent) are sceptical about their ability to do so. If refugees view demands for cultural integration as antagonistic to the desire for cultural maintenance, they may opt for separation as a resolution strategy (Birman and Tyler, 1994). While cultural preservation has been associated with mental health benefits (Abe, Zane and Chun, 1994; Beiser *et al.*, 1995), some refugees who retain strong emotional ties to their native lands have more difficulty developing positive attitudes toward the country of resettlement and are less motivated to integrate (Nicassio, 1985).

In other cases refugees view the demands for cultural conformity exerted by the host country and the pressures for cultural maintenance arising from their own community as largely compatible. This was evident in Donà and Berry's (1994) study of the acculturation strategies of 101 Central American refugees in Canada. Their findings confirmed that integration was, by far, the most preferred mode of acculturation, i.e. 77 per cent of the refugees held favourable attitudes to both Latin American and Canadian cultures. Only 18 per cent adopted a separatist position, maintaining positive attitudes toward Latin American, but not Canadian, culture, and even fewer (4 per cent) assumed an assimilationist position, favouring Canadian culture. None of the refugees in their sample could be described as marginalised or having negative attitudes toward both Latin American and Canadian cultures.

The refugees in Donà and Berry's research adopted a range of strategies for dealing with the pressures of acculturation, and those strategies related to specific behavioural and psychological outcomes. Assimilated individuals exhibited less cultural maintenance than either the integrated or separated; in contrast, the separated refugees had the least experience with things 'Canadian', media, food, organisations, and social interactions with members of the host community. Donà and Berry reported that integrated refugees had fewer psychological problems than either the assimilated or separated; however, the study also found a curvilinear relationship between cultural maintenance and acculturative stress. Those individuals who endorsed high or low cultural preservation exhibited more psychological problems than those with an intermediate amount of cultural involvement and intra-ethnic contact.

Cheung's (1995) study of Cambodian refugees in New Zealand reported a similar preference for integration as an acculturation style. Integration, however, is not always easy to attain. Dompierre and Lavallée's (1990) research with African refugees in Québec revealed that separation was perceived as the easiest acculturation strategy; 45 per cent found it easy to retain their original cultural identity but difficult to relate to the Québecois. Only 31 per cent found integration (biculturalism) an easy strategy to achieve; 16 per cent found assimilation an easy option, acknowledging that relationships with co-nationals were more difficult than with host nationals; and 13 per cent found relations with both African and French Canadian cultural groups difficult to maintain. Although the incidence of marginality, on the whole, is relatively low in refugees, it is found more frequently in refugee populations than members of the receiving community (Smither and Rodriguez-Giegling, 1979).

Refugees experience acculturation and adaptation in a variety of ways, and distinctive differences are readily observable across refugee groups and generations. Vietnamese in the United States, for example, compared with Laotians and Cambodians, have better language ability and better access to jobs (Chung and Kagawa-Singer, 1993). This makes integration a more viable option for the Vietnamese. Younger refugees are also more easily accepted into the receiving culture; they generally have greater language proficiency, identify more strongly with the host culture and have less positive attitudes toward cultural maintenance (Liebkind, 1994, 1996). Older refugees may feel 'left behind' and suffer increasing social isolation as younger members of their families become socialised into the host culture at a more rapid pace (Nguyen, 1982). This is particularly the case for women who are frequently left on the fringe of the resettlement society with much less opportunity for social integration due to limited language ability and poor job skills. There is also some evidence that women have more negative attitudes toward cultural assimilation than do men (Liebkind, 1996).

Differences in attitudes and behaviours often lead to conflict in the home (also refer to the discussion of intergenerational discord in immigrant families in Chapter 9). In refugee families increasing tension is frequently associated with changes in public and private roles. As younger refugees acculturate more quickly and often relate to the host culture more effectively, they become cultural brokers, linking their older family members to the new society. This affords children greater status and power within the family and places older adults in an unaccustomed position of dependency (Matsuoka, 1990; Rick and Forward, 1992). For male heads of households the situation may be further exacerbated by unemployment or underemployment. The inability to assume the breadwinner role and to provide economic security for the family may undermine parental authority and negatively affect self-concept. For women strong feelings of dependency are frequently accompanied by conflict over cultural maintenance. Children's emerging cultural knowledge and skills, which permit access to the country of resettlement, are often perceived as threats to cultural preservation.

While Yee's (1990, 1992) studies of Vietnamese refugees in the United States graphically illustrate these phenomena, she interprets intrafamilial conflict within a theoretical framework that emphasises the significance of cultural differences in attitudes toward ageing. Yee notes that Vietnamese refugees have relocated from a society that values, esteems and respects the elderly. In the United States, by contrast, any status associated with ageing is achieved rather than ascribed. Conventional means of attaining status, such as achieving professional recognition, accumulating wealth or establishing routes to social and political power, are often blocked for Vietnamese refugees; they frequently lack language skills, cultural familiarity and even the economic means for establishing credibility as figures of authority in their new homes. As older refugees become increasingly economically and culturally dependent upon their children and grandchildren, and as filial piety declines, tensions regarding cultural maintenance also heighten. Indeed, two of the most negative aspects of life in the United States as reported by the elderly Vietnamese women in Yee's studies were lack of preservation of Vietnamese culture and assimilation of negative aspects of American culture. It is not surprising that these are fundamental concerns for older refugees. While the retention of traditional cultural values facilitates cultural preservation for future generations, it also affords the more immediate benefit of restoring authority and status to the elderly.

Refugee families experience the tension between heritage and host culture traditions and values both inside and outside the home. Adolescents often face conflicts between peer pressures and parental expectations. Young refugees who sustain friendships with members of the dominant culture are less susceptible to emotional disturbances; on the other hand, those who have strong ties with host country peers often experience more conflict with their parents (Charron and Ness, 1983). Adults, in contrast, are more likely to encounter problems arising from conflicts between traditional parental roles and broader sociocultural demands. Parents who assimilate more slowly face difficulties with cross-cultural adaptation. They may also lose status within their families; they have children, however, who perform better academically (Wehrly, 1990). Nevertheless, conflict takes its toll. Tran (1991) reported that older Vietnamese who lived in homes with children under the age of 16 experienced poorer adjustment. Although there may be many reasons for this finding, such as economic hardship or overcrowded living conditions, Tran speculated that intergenerational conflicts may be especially stressful, particularly in families where the children have become too Westernised.

Compared with research on refugee migration and mental health, less is known about acculturation processes and pressures. The data that are available, however, seem to converge with studies of immigrants (see Chapter 9). Cultural identity, maintenance of traditional language, customs and values, and establishing harmonious relationships with members of the resettlement society are important considerations. These cultural and relational domains are affected and shaped by intercultural contact and are experienced differently not only by men and women, but also across generations and refugee groups. Further research is recommended to understand the complexities of the acculturation process in refugees.

CHAPTER SUMMARY

This chapter has described the cross-cultural transition and adaptation problems of refugees. Although refugees encounter many of the same challenges and pressures as do other acculturating groups, their traumatic premigration experiences and the involuntary 'push' into alien environments distinguish them from sojourners and immigrants. As such, much of the theory and research on refugees has concentrated on migration and mental health. Studies have routinely demonstrated that psychological dysfunction is associated with refugee status and that both depression and posttraumatic stress disorders are frequently diagnosed in refugee populations.

Stress and coping perspectives on refugee settlement have examined both pre- and postmigration experiences and their effects on psychological and social adjustment. Evidence has suggested that premigration factors exert stronger influences on refugee adaptation, which is not surprising in light of traumatic experiences, such as war, loss, injury, internment and involuntary displacement. Refugee research on postmigration factors, however, converges with studies of other migrant groups. Investigations have shown that personal resources, such as positive self-concept and perceptions of self-efficacy, facilitate the adaptation process. The same is true for social support, whether offered by nuclear, extended or foster families or by other members of the refugee community. Skills that facilitate culture learning, such as education, language fluency and effective interaction with members of the receiving community, also positively influence the adjustment process.

Finally, studies have considered the process of acculturation and the cognitive and behavioural changes resulting from intercultural interactions with host nationals. Although most refugees prefer an integrated, bicultural approach to acculturation, and this strategy has been associated with better psychological and social adaptation, integration is not always easy to achieve. Tensions often arise between changing identities and conflicting lifestyles. The young more readily incorporate the attitudes and values of the receiving cultures, frequently causing intergenerational conflict in refugee families. Despite these tensions, however, the majority of refugees are able to manage intercultural contact and acculturative changes and learn to adapt to life in a new and different environment.

NOTES

1 There are also economic migrants who seek political asylum by falsely claiming persecution. They represent a small but growing number of migrants who nearly always seek asylum in Europe and North America (UNHCR, 1998).
2 This is particularly the case in the English literature on refugees which is based on research conducted primarily in North America and Europe and most frequently, though not exclusively, involves Indochinese migrants.

Part IV

Applications and conclusions

In this section of the book we look at applying psychological theory and research findings to solving the kinds of problems that result from intercultural contact and change. In Chapter 11 we consider how culture learning, stress and coping, and social identification theories can be used to facilitate the social and psychological adaptation of culture travellers. The model we present provides a comprehensive approach to selection, preparation, and training; it also includes an evaluative component for applied interventions. Based on the broader training literature as well as some fundamental principles of industrial and organisational psychology, the model places special emphasis on culture learning theory and its usefulness for preventive and remedial measures. Although the programmes discussed are particularly geared towards expatriate executives, the selection and training principles can also be applied to international students, diplomats and aid workers. It is acknowledged, however, that our model, which relies upon the identification of culturally relevant knowledge, skills, abilities and attitudes, is an idealistic one and that in fact few cross-cultural travellers are systematically exposed to selection and preparation programmes for their overseas sojourns.

In the final chapter we briefly summarise the historical and current trends in theory and research on culture contact, making specific reference to developments arising since the first edition of this book. We also elaborate our new 'ABC Model of Culture Shock'. The Affect, Behaviours and Cognitions associated with culture contact are discussed, and the theoretical paradigms that provide a foundation for empirical studies and remedial interventions are reviewed. The ABC model serves to unify the major theoretical approaches to culture contact and to integrate the diverse literature on tourists, sojourners, immigrants and refugees. It may be seen as a response to and a reflection of significant advances in the field. Finally, we consider trends in between-society and within-society cultural contact and make cautious predictions about the future.

11 Culture training

In Chapter 3 on culture learning, we reviewed the various ways in which people react to culturally novel or unfamiliar environments, classifying the responses according to whether the adaptations entail changes in cognitions, emotions, or behaviours. For most culture travellers, coping with and adjusting to a novel environment are achieved on a do-it-yourself, trial-and-error basis. People might consult popular guidebooks, listen to 'old hands' talking about their experiences, and generally do the best they can to acquire the necessary knowledge and skills. Muddling through like this can be a highly unsatisfactory experience and accounts for the many reported failures in psychological and sociocultural adaptation.

There is now sufficient evidence, accumulated over several decades, to suggest that most people who cross cultures would benefit from some kind of systematic preparation and training to assist them in coping with culture-contact induced stress. Simply dropping culture travellers in at the deep end after some limited introductory information sessions can be costly, both in financial and personal terms. For example, the early repatriation of inadequately performing executives and their families is a fiscal burden on companies, not to mention lost or botched business deals. It is estimated that between 20 and in some cases up to 50 per cent of expatriate executives return prematurely (Black, 1988, 1990; Black and Gregersen, 1990; Harris and Moran, 1991; Tung, 1987). In monetary terms the overall cost to an employer may be between three and five times the employee's annual salary; the cost of each failure can range from one quarter to one million US dollars per employee; and the total annual cost for United States industry alone may be up to US$2 billion (Bhagat and Prien, 1996; Cascio, 1992; Guzzo, Noonan and Elron, 1994; Van Pelt and Wolniansky, 1990). Even allowing for a certain amount of exaggeration in these estimates, a great deal of money is being wasted on what should, in principle, be a preventable problem.

This problem is not confined to expatriate executives. The Peace Corps, an organisation of volunteer workers that from its inception was advised and evaluated by professional psychologists (Guthrie, 1975, 1981), reported attrition rates of between 40 and 50 per cent for the decade 1961 to 1971 (Harris, 1973). Similarly, foreign students who do badly in their courses represent a poor investment for their countries, families and the universities that they attend. Even those individuals who make a more permanent commitment to a new culture, such as immigrants and refugees, may experience unnecessary hardships which decrease the likelihood of successful adaptation. In all instances of failure, there is a personal cost in terms of impaired self-esteem, delayed career progression and general unhappiness. And it is not only the focal persons who suffer, but their families as well (Arvey, Bhagat and Salas, 1991; De Verthelyi, 1995; Fontaine, 1996). There are also hidden costs, in particular the cumulative effect of such incidents on international and intergroup harmony.

Altogether, there is ample empirical and theoretical justification for providing systematic training for persons exposed to unfamiliar cultures. However, the majority of persons entering into culture contact receive no formal training whatsoever, or only a perfunctory amount, usually insufficient to give them the intellectual and personal resources they need. There are good reasons why training is absent or under-emphasised. Culture training is expensive. There are also practical difficulties regarding the delivery of training courses. For instance, intending culture travellers may either be unwilling to participate in training or they may be difficult to identify and reach. Refugees are a case in point. The urgency of their flight, the need to resettle them quickly, and the general turmoil that precipitated their abrupt relocation are unlikely to leave room for culture orientation. With tourists, it would be impractical to do more than provide some general information about the geography, history and some of the distinguishing customs of their destinations.

In the case of overseas students, those sponsored by their governments or universities often do receive some training, but it is usually delivered by non-specialists and therefore tends to lack a firm theoretical and empirical base. However, most overseas students are now privately supported by their families and usually do not come to the notice of potential formal culture-trainers unless they get into trouble. In practice this means when they start to fail in their courses, become medical or psychological casualties, or attract the attention of the law.

Sojourners are more likely to receive systematic training than tourists, immigrants or refugees, and of the various sojourning groups, expatriate executives are most often targeted. This is because an increasing number of multinational companies have done their homework on the cost-effectiveness of such interventions. Other sojourner groups that undergo some training tend to be those sponsored by government or voluntary agencies and include the Peace Corps, health workers and technical assistance personnel (Brislin, 1993; Dinges and Baldwin, 1996; Seidel, 1981).

Brislin and Yoshida (1994), in reviewing the empirical literature, make a number of claims about the benefits of intercultural training. These include greater understanding of one's own culture; an increase in what has been called 'world-mindedness'; a decrease in stereotyping members of other cultures; a greater likelihood of thinking about other cultures in more complex terms; the capacity to solve problems that require an understanding of cultural differences; increases in confidence about the ability to deal with cultural differences; more ease and greater enjoyment from intercultural interactions; decreased stress; better interpersonal relations and more effective work performance in heterogeneous work groups; and more realistic expectations about goals and achievements in other cultures.

There is a debate in the literature, however, as to whether this is more in the nature of a wish list than an objective assessment of outcomes. This question will be raised throughout this chapter and specifically considered in the section on the evaluation of training programmes. Whatever the verdict, at least Brislin and Yoshida's list provides an explicit set of objectives against which the effectiveness of particular procedures can be evaluated.

What follows is a description of a comprehensive approach to culture training. It is framed in terms of what should ideally be done to prepare culture travellers for their overseas experiences, and it places particular emphasis on training sojourners for international assignments. A critical, empirically based evaluation of the underlying assumptions is also included. However, we acknowledge that in practice most training programmes will not meet the requirements of the model we will now present. Still, it does have practical utility because it can be used to devise interventions that have a sound theoretical and empirical foundation.

As in previous sections of this book, we differentiate two types of culture contact: between-culture contact, where persons from one society travel as temporary sojourners abroad to achieve specific aims; and culture contact that occurs within multicultural societies. This distinction is particularly useful in the present context because the training requirements of sojourners differ from the needs of newcomers and members of minority and majority groups in culturally diverse societies.

The task for sojourners is to cope with and adjust to the requirements of their new cultures, to develop what is sometimes referred to as 'sociocultural competence' (Mak *et al.*, 1999). In reviewing and interpreting the training literature, we have followed the theoretical approach used in previous sections of this book, in distinguishing between cognitive, affective, and behavioural processes. On the cognitive front, newcomers have to acquire information about the host country's political, social and administrative prescriptions, particularly those that directly affect and regulate their lives. They will have to realise that these rules may have both formal and informal manifestations. Emotionally, they will have to learn to cope with the absence of familiar places, social networks and practices, deal with the anxiety which such loss produces, and try to find pleasure and satisfaction in their new circumstances. Behaviourally, they will have to acquire a new repertoire of interpersonal and social skills in order to interact effectively with their local counterparts.

In the training literature, these three domains are sometimes referred to by the acronym **MUD**, standing for **M**emory, **U**nderstanding, and **D**oing

(Hesketh and Bochner, 1994). Effective training programmes should contain elements that increase competence in each of these areas (Brislin, 1994). Training entails providing relevant useful information which the participants have to commit to **M**emory; the programme must provide a rationale for what is being learned, so that the participants gain an **U**nderstanding of the underlying issues, giving meaning to the newly acquired material. And because research has shown that abstract learning may not translate into action, training programmes should contain behavioural exercises that impart concrete skills to the participants. It is also important to include explicit procedures for evaluating the effectiveness of the interventions. Another way of stating the aims of training is in terms of the three Ws: Tell the participants WHAT they have to do, WHEN the action is appropriate, and WHY it is the correct response. In the review of the cross-cultural training literature that follows, we will organise the material in terms of the **MUD** principle, that is, look at the procedures in terms of how well they achieve mastery in each of the three areas.

There is another aspect of cross-cultural training which is not usually made explicit, namely, as Otto Klineberg (1981) pointed out a quarter of a century ago, that the sojourn forms part of a cycle. At least five stages have been identified, and ideally each of these requires a managed intervention. The process starts with selecting the persons destined for an overseas sojourn, presumably based on criteria deemed to be relevant to the assignment. Those selected are then given predeparture orientation. Once in the field, the sojourners are provided with ongoing, during-sojourn social and informational support. Fontaine (1996) uses the term 'international microcultures' to refer to the basis on which participants and their support structures and networks develop shared perceptions about how to achieve their aims. Towards the end of their assignment, sojourners will undergo re-entry training (Martin and Harrell, 1996) to minimise what has been called 'reverse culture shock' (Hickson, 1994; Tung, 1988a,b).

Finally, after having returned home to their jobs or educational institutions and their erstwhile social networks, further training, sometimes called 'inpatriation' (Harvey, 1997b), is required to facilitate the transition. This is particularly relevant in the case of sojourners who have been abroad for a long period, and paradoxically, were successful in their culture learning while overseas (Harris and Moran, 1991). A particular issue is professional integration. After several years abroad, professional sojourners can return to work settings that may seem more unfamiliar than the overseas environment. In sum, culture learning is not something that occurs in isolation from the rest of the sojourner's activities, nor does it necessarily commence at the onset of the sojourn and cease at its termination.

Perhaps the best illustration of this is Klineberg's (1981) treatment of the academic sojourn as a life history. Klineberg notes that predeparture experiences, levels of competence, and degree of preparation will affect what happens to the person while abroad, which in turn will influence the individual's course after returning home. This approach makes it explicit that the difficulties that sojourners might experience, including contracting 'culture shock', are the result of a complex set of social-psychological influences played out over a long period. As Klineberg notes, the seeds of many during-sojourn disasters are sown years previously due to poor selection and preparation.

Once again, most actual training programmes do not follow the cycle we have described. Nevertheless, it is useful to identify the components that should ideally be taken into account, and our review of the literature is organised accordingly.

The training requirements for members of culturally diverse societies are different. With some exceptions, host members do not receive any second-culture training, nor do they see it as necessary. In any case it would not be feasible or cost-effective to implement such training, other than to raise the general level of awareness about the advantages of multiculturalism (Pedersen, 1999). The exception is the training that is (or should be) provided to host-society members whose professional or occupational roles bring them into close contact with either sojourners or members of minority groups. These include persons working in the tourist industry (Bochner and Coulon, 1997), foreign student advisers, immigration officials, and the providers of medical and psychological services to non-mainstream clients (Leach, 1997; Lonner, 1997; Pedersen, 1994a,b), and some of this work will be described later in this chapter.

The literature does contain references to the training of members of minority groups in multicultural societies, including the original inhabitants of countries that were settled, or perhaps more accurately described as conquered, by technologically superior colonisers. The main purpose of these training programmes is to make the participants biculturally competent so that they can function effectively in their dealings with the majority culture while at the same time retaining the skills and values that enable them to continue participating in their culture of origin (LaFromboise, Coleman and Gerton 1993). Later in this chapter, we will describe some training programmes aimed at achieving these goals.

TRAINING PRINCIPLES, ISSUES AND AIMS

Training is an established component of applied psychology, where it is used systematically to improve the effectiveness of workers in industry and commerce (Goldstein, 1993). The aim is to impart or increase job-related competencies, sometimes summarised by the acronym KSAA (Goldstein, 1991), that is, the Knowledge, Skills, Abilities, and Attitudes that workers need to do their jobs effectively. In terms of our distinction between cognitions, emotions and behaviours, the competencies relate to what workers know, what they are willing to do, and what they can do. Furthermore, in terms of the **MUD** principles, some KSAAs are better acquired by emphasising rote

Memory, some by imparting Understanding, and some by Doing; others require all three techniques. Thus, facts and rules lend themselves to rote learning; concepts, principles and affective evaluations are best acquired by achieving an understanding of the underlying logical connections; and procedures need to be rehearsed, often on a repetitive basis, until the acts become part of the learner's behavioural repertoire.

A major problem in training is the issue of the transfer of skills, that is, the extent to which the learning that was acquired in the classroom will transfer to the workplace and the extent to which the training acquired in one workplace will transfer to another (Hesketh, 1997). Both of these issues are highly relevant in cross-cultural training, most of which occurs in the 'classroom' and tends to be generic. It is assumed that such training will prepare the participants for overseas assignments irrespective of the particular destination of the individuals being trained or their sojourn-specific tasks (e.g. Brislin, 1986, 1995). As we will note later, this assumption lacks strong empirical support.

Finally, it is necessary to establish the KSAAs that are relevant in particular jobs. Thus, motor mechanics will need knowledge, skills, abilities and attitudes that differ from the KSAAs for sales assistants or police officers. There may also be some attributes common to all three occupations that contribute to successful performance. In industrial psychology the procedure used to establish minimum occupational competencies is called a job analysis (Harvey, 1991), which consists of an empirical investigation of the actual KSAAs that a particular job entails. The technique usually includes systematic observation of a representative sample of workers, backed up by assessments of satisfactory performance and interviews with supervisors and co-workers. Theoretical considerations are also taken into account.

The results of the job analysis are then used to develop three empirically-based benchmarks: (1) job-specific selection criteria, that is, the minimum competencies candidates should have before they will be considered for a particular job; (2) the content of on-the-job training programmes, that is, the additional training that recruits will need in order to cope with the demands of their job; and (3) evaluation criteria, that is, a set of indicators against which workers can be assessed to determine the level of their performance in the job.

Translating this model into the present context, the 'job' can be construed at two levels of abstraction. At the most general level, the job or task consists of cross-cultural adaptation. From this it follows that sojourners should be selected on the basis of their potential to adapt to novel cultural environments, they should be trained to survive and thrive in such settings, and their success overseas should be appraised in terms of objective measures. In more specific terms, the 'job' consists of the actual tasks being performed, such as students acquiring a particular degree, executives managing a particular business, or technical experts advising on a particular project. The content of

managing); (2) an ability to work in teams containing people from different disciplines, companies and industrial backgrounds; and (3) an ability to manage and work with people from different ethnic backgrounds. In turn, these abilities must be supported by good communication, language and negotiating skills, and an awareness and acceptance of differences. Tung (1997) provides some evidence that possessing these KSAAs does enhance overseas performance. According to Dunbar (1992), possessing culturally relevant knowledge, motivation and skills is related to general satisfaction with the overseas sojourn although this is not the same as saying that the sojourner's performance was effective.

In a comprehensive review of the literature, Dinges and Baldwin (1996) have identified a comparable set of dimensions and particular KSAAs that affect intercultural performance. The items that seem to have the best empirical support include low ethnocentrism, previous intercultural experience, awareness of self and culture, verbal and non-verbal communication skills, personality traits such as flexibility, empathy and tolerance, and technical competence. Applied research by Kelley and Meyers (1989), who identified emotional resilience, flexibility/openness, perceptual acuity, and personal autonomy as the defining features of sojourner effectiveness in the development of their Cross-Cultural Adaptability Inventory (CCAI), is consistent with these dimensions. A similar but expanded list has been offered by Kealey (1996) and includes empathy, respect, listening ability, realistic expectations, interest in local culture, flexibility, tolerance, technical skills, initiative, open-mindedness, sociability and positive self-image.

In general, there is reasonable agreement about the KSAAs that should contribute to intercultural competence, effectiveness and adjustment, both with respect to those that facilitate general adaptation during the cross-cultural transition and those that are job specific. However, as Dinges and Baldwin (1996) indicate in their review of this literature, many of the conclusions depend on anecdotal and impressionistic accounts rather than rigorous, quantitative empirical research.

Training techniques for crossing cultures

In this section we will describe the various training techniques used in cross-cultural orientation programmes, their strengths and weaknesses, and the training models from which they were derived. We will also provide examples of some of the items, exercises and procedures. A comprehensive review of specific instruments, simulations, films, videotapes, and other resources and teaching aids can be found in Cushner and Brislin (1996), Fowler and Mumford (1995), Gudykunst, Guzley and Hammer (1996) and Seelye (1996). Appendices A, B, and C in Kohls and Knight (1994) contain an annotated list of many of the most commonly used procedures.

Information-giving

The most common type of cross-cultural orientation takes the form of pro-viding prospective sojourners with information about the destination culture using a didactic approach (Gudykunst and Hammer, 1983). Travellers are presented with facts and figures, either in written or graphic form, about the climate, food, social relations, religious customs, and anything else the trainer may consider important. Techniques used include lectures, pamphlets, panel discussions, and question and answer sessions. There is also a growing body of popular books aimed at the culture traveller, some of which were cited in the chapter on Culture Learning (e.g. Axtell, 1993), as well as travel guides such as *The Lonely Planet* series, which contain some tips on how to negotiate cultural pitfalls. This kind of information is relatively easy to assemble and deliver and is based on the (**M**)emory principle of training. However, the effectiveness of such cognitive programmes is limited because: (a) the facts are often too general to have any clear, specific application in particular circumstances; (b) the facts tend to emphasise the exotic, such as what to do in a Buddhist temple, but ignore mundane but more commonly occurring events, such as how to hail a taxi; (c) such programmes give the false impres-sion that a culture can be learned in a few easy lessons, whereas all that they mostly convey is a superficial, incoherent and often misleading picture which glosses over that culture's hidden agenda (Hall, 1966); and (d) finally, even if the facts are retained (itself a doubtful proposition), they do not necessarily lead to action, or to the correct action. Not all didactic orientations suffer from all of these deficiencies, and the better ones provide information that can be quite useful. Nevertheless, it would be absurd to teach people how to drive a car by only giving them information about how to do it, yet that is exactly the principle on which programmes relying mainly on information-giving are based. It is therefore highly desirable that cognitive training should be combined with some form of experiential learning.

Cultural sensitisation

Programmes based on the principle of cultural sensitisation not only provide trainees with information about other cultures, but also try to increase the awareness of the participants about the cultural biases of their own behaviour. The aims are to compare and contrast their own cultural practices with what prevails elsewhere and to look at various behaviours from the perspective of each society. The underlying assumption of this approach is that it will increase sensitivity to and awareness of cultural relativity by accepting, or at least entertaining, the view that very few human values, beliefs and behaviours are absolute and universal (Adamopoulos and Lonner, 1994). The technique relies on the (**U**)nderstanding principle of training, and such programmes often operate with objectives at two levels: (1) to achieve self-awareness about the values and attitudes that are typically held by members of one's society, but may be rejected by other cultural groups; and (2) to gain insight into one's own personal traits, attitudes and prejudices.

A major psychological dimension on which people differ, both across and within cultures, is the extent to which they favour individualism or collectivism (I–C; Triandis, 1995a), a topic that was covered in the first chapter of this book. Research has suggested that the interpersonal effectiveness of individualists in contact with collectivists (and vice versa) increases if they can place themselves into the framework of the other cultural orientation (Bhawuk and Brislin, 1992; Singelis, 1994). Triandis and Singelis (1998) have argued that it is feasible to train people to become aware of and accept individual differences in collectivism and individualism; they also claim that this can be achieved by a questionnaire that gives participants feedback regarding their own I–C preferences. Gudykunst (1998b) likewise regards individualism–collectivism as a relevant dimension for inclusion in intracultural training programmes. However, we should acknowledge that no amount of training can resolve conflicts based on core value differences.

Simulations

Simulations have been defined as operating imitations of real-life processes (Sisk, 1995). In this section we will describe some procedures used to develop awareness of cultural differences utilising the simulation technique. Probably the best known and most widely used simulations are the Contrast-American and BAFA BAFA simulations (for a fuller description of these methods and their origins see Gudykunst and Hammer, 1983). In the Contrast-American role-plays, American trainees interact with persons who simulate values and beliefs that are diametrically opposed to American presumptions. The sessions are followed by discussions in which the contrasting underlying assumptions are explored.

In the BAFA BAFA game (Shirts, 1973), participants are randomly allocated to two hypothetical cultural groups that differ in their core values. The teams are given names (Alpha and Beta) and provided with written descriptions of the customs of their respective societies. The two teams are sent to separate rooms and are instructed to learn their own cultures. The groups then exchange visitors, simulating the sojourner and host experience for both Alpha and Beta members. The objective of this phase of the exercise is to learn about the other culture, gain an understanding of it, and brief members of their own culture on it.

Typically, returning participants report that they tried to understand the other culture by using their own culture as a frame of reference, leading to the observation that 'they are weird'. Other comments included 'good intentions are not enough . . . (you can still) completely misunderstand and offend the other culture' (Shirts, 1995, p. 95). Trainers can draw on such statements to get participants to analyse their experiences and reactions. In particular, the aim is to bring into awareness the strong tendencies towards ethnocentrism that the game evokes despite the totally arbitrary nature of the Alpha and Beta cultural norms.

BAFA BAFA has been used with school children, business organisations and government departments. Although the simulation has intuitive appeal, hard evidence for its effectiveness is scarce. In an experiment in which a group of trainees playing the BAFA BAFA game was compared with a group that received lecture-based training only, there were no between-group differences on quantitative measures of cultural sensitivity (Pruegger and Rogers, 1994). However, a subsidiary analysis showed that experiential learning had a greater effect than information-giving on one of the measures used in the study, a content analysis of comments made by the participants. In other words, although a quantitative analysis did not support the hypotheses, a qualitative analysis did, not an unusual outcome in this field. These results highlight some of the difficulties of evaluating culture training techniques, particularly those using an experiential approach.

In the Barnga game (Steinwachs, 1995), groups of players receive a modi-fied set of playing cards and a sheet of rules for playing a new card game called 'Five Tricks'. Once everyone has mastered the rules, the written instructions are taken away, and the trainer informs the players that they will now be taking part in a tournament during which they can no longer speak or write words. However, they are allowed to make gestures or draw pictures. When the game is over, the participants discuss their experiences. The aim of Barnga is to simulate intercultural communication difficulties.

In the Markhall simulation (Blohm, 1995), participants are assigned to two contrasting organisations with different management styles and values. The Creative Card Company follows practices that are characteristic of large Jap-anese corporations while the Ace Card Company is based on the American industrial model. For several hours the participants role-play working for these organisations, designing, producing and marketing greeting cards. The simulation has been used to facilitate the re-entry of American exchange students returning from Japan, in programmes aimed at preparing business persons for overseas assignments, and in raising the awareness of managers of multinational companies about cultural differences among their overseas branches.

Another simulation used in training international business personnel is Ecotonos (Saphiere, 1995). Participants are divided into three 'cultures' and provided with cards listing the rules in each culture. Each group talks about the meaning and manifestation of these rules. On the basis of these discus-sions they then create a story about how their culture developed. After the participants become acculturated to their own 'society', the individuals are assigned to 'multicultural' groups, that is, groups containing persons from each of the three original cultures, and given a task, such as preparing a budget or designing a marketing strategy. The participants learn to accommodate to each other's cultural negotiating styles and preferences.

Culture sensitisation and self-awareness programmes suffer from some of the same limitations as information-giving, particularly with respect to whether the learning will transfer from the classroom into the field. For instance, it is all very well for a Westerner to accept intellectually that gender inequality favouring males is the norm in some cultures. But it is another matter, when the person becomes a sojourner, to participate willingly in social interactions that at home would be regarded as harassing or oppressive. One of the authors of this book, whose publications include a learned analysis of the construct of cultural relativism (Bochner, 1979), offended his Filipino hosts by declining to accompany them to a cockfight, a popular sport in that country. Finally, although the simulations have face validity, and participants often become highly involved in the exercises (Gannon and Poon, 1997), empirical support for their effectiveness is sparse. This is not surprising because the issue here is not just whether the simulations have an immediate effect, but also whether the effects will generalise out of the classroom into the field and over time. Such empirical evaluations are extremely difficult to implement.

The critical incident technique

A number of authors have used the critical incident technique (Flanagan, 1954) as a training tool (Bennett, 1995; Dant, 1995; Pedersen, 1995; Wight, 1995). The method consists of a series of brief descriptions of social episodes where there is a misunderstanding or conflict arising from cultural differences between the actors. The incidents merely describe what happened and some of the feelings and reactions of the parties involved. The text does not explain why the misunderstanding occurred or the cultural basis for the conflict. The aim of the exercise is for the trainees to discover this during the debriefing sessions when these issues are explored in detail with the help of a facilitator.

For instance, one incident consists of a vignette about a Japanese exchange student staying with an America host family. The pupil spends all her time studying. Her American hosts try to persuade her to take some time off so that she can join in the family's activities. The student does not want to offend her hosts but is also worried that she will not do well in her exams if she takes their advice. In another example, an American administrator of an international residence hall on campus receives a complaint from an American student that his Middle Eastern roommate's predawn rituals, associated with the observance of the holy month of Ramadan, are extremely disturbing (Bennett, 1995). As with the other methods described previously, the purpose of the critical incidents technique is to increase the participants' awareness of their own culturally determined attitudes and their interpretations of the behaviour of other people.

Using a similar approach, Sorti (1994) generated a number of episodes describing brief, failed encounters between culturally disparate individuals. The misunderstandings are then explained in cultural terms. To illustrate, in an encounter involving what a mainstream American manager would regard as giving routine performance evaluation feedback to a subordinate from a Middle Eastern culture, the supervisor used the standard Anglo approach of listing the employee's strengths and weaknesses. The worker was gravely offended by the encounter, and because the supervisor's motivation was to help the employee to become more effective, the manager also was not pleased. The commentary noted that in Middle Eastern societies, shame or the public loss of face should be avoided, and if that is not possible, criticisms should be expressed discreetly and indirectly. It recommended that in such circumstances, supervisors should spend most of the interview in lavishing praise on the subordinate and mention any shortcomings only in passing. The subordinate would have understood what was being said, but honour would have been preserved.

Culture assimilators

Culture assimilators are based on a more sophisticated version of the critical incident technique and are informed by an explicit theoretical model that concerns the role that isomorphic attributions play in facilitating inter-personal communication. According to Triandis (1975), a major obstacle to effective cross-cultural communication is the inability of the participants to understand the causes of each other's behaviour, that is, to make correct attributions about the reasons for the other person's actions (Jaspars and Hewstone, 1982; Jones and Nisbett, 1971; Kelley, 1972). Effective intercultural relations require isomorphic attributions that correspond to the idea 'I assign the same cause for the other person's behaviour as they would for themselves'. The likelihood of making isomorphic attributions decreases as the divergence between the subjective cultures of the participants increases, and this is a major cause of mutual hostility and misunderstanding. Training involves teaching participants how to make 'accurate' behavioural attributions about each other's actions (Fiedler, Mitchell and Triandis, 1971; Foa and Chemers, 1967).

This is achieved through a device called the culture assimilator, also some-times called the intercultural sensitiser, which in effect is a programmed learning manual (Albert, 1983, 1995; Bochner and Coulon, 1997; Brislin, 1986, 1995; Brislin *et al.*, 1986; Cushner, 1989; Fiedler *et al.*, 1971; Hannigan, 1990; Mitchell *et al.*, 1972; Pearce, Kim and Lussa, 1998; Triandis, 1984). Earlier formats consisted of a booklet containing descriptions of episodes in which two culturally disparate individuals meet, but the procedure also lends itself to a computerised presentation. Each incident terminates in embarrassment, misunderstanding or interpersonal hostility. The trainee is then presented with four or five alternative explanations of what went wrong, which corres-pond to assigning different attributions to the observed behaviour. Only one of these attributions is correct from the perspective of the culture being learned. For instance, if the meeting is between an American and an Arab, and the American is the person being trained, then the 'correct' attribution is the one that most Arabs would make. The other three attributions are plausible and usually consistent with the attributions that Americans would make in such a situation, but which are wrong in the Arab context. The trainees select the answer they regard as correct and are then instructed to turn to a subsequent page where they are either praised if they have selected the 'right' answer or told why they were wrong if they selected an 'incorrect' answer. The excerpt from the Arab Culture Assimilator (see table 11.1), developed by the Training Research Laboratory at the University of Illinois (Symonds *et al.*, 1966), is typical of the technique.

Both culture-general and culture-specific assimilators have been developed. The former dwell on the generic issues that arise during most intercultural interactions, irrespective of the particular cultures involved or the roles of the individuals in contact. According to Brislin (1995), American business people in Japan, African foreign students in Western universities, or Palestinian Arabs in Israel, all share common problems – particularly the need to become aware of and respond appropriately to differences between their own and their hosts' cultures. However, most culture assimilators have been developed to train particular categories of persons-in-contact to cope with particular cultural conditions (Triandis, 1995b).

Culture-specific instruments have been developed for use in two contexts: for sojourners headed for particular destinations and in multicultural societies, for people from mainstream cultures dealing with members of subcultural groups (and vice versa). Examples of the latter include Australian hospitality industry workers serving Japanese tourists (Bochner and Coulon, 1997), mainstream Australian nurses interacting with Pitjantjatjara Australian Aborigines (O'Brien and Plooij, 1976), mainstream Americans interacting with Chinese (Leong and Kim, 1991), Korean, East Indian (Nitsche and Green, 1977), and Hispanic immigrants, Hispanic school children interacting with Anglo-American teachers, mainstream American social workers interacting with Mexican-Americans, white American supervisors interacting with African-American soldiers and subordinates respectively, and non-Navajos interacting with Navajos (cited in Albert, 1995). Examples of culture-specific assimilators designed for sojourners include American student volunteers going to Honduras to vaccinate villagers (O'Brien, Fiedler and Hewett, 1971), Americans working in China and Chinese working in the United States (Cushner and Brislin, 1997), American civilian employees destined to work in an American military establishment in Japan (Harrison, 1992), American Reserve Officer Training Corps cadets headed for Thailand (Mitchell and Foa, 1969), Americans working in Iran (Chemers, 1969), and American Peace Corps workers in various Asian and South American locations (Downs, 1969).

The culture assimilator technique relies on cognitive learning and the (U)nderstanding principle of training and, therefore, suffers from the already mentioned limitations inherent in such an approach. One of its strengths is that it is based on a sound theoretical principle, namely the importance of

Table 11.1 An example from the Arab Culture Assimilator

An American Peace Corps worker, living in an Arab village, must go into the large city nearby. He knows that the period he will be travelling is the period of Moslem religious observance which requires fasting during the daylight hours. However, he believes that the restaurants will remain open to serve those who wish to eat. Upon arriving at one of the city's largest restaurants, he is suprised to find it closed. What would explain this occurrence?

1. The owner was probably a Moslem, and since he was not able to eat, he did not wish anyone else to eat. Go to p. 136.
2. The Moslems are very hungry during this period, and if there were any restaurants open, they would not be able to maintain their fast. Go to p. 137.
3. The restaurant was probably open only for certain daylight hours, and the Peace Corps worker was not there at the right time. Go to p. 138.
4. Even if the restaurant remained open during the day, there would not be anyone who wished to eat. Go to p. 139.

p. 136. Your answer was 1: *The owner was probably a Moslem, and since he was not able to eat, he did not wish anyone else to eat.*
This answer is incorrect. The restaurant owner is a businessman as well as a Moslem. For him to close his restaurant so that others would be as hungry as he would be bad business.
Return to the scenario and try again.

p. 137. You chose your answer 2: *The Moslems are very hungry during this period, and if there were any restaurants open, they would not be able to maintain their fast.*
This is entirely incorrect. You did not think about your answer thoroughly.
Most Arabs are staunch Moslems who are quite willing to undergo great hardships to observe religious custom.
Return to the scenario and try again.

p. 138. You chose answer 3: *The restaurant was probably open only for certain daylight hours, and the Peace Corps worker was not there at the right time.*
It is evident by your response that you have completely missed the point.
This answer is incorrect. The restaurant remained closed throughout the daylight hours during the fasting period. If it remained open during daylight hours, the Peace Corps worker probably could have eaten a little later.
Return to the scenario and try again.

p. 139. Your choice was answer 4: *Even if the restaurant remained open during the day, there would not be anyone who wished to eat.*
This alternative is right. In choosing this answer you have shown that you are thinking.
The Arab countries are quite homogeneous in regard to religion, with 90–99% of the population being Moslem in some areas. Since these people are quite religious and observe religious customs rigorously, even if the restaurant remained open during the day, it would be largely without customers.
Go on to the next scenario.

isomorphic attributions in cross-cultural communication. It also has the advantage of giving immediate feedback, an important point in its favour. But a great deal depends on which particular critical incidents are selected to form the basic curriculum. Sometimes exotic, strange and hence less common events tend to be given greater prominence than the more frequently encountered day-to-day problems that make up the bread-and-butter content of intercultural contacts. Many of the authors cited in this section have noted the importance of selecting or generating appropriate incidents.

Experiential learning by doing

The limitations of information-based orientation programmes led to various attempts to expose trainees to supervised real or simulated second-culture experiences. Perhaps the most elaborate of these schemes was undertaken in the 1960s by the Peace Corps, who built a model Southeast Asian village on the Big Island of Hawaii and hired natives of the target countries to inhabit the site. American trainees spent several days or weeks in this village under expert guidance, gaining first-hand experience of what it is like to live in an Asian rural settlement (Downs, 1969; Textor, 1966). This approach is explicitly informed by the (**D**)oing principle of training, and there is some evidence that experiential learning is more effective than mere information-giving in the transfer of training from the classroom to the field (McDaniel, McDaniel and McDaniel, 1988).

Most organisations do not have, or are unwilling to commit, such massive resources to experiential culture training. More typically, behaviourally based culture-training programmes rely on role-playing encounters between trainees and persons pretending to come from some other culture, or if other-culture professional personnel are available, with them. The better pro-grammes also contain an evaluation component, which may take the form of a team of psychologists evaluating and perhaps fine-tuning the behaviour of the candidates in the field, as well as monitoring their sociocultural adjustment.

Thus, when the literature refers to experiential training, contrasting it with the didactic approach (e.g. Basadur, Wakabayashi and Takai, 1992; Gudykunst and Hammer, 1983), what is really being described are simula-tions whose verisimilitude to real life events may range from the very high to the slight. One reason why simulated interactions are said to be more effective than lectures is because it is assumed that they will achieve a greater level of trainee involvement. Still, that does not necessarily lead to more effective training outcomes. Indeed, that is exactly what Gannon and Poon (1997) found in a study in which they randomly assigned trainees to three conditions: what they called the 'integrative' approach, which consisted of brief lectures, discussions, video clips and group exercises; a video-based approach, in which participants watched three videos about cross-cultural experiences; and an experiential condition consisting of the BAFA BAFA simulation. No differences were found between the three conditions on the focal dependent variable of cultural awareness. However, participants in the experiential training condition reported more favourable reactions towards the training than the subjects in the other two groups. They were more satis-fied with the training process and perceived it to be more useful and relevant, suggesting that the experiential approach was more motivating. But none of this translated into higher levels of cultural awareness.

Evaluation

Kohls (1995) reviewed the advantages and disadvantages of the various training methods, including lectures, debriefing, interviews, discussions, case studies, critical incidents, role-plays, simulations, games, films, slide shows, videos, and on the job training. Up to fifteen advantages and disadvantages are listed in each category. Aspects that are regarded as positive include structure, goal directedness, not too long, interactive, attention-grabbing, real-life application, skill and process oriented, experiential, and fun. However, it should be noted that this is a list of desirable attributes, not characteristics whose effectiveness has been confirmed empirically.

As has already been noted, reviews evaluating the effectiveness of cross-cultural training come up with only qualified support for their usefulness in terms of the criteria presented earlier in this chapter (e.g. Black and Mendenhall, 1990). One reason for the gap between promise and delivery is the unsystematic nature of most training programmes. Another is their emphasis on information-giving and cognitive methods of delivery rather than on procedures with a behavioural and affective emphasis (Kealey and Protheroe, 1996). And yet, behaviourally oriented interventions lend themselves more readily to empirical evaluations. As George Guthrie wrote a quarter of a century ago, 'If a supplementary school feeding program is accomplishing its objectives, the results should show up on a set of bathroom scales rather than attitude scales' (Guthrie, 1977, p. 137).

Landis, Brislin and Hulgus (1985) demonstrated this in a laboratory study that measured the effects of culture assimilator training in terms of subsequent behavioural ratings involving interactions with minority group confederates. Appropriate control groups were included in the design of the experiment. The study found a significant improvement in making isomorphic attributions among those participants who had been exposed to the assimilator training. Because the culture assimilator technique does lend itself to being evaluated against specific behavioural outcomes, the literature contains a number of studies that provide qualified evidence for its usefulness (e.g. Harrison, 1992; Mitchell *et al.*, 1972; O'Brien, Fiedler and Hewett, 1971; O'Brien and Plooij, 1976; Weldon *et al.*, 1975; Worchell and Mitchell, 1972).

Finally, to put the entire preceding material into perspective, the vast majority of culture travellers, as well as those who come into contact with members of other cultures in their own societies, receive no systematic culture-training whatsoever (Harris and Moran, 1991). In practice, most organisations select their staff on the basis of technical competence and experience, ignoring the non-technical skills and knowledge required for success in another culture (Kealey, 1996). Nor are substantial resources devoted to pre-departure briefing (Kealey and Protheroe, 1996). It is assumed that high performing people at home will also perform well overseas. The little 'training' that does occur is done informally by 'old hands' who pass on useful information to the 'new chums'. This in itself may not be such a bad thing. One of the requirements of a successful culture-trainer is to be a mediating person (Bochner, 1981), that is, a person who is intimately familiar with both cultures and can act as a link between them, representing each to the other. In theory 'old hands' should have that rare capacity but, in practice, some may have highly specialised, distorted or even prejudiced views of one or both of the cultures and perpetuate these distortions in the informal training they impart to highly impressionable newcomers.

TRAINING FOR MULTICULTURAL LIVING

A great deal has been written about intrasocietal multicultural relations. Groups and interactions that have been studied include immigrants (Eitinger and Schwarz, 1981; Stoller, 1966; Taft, 1966, 1973; Watson, 1977); guest workers (Böker, 1981); black–white contact in Britain, the United States, and South Africa (Banton, 1965, 1967; Bloom, 1971; Jones, 1994; Katz, 1976; Klineberg, 1971; Pettigrew, 1964, 1969); and relations between mainstream and aboriginal inhabitants of countries such as Australia (Kearney and McElwain, 1976; Stevens, 1971, 1972; Throssell, 1981), New Zealand (Ritchie, 1981), the United States (Bennett, 1994; Darnell, 1972; Daws, 1968; Gallimore, Boggs and Jordan, 1974; Trimble, 1976), and Canada (Berry, 1975). However, until quite recently, culture orientation has not been a feature in this area.

This is changing. Three groups in particular are now being given systematic training: the original inhabitants of some of the more developed countries; various minority groups within multicultural societies; and specific occupational groups whose work entails interacting with foreigners and members of various subcultures. Training programmes with indigenous and minority people are based on the principle of imparting bicultural competence, that is, assisting the participants to function effectively in both their culture of origin as well as the dominant culture that engulfed them. A specific, core aim of these programmes is to ensure that trainees do not lose their original cultural identity and that they are not pushed into having to choose one culture over the other (LaFromboise *et al.*, 1993; Rashid, 1984). The aim of occupationally-based training programmes is to assist mainstream members to interact effectively with clients, customers or patients from particular minority or foreign groups. Examples of each type of training programme will now be presented.

Training for bicultural competence

LaFromboise and Rowe (1983) described an assertion programme aimed at teaching native Americans to function effectively in their tribal groups as well as in the wider American society. The following target situations were included: teaching clients to make their desires or preferences known in both native and non-native settings; challenging employers who stereotype native Americans; openly expressing disagreement with natives and non-natives; maintaining composure when called names such as 'Chief', 'Injun', 'Squaw', or 'Brave'; standing up to programme administrators; dealing with interference and unwanted help; refusing unreasonable requests from both natives and non-natives; and making complaints. The list was formed after lengthy discussions with mental health providers, tribal leaders and programme administrators. Video and live-modelling techniques were used and included items such as eye contact, timing, loudness of voice, content of message, and cultural appropriateness. Both intracultural and intercultural (native-to-white) feedback was provided, and the effectiveness of the programme was evaluated by judges rating videotapes of the participants in pre- and post-training role-plays. The LaFromboise and Rowe (1983) study provides an excellent model for training programmes aimed at improving the social competence of minority persons, both in their dealings with the majority culture, particularly its officialdom, and in their contacts with members of their own ethnic group. It employs techniques based on all three **MUD** principles and includes an explicit evaluation component. Very few training programmes meet these high standards.

Training for occupational skills for workers with minority clients

The issue of providing culturally appropriate counselling and psychotherapy to non-mainstream clients was discussed elsewhere in this book (see Chapter 3 on culture learning). Paralleling the acknowledgement of that problem, there is now a growing literature on how to train counsellors in cultural skills. It is beyond the scope of this book to deal in detail with this topic, other than to identify and list the core principles of multicultural counselling.

The main obstacle to the delivery of appropriate interventions to minority clients is the Eurocentric bias of contemporary psychology. The theoretical orientation underlying service delivery, how it is organised, taught, and practised, and its intellectual roots have all been dominated by Western thought. As Lunt and Poortinga (1996) noted, most psychologists live and work in the United States. They also publish and read books and journals that are produced there, with a few British contributions making up the rest. Furthermore, the science and practice of psychology in the United States is dominated by white, middle-class, male attitudes and values (Leach and Carlton, 1997; Pedersen, 1994a,b; Sue, Ivey and Pedersen, 1996; Sue and Sue,

1990), and traditional training programmes reflect these values. To correct this bias, there is currently a concerted move in the United States to train psychological practitioners to develop a more multicultural orientation in their work (for recent reviews of this literature see Leach, 1997; Lonner, 1997; Sue, 1997). There have also been some attempts to make the teaching of psychology more culturally diverse (Lonner and Malpass, 1994), but these have met with only limited success.

Other occupational groups who are now beginning to receive specific training to deal more effectively with non-mainstream clients include police officers (Holdaway, 1998; Oakley, 1989, 1993), employees in the tourist and hospitality industries (Bochner and Coulon, 1997; Laws, Moscardo and Faulkner, 1998), and bank officers (Bochner and Hesketh, 1994). More generally, three sets of influences have sparked organisations across the whole industrial and commercial spectrum to provide their employees with at least a minimum of diversity training (Ferdman and Brody, 1996). These are moral, legal and competitive pressures, respectively.

Cultural pluralism or multiculturalism is often represented as a moral imperative (Fowers and Richardson, 1996), which in practice means increasing awareness of unjust practices based on ethnic background and reducing intergroup inequities. Organisations which engage in diversity training do so from a mixture of moral considerations and self-interest based on the belief that their equity initiatives will result in the more effective use of their human resources (Buntaine, 1994). It is also assumed that there will be an increase in customer approval and a reduction in lawsuits and complaints. Although all of this makes intuitive sense, there is very little empirical evidence available to support these claims.

Finally, how best to train cross-cultural trainers has also received considerable attention (Paige, 1986; Ptak, Cooper and Brislin, 1995). It is beyond the scope of this chapter to go into details, other than to note that the issues relating to sojourner training are duplicated with respect to those conducting the training. Thus, the list of desirable KSAAs for culture trainers includes personal characteristics such as self-awareness, tolerance for ambiguity, and cognitive and behavioural flexibility; past cross-cultural experience; motivation; interpersonal and communication skills; and knowledge of the field. Respect for the local culture is also a desirable trait as it is being increasingly recognised that intercultural training has ethical implications, in particular with respect to the consequences of the asymmetrical power that often characterises the relationship between trainers and trainees (Paige and Martin, 1996). But again, most of the trainer attributes have been identified on intuitive grounds rather than on the basis of a thorough job analysis, and most trainers do not receive a great deal of formal training, their main qualification being personal cross-cultural experience.

CHAPTER SUMMARY

Culture training has application in two broad areas. The first and major effort has been to provide pre-departure orientation to individuals about to undertake an extended sojourn abroad. A second, less-developed field has concentrated on teaching members of multicultural societies to become more aware of and sensitive to each other's values and practices and to impart specific job-related skills to majority members who work with minority clients or customers.

Several training models exist, each with its own implications for intervention and practice. The main training techniques include information-giving, cultural sensitisation simulations and games, attribution exercises, and culture-based social-skills training. The various techniques reflect the **MUD** principles of training, that is, they emphasise either **M**emory, **U**nderstanding, or **D**oing in their approaches. The techniques also differ according to whether the training methods are didactic or experiential.

It was suggested that the content of training curricula should be based on a 'job analysis' of the KSAAs – the knowledge, skills, abilities, and attitudes, required to function effectively in the destination culture. In the case of training for multicultural living an analysis of the competencies required to perform proficiently in both the original and the contact cultural networks should guide the curriculum planning. Evidence suggests that although all of the methods have some utility, the more practical and less abstract they are, the more successful they will be. The most effective training combines a cognitive and informational approach with systematically developed behavioural exercises and includes an explicit evaluation component.

Social skills and behavioural techniques are particularly suited for the training of minority members in multicultural societies. The aim of such programmes is to help non-mainstream members to become more competent in their dealings with the dominant culture while retaining the practices and values of their own ethnic group. The social skills approach has also been used to train mainstream service-providers to take the cultural backgrounds of their clients into account.

12 Conclusion

THE ABCs OF 'CULTURE SHOCK'

The aim of this book has been to review the current state of knowledge about the determinants, effects and correlates of culture contact, the expression we have used to refer to interpersonal interactions between people from different cultural or ethnic backgrounds. The term 'culture shock' appears in the title of the book to draw attention to the fact that such interactions can be, and usually are, difficult, awkward and stressful. However, we have gone well beyond the original meaning of the term that was introduced by Oberg in 1960. First, unlike his early formulation that regarded 'culture shock' as a negative, passive reaction to a set of noxious circumstances, we have treated people's responses to unfamiliar cultural environments as an active process of dealing with change. Second, we have introduced a model of 'culture shock' that explicitly distinguishes three components of this process: Affect, Behaviour and Cognitions, that is, how people feel, behave, think and perceive when exposed to second-culture influences. In turn, we have linked each of these elements to particular theoretical frameworks that provide a foundation for the empirical research exploring these issues. Finally, we have used the principle of cultural distance to account for the differences in the extent to which people experience and cope with 'culture shock'.

The affective component of culture contact closely resembles Oberg's initial representation of 'culture shock' as a buzzing confusion. Oberg had in mind people who were more or less suddenly exposed to a completely unfamiliar setting and largely overwhelmed by it. Some of the affective responses consistently mentioned in the literature included confusion, anxiety, disorientation, suspicion, bewilderment, perplexity and an intense desire to be elsewhere. Early theoretical accounts of these responses and remedial action to reduce 'culture shock' relied heavily on clinical constructs. Personality traits were also invoked to explain why some people are more prone to suffer from 'culture shock' than others.

More recent formulations emphasising the affective component of intercultural contact draw on the stress and coping literature, particularly the work of Lazarus, to account for the negative emotions aroused by exposure to unfamiliar cultural settings. This approach highlights the factors that reduce the distress of culture contact, including personal resources, such as self-efficacy and emotional resilience, and interpersonal assets, such as social support. It also suggests various interventions. For example, personal characteristics may be considered in the selection of candidates for overseas assignments in an effort to increase the likelihood of successful adaptation. Interpersonal assets may be enhanced by on site mentoring, participation in ethnic organisations, and the systematic provision of social support. And traditional counselling, particularly interventions that assist in the development of effective coping skills, is useful for remediation.

The behavioural component of 'culture shock' is associated with the concept of culture learning, an extension of the social skills approach, which in turn is based on Michael Argyle's model of interpersonal behaviour as a mutually skilled performance. The core idea is that the rules, conventions and assumptions that regulate interpersonal interactions, including both verbal and non-verbal communication, vary across cultures. Visitors or sojourners in unfamiliar settings who lack culturally relevant social skills and knowledge will have difficulty in initiating and sustaining harmonious relations with their hosts. Their culturally inappropriate behaviour will lead to misunderstandings and may cause offence. It is also likely to make them less effective in both their professional and personal lives. In other words, culturally unskilled persons are less likely to achieve their goals, whatever they might be. Expatriate executives may alienate their local counterparts, overseas students may underachieve academically, hospitality industry workers may offend tourists (and vice versa), and the job prospects of migrants may be adversely affected.

The intervention techniques implied by the behavioural model are quite straightforward. A necessary condition of functioning effectively in a second-culture environment is to acquire relevant basic social skills through behavioural culture training, mentoring and learning about the historical, philosophical and sociopolitical foundations of the host society. Incidentally, the culture learning or behavioural component of 'culture shock' is also related to much of the negative affect associated with culture contact. People who stumble about socially like the proverbial bull in a china shop are quite likely to develop a sense of anxiety, uncertainty and ultimately lowered self esteem. Conversely, people who are anxious, depressed and withdrawn are less likely to make efforts to develop culture-appropriate skills.

The third element of the model is the cognitive component. Several theoretical traditions were brought into play in this regard. Perhaps the broadest is the notion that culture consists of shared meanings. People interpret material, interpersonal, institutional, existential and spiritual events as cultural manifestations, and these vary across cultures. When cultures come into contact, such established 'verities' lose their apparent inevitability. For instance, when persons from a male-dominated culture find themselves in a society that practices gender equality, the conflict between these two irreconcilable positions spills over into the cognitive workings of both visitors and hosts. It affects how the participants see each other, how they regard themselves, and whether either party will be influenced to change their views as a consequence of the contact. In our treatment of this issue, we have concentrated on the interpersonal beliefs and perceptions that culture contact evokes and on the changes or resistance to change in the participants' self-construals.

As such, we have made a distinction between looking outward and looking inward. In the former case, we have referred to attribution theory and research to explain some of the otherwise irrational behaviour that is the hallmark of intergroup prejudice and discrimination. We have also discussed stereotypes and how these may facilitate or impede intergroup relations. In the latter case, we have considered how people define their own identity in order to cope with an assault on their definition of social reality. In doing this we have drawn on the writings of John Berry and the early work by Bochner on the four alternatives open to people facing this predicament.

First, individuals can respond to second-culture influences by remaining staunchly monocultural in their traditions of origin and, if anything, becoming more ethnocentric in the process. Second, newcomers can succumb utterly to their new culture. They can assimilate, identifying with it totally, and become monocultural in it. Usually, such people will also abandon their culture of origin. Third, persons in contact can synthesise the best elements of both cultural traditions and become bicultural or mediating persons. The fourth alternative harks back to the early days of the twentieth century when sociologists such as Park and Stonequist talked about the marginal syndrome, referring to people who vacillate between their various cultures, identifying with neither, nor for that matter being accepted in either.

Tajfel's Social Identity Theory was used to put these responses into the context of intergroup relations. The 'selves' (the Who Am I?s) that individuals develop, maintain and sometimes change, largely derive from and are supported by the various groups to which they belong. These 'selves' are also influenced by the nature and quality of the relationships across various social, cultural, ethnic, and national groups. Consequently, interventions drawing their theoretical sustenance from the cognitive/social identity component of 'culture shock' usually involve some form of sensitivity training, emphasising the cultural relativity of most values, the advantages of cultural diversity, the validity of all cultural systems and tolerance of ambiguity.

Although it is relatively straightforward to point to the defining criteria of 'culture shock' with respect to its affective and behavioural elements and their adaptive and maladaptive outcomes, the specification of the cognitive indicators of 'culture shock' is a more complex matter. There would be widespread agreement that anxiety, confusion, low self-esteem and a sense of helplessness are undesirable experiences. And as Plato reminded us, knowledge is power, and most commentators would agree that culture travellers who are socially unskilled and uninformed with respect to their new society operate under a handicap. However, when it comes to second-culture induced perceptions, cognitions and self-definitions, the answer as to which of these will be advantageous or adaptive for the individuals and groups concerned will depend on the specific circumstances that have evoked them. Consequently, although we have discussed psychological and sociocultural outcomes of intercultural contact as indicators of affective and behavioural adaptation, we have not referred to a cognitive-based equivalent. This is graphically illustrated in Figure 12.1, which shows that the adaptive and maladaptive consequences of intrapersonal, interpersonal and intergroup cognitions may ultimately manifest themselves in affective and behavioural domains.

The difficulties involved in defining 'adaptiveness' can be illustrated with reference to both inward and outward-looking cognitions. For instance, in many cases a prejudiced attitude towards culturally different individuals and groups can be highly functional for the holder of these opinions, which is why such beliefs are so difficult to change. The social identity literature that we reviewed provides many examples where in-group esteem is increased by means of the active denigration of selected out-groups. Although such ethnocentric opinions may lack an empirical base, they are nevertheless adhered to because of the reassurance and heightened self-worth they produce in the holder of these beliefs. One therefore has to conclude that although racist and prejudiced practices may be seen as fundamentally objectionable and as causing havoc at the level of international relations, they are also capable of bestowing measurable psychological benefits on particular individuals.

The same problem arises with respect to the inward-looking side of the equation. In tight, predominantly monocultural societies it appears adaptive for newcomers to assimilate and for mainstreamers to avoid other cultural influences. As an example of the latter point, we reviewed studies of returning Japanese expatriates. These returnees frequently experienced social rejection due to a perceived loss of the core features of Japanese cultural identity.

A similar issue arises in societies that contain ethnic groups who are descended from the original, precontact inhabitants of the territory, such as native Americans and aboriginal Australians. Some members of these groups have argued that it would be in their interests to develop and maintain separatist, monocultural social structures and identities as a way of preserving the distinctiveness of their cultures. They may well have a point. Not only are there genuine social and political considerations, but there are also a number of studies that have shown separatism is positively associated with psychological well-being in members of native cultures.

In societies that genuinely value cultural diversity, it is clearly adaptive to develop and maintain a bicultural, mediating identity. This will give such persons greater social access to the various subgroups that make up these societies, as well as affording increased employment opportunities in those industries that operate in culturally heterogeneous environments. In addition

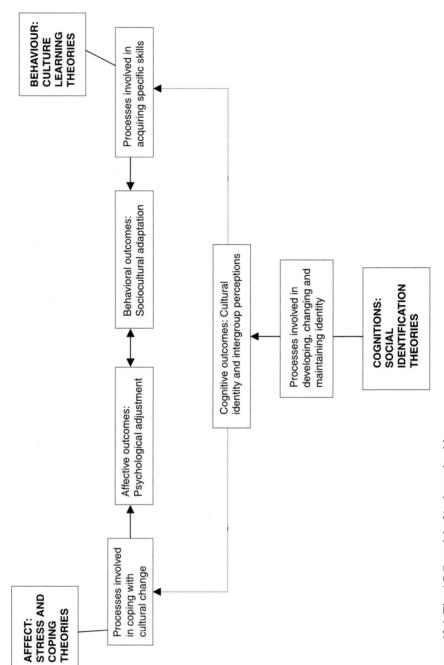

Figure 12.1 The ABC model of 'culture shock'

to these social benefits, a bicultural identity has also been associated with a number of positive psychological outcomes.

About the only cognitive response to second-culture influences that has fairly obvious adverse consequences is the marginal syndrome, and even here the evidence is not completely unequivocal. The literature contains many studies showing that the mental and physical health of marginal persons is adversely affected by their in-between status. However, some researchers have suggested that marginalised people voluntarily choose that option and that as archetypal individualists, they are not adversely affected by the consequences. There are also studies showing that some persons are motivated by their marginality to become high achievers, driving them to succeed in their occupation or profession. So once again, even a marginal identity resulting from culture contact must be regarded as a mixed blessing, because of its potential to have some positive outcomes.

INTERCULTURAL INTERACTIONS: THEN AND NOW

Between-society contact

Another core feature of our approach to 'culture shock' is that it explicitly distinguishes within-culture from between-culture contact. The earlier treatments of 'culture shock' were mainly concerned with the effects of contact that occurs between members of different societies, that is, where a person from one culture travels to or visits another. These culture travellers have been called visitors or sojourners in the literature, and members of the receiving country have been referred to as hosts. One of the distinguishing features of visitors is that their journeys have specifiable purposes and definitive time frames. Visitors are expected to return to their country of origin after fulfilling their goals although the time period can range from a few days, as in the case of tourists, to several years with students and expatriates. Another aspect of the short-term sojourn is that the duration and extent of non-trivial contact between visitors and members of the host societies vary considerably.

Many sojourners tend to be relatively inexperienced, untrained travellers who undergo an abrupt transition from their own culture to a new and unfamiliar environment. Oberg's version of 'culture shock' as buzzing confusion was a reasonably accurate description of what people in such circumstances actually experience. Despite the popularity of this construct in the sojourner literature, however, it has provided us only with a limited understanding of culture contact and change. Early writings about 'culture shock' were largely atheoretical in nature, narrowly focused on feelings and affect, and relatively silent about effective, theory-driven remedial action. A more comprehensive perspective, such as the ABC framework that informs this book, is required to do justice to the topic.

One other aspect of between-society contact is worth noting. Because sojourners embark on journeys to achieve particular purposes, the outcomes of the transition are capable of being evaluated. In theory, tourists can be measured on how satisfied they are with their visits; the academic achievements of students can be assessed; the performance of business travellers can be quantified in terms of various indicators, as can the efforts of medical, technical and aid workers. Evaluation studies are now being conducted more frequently; however, there is still room for more systematic studies of sojourn outcomes.

Early work on tourists and sojourners usually ignored any effects of their presence on the members and institutions of their host societies. The assumptions were that the sojourn is basically a one-way process and that a host society is too monolithic to be affected significantly by the strangers in its midst. If anyone's psychology should be influenced by the contact, it should be the visitors – not their hosts. This view is now changing, particularly with respect to tourists, but also in the case of student sojourners. Both tourists and students have become significant contributors to the export earnings of many receiving countries, and it makes pragmatic sense to assess what impact, if any, their presence has on the physical and sociopolitical environments of the host countries. Finally, those wishing to use between-society contact as a means of increasing intergroup harmony and mutual understanding across cultures have a special interest in monitoring the effects of such contact in both hosts and visitors.

Within-society contact

We have referred to the second category of cross-cultural interaction as within-society contact. The defining characteristic of these contacts is that they occur among culturally diverse members of groups within the borders of particular nation states. What distinguishes these contacts from between-society sojourns is their permanency. Newcomers are residents and have no intention of leaving after a set period of time – their new location is their home. The main categories of these culture travellers include immigrants, refugees and the offspring of both groups, usually including at least the second generation.

As was the case with the sojourn literature, early psychological research on within-society contact dealt mainly with the affective correlates of being a newcomer and an outsider. A major aspect of this research was a preoccupation with the potential association between mental health and migration. And because until relatively recently the official policy of most receiving countries was to encourage migrants to assimilate, the various alternate ways of establishing a migrant identity received very little attention. It was assumed that in time the immigrants would develop a core monocultural identity resembling that of their hosts. The same assumption was made with respect to the cultural composition of the receiving societies, the expectation being that they would absorb the newcomers without sustaining any major changes.

The notion of a multicultural society is a relatively recent development. Although the idea was discussed in the first edition of this book, it did not receive the emphasis that we have given it in the present work. At that time examples of between-society culture contact were still the major focus of the 'culture shock' literature. Since then, there has been a gradual increase in interest in intercultural relations that take place within societies, reflecting the greater cultural diversity characterising many contemporary nation states. These trends reflect the increase in immigration and refugee movements.

Another significant contribution to within-society ethnic diversity has been the gradual elimination of race as a criterion for admitting or excluding immigrants. Australia, for instance, maintained an official White Australia immigration policy well into the early 1970s. Other Western receiving societies also tended to favour immigrants from European countries over migrants from Asia or Africa. These policies have now been declared discriminatory, opening the doors to immigrants and refugees from all over the world.

The practical consequences of these changes have seen the establishment of substantial Southeast and East Asian communities in the larger Australian, Canadian, British, and American cities, as well as large Hispanic communities in parts of the United States, and African and Caribbean communities in Britain. One of the effects of these developments has been to increase the perceived cultural distance between the receiving and immigrant groups in those cities experiencing a large influx of non-traditional migrants. For instance, since the end of the Second World War, Sydney has absorbed a steady stream of European migrants from countries such as Britain, Poland, Yugoslavia, Hungary, Greece, Italy and the Netherlands. Because the appearance of these newcomers did not differ markedly from the majority ethnic group in Australia, their culture-distance (similarity) index, had it been measured, would have ranged from low in the case of the Northern Europeans to medium with respect to Southern Europeans. However, the large numbers of newcomers from Vietnam, China, Indonesia, Hong Kong, and other countries in Asia, constitute a highly visible and distinctive group of culturally distant immigrants. It has now dawned on the long-standing members of the receiving society, as well as the recently established European migrant communities, that the ethnic composition of their society is changing. In particular there has been the realisation that they are now sharing their country with relatively large numbers of people whose cultures differ significantly from the mainstream ethos. This increase in the range of cultural diversity also has implications for core state institutions such as the education system, industrial and organisational practices, and the administration of law and order. The Australian experience is replicated in most of the other major receiving countries and is now being reflected in a growth in research on within-society culture contact, some of which we reviewed in this book.

THE FUTURE

Predicting the future is a hazardous business. Nevertheless, there are distinctive trends that can serve as a basis for cautious forecasting. In this final section of the book we set out our views about what we believe will be some of the main developments in cross-cultural relations. As in previous treatments of this topic, we will distinguish within- from between-society culture contact.

Between-society relations

The carriers of between-society contact are the various sojourning groups described in Chapters 6, 7 and 8. A world-wide convergence can be observed among the institutional structures that provide the behaviour settings for these groups. International business practices are being unified through the globalisation of industry and commerce. Ownership is becoming increasingly centralised through mergers and acquisitions. The bigger multinationals now have operations in most of the countries of the world, and their brands are recognised everywhere. Their products have been standardised to the extent that a McDonald's hamburger, a Coca Cola drink, a chocolate Mars Bar, a Toyota car, or a Holiday Inn room are virtually identical irrespective of where on earth they are being consumed or used. This means that work and organisational structures also tend to become standardised.

In terms of the central interest of the book, one consequence of this structural convergence has been a gradual decrease in the cultural distance of the work environments of international business people. Expatriates will still have to adjust to aspects of their wider host society, the ease of their adjustment being a function of the distance between it and their culture of origin. But in the future, the work-related adjustment of expatriates is likely to depend much more on conventional industrial and commercial issues and increasingly less on the sorts of cultural factors discussed in this book.

Tertiary education is also undergoing global homogenisation. The students who study abroad are often members of the middle class and are likely to have attended local secondary schools or colleges that are patterned on Western educational institutions. There is also an increasing trend for British, Australian, and American universities to own and operate junior colleges in emerging Southeast Asian countries, which they then use as feeders to their own institutions. Such subsidiaries act not just as educational preparatory schools, but also orient the students towards Western educational practices and expectations. As in the case of international business travellers, the cumulative effect of these developments is to reduce the cultural distance between international students and their overseas host institutions.

Finally, the trend towards global homogenisation is particularly evident in the tourist industry which, when viewed through the eyes of a cross-cultural psychologist, has as one of its main goals the reduction or elimination of cultural distance between tourists and their destinations. As we saw in Chapter 6, this is achieved by sanitising the experiences of tourists from the more extreme aspects of the local scene. It is also accomplished by protecting tourists from possible cultural affronts by cocooning them in package tours and international hotels where the only locals they encounter are service staff trained not to disturb their sensibilities.

Expatriate executives, student sojourners, and 'package' tourists are likely to find their intercultural encounters easier to manage as certain aspects of their work, study and recreational environments become more homogenised. This does not imply, however, that societies world-wide are uniformly heading towards social and psychological convergence. No doubt there are broad homogenising influences such as the globalisation of the entertainment business, the news media, and the internet. Still, there is considerable debate as to whether these factors drastically reduce or eliminate fundamental cross-cultural differences (Poortinga, 1997; Smith and Bond, 1998). Rather than wholesale endorsement of the view that cultures are becoming increasingly homogeneous, we favour the principle of functional convergence, that is, the homogenisation of psychological and social attributes that are functional in adapting to the demands of increasing industrial and technological development (Yang, 1988). We also believe that 'modern' and 'traditional' values can coexist without conflict and that these values are likely to be played out in different domains or social contexts (Kâğitçibaşi, 1994). If this is the case, there will always be broader sociocultural issues, traditions, values and practices that sojourners must be equipped to handle while living in a new and different cultural environment.

The functional convergence view of the future suggests that because aspects of between-society sojourns will become increasingly less like those of a cross-cultural encounter, the adjustment, coping and culture learning requirements of sojourners will also become less critical. One of the benefits of this may be a slight increase in the level of harmonious intercultural relations. More widespread convergence, however, would be costly to societies on at least two counts. First, cultural diversity, like biodiversity, provides insurance for the survival of the species by guaranteeing that all its adaptive 'eggs' are not put into one 'basket'. Second, if variety is the spice of life, and widespread convergence occurs, the next 50 years will see a slide towards the dulling of societies.

Within-society relations

Based on present trends, it is difficult to be sanguine about the future with respect to the nature of intergroup relations in multicultural societies. Since the end of the Second World War, the world has technically been at peace, and no major international armed conflicts have been recorded during that time. However, millions of people, most of them civilian bystanders, have died in a continuous stream of vicious civil wars. Very few parts of the world have been untouched by this modern version of the plague. A partial list of afflicted places where murder and mayhem are a depressingly frequent occurrence includes the former Yugoslavia, the former Soviet Union, India, Pakistan, Sri Lanka, parts of Africa and South America, Northern Ireland, the Middle East, Spain, Cyprus, and Indonesia. In a recent review of the literature on interethnic conflict, Isajiw (2000) states that in addition to the high profile conflicts that stand out because they are continuously in the media, many interethnic clashes are rarely reported. Various authorities cited by Isajiw estimate that in the post-Second World War period, between 233 and 295 groups were involved in hostilities directly related to interethnic issues.

Interethnic hostilities may be dependent upon a number of factors that have been discussed in this book: social categorisation, group-serving biases, unequal or limited access to resources, differences in values and ideologies, prejudice, and perceived threat. It is paradoxical that while between-society culture contact is becoming more benign, relations within some culturally heterogeneous nations are increasingly fraught. Indeed, acrimonious intergroup relations within nations have been largely responsible for the steadily increasing number of refugees, and this shows no signs of abating.

To balance this depressing account and conclude on a more cheerful note, the world also contains many examples of apparently successful multicultural societies, such as Australia, Canada, and Singapore. In these instances we find national policies designed to improve intergroup relations by simultaneously encouraging the development of vital ethnic communities and promoting mutual interaction and sharing. And there is at least some empirical evidence that increased intergroup contact under conditions of high ethnic vitality and low threat fosters more harmonious relations.

Admittedly, the acid test for these countries is yet to come. Many multicultural nations still have a dominant majority composed of established ethnic groups, and most have a fairly homogeneous mainstream that defines the ethnic identity of the respective nation state. However, if present immigration trends persist, this may change. For instance, there has been considerable debate in the media about the increasing Southeast Asian presence in Australia and Canada, and alarm has been raised in Singapore about the threat of Western values. There may come a point when the mainstream will start to actively resist a further transformation of their societies. Such trends are already evident in European countries such as Germany and France with large and growing non-European immigrant communities. If societies are to be truly multicultural, however, they must acknowledge the 'mutuality of accommodation' and recognise that both newcomers and members of the receiving society change as a result of contact (Beiser, 1999, p. 45).

FINAL REMARKS

In this book we have attempted to review the recent literature on culture contact and to relate contemporary theory and research to earlier work described in the first edition of *Culture Shock*. Our review has shown that the quantity of research on intercultural contact has increased dramatically over the last 15 years. In connection with this exponential increment, the quality of contemporary research has also improved. Studies are now more systematically guided by theories taken from various areas of psychology – social, developmental, personality, cross-cultural, and health. Research designs are more robust, and statistical analyses are more sophisticated. We regard all of these initiatives as healthy developments in the field.

Despite the positive developments, there is still a tendency for research on culture contact to be fragmented and disjointed. To a large extent the literature on tourists, sojourners, immigrants and refugees has evolved in parallel streams, and while there have been some examples of cross-fertilisation, there have been only limited attempts at integration. We believe that there are common themes running through the culture contact literature, and despite differences in emphases, that theory and research can be synthesised into a coherent body of knowledge. This has been a major objective of this book and our modest contribution to the field.

References

Abbott, M. (Ed.). (1989). *Refugee resettlement and well-being*. Auckland: Mental Health Foundation of New Zealand.

Abe, H. and Wiseman, R. (1983). 'A cross-cultural confirmation of the dimensions of intercultural effectiveness'. *International Journal of Intercultural Relations, 7*, 53–67.

Abe, J., Talbot, D. M. and Geelhoed, R. J. (1998). 'Effects of a peer program on international student adjustment'. *Journal of College Student Development, 39*, 539–547.

Abe, J., Zane, N. and Chun, K. (1994). 'Differential responses to trauma: Migration-related discriminants of Posttraumatic Stress Disorder among Southeast Asian refugees'. *Journal of Community Psychology, 22*, 121–135.

Abo, T. (1994). *Hybrid factory: The Japanese production system in the United States*. New York: Oxford University Press.

Aboud, F. (1987). 'The development of ethnic self-identification and attitudes'. In J. S. Phinney and M. Rotheram (Eds), *Children's ethnic socialization: Pluralism and development* (pp. 32–55). Newbury Park, CA: Sage.

Aboud, F. and Skerry, S. (1984). 'The development of ethnic attitudes: A critical review'. *Journal of Cross-cultural Psychology, 15*, 3–34.

Abrams, D., and Hogg, M. A. (Eds). (1990). *Social identity theory: Constructive and critical advances*. London: Harvester Wheatsheaf.

Abramson, N. R. and Ai, J. X. (1999). 'Canadian companies doing business in China: Key success factors'. *Management International Review, 39*, 7–35.

Adamopoulos, J. and Lonner, W. J. (1994). 'Absolutism, relativism and universalism in the study of human behavior'. In W. J. Lonner and R. Malpass (Eds), *Psychology and culture* (pp. 129–134). Needham Heights, MA: Allyn & Bacon.

Adams, A., Bochner, S. and Bilik, L. (1998). *The effectiveness of warning signs in hazardous work places: Cognitive and social determinants. Applied Ergonomics, 29*, 247–254.

Adelman, M. B. (1988). 'Cross-cultural adjustment: A theoretical perspective on social support'. *International Journal of Intercultural Relations, 12*, 183–205.

Adler, J. and Waldman, S. (1995, July 10). 'Sweet land of liberties'. *Newsweek*, pp. 18–23.

Adler, N. J. (1997). *International dimensions of organizational behavior* (3rd edn). Cincinnati, OH: Southwestern College Publishing.

Adler, P. S. (1975). 'The transitional experience: An alternative view of "culture shock"'. *Journal of Humanistic Psychology, 15*, 13–23.

Ady, J. C. (1995). 'Toward a differential demand model of sojourner adjustment'. In R. L. Wiseman (Ed.), *Intercultural communication theory* (pp. 92–114). London: Sage.

Aiello, J. R. and Jones, S. E. (1971). 'Field study of the proxemic behavior of young school children in three subcultural groups'. *Journal of Personality and Social Psychology, 19*, 351–356.

Ajdukovic, M. and Ajdukovic, D. (1993). 'Psychological well-being of refugee children'. *Child Abuse and Neglect, 17*, 843–854.

Alatas, S. H. (1972). 'The captive mind in development studies: Some neglected problems and the need for an autonomous social science tradition in Asia'. *International Social Science Journal, 24*, 9–25.

Alatas, S. H. (1975). 'The captive mind and creative development'. *International Social Science Journal, 27*, 691–700.

Albert, R. D. (1983). 'The intercultural sensitizer or culture assimilator: A cognitive approach'. In D. Landis and R. Brislin (Eds), *Handbook of intercultural training: Vol. 2. Issues in training methodology* (pp. 186–217). Elmsford, NY: Pergamon.

Albert, R. D. (1995). 'The intercultural sensitizer/culture assimilator as a cross-cultural training method'. In S. M. Fowler and M. G. Mumford (Eds), *Intercultural sourcebook: Cross-cultural training methods* (Vol. 1, pp. 157–168). Yarmouth, MN: Intercultural Press.

Alford, R. D. (1988). *Naming and identity: A cross-cultural study of personal naming practices*. New Haven, CT: HRAF Press.

Allen, L. R., Long, P. T., Perdue, R. R. and Kieselbach, S. (1988). 'The impact of tourism development on citizens' perceptions of community life'. *Journal of Travel Research, 27*, 16–21.

Allodi, F. (1989). 'The children of victims of political persecution and torture: A psychological study of a Latin American refugee community'. *International Journal of Mental Health, 18*, 3–15.

Allport, G. W. (1937). *Personality: A psychological interpretation*. New York: Henry Holt.

Altrocchi, J. and Altrocchi, L. (1995). 'Polyfaceted psychological acculturation in Cook Islanders'. *Journal of Cross-cultural Psychology, 26*, 426–440.

Alzua, A., O'Leary, J. T. and Morrison, A. (1998). 'Cultural heritage tourism: Identifying niches for international travelers'. *The Journal of Tourism Studies, 9*, 2–13.

Amaral Dias, C. A., Vicente, T. N., Cabrita, M. F. and de Mendon, A. R. (1981). 'Transplantation, identity and drug addiction'. *Bulletin of Narcotics, 33*, 21–26.

Amir, Y. and Ben-Ari, R. (1985). 'International tourism, ethnic contact and attitude change'. *Journal of Social Issues, 41*, 105–116.

Amir, Y. and Ben-Ari, R. (1988). 'A contingency approach for promoting intergroup relations'. In J. W. Berry and R. C. Annis (Eds), *Ethnic psychology: Research and practice with immigrants, refugees, native peoples, ethnic groups and sojourners* (pp. 287–296). Lisse, The Netherlands: Swets & Zeitlinger.

Andersen Consulting (1995). *Moving China ventures out of the red into the black: Insights from best and worst performers*. London: The Economist Intelligence Unit.

Anderson, J., Moeschberger, M., Chen, M. S., Kunn, P., Wewers, M. E. and Guthrie, R. (1993). 'An acculturation scale for Southeast Asians'. *Social Psychiatry and Psychiatric Epidemiology, 28, 134–141*.

Andersen, P. (1994). 'Explaining intercultural differences in nonverbal communication'. In L. Samovar and R. Porter (Eds), *Intercultural communication* (pp. 229–240). Belmont, CA: Wadsworth.

Ap, J. (1990). 'Residents' perceptions: Research on the social impact of tourism'. *Annals of Tourism Research, 17,* 610–616.

Ap, J. (1992). 'Residents' perceptions on tourism impacts'. *Annals of Tourism Research, 19,* 665–690.

Arce, C. (1981). 'A reconsideration of Chicano culture and identity'. *Daedalus, 110,* 177–192.

'Are foreign workers taking away local jobs?' (1998, September 6). *The Sunday Times,* p. 33.

Argyle, M. (1969). *Social interaction.* London: Methuen.

Argyle, M. (1975). *Bodily communication.* London: Methuen.

Argyle, M. (1980). 'Interaction skills and social competence'. In P. Feldman and J. Orford (Eds), *Psychological problems: The social context* (pp. 123–150). Chichester, UK: Wiley.

Argyle, M. (1981). 'The nature of social skill'. In M. Argyle (Ed.), *Social skills and health* (pp. 1–30). London: Methuen.

Argyle, M. (1982). 'Intercultural communication'. In S. Bochner (Ed.), *Cultures in contact: Studies in cross-cultural interaction* (pp. 61–80). Oxford: Pergamon.

Argyle, M., Henderson, M., Bond, M., Iizuka, Y. and Contarello, A. (1986). 'Cross-cultural variations in relationship rules'. *International Journal of Psychology, 21,* 287–315.

Argyle, M. and Kendon, A. (1967). 'The experimental analysis of social performance'. In L. Berkowitz (Ed.), *Advances in experimental social psychology* (Vol. 3, pp. 55–98). New York: Academic Press.

Arieli, A. (1992). 'Psychopathology among Jewish Ethiopian immigrants to Israel'. *Journal of Nervous and Mental Diseases, 180,* 465–466.

Armes, K. and Ward, C. (1989). 'Cross-cultural transitions and sojourner adjustment in Singapore'. *Journal of Social Psychology, 12,* 273–275.

Arvey, R. D., Bhagat, R. S. and Salas, E. (1991). 'Cross-cultural and cross-national issues in personnel and human resources management: Where do we go from here?'. *Research in Personnel and Human Resources Management, 9,* 367–407.

Ataca, B. (1996, August). 'Psychological and sociocultural adaptation of Turkish immigrants, Canadians and Turks'. Paper presented at the XIII Congress of the International Association for Cross-cultural Psychology, Montreal, Canada.

Atkinson, D. R., Morten, G. and Sue, J. (1983). *Counselling American minorities* (2nd edn). Dubuque, IA: William Brown.

Australian Department of Immigration and Multicultural Affairs. (1999). *Immigration statistics.* Available: http://www./immi.gov.au/statistics/migrant.htm.

Averill, J. R. (1973). 'Personal control over aversive stimuli and its relationship to stress'. *Psychological Bulletin, 80,* 286–303.

Axtell, R. E. (1993). *Do's and taboos around the world.* New York: Wiley.

Aycan, Z. (1997). 'Expatriate adjustment as a multifaceted phenomenon: Individual and organizational level predictors'. *The International Journal of Human Resource Management, 8,* 434–456.

Aycan., Z. and Berry, J. W. (1994). 'The influences of economic adjustment of immigrants on their psychological well-being and adaptation'. Paper presented at the XII International Congress of the International Association for Cross-cultural Psychology, Pamplona, Spain.

Aycan, Z. and Berry, J. W. (1996). 'Impact of employment-related experiences on immigrants' psychological well-being and adaptation to Canada'. *Canadian Journal of Behavioural Science, 28*, 240–251.

Aycan, Z., Kanungo, R. N. and Sinha, J. B. P. (1999). 'Organizational culture and human resource management practices: The model of culture fit'. *Journal of Cross-cultural Psychology, 30*, 501–526.

Babiker, I. E., Cox, J. L. and Miller, P. (1980). 'The measurement of cultural distance and its relationship to medical consultations, symptomatology, and examination performance of overseas students at Edinburgh University'. *Social Psychiatry, 15*, 109–116.

Bachner, D. J., Zeutschel, U. and Shannon, D. (1993). 'Methodological issues in researching the effects of U.S.–German Educational youth exchange: A case study'. *International Journal of Intercultural Relations, 17*, 41–72.

Bagley, C. R. (1993). 'Mental health and social adjustment of elderly Chinese immigrants in Canada'. *Canada's Mental Health, 41*, 6–10.

Baker, J. E. (1997). 'Trophy hunting as a sustainable use of wildlife resources in Southern and Eastern Africa'. *Journal of Sustainable Tourism, 5*, 306–321.

Balarayan, R. (1995). 'Ethnicity and variations in the nation's health'. *Health Trends, 27*, 1149.

Baldacchino, G. (1997). *Global tourism and informal labour relations: The small–scale syndrome at work*. London: Mansell.

Baldrige, L. (1993). *Letitia Baldrige's new complete guide to executive manners*. New York: Rawson.

Ballantyne, R., Packer, J. and Beckmann, E. (1998). 'Targeted interpretation: Exploring relationships among visitors' motivations, activities, attitudes, information needs and preferences'. *The Journal of Tourism Studies, 9*, 14–25.

Ballard, B. and Clanchy, J. (1984). *Study abroad: A manual for Asian students*. Kuala Lumpur: Longmans.

Banai, M. and Reisel, W. D. (1999). 'Would you trust your foreign manager? An empirical investigation'. *The International Journal of Human Resource Management, 10*, 477–487.

Bandura, A. (1986). *Social foundations of thought and action: A social-cognitive view*. Englewood Cliffs, NJ: Prentice-Hall.

Banks, J. A. and Banks, C. A. M. (Eds). (1995). *Handbook of research on multicultural education* (pp. 484–497). New York: Macmillan.

Banton, M. P. (1965). *Roles: An introduction to the study of social relations*. London: Tavistock.

Banton, M. P. (1967). *Race relations*. London: Tavistock.

Barankin, T., Konstantareas, M. M. and de Bossett, F. (1989). 'Adaptation of recent Soviet Jewish immigrants and their children to Toronto'. *Canadian Journal of Psychiatry, 34*, 512–518.

Barker, J. (1991). 'Pacific Island migrants in the United States: Some implications for aging services'. *Journal of Cross-cultural Gerontology, 6*, 173–192.

Barker, M., Child, C., Gallois, C., Jones, E. and Callan, V. C. (1991). 'Difficulties of overseas students in social and academic situations'. *Australian Journal of Psychology, 43*, 79–84.

Barona, A. and Miller, J. A. (1994). 'Short Acculturation Scale for Hispanic Youth (SASH-Y): A preliminary report'. *Hispanic Journal of Behavioral Sciences, 16*, 155–162.

Barthes, R. (1973). *Mythologies*. London: Paladin.

Basadur, M., Wakabayashi, M. and Takai, J. (1992). 'Training effects on the divergent thinking attitudes of Japanese managers'. *International Journal of Intercultural Relations, 16*, 329–345.

Bass, B. M. (1997). 'Does the transactional–transformational leadership paradigm transcend organizational and national boundaries?'. *American Psychologist, 52*, 130–139.

Bass, B. M. and Avolio, B. J. (1994). *Improving organizational effectiveness through transformational leadership*. Thousand Oaks, CA: Sage.

Baxter, J. C. (1970). 'Interpersonal spacing in natural settings'. *Sociometry, 33*, 444–456.

Becker, C. B. (1990). 'Higher education in Japan: Facts and implications'. *International Journal of Intercultural Relations, 14*, 425–448.

Beiser, M. (1987). 'Changing time perspective and mental health among Southeast Asian refugees'. *Culture, Medicine and Psychiatry, 11*, 437–464.

Beiser, M. (1988). 'Influences of time, ethnicity, and attachment on depression in Southeast Asian refugees'. *American Journal of Psychiatry, 145*, 46–51.

Beiser, M. (1999). *Strangers at the gate: The 'boat people's' first ten years in Canada*. Toronto: University of Toronto Press.

Beiser, M., Barwick, C., Berry, J. W., da Costa, G., Fantino, A., Ganesan, S., Lee, C., Milne, W., Naidoo, J., Prince, R., Tousignant, M. and Vela, E. (1988). *Mental health issues affecting immigrants and refugees*. Ottawa: Health and Welfare Canada.

Beiser, M., Dion, R., Gotowiec, A., Hyman, I. and Vu, N. (1995). Immigrant and refugee children in Canada. *Canadian Journal of Psychiatry, 40*, 67–72.

Beiser, M. and Fleming, J. A. E. (1986). 'Measuring psychiatric disorder among Southeast Asian refugees'. *Psychological Medicine, 16*, 627–639.

Beiser, M., Johnson, P. and Turner, J. (1993). 'Unemployment, underemployment and depressive affect among Southeast Asian refugees'. *Psychological Medicine, 23*, 731–743.

Beiser, M., Turner, J. and Ganesan, S. (1989). 'Catastrophic stress and factors affecting its consequences among Southeast Asian refugees'. *Social Science and Medicine, 28*, 183–195.

Bemak, F. and Greenberg, B. (1994). 'Southeast Asian refugee adolescents: Implications for counselling'. *Journal of Multicultural Counselling and Development, 22*, 115–124.

Bennett, J. W., Passin, H. and McKnight, R. K. (1958). *In search of identity: The Japanese overseas scholar in America and Japan*. Minneapolis, MN: University of Minnesota Press.

Bennett, M. J. (1995). 'Critical incidents in an intercultural conflict–resolution exercise'. In S. M. Fowler and M. G. Mumford (Eds), *Intercultural sourcebook: Cross-cultural training methods* (Vol. 1, pp. 147–156). Yarmouth, MN: Intercultural Press.

Bennett, S. K. (1994). 'The American Indian: A psychological overview'. In W. J. Lonner and R. Malpass (Eds), *Psychology and culture* (pp. 35–39). Needham Heights, MA: Allyn & Bacon.

Benson, P. G. (1978). 'Measuring cross-cultural adjustment: The problem of criteria'. *International Journal of Intercultural Relations, 2*, 21–37.

Berno, T. (1995). 'The sociocultural and psychological effects of tourism on indigenous cultures'. Unpublished doctoral thesis, University of Canterbury, Christchurch, New Zealand.

Berno, T. (1999). 'When a guest is a guest: Cook Islanders view tourism'. *Annals of Tourism Research, 26*, 656–675.

Berno, T. and Ward, C. (1998, April). 'Psychological and sociocultural adjustment of international students in New Zealand'. Paper presented at the Annual Meeting of the Society of Australasian Social Psychologists, Christchurch, New Zealand.

Berry, J. W. (1974). 'Psychological aspects of cultural pluralism'. *Topics in Culture Learning, 2*, 17–22.

Berry, J. W. (1975). 'Ecology, cultural adaptation, and psychological differentiation: Traditional patterning and acculturative stress'. In R. W. Brislin, S. Bochner and W. J. Lonner (Eds), *Cross-cultural perspectives on learning* (pp. 207–229). New York: Wiley.

Berry, J. W. (1980). 'Acculturation as varieties of adaptation'. In A. M. Padilla (Ed.), *Acculturation: Theories, models and findings* (pp. 9–25). Boulder, CO: Westview.

Berry, J. W. (1984a). 'Cultural relations in plural societies'. In N. Miller and M. Brewer (Eds.), *Groups in contact* (pp. 11–27). New York: Academic Press.

Berry, J. W. (1984b). 'Multicultural policy in Canada: A social psychological analysis'. *Canadian Journal of Behavioral Science, 16*, 353–370.

Berry, J. W. (1990). 'Psychology of acculturation: Understanding individuals moving between cultures'. In R. Brislin (Ed.), *Applied cross-cultural psychology* (pp. 232–253). Newbury Park, CA: Sage.

Berry, J. W. (1994a). 'Acculturative stress'. In W. J. Lonner and R. Malpass (Eds), *Psychology and culture* (pp. 211–215). Needham Heights, MA: Allyn & Bacon.

Berry, J. W. (1994b). 'Acculturation and psychological adaptation'. In A.-M. Bouvy, F. J. R. van de Vijver, P. Boski and P. Schmitz (Eds), *Journeys into cross-cultural psychology* (pp. 129–141). Lisse, The Netherlands: Swets & Zeitlinger.

Berry, J. W. (1997). 'Immigration, acculturation and adaptation'. *Applied Psychology: An International Review, 46*, 5–34.

Berry, J. W. and Annis, R. C. (1974). 'Acculturative stress'. *Journal of Cross-cultural Psychology*, 5, 382–406.

Berry, J. W. and Blondel, T. (1982). 'Psychological adaptation of Vietnamese refugees in Canada'. *Canadian Journal of Community Mental Health, 1*, 81–88.

Berry, J. W. and Kalin, R. (1995). 'Multicultural and ethnic attitudes in Canada: An overview of the 1991 National Survey'. *Canadian Journal of Behavioural Science, 27*, 301–320.

Berry, J. W., Kalin, R. and Taylor, D. (1977). *Multiculturalism and ethnic attitudes in Canada*. Ottawa: Minister of Supply and Services.

Berry, J. W. and Kim, U. (1988). 'Acculturation and mental health'. In P. Dasen, J. W. Berry and N. Satorius (Eds.), *Health and cross-cultural psychology* (pp. 207–236). London: Sage.

Berry, J. W., Kim, U., Minde, T. and Mok, D. (1987). 'Comparative studies of acculturative stress'. *International Migration Review, 21*, 491–511.

Berry, J. W., Kim, U., Power, S., Young, M. and Bujaki, M. (1989). 'Acculturation attitudes in plural societies'. *Applied Psychology, 38*, 185–206.

Berry, J. W. and Kostovcik, N. (1990). 'Psychological adaptation of Malaysian students in Canada'. In Abdul Halim Othman and Wan Rafaei Adbul Rahman (Eds), *Psychology and socioeconomic development* (pp. 155–162). Bangi, Malaysia: National University Press.

Berry, J. W., Wintrob, R., Sindell, P. S. and Mawhinney, T. A. (1982). 'Psychological adaptation to culture change among the James Bay Cree'. *Naturaliste Canadien, 109*, 965–975.

Berthoud, R. and Nazroo, J. (1997). 'The mental health of ethnic minorities'. *New Community, 23*, 309–324.

Betts, K. (1991). 'Australia's distorted immigration policy'. In D. Goodman, D. J. O'Hearn and C. Wallace-Crabbe (Eds), *Multicultural Australia: The challenges of changes* (pp. 149–177). Newham, Australia: Scribe.

Bhagat, R. S. and Prien, K. O. (1996). 'Cross-cultural training in organizational context'. In D. Landis and R. S. Bhagat (Eds), *Handbook of intercultural training* (2nd edn, pp. 216–230). Thousand Oaks, CA: Sage.

Bhawuk, D. P. S. and Brislin, R. W. (1992). 'The measurement of intercultural sensitivity using the concepts of individualism and collectivism'. *International Journal of Intercultural Relations, 16*, 413–436.

Biegel, D., Naparstek, A. and Khan, M. (1980, September). 'Social support and mental health: An examination of interrelationships'. Paper presented at the Eighty-eighth Annual Convention of the American Psychological Association, Montreal, Canada.

Bierbrauer, G. and Pedersen, P. B. (1996). 'Culture and migration'. In G. R. Semin and K. Fiedler (Eds), *Applied social psychology* (pp. 399–422). London: Sage.

Birman, D. and Tyler, F. B. (1994). 'Acculturation and alienation of Soviet Jewish refugees in the United States'. *Genetic, Social and General Psychology Monographs, 120*, 101–115.

Black, J. S. (1988). 'Work role transitions: A study of American expatriate managers in Japan'. *Journal of International Business Studies, 19*, 533–546.

Black, J. S. (1990). 'The relationship of personal characteristics with the adjustment of Japanese expatriate managers'. *Management International Review, 30*, 119–134.

Black, J. S. (1992). 'Socializing American expatriate managers overseas'. *Group and Organization Management, 17*, 171–192.

Black, J. S. and Gregersen, H. B. (1990). 'Expectations, satisfaction, and intention to leave of American expatriate managers in Japan'. *International Journal of Intercultural Relations, 14*, 485–506.

Black, J. S., Gregersen, H. B. and Mendenhall, M. E. (1992). *Global assignments*. San Francisco: Jossey-Bass.

Black, J. S. and Mendenhall, M. (1990). 'Cross-cultural training effectiveness: A review and a theoretical framework for future research'. *Academy of Management Review, 15*, 113–136.

Black, J. S. and Stephens, G. K. (1989). 'The influence of the spouse on American expatriate adjustment in Pacific Rim overseas assignments'. *Journal of Management, 15*, 529–544.

Blamey, R. K. (1997). 'Ecotourism: The search for an operational definition'. *Journal of Sustainable Tourism, 5*, 109–130.

Blohm, J. D. (1995). 'Markhall: A comparative corporate-culture simulation'. In S. M. Fowler and M. G. Mumford (Eds), *Intercultural sourcebook: Cross-cultural training methods* (Vol. 1, pp. 109–115). Yarmouth, MN: Intercultural Press.

Bloom, L. (1971). *The social psychology of race relations*. London: Allen & Unwin.

Bochner, S. (1972). 'Problems in culture learning'. In S. Bochner and P. P. Wicks (Eds), *Overseas students in Australia* (pp. 65–81). Sydney: The New South Wales University Press.

Bochner, S. (1976). 'Religious role differentiation as an aspect of subjective culture'. *Journal of Cross-cultural Psychology, 7*, 3–19.

Bochner, S. (1979). 'Cultural diversity: Implications for modernization and international education'. In K. Kumar (Ed.), *Bonds without bondage: Explorations in transcultural interactions* (pp. 231–256). Honolulu: University of Hawaii Press.

Bochner, S. (1981). 'The social psychology of cultural mediation'. In S. Bochner (Ed.), *The mediating person: Bridges between cultures* (pp. 6–36). Cambridge, MA: Schenkman.

Bochner, S. (1982). 'The social psychology of cross-cultural relations'. In S. Bochner (Ed.), Cultures in contact: *Studies in cross-cultural interaction* (pp. 5–44). Oxford: Pergamon.

Bochner, S. (1986). 'Coping with unfamiliar cultures: Adjustment or culture learning?'. *Australian Journal of Psychology, 38*, 347–358.

Bochner, S. (1992). 'The diffusion of organizational psychology across cultural boundaries: Issues and problems'. In J. Misumi, B. Wilpert and H. Motoaki (Eds), *Organisational and work psychology* (pp. 89–94). Hove, UK: Lawrence Erlbaum Associates Ltd.

Bochner, S. (1994). 'Cross-cultural differences in the self concept: A test of Hofstede's individualism/collectivism distinction'. *Journal of Cross-cultural Psychology, 25*, 273–283.

Bochner, S. (1996). 'Pre-election perceptions of politicians and their promises as a function of the reference group match between speaker and listener'. *Asian Journal of Communication, 6*, 89–110.

Bochner, S. (1999). 'Cultural diversity within and between societies: Implications for multicultural social systems'. In P. B. Pedersen (Ed.), *Multiculturalism as a fourth force* (pp. 19–60). Washington, DC: Taylor & Francis.

Bochner, S., Brislin, R. W. and Lonner, W. J. (1975). 'Introduction'. In R. W. Brislin, S. Bochner and W. J. Lonner (Eds), *Cross-cultural perspectives on learning* (pp. 3–36). New York: Sage.

Bochner, S., Buker, E. A. and McLeod, B. M. (1976). 'Communication patterns in an international student dormitory: A modification of the "small world" method'. *Journal of Applied Social Psychology, 6*, 275–290.

Bochner, S. and Cairns, L. G. (1976). 'An unobtrusive measure of helping behaviour toward Aborigines'. In G. E. Kearney and D. W. McElwain (Eds), *Aboriginal cognition: Retrospect and prospect* (pp. 344–356). Canberra: Australian Institute of Aboriginal Studies.

Bochner, S. and Coulon, L. (1997). 'A culture assimilator to train Australian hospitality industry workers serving Japanese tourists'. *The Journal of Tourism Studies, 8*, 8–17.

Bochner, S. and Hesketh B. (1994). 'Power distance, individualism/collectivism, and job-related attitudes in a culturally diverse work group'. *Journal of Cross-cultural Psychology, 25*, 233–257.

Bochner, S., Hutnik, N. and Furnham, A. (1985). 'The friendship patterns of overseas and host students in an Oxford student residence'. *Journal of Social Psychology, 125*, 689–694.

Bochner, S., Lin, A. and McLeod, B. M. (1979). 'Cross-cultural contact and the development of an international perspective'. *Journal of Social Psychology, 107*, 29–41.

Bochner, S., Lin, A. and McLeod, B. M. (1980). 'Anticipated role conflict of returning overseas students'. *Journal of Social Psychology, 110*, 265–272.

Bochner, S., McLeod, B. M. and Lin, A. (1977). 'Friendship patterns of overseas students: A functional model'. *International Journal of Psychology, 12*, 277–297.

Bochner, S. and Orr, F. E. (1979). 'Race and academic status as determinants of friendship formation: A field study'. *International Journal of Psychology, 14*, 37–46.

Bochner, S. and Perks, R. W. (1971). 'National role evocation as a function of cross-national interaction'. *Journal of Cross-cultural Psychology, 2*, 157–164.

Bochner, S. and Wicks, P. (Eds). (1972). *Overseas students in Australia*. Sydney: University of New South Wales Press.

Boekestijn, C. (1988). 'Intercultural migration and the development of personal identity: The dilemma between identity maintenance and cultural adaptation'. *International Journal of Intercultural Relations, 12*, 83–105.

Bojanic, D. C. and Rosen, L. D. (1994). 'Measuring service quality in restaurants: An application of the SERVQUAL instrument'. *Hospitality Research Journal, 18*, 3–14.

Böker, W. (1981). 'Psycho(patho)logical reactions among foreign labourers in Europe'. In L. Eitinger and D. Schwarz (Eds), *Strangers in the world* (pp. 186–201). Bern, Switzerland: Hans Huber.

Bolinger, D. (1975). *Aspects of language* (2nd edn). New York: Harcourt Brace Jovanovich.

Boman, B. and Edwards, M. (1984). 'The Indochinese refugee: An overview'. *Australian and New Zealand Journal of Psychiatry, 18*, 40–52.

Bond, M. H. (1986). 'Mutual stereotypes and the facilitation of interaction across cultural lines'. *International Journal of Intercultural Relations, 10*, 259–276.

Bond, M. H. (1988). 'Finding universal dimensions of individual variation in multi-cultural studies of values: The Rokeach and Chinese value surveys'. *Journal of Personality and Social Psychology, 55*, 1009–1015.

Bond, M. H. (Ed.). (1996). *The handbook of Chinese psychology*. Hong Kong: Oxford University Press.

Bond, M. H. and Cheung, T. S. (1983). 'The spontaneous self-concept of college students in Hong Kong, Japan, and the United States'. *Journal of Cross-cultural Psychology, 14*, 153–171.

Borjas, G. J. (1988). 'Economic theory and international migration'. *International Migration Review, 23*, 457–485.

Boski, P. (1990). 'Correlative national self-identity of Polish immigrants in Canada and the United States'. In N. Bleichrodt and P. J. D. Drenth (Eds), *Contemporary issues in cross-cultural psychology* (pp. 207–216). Lisse, The Netherlands: Swets & Zeitlinger.

Boski, P. (1994). 'Psychological acculturation via identity dynamics: Consequences for subjective well-being'. In A.-M. Bouvy, F. J. R. van de Vijver, P. Boski and P. Schmitz (Eds), *Journeys into cross-cultural psychology* (pp. 197–215). Lisse, The Netherlands: Swets & Zeitlinger.

Boski, P. (1998, August). 'A quest for a more cultural and a more psychological model of acculturation'. Paper presented at the XIV International Congress of the International Association for Cross-cultural Psychology, Bellingham, WA.

Bourhis, R. and Giles, H. (1977). 'The language of intergroup distinctiveness'. In H. Giles (Ed.), *Language, ethnicity and intergroup relations* (pp. 119–135). London: Academic Press.

Bourhis, R. Y., Moïse, C., Perreault, S. and Senécal, S. (1997). 'Towards an interactive acculturation model: A social psychological approach'. *International Journal of Psychology, 32*, 369–386.

Bowen, D. J., Carscadden, L., Beighle, K. and Fleming, I. (1992). 'Posttraumatic stress disorder among Salvadoran women: Empirical evidence and description of treatment'. *Women and Therapy*, 13, 267–280.

Bowlby, J. (1969). *Attachment and loss.* London: Hogarth.

Boxer, A. H. (1969). *Experts in Asia: An inquiry into Australian technical assistance.* Canberra: Australian National University Press.

Boyacigiller, N. A. and Adler, N. J. (1991). 'The parochial dinosaur: Organizational science in a global context'. *Academy of Management Review, 16*, 262–290.

Brabant, S., Palmer, E. C. and Gramling, R. (1990). 'Returning home: An empirical investigation of cross-cultural re-entry'. *International Journal of Intercultural Relations, 14*, 387–404.

Braganti, N. L. and Devine, E. (1992). *European customs and manners.* New York: Meadowbrook Press.

Branscombe, N. R. and Wann, D. L. (1994). 'Collective self-esteem consequences of outgroup derogation when a valued social identity is on trial'. *European Journal of Social Psychology, 24*, 641–657.

Breakwell, G. M. (1986). *Coping with threatened identities.* London: Methuen.

Breakwell, G. M. and Lyons, E. (Eds). (1996). *Changing European identities: A social psychological analysis of social change.* Oxford: Butterworth-Heinemann.

Brein, M. and David, K. H. (1971). 'Intercultural communication and the adjustment of the sojourner'. *Psychological Bulletin, 76*, 215–230.

Brewer, M. B. (1993). 'Social identity, distinctiveness, and in-group homogeneity'. *Social Cognition, 11*, 150–164.

Brewer, M. B. (1996). 'When contact is not enough: Social identity and intergroup cooperation'. *International Journal of Intercultural Relations, 20*, 291–304.

Brewer, M. B. (1999). 'Multiple identities and identity transition: Implications for Hong Kong'. *International Journal of Intercultural Relations, 23*, 187–198.

Brewin, C. (1980). 'Explaining the lower rates of psychiatric treatment among Asian immigrants to the United Kingdom: A preliminary study'. *Social Psychiatry, 15*, 17–19.

Brewster, C., Tregaskis, O., Hegewisch, A. and Mayne, L. (1996). 'Comparative research in human resource management: A review and an example'. *The International Journal of Human Resource Management, 7*, 586–604.

Brickman, W. W. (1965). 'Historical development of governmental interest in international higher education'. In S. Fraser (Ed.), *Government policy and international education* (pp. 17–46). New York: Wiley.

Brislin, R. W. (1981). *Cross-cultural encounters.* New York: Pergamon.

Brislin, R. W. (1986). 'A culture-general assimilator: Preparation for various types of sojourns'. *International Journal of Intercultural Relations, 10*, 215–234.

Brislin, R. W. (1993). *Understanding culture's influence on behavior.* Fort Worth, TX: Harcourt Brace Jovanovich.

Brislin, R. W. (1994). 'Preparing to live and work elsewhere'. In W. J. Lonner and R. Malpass (Eds), *Psychology and culture* (pp. 239–244). Needham Heights, MA: Allyn & Bacon.

Brislin, R. W. (1995). 'The culture-general assimilator'. In S. M. Fowler and M. G. Mumford (Eds), *Intercultural sourcebook: Cross-cultural training methods* (Vol. 1, pp. 169–177). Yarmouth, MN: Intercultural Press.

Brislin, R. W. and Baumgardner, S. R. (1971). 'Non-random sampling of individuals in cross-cultural research'. *Journal of Cross-cultural Psychology, 2*, 397–400.

Brislin, R. W., Cushner, K., Cherrie, C. and Yong, M. (1986). *Intercultural interactions: A practical guide*. Beverly Hills: Sage.

Brislin, R.W., Landis, D. and Brandt, M. E. (1983). 'Conceptualizations of intercultural behavior and training'. In D. Landis and R. W. Brislin (Eds), *Handbook of intercultural training* (pp. 1–35). New York: Pergamon.

Brislin, R. W., and Yoshida, T. (1994). *Intercultural communication training: An introduction*. Thousand Oaks, CA: Sage.

Broad, S. and Weiler, B. (1998). 'Captive animals and interpretation: A tale of two tiger exhibits'. *The Journal of Tourism Studies, 9*, 14–27.

Brown, D. (1996). 'Genuine fakes'. In T. Selwyn (Ed.), *The tourist image: Myths and myth making in tourism* (pp. 33–47). Chichester: Wiley.

Brown, R. J., Hinkle, S., Ely, P. G., Fox-Cardamone, L., Maras, P. and Taylor, L. A. (1992). 'Recognising group diversity: Individualist–collectivist and autonomous–relational social orientations and their implications for intergroup processes'. *British Journal of Social Psychology, 31*, 327–342.

Brunt, P. and Courtney, P. (1999). 'Host perception of sociocultural impacts'. *Annals of Tourism Research, 26*, 493–515.

Buckley, R. (1994). 'A framework for ecotourism'. *Annals of Tourism Research, 21*, 629–642.

Budhwar, P. S. and Sparrow, P. R. (1998). 'National factors determining Indian and British HRM Practices: An empirical study'. *Management International Review, 38*, 105–121.

Buntaine, C. S. (1994). 'Beyond smiling faces'. In E. Y. Cross, J. H. Katz, F. A. Miller and E. W. Seashore (Eds), *The promise of diversity: Over 40 voices discuss strategies for eliminating discrimination in organizations* (pp. 219–221). Burr Ridge, IL: Irwin.

Burgoon, J. K. (1995). 'Cross-cultural and intercultural applications of expectancy violations theory'. In R. L. Wiseman (Ed.), *Intercultural communication theory* (pp. 194–214). Thousand Oaks, CA: Sage.

Burgoon, J. K., Buller, D. B. and Woodall, W. G. (1989). *Nonverbal communication: The unspoken dialogue*. New York: Harper Collins.

Burgoon, J. K., Coker, D. A. and Coker, R. A. (1986). 'Communicative effects of gaze behavior: A test of two contrasting explanations'. *Human Communications Research, 12*, 495–524.

Buriel, R., Calzada, S. and Vasquez, R. (1982). 'Relationship of traditional Mexican American culture to adjustment and delinquency among three generations of Mexican-American male adolescents'. *Hispanic Journal of Behavioral Sciences, 1*, 41–55.

Byrne, D. (1969). 'Attitudes and attraction'. In L. Berkowitz (Ed.), *Advances in experimental social psychology* (Vol. 4, pp. 35–89). New York: Academic Press.

Bystrzanowski, J. (Ed.). (1989). *Tourism as a factor of change: A sociocultural study*. Vienna: European Coordination Centre for Research and Documentation in Social Sciences.

Caligiuri, P. M. and Cascio, W. (1998). 'Can we send her there? Maximizing the success of Western women on global assignments'. *Journal of World Business, 33*, 394–416.

Caligiuri, P. M., Joshi, A. and Lazarova, M. (1999). 'Factors influencing the adjustment of women on global assignments'. *The International Journal of Human Resource Management, 10*, 163–179.

Caligiuri, P. M. and Tung, R. (1999). 'Comparing the success of male and female expatriates from a US-based multinational company'. *The International Journal of Human Resource Management*, 10, 763–782.

Camilleri, C. and Malewska-Peyre, H. (1997). 'Socialization and identity strategies'. In J. W. Berry, P. R. Dasen and T. S. Saraswathi (Eds), *Handbook of cross-cultural psychology: Vol. 2. Basic processes and human development* (pp. 41–67). Boston: Allyn & Bacon.

Campbell, L. M. (1999). 'Ecotourism in rural developing communities'. *Annals of Tourism Research, 26*, 534–553.

Carey, A. T. (1956). *Colonial students*. London: Secker & Warburg.

Carlyn, M. (1977). 'An assessment of the Myers–Briggs Type Indicator'. *Journal of Personality Assessment, 41*, 461–473.

Carver, C. S., Scheier, M. F. and Weintraub, J. K. (1989). 'Assessing coping strategies: A theoretically based approach'. *Journal of Personality and Social Psychology, 56*, 267–283.

Cascio, W. F. (1992). *Managing human resources: Productivity, quality of work life, profits* (3rd edn). New York: McGraw-Hill.

Cascio, W. F. (1995). 'Whither industrial and organizational psychology in a changing world of work?'. *American Psychologist, 50*, 928–939.

Celano, M. P. and Tyler, F. B. (1991). 'Behavioral acculturation among Vietnamese refugees in the United States'. *Journal of Social Psychology, 13*, 373–385.

Chance, N. A. (1965). 'Acculturation, self-identification and personality adjustment'. *American Anthropologist, 67*, 372–393.

Chaney, L. H. and Martin, J. S. (1995). *Intercultural business communication*. Upper Saddle River, NJ: Prentice-Hall.

Chang, H.-B. (1973). 'Attitudes of Chinese students in the United States'. *Sociology and Social Research, 58*, 66–77.

Chang, W. C., Chua, W. L. and Toh, Y. (1997). 'The concept of psychological control in the Asian context'. In K. Leung, U. Kim, S. Yamaguchi and Y. Kashima (Eds), *Progress in Asian social psychology* (Vol. 1, pp. 95–117). New York: John Wiley.

Chao, G., Walz, P. M. and Gardner, P. (1992). 'Formal and informal mentorship: A comparison of mentoring functions and contrast with nonmentored counterparts'. *Personnel Psychology, 45*, 619–636.

Charron, D. and Ness, R. (1983). 'Emotional distress among Vietnamese adolescents'. *Journal of Refugee Resettlement, 1*, 7–15.

Chataway, C. J. and Berry, J. W. (1989). 'Acculturation experiences, appraisal, coping and adaptation: A comparison of Hong Kong Chinese, French and English students in Canada'. *Canadian Journal of Behavioral Science, 21*, 295–301.

Chemers, M. M. (1969). 'Cross-cultural training as a means for improving situational favorableness'. *Human Relations, 22*, 531–546.

Chen, L. (1995). 'Interaction involvement and patterns of topical talk: A comparison of intercultural and intracultural dyads'. *International Journal of Intercultural Relations, 19*, 463–482.

Chen, M. J. (1994). 'Chinese and Australian concepts of intelligence'. *Psychology and Developing Societies, 6*, 103–117.

Cheung, P. (1995). 'Acculturation and psychiatric morbidity among Cambodian refugees in New Zealand'. *International Journal of Social Psychiatry, 41*, 108–119.

Child, J. (1994). *Management in China during the age of reform*. Cambridge: Cambridge University Press.

Chinese Culture Connection (1987). 'Chinese values and the search for culture-free dimensions of culture'. *Journal of Cross-cultural Psychology, 18*, 143–164.

Chirgwin, S. and Hughes, K. (1997). 'Ecotourism: The participants' perceptions'. *The Journal of Tourism Studies, 8*, 2–7.

Chu, H. M. (1972). 'Migration and mental disorder in Taiwan'. In W. Lebra (Ed.), *Transcultural research in mental health* (pp. 295–325). Honolulu: East West Center Press.

Chung, R. C.-Y. and Kagawa-Singer, M. (1993). 'Predictors of psychological distress among Southeast Asian refugees'. *Social Science and Medicine, 36*, 631–639.

Church, A. T. (1982). 'Sojourner adjustment'. *Psychological Bulletin, 91*, 540–572.

Citizenship and Immigration Canada (1999). *Immigration statistics*. Available: http://www.cicnet.ci.gc.ca/english/pub/anrep99e.html#plan10.

Clarke, G., Sack, W. H. and Goff, B. (1993). 'Three forms of stress in Cambodian adolescent refugees'. *Journal of Abnormal Child Psychology, 21*, 65–77.

Clément, R. (1986). 'Second language proficiency and acculturation: An investigation of the effects of language status and individual characteristics'. *Journal of Language and Social Psychology, 5*, 271–290.

Clément, R. and Bourhis, R. (1996). 'Bilingualism and intergroup communication'. *International Journal of Psycholinguistics, 12*, 171–191.

Clément, R., Gardner, R. C. and Smythe, P. C. (1977). 'Interethnic contact: Attitudinal consequences'. *Canadian Journal of Behavioural Sciences, 9*, 205–215.

Cochrane, R. (1977). 'Mental illness in immigrants to England and Wales: An analysis of mental hospital admissions, 1971'. *Social Psychiatry, 12*, 25–35.

Cochrane, R. and Sobol, M. (1980). 'Life stresses and psychological consequences'. In P. Feldman and J. Orford (Eds), *Psychological problems: The social context* (pp. 151–182). Chichester, UK: Wiley.

Cochrane, R. and Stopes-Roe, M. (1977). 'Psychological and social adjustment of Asian immigrants to Britain: A community survey'. *Social Psychiatry, 12*, 195–206.

Coelho, G. V. (1958). *Changing images of America*. Glencoe, IL: Free Press.

Cohen, E. (1995). 'Contemporary tourism – trends and challenges: Sustainable authenticity or contrived post-modernity?'. In R. Butler and D. Pearce (Eds), *Change in tourism: People, places, processes* (pp. 12–29). London: Routledge.

Coleman, D. (1995). 'Immigration policy in Great Britain'. In F. Heckmann and W. Bosswick (Eds), *Migration policies: A comparative perspective* (pp. 105–128). Stuttgart: Enke.

Collett, P. (1982). 'Meetings and misunderstandings'. In S. Bochner (Ed.), *Cultures in contact: Studies in cross-cultural interaction* (pp. 81–98). Oxford: Pergamon.

Collett, P. (1994). *Foreign bodies: A guide to European mannerisms*. London: Simon and Schuster.

Constantinou, S. and Harvey, M. (1985). 'Dimensional structure and intergenerational differences in ethnicity: The Greek Americans'. *Sociology and Social Research, 69*, 234–254.

Cope, A. M., Doxford, D. and Hill, T. (1998). 'Monitoring tourism on the UK's first long-distance cycle route'. *Journal of Sustainable Tourism, 6*, 210–223.

Cort, D. A. and King, M. (1979). 'Some correlates of culture shock among American tourists in Africa'. *International Journal of Intercultural Relations, 3*, 211–225.

Cortazzi, M. and Jin, L. (1997). 'Communication for learning across cultures'. In D. McNamara and R. Harris (Eds), *Overseas students in higher education* (pp. 76–90). London: Routledge.

Cortés, D. E., Rogler, L. H. and Malgady, R. G. (1994). 'Biculturality among Puerto Rican adults in the United States'. *American Journal of Community Psychology, 22*, 707–721.

Cousins, S. (1989). 'Culture and selfhood in Japan and the U.S.'. *Journal of Personality and Social Psychology, 56*, 124–131.

Cox, T. H. and Blake, S. (1991). 'Managing cultural diversity: Implications for organizational competitiveness'. *The Executive, 5*, 45–56.

Cox, T. H., Lobel, S. A. and McLeod, P. L. (1991). 'Effects of ethnic group cultural differences on cooperative and competitive behavior on a group task'. *Academy of Management Journal, 34*, 827–847.

Crano, S. L. and Crano, W. D. (1993). 'A measure of adjustment strain in international students'. *Journal of Cross-cultural Psychology, 24*, 267–283.

Cross, S. (1995). 'Self-construals, coping, and stress in cross-cultural adaptation'. *Journal of Cross-cultural Psychology, 26*, 673–697.

Cuéllar, I. and Arnold, B. (1988). 'Cultural considerations and rehabilitation of Mexican Americans'. *Journal of Rehabilitation, 54*, 35–40.

Cuéllar, I., Arnold, B. and González, G. (1995). 'Cognitive referents of acculturation: Assessment of cultural constructs of Mexican Americans'. *Journal of Community Psychology, 23*, 339–356.

Cuéllar, I., Arnold, B. and Maldonado, R. (1995). 'Acculturation rating scale for Mexican Americans-II: A revision of the original ARMSA scale'. *Hispanic Journal of Behavioral Sciences, 17*, 275–304.

Cuéllar, I., Harris, L. C. and Jasso, R. (1980). 'An acculturation scale for Mexican American normal and clinical populations'. *Hispanic Journal of Behavioral Sciences, 2*, 199–217.

Cui, G. and Awa, N. E. (1992). 'Measuring intercultural effectiveness: An integrative approach'. *International Journal of Intercultural Relations, 16*, 311–328.

Cushner, K. (1989). 'Assessing the impact of a culture-general assimilator'. *International Journal of Intercultural Relations, 13*, 125–146.

Cushner, K. and Brislin, R. W. (1996). *Intercultural interaction; A practical guide* (2nd edn). Thousand Oaks, CA: Sage.

Cushner, K. and Brislin, R. W. (1997). 'Key concepts in the field of cross-cultural training: An introduction'. In K. Cushner and R. W. Brislin (Eds), *Improving intercultural interactions: Modules for cross-cultural training programs* (Vol. 2, pp. 1–17). Thousand Oaks, CA: Sage.

Dadfar, A. (1994). 'The Afghans: Bearing the scars of a forgotten war'. In A. J. Marsella, T. Bornemann, S. Ekblad and J. Orley (Eds), *Amidst the peril and pain: The mental health and well-being of the world's refugees* (pp. 125–139). Washington, DC: American Psychological Association.

Daly, S. and Carpenter, M. (1985). 'Adjustment of Vietnamese refugee youths: A self-report'. *Psychological Reports, 56*, 971–976.

D'Amore, L. (1988). 'Tourism: The world's peace industry'. *Journal of Travel Research, 27*, 35–40.

Dane, L. F. (1981). 'The use of the paraprofessional for treatment of Americans abroad: A survey of theory and practice'. In S. Bochner (Ed.), *The mediating person: Bridges between cultures* (pp. 169–183). Cambridge, MA: Schenkman.

Dann, G. (1999). 'Writing out the tourist in space and time'. *Annals of Tourism Research, 26*, 159–187.

Dant, W. (1995). 'Using critical incidents as a tool for reflection'. In S. M. Fowler and

M. G. Mumford (Eds), *Intercultural Sourcebook: Cross-cultural training methods* (Vol. I, pp. 141–146). Yarmouth, MN: Intercultural Press.

Darnell, F. (Ed.). (1972). *Education in the North.* Fairbanks: University of Alaska Press.

David, K. (1971). 'Culture shock and the development of self-awareness'. *Journal of Contemporary Psychotherapy, 4,* 44–48.

Davies, H. (1995). 'Interpreting *guanxi*: The role of personal connections in a high context transitional economy'. In H. Davies (Ed.), *China business: Context and issues* (pp. 155–169). Hong Kong: Longman.

Davis, F. J. (1971). 'The two-way mirror and the U-curve: America as seen by Turkish students returned home'. *Sociology and Social Research, 56,* 29–43.

Daws, G. (1968). *Shoal of time: A history of the Hawaiian Islands.* Honolulu: University of Hawaii Press.

de Kadt, E. (1979). *Tourism: Passport to development?* Washington, DC: Oxford University Press.

De Verthelyi, R. F. (1995). 'International students' spouses: Invisible sojourners in the culture shock literature'. *International Journal of Intercultural Relations, 19,* 387–411.

Deaux, K. (1976). *The behavior of women and men.* Monterey, CA: Brooks/Cole.

Deaux, K. (1996). 'Social identification'. In E. T. Higgins and A. W. Kruglanski (Eds), *Social psychology: Handbook of basic principles* (pp. 777–798). New York: Guildford Press.

Department of Labour and Immigration, Committee on Community Relations (1975). *Final report.* Canberra: Australian Government Publishing Service.

Department of Social Security (1990). *Naming systems of ethnic groups: A language guide for departmental staff.* Canberra: Australian Government Printing Service.

Der-Karabetian, A. (1980). 'Relation of two cultural identities of Armenian-Americans'. *Psychological Reports, 47,* 123–128.

Deshpande, S. P. and Viswesvaran, C. (1992). 'Is cross-cultural training of expatriate managers effective? A meta-analysis'. *International Journal of Intercultural Relations, 16,* 295–310.

Deutsch, S. E. and Won, G. Y. M. (1963). 'Some factors in the adjustment of foreign nationals in the United States'. *Journal of Social Issues, 19,* 115–122.

Devine, E. and Braganti, N. L. (1988). *The travelers' guide to Latin American customs and manners.* New York: St Martin's Press.

Dew, A.-M. and Ward, C. (1993). 'The effects of ethnicity and culturally congruent and incongruent nonverbal behaviors on interpersonal attraction'. *Journal of Applied Social Psychology, 23,* 1376–1389.

Diener, E. and Diener, M. (1995). 'Factors predicting the subjective well-being of nations'. *Journal of Personality and Social Psychology, 69,* 851–864.

Dillard, J. P., Wilson, S. R., Tusing, K. J. and Kinney, T. A. (1997). 'Politeness judgments in personal relationships'. *Journal of Language and Social Psychology, 16,* 297–325.

Dimanche, F. and Lepetic, A. (1999). 'New Orleans tourism and crime: A case study'. *Journal of Travel Research, 38,* 19–23.

Dinges, N. G. and Baldwin, K. D. (1996). 'Intercultural competence: A research perspective'. In D. Landis and R. S. Bhagat (Eds), *Handbook of intercultural training* (2nd edn, pp. 106–123). Thousand Oaks, CA: Sage.

Ditchburn, G. J. (1996). 'Cross-cultural adjustment and psychoticism'. *Personality and Individual Differences, 21,* 295–296.

Dogan, H. (1989). 'Forms of adjustment: Sociocultural impacts of tourism'. *Annals of Tourism Research, 16*, 216–236.

Dohrenward, B. P. and Dohrenward, B. S. (1974). 'Social and cultural influences on psychopathology'. *Annual Review of Psychology, 25*, 417–452.

Dompierre, S. and Lavallée, M. (1990). 'Degré de contact et stress acculturatif dans le processus d'adaptation des réfugiés Africains'. *International Journal of Psychology, 25*, 417–437.

Donà, G. and Berry, J. W. (1994). 'Acculturation attitudes and acculturative stress of Central American refugees'. *International Journal of Psychology, 29*, 57–70.

Dorfman, P. W. and Howell, J. P. (1997). 'Managerial leadership in the United States and Mexico'. In C. S. Granrose and S. Oskamp (Eds), *Cross-cultural work groups* (pp. 163–185). Thousand Oaks, CA: Sage.

Downs, J. F. (1969). 'Fables, fancies and failures in cross-cultural training'. *Trends, 2*, (whole no. 3).

Draguns, J. G. (1997). 'Abnormal behavior patterns across cultures: Implications for counselling and psychotherapy'. *International Journal of Intercultural Relations, 21*, 213–248.

Dreher, G. and Ash, R. (1990). 'A comparative study of mentoring among men and women in managerial, professional and technical positions'. *Journal of Applied Psychology, 75*, 539–546.

Driskill, G. W. and Downs, C. W. (1995). 'Hidden differences in competent communication: A case study of an organization with Euro-Americans and first generation immigrants from India'. *International Journal of Intercultural Relations, 19*, 505–522.

Du Bois, C. (1956). *Foreign students and higher education in the United States.* Washington, DC: American Council on Education.

Dube, K. C. (1968). 'Mental disorder in Agra'. *Social Psychiatry, 3*, 139–143.

Duke, K. (1996). 'The resettlement of refugees in the United Kingdom'. *New Community, 22*, 461–478.

Dunbar, E. (1992). 'Adjustment and satisfaction of expatriate U.S. personnel'. *International Journal of Intercultural Relations, 16*, 1–16.

Dunbar, E. (1994). 'The German executive in the U.S. work and social environment: Exploring role demands'. *International Journal of Intercultural Relations, 18*, 277–291.

Duncan, S. (1969). 'Nonverbal communication'. *Psychological Bulletin, 72*, 118–137.

Dyal, J. A. (1984). 'Cross-cultural research with the locus of control construct'. In H. M. Lefcourt (Ed.), *Research with the locus of control construct* (Vol. 3, pp. 209–306). New York: Academic Press.

Dyal, J. A., Rybensky, L. and Somers, M. (1988). 'Marital and acculturative strain among Indo-Canadian and Euro-Canadian women'. In J. W. Berry and R. C. Annis (Eds), *Ethnic psychology: Research and practice with immigrants, refugees, native peoples, ethnic groups, and sojourners* (pp. 80–95). Lisse, The Netherlands: Swets & Zeitlinger.

Dyer, J., Vedlitz, A. and Worchel, S. (1989). 'Social distance among racial and ethnic groups in Texas: Some demographic correlates'. *Social Science Quarterly, 70*, 607–615.

Earley, P. C. (1989). 'Social loafing and collectivism: A comparison of the United States and the People's Republic of China'. *Administrative Science Quarterly, 34*, 565–581.

Earley, P. C. (1993). 'East meets West meets Mideast: Further explorations of collectivistic and individualistic work groups'. *Academy of Management Journal, 36*, 319–348.

Earley, P. C. and Randel, A. E. (1997). 'Self and other: "Face" and work group dynamics'. In C. S. Granrose and S. Oskamp (Eds), *Cross-cultural work groups* (pp. 113–133). Thousand Oaks, CA: Sage.

Ebata, K. and Miyake, Y. (1989). 'A mental health survey of the Vietnamese refugee in Japan'. *International Journal of Social Psychiatry, 35*, 164–172.

Ecotourism Society (1998). *Ecotourism statistical fact sheet: General tourism statistics.* Washington, DC: Ecotourism Society.

Edgell, D. L. (1990). *International tourism policy.* New York: Van Nostrand.

Eide, I. (Ed.). (1970). *Students as links between cultures.* Paris: UNESCO.

Eisenbruch, M. (1991). 'From Posttraumatic Stress Disorder to cultural bereavement: Diagnosis of Southeast Asian refugees'. *Social Science and Medicine, 33*, 673–680.

Eitinger, L. and Grunfeld, B. (1966). 'Psychosis among refugees in Norway'. *Acta Psychiatrica Scandinavia, 42*, 315–328.

Eitinger, L. and Schwarz, D. (Eds). (1981). *Strangers in the world.* Bern, Switzerland: Hans Huber.

Ekblad, S. (1993). 'Psychosocial adaptation of children while housed in a Swedish refugee camp: Aftermath of the collapse of Yugoslavia'. *Stress Medicine, 9*, 159–166.

Ekman, P. and Friesen, W. V. (1972). 'Hand movements'. *The Journal of Communication, 22*, 353–374.

Ekman, P. and Friesen, W. V. (1975). *Unmasking the face: A guide to recognizing emotions from facial clues.* Englewood Cliffs, NJ: Prentice-Hall.

Elich, J. H. and Blauw, P. W. (1981). *En toch terug* [Yet returned]. Rotterdam, The Netherlands: Department of Sociology, Erasmus University.

Emery, F. E. (Ed.). (1969). *Systems thinking.* Harmondsworth, UK: Penguin Books.

Eng, L. L. and Manthei, R. J. (1984). 'Malaysian and New Zealand students' self-reported adjustment and academic performance'. *New Zealand Journal of Educational Studies, 19*, 179–184.

English, E. P. (1986). *The great escape: An examination of North–South tourism.* Ottawa: The North South Institute.

Enloe, W. and Lewin, P. (1987). 'Issues of integration abroad and readjustment to Japan of Japanese returnees'. *International Journal of Intercultural Relations, 11*, 223–248.

Ensel, W. M. and Lin, N. (1991). 'The life stress paradigm and psychological distress'. *Journal of Health and Social Behavior, 32*, 321–342.

Erez, M. (1994). 'Toward a model of cross-cultural industrial and organizational psychology'. In H. C. Triandis, M. D. Dunnette and L. M. Hough (Eds), *Handbook of industrial and organizational psychology* (2nd edn, Vol. 4, pp. 559–607). Palo Alto, CA: Consulting Psychologists Press.

Erez, M. and Earley, P. C. (1993). *Culture, self-identity, and work.* New York: Oxford University Press.

Erez, M. and Somech, A. (1996). 'Is group productivity loss the rule or the exception? Effects of culture and group-based motivation'. *Academy of Management Journal, 39*, 1513–1537.

Espenshade, T. J. and Hempstead, K. (1996). 'Contemporary American attitudes toward U.S. immigration'. *International Migration Review, 30*, 533–570.

Espin, O. M. (1987). 'Psychological impact of migration on Latinas'. *Psychology of Women Quarterly, 11*, 489–503.

Esquivel, G. and Keitel, M. (1990). 'Counselling immigrant children in schools'. *Elementary School and Guidance Counselling, 24*, 213–221.

Esses, V. M., Jackson, L. M. and Armstrong, T. L. (1998). 'Intergroup competition and attitudes toward immigrants and immigration'. *Journal of Social Issues, 54*, 699–724.

Evans, J. R. and Berman, B. (Eds). (1992). *Marketing* (6th edn). New York: Macmillan.

Evans-Pritchard, D. (1993). 'Mobilization of tourism in Costa Rica'. *Annals of Tourism Research, 20*, 778–779.

Eylon, D. and Au, K. Y. (1999). 'Exploring empowerment cross-cultural differences along the power distance dimension'. *International Journal of Intercultural Relations, 23*, 373–385.

Farias, P. J. (1991). 'Emotional distress and its sociopolitical correlates in Salvadoran refugees: Analysis of a clinical sample'. *Culture, Medicine and Psychiatry, 15*, 167–192.

Farmer, R. J. S. and Hafeez, A. (1989). 'The contribution and needs of Southeast Asian refugees in New Zealand'. In M. Abbott (Ed.), *Refugee resettlement and well-being* (pp. 161–198). Auckland: Mental Health Foundation of New Zealand.

Farrell, B. H. (1979). 'Tourism's human conflicts: Cases from the Pacific'. *Annals of Tourism Research, 6*, 122–136.

Farver, J. A. M. (1984). 'Tourism and employment in the Gambia'. *Annals of Tourism Research, 11*, 249–265.

Faulkner, B. and Tideswell, C. (1997). 'A framework for monitoring community impacts of tourism'. *Journal of Sustainable Tourism, 5*, 3–28.

Fayerweather, J. (1959). *The executive overseas: Administrative attitudes and relationships in a foreign culture*. Syracuse: Syracuse University Press.

Fazel, M. K. and Young, D. M. (1988). 'Life quality of Tibetans and Hindus: A function of religion'. *Journal for the Scientific Study of Religion, 27*, 229–242.

Feghali, E. (1997). 'Arab cultural communication patterns'. *International Journal of Intercultural Relations, 21*, 345–378.

Feldman, D. C. and Bolino, M. C. (1999). 'The impact of on-site mentoring on expatriate socialization: A structural equation modelling approach'. *The International Journal of Human Resource Management, 10*, 54–71.

Feldman, D. C. and Thomas, D. (1992). 'Career issues facing expatriate managers'. *Journal of International Business Studies, 23*, 271–294.

Feldman, D. C. and Tompson, H. B. (1993). 'Expatriation, repatriation, and domestic geographic relocation: An empirical investigation of adjustment to new job assignments'. *Journal of International Business Studies, 24*, 507–529.

Feldman, S. S., Mont-Reynaud, R. and Rosenthal, D. (1992). 'When East moves West: The acculturation of values of Chinese adolescents in the U.S. and Australia'. *Journal of Research on Adolescence, 2*, 147–173.

Feldman, S. S. and Rosenthal, D. (1990). 'The acculturation of autonomy expectations on Chinese high schoolers in two Western nations'. *International Journal of Psychology, 25*, 259–281.

Felix-Ortiz, C. M., Newcomb, M. D. and Meyers, H. (1994). 'A multidimensional measure of cultural identity for Latino and Latina adolescents'. *Hispanic Journal of Behavioral Sciences, 16*, 99–115.

Ferdman, B. M. (1995). 'Cultural identity and diversity in organizations: Bridging the gap between group differences and individual uniqueness'. In M. Chemers,

S. Oskamp and M. Constanzo (Eds), *Diversity in organizations: New perspectives for a changing workplace* (pp. 37–61). Thousand Oaks, CA: Sage.

Ferdman, B. M. and Brody, S. E. (1996). 'Models of diversity training'. In D. Landis and R. S. Bhagat (Eds), *Handbook of intercultural training* (2nd edn, pp. 282–303). Thousand Oaks, CA: Sage.

Fernando, S. (1993). 'Racism and xenophobia'. *Innovation in Social Sciences Research, 6*, 9–19.

Fiedler, F. E., Mitchell, T. and Triandis, H. C. (1971). 'The culture assimilator: An approach to cross-cultural training'. *Journal of Applied Psychology, 55*, 95–102.

Fisher, F. (1995). *Culture shock! A global traveler's guide.* Singapore: Times Books.

Flanagan, J. C. (1954). 'The critical incident technique'. *Psychological Bulletin, 51*, 327–358.

Florkowski, G. W. and Fogel, D. S. (1999). 'Expatriate adjustment and commitment: The role of host-unit treatment'. *The International Journal of Human Resource Management, 10*, 783–807.

Foa, U. G. and Chemers, M. M. (1967). 'The significance of role behavior differentiation for cross-cultural interaction training'. *International Journal of Psychology, 2*, 45–57.

Folkman, S. and Lazarus, R. S. (1985). 'If it changes it must be a process: Studies of emotion and coping in three stages of a college examination'. *Journal of Personality and Social Psychology, 48*, 150–170.

Folkman, S., Schaeffer, C. and Lazarus, R. S. (1979). 'Cognitive processes as mediators of stress and coping'. In V. Hamilton and D. M. Warburton (Eds), *Human stress and cognition* (pp. 265–298). New York: Wiley.

Fontaine, G. (1986). 'Roles of social support in overseas relocation: Implications for intercultural training'. *International Journal of Intercultural Relations, 10*, 361–378.

Fontaine, G. (1996). 'Social support and the challenges of international assignments: Implications for training'. In D. Landis and R. S. Bhagat (Eds), *Handbook of intercultural training* (2nd edn, pp. 264–281). Thousand Oaks, CA: Sage.

Fowers, B. J. and Richardson, F. C. (1996). 'Why is multiculturalism good?'. *American Psychologist, 51*, 609–621.

Fowler, S. M. and Mumford, M. G. (Eds). (1995). *Intercultural sourcebook: Cross-cultural training methods* (Vol. 1). Yarmouth, MN: Intercultural Press.

Fox, C. (1997). 'The authenticity of intercultural communication'. *International Journal of Intercultural Relations, 21*, 85–103.

Fox, P. G., Cowell, J. M. and Montgomery, A. C. (1994). 'The effects of violence on health and adjustment of Southeast Asian refugee children: An integrative review'. *Public Health Nursing, 11*, 195–201.

Fox, W. M. (1995). 'Sociotechnical system principles and guidelines: Past and present'. *Journal of Applied Behavioral Science, 31*, 91–105.

Fransella, F. and Bannister, D. (1977). *A manual for repertory grid technique.* London: Academic Press.

Fraser, M. W. and Pecora, P. J. (1985–6). 'Psychological adaptation among Indochinese refugees'. *Journal of Applied Social Sciences, 10*, 20–21.

Fraser, S. E. and Brickman, W. W. (1968). *A history of international and comparative education.* Glenview, IL: Scott Foresman.

Freeman, M. A. (1997). 'Demographic correlates of individualism and collectivism: A study of social values in Sri Lanka'. *Journal of Cross-cultural Psychology, 28*, 321–341.

Fry, J. N. and Killing, J. P. (1989). *Strategic analysis and action* (2nd edn). Scarborough: Prentice-Hall.

Furnham, A. (1979). 'Assertiveness in three cultures: Multidimensionality and cultural differences'. *Journal of Clinical Psychology, 35,* 522–527.

Furnham, A. (1983). 'Social difficulty in three cultures'. *International Journal of Psychology, 18,* 215–228.

Furnham, A. (1984). 'Tourism and culture shock'. *Annals of Tourism Research, 11,* 41–57.

Furnham, A. (1985). 'Why do people save? Attitudes to, and habits of, saving money in Britain'. *Journal of Applied Social Psychology, 15,* 354–373.

Furnham, A. (1993). 'Communicating in foreign lands: The cause, consequences and cures of culture shock'. *Language, Culture and Curriculum, 6,* 91–109.

Furnham, A. and Alibhai, N. (1985). 'The friendship networks of foreign students: A replication and extension of the functional model'. *International Journal of Psychology, 20,* 709–722.

Furnham, A. and Bochner, S. (1982). 'Social difficulty in a foreign culture: An empirical analysis of culture shock'. In S. Bochner (Ed.), *Cultures in contact: Studies in cross-cultural interactions* (pp. 161–198). Oxford: Pergamon.

Furnham, A. and Bochner, S. (1986). *Culture shock: Psychological reactions to unfamiliar environments.* London: Methuen.

Furnham, A. and Erdmann, S. (1995). 'Psychological and sociocultural variables as predictors of adjustment in cross-cultural transitions'. *Psychologia, 38,* 238–251.

Furnham, A. and Li, Y. H. (1993). 'The psychological adjustment of the Chinese community in Britain: A study of two generations'. *British Journal of Psychiatry, 162,* 109–113.

Furnham, A. and Shiekh, S. (1993). 'Gender, generational and social support correlates of mental health in Asian immigrants'. *International Journal of Social Psychiatry, 39,* 22–33.

Furnham, A. and Tresize, L. (1981). 'The mental health of foreign students'. *Social Science and Medicine, 17,* 365–370.

Furukawa, T. (1997). 'Sojourner readjustment: Mental health of international students after one year's foreign sojourn and its psychosocial correlates'. *Journal of Nervous and Mental Diseases, 185,* 263–268.

Furukawa, T. and Shibayama, T. (1993). 'Predicting maladjustment of exchange students in different cultures: A prospective study'. *Social Psychiatry and Psychiatric Epidemiology, 28,* 142–146.

Furukawa, T. and Shibayama, T. (1994). 'Factors influencing adjustment of high school students in an international exchange program'. *Journal of Nervous and Mental Disease, 182,* 709–714.

Gabrielidis, C., Stephan, W. G., Ybarra, O., Pearson, V. M. D. S. and Villareal, L. (1997). 'Preferred styles of conflict resolution: Mexico and the United States'. *Journal of Cross-Cultural Psychology, 28,* 661–677.

Gaertner, S. L., Dovidio, J. F. and Bachman, B. A. (1996). 'Revisiting the contact hypothesis: The induction of a common ingroup identity'. *International Journal of Intercultural Relations, 20,* 271–290.

Gallimore, R., Boggs, J. W. and Jordan, C. (1974). *Culture, behavior and education: A study of Hawaiian-Americans.* Beverly Hills, CA: Sage.

Gallois, C., Franklyn-Stokes, A., Giles, H. and Coupland, N. (1988). 'Communication accommodation theory and intercultural encounters: Intergroup and interpersonal considerations'. In Y. Y. Kim and W. B. Gudykunst (Eds), *International and intercultural communication annual: Vol. 12. Theories in intercultural communication* (pp. 157–185). Newbury Park, CA: Sage.

Gallois, C., Giles, H., Jones, E., Cargile, A. A. and Ota, H. (1995). 'Accommodating intercultural encounters: Elaborations and extensions'. In R. L. Wiseman (Ed.), *Intercultural communication theory* (pp. 115–147). Thousand Oaks, CA: Sage.

Gannon, M. J. and Poon, J. M. L. (1997). 'Effects of alternative instructional approaches on cross-cultural training outcomes'. *International Journal of Intercultural Relations, 21*, 429–446.

Gao, G. (1998). '"Don't take my word for it." – Understanding Chinese speaking practices'. *International Journal of Intercultural Relations, 22*, 163–186.

Garcia, M. and Lega, L. (1979). 'Development of a Cuban ethnic identity questionnaire'. *Hispanic Journal of Behavioral Sciences, 1*, 247–261.

Gardner, G. H. (1962). 'Cross-cultural communication'. *Journal of Social Psychology, 58*, 241–256.

Garza-Guerrero, A. (1974). 'Culture shock: Its mourning and the vicissitudes of identity'. *Journal of American Psychoanalytic Association, 22*, 408–429.

Gaw, K.F. (2000). 'Reverse culture shock in students returning from overseas'. *International Journal of Intercultural Relations, 24*, 83–104.

Gelfand, D. (1989). 'Immigration, aging and intergenerational relationships'. *The Gerontologist, 29*, 366–372.

Georgas, J. (1998, August). 'Intergroup contact and acculturation of immigrants'. Paper presented at the XIV International Congress of the International Association for Cross-cultural Psychology, Bellingham, WA.

Georgas, J. and Papastylianou, D. (1996). 'Acculturation and ethnic identity: The remigration of ethnic Greeks to Greece'. In H. Grad, A. Blanco and G. Georgas (Eds), *Key issues in cross-cultural psychology* (pp. 114–127). Lisse, The Netherlands: Swets & Zeitlinger.

Gerdes, H. and Mallinckrodt, B. (1994). 'Emotional, social and academic adjustment of college students'. *Journal of Counselling and Development, 72*, 281–288.

Ghaffarian, S. (1987). 'The acculturation of Iranians in the United States'. *Journal of Social Psychology, 127*, 565–571.

Ghuman, P. (1994). 'Canadian or Indo-Canadian: A study of South Asian adolescents'. *International Journal of Adolescence and Youth, 4*, 229–243.

Gibson, C. B. (1997). 'Do you hear what I hear? A framework for reconciling intercultural communication difficulties arising from cognitive styles and cultural values'. In P. C. Earley and M. Erez (Eds), *New perspectives on international industrial/organizational psychology* (pp. 335–362). San Francisco: The New Lexington Press.

Gibson, M. (1993). 'Accommodation without assimilation'. Paper presented at the Conference of Immigrant Students in California, University of California, San Diego, Center for U.S.–Mexican Studies.

Gil, A. G., Vega, W. A. and Dimas, J. M. (1994). 'Acculturative stress and personal adjustment among Hispanic adolescent boys'. *Journal of Community Psychology, 22*, 42–54.

Giles, H. (1973). 'Accent mobility: A model and some data'. *Anthropological Linguistics, 15*, 87–105.

Giles, H., Bourhis, R. and Taylor, D. M. (1977). 'Towards a theory of language in ethnic group relations'. In H. Giles (Ed.), *Language, ethnicity and intergroup relations* (pp. 307–348). London: Academic Press.

Gish, D. (1983). 'Sources of missionary stress'. *Journal of Psychology and Theology, 11*, 243–250.

Golden, J. G. (1987). 'Acculturation, biculturalism and marginality: A study of Korean-American high school students'. *Dissertation Abstracts International, 48*, 1135A. (University Microfilms No. DA8716257)

Goldenberg, V. and Saxe, L. (1996). 'Social attitudes of Russian immigrants to the United States'. *Journal of Social Psychology, 136*, 421–434.

Golding, J. M. and Burnam, M. A. (1990). 'Immigration, stress, and depressive symptoms in a Mexican-American community'. *Journal of Nervous and Mental Disease, 178*, 161–171.

Goldstein, I. L. (1991). 'Training in work organizations'. In M. D. Dunnette and L. M. Hough (Eds), *Handbook of industrial and organizational psychology* (2nd edn, Vol. 2., pp. 507–619). Palo Alto, CA: Consulting Psychologists Press.

Goldstein, I. L. (1993). *Training in organizations: Needs assessment, development, and evaluation* (3rd edn). Pacific Grove, CA: Brooks/Cole.

Gollwitzer, P. M., Heckhausen, H. and Ratajczak, H. (1990). 'From weighing to willing: Approaching a change decision through pre- or postdecisional mentation'. *Organizational Behavior and Human Decision Processes, 45*, 41–65.

Gomez, M. J. and Fassinger, R. E. (1994). 'An initial model of Latina achievement: Acculturation, biculturalism and achieving styles'. *Journal of Counselling Psychology, 41*, 205–215.

Goodman, M. E. (1967). *The individual and culture*. Homewood, IL: The Dorsey Press.

Goot, M. (1993). 'Multiculturalists, monoculturalists and the many in between: Attitudes to cultural diversity and their correlates'. *Australian and New Zealand Journal of Sociology, 99*, 226–253.

Graen, G. B. and Wakabayashi, M. (1994). 'Cross-cultural leadership making: Bridging American and Japanese diversity for team advantage'. In H. C. Triandis, M. D. Dunnette and L. M. Hough (Eds), *Handbook of industrial and organizational psychology* (2nd edn, Vol. 4, pp. 415–446). Palo Alto, CA: Consulting Psychologists Press.

Granrose, C. S. and Oskamp, S. (Eds). (1997). *Cross-cultural work groups*. Thousand Oaks, CA: Sage.

Grassby, A. J. (1973). *A multicultural society for the future*. Canberra: Australian Government Publishing Service.

Graves, T. D. (1967). 'Psychological acculturation in a tri-ethnic community'. *Southwestern Journal of Anthropology, 23*, 337–350.

Green, B. C. and Chalip, L. (1998). 'Sport tourism as the celebration of subculture'. *Annals of Tourism Research, 25*, 275–291.

Gudykunst, W. B. (1983a). 'Similarities and differences in perceptions of initial intracultural and intercultural interactions'. *The Southern Speech Communication Journal, 49*, 40–65.

Gudykunst, W. B. (1983b). 'Toward a typology of stranger-host relationships'. *International Journal of Intercultural Relations, 7*, 401–415.

Gudykunst, W. B. (1985). 'A model of uncertainty reduction in intercultural encounters'. *Journal of Language and Social Psychology, 4*, 79–98.

Gudykunst, W. B. (1995). 'Anxiety/uncertainty management (AUM) theory'. In R. L. Wiseman (Ed.), *Intercultural communication theory* (pp. 8–58). Thousand Oaks, CA: Sage.

Gudykunst, W. B. (1998a). 'Individualistic and collectivistic perspectives on communication: An introduction'. *International Journal of Intercultural Relations, 22*, 107–134.

Gudykunst, W. B. (1998b). 'Applying anxiety/uncertainty management (AUM) theory to intercultural adjustment training'. *International Journal of Intercultural Relations, 22*, 227–250.

Gudykunst, W. B., Guzley, R. M. and Hammer, M. R. (1996). 'Designing intercultural training'. In D. Landis and R. S. Bhagat (Eds), *Handbook of intercultural training* (2nd edn, pp. 61–80). Thousand Oaks, CA: Sage.

Gudykunst, W. B. and Hammer, M. R. (1983). 'Basic training design: Approaches to intercultural training'. In D. Landis and R. W. Brislin (Eds), *Handbook of intercultural training: Volume 1. Issues in theory and design* (pp. 118–154). New York: Pergamon.

Gudykunst, W. B. and Hammer, M. R. (1984). 'Dimensions of intercultural effectiveness: Culture specific or culture general?'. *International Journal of Intercultural Relations, 8*, 1–10.

Gudykunst, W. B. and Hammer, M. R. (1988). 'Strangers and hosts: An uncertainty reduction based theory of intercultural adaptation'. In Y. Y. Kim and W. B. Gudykunst (Eds), *Cross-cultural adaptation: Current approaches* (pp. 106–139). Newbury Park, CA: Sage.

Gudykunst, W. B. and Kim, Y. Y. (1984). *Communicating with strangers: An approach to intercultural communication.* New York: Random House.

Gudykunst, W. B. and Matsumoto, Y. (1996). 'Cross-cultural variability of communication in interpersonal relationships'. In W. B. Gudykunst and S. Ting-Toomey (Eds), *Communication in personal relationships across cultures* (pp. 19–56). Thousand Oaks, CA; Sage.

Gudykunst, W. B. and Nishida, T. (1986). 'The influence of cultural variability on perceptions of communication behavior associated with relationship terms'. *Human Communication Research, 13*, 147–166.

Gudykunst, W. B. and Shapiro, R. B. (1996). 'Communication in everyday interpersonal and intergroup encounters'. *International Journal of Intercultural Relations, 20*, 19–45.

Gudykunst, W. B., Sodetani, L. and Sonoda, K. (1987). 'Uncertainty reduction in Japanese–American–Caucasian relationships in Hawaii'. *Western Journal of Speech Communication, 51*, 256–278.

Gudykunst, W. B., Yoon, Y. C. and Nishida, T. (1987). 'The influence of individualism–collectivism on perceptions of communication in in-group and out-group relationships'. *Communication Monographs, 54*, 295–306.

Gullahorn, J. E. and Gullahorn, J. T. (1966). 'American students abroad: Professional vs. personal development'. *The Annals, 368*, 43–59.

Gullahorn, J. T. and Gullahorn, J. E. (1962). 'Visiting Fulbright professors as agents of cross-cultural communication'. *Sociology and Social Research, 46*, 282–293.

Gullahorn, J. T. and Gullahorn, J. E. (1963). 'An extension of the U-curve hypothesis'. *Journal of Social Issues, 19*, 33–47.

Guskin, A. E. (1966). 'Tradition and change in a Thai university'. In R. B. Textor (Ed.), *Cultural frontiers of the Peace Corps* (pp. 87–106). Cambridge, MA: MIT Press.

Guthrie, G. M. (1966). 'Cultural preparation for the Philippines'. In R. B. Textor (Ed.), *Cultural frontiers of the Peace Corps* (pp. 15–34). Cambridge, MA: MIT Press.

Guthrie, G. M. (1975). 'A behavioral analysis of culture learning'. In R. W. Brislin, S. Bochner and W. J. Lonner (Eds), *Cross-cultural perspectives on learning* (pp. 95–115). New York: Sage.

Guthrie, G. M. (1977). 'Problems of measurement in cross-cultural research'. *Annals of the New York Academy of Sciences, 285*, 131–140.

Guthrie, G. M. (1981). 'What you need is continuity'. In S. Bochner (Ed.), *The mediating person: Bridges between cultures* (pp. 96–112). Cambridge, MA: Schenkman.

Guthrie, G. M. and Zektick, I. N. (1967). 'Predicting performance in the Peace Corps'. *Journal of Social Psychology, 71*, 11–21.

Guzzo, R. A., Noonan, K. A. and Elron, E. (1994). 'Expatriate managers and the psychological contract'. *Journal of Applied Psychology, 79*, 617–626.

Hailey, J. (1996). 'Breaking through the glass ceiling'. *People Management, 2*, 32–34.

Hakstian, A. R., Woolsey, L. K. and Schroeder, M. L. (1986). 'Development and application of a quickly-scored in-basket exercise in an organizational setting'. *Educational and Psychological Measurement, 46*, 385–396.

Hall, C. M. and O'Sullivan, V. (1996). 'Tourism, political stability and violence'. In A. Pizam and Y. Mansfeld (Eds), *Tourism, crime and international security issues* (pp. 105–121). Chichester, UK: Wiley.

Hall, E. T. (1959). *The silent language*. Garden City, NY: Doubleday.

Hall, E. T. (1966). *The hidden dimension*. Garden City, NY: Doubleday.

Hall, J. and Beil-Warner, D. (1978). 'Assertiveness of male Anglo- and Mexican-American college students'. *Journal of Social Psychology, 105*, 175–178.

Hammer, M. R. (1987). 'Behavioral dimensions of intercultural effectiveness: A replication and extension'. *International Journal of Intercultural Relations, 11*, 65–88.

Hammer, M. R. (1992). 'Research mission statements and international students advisory offices'. *International Journal of Intercultural Relations, 16*, 217–236.

Hammer, M. R., Gudykunst, W. B. and Wiseman, R.L. (1978). 'Dimensions of intercultural effectiveness: An exploratory study'. *International Journal of Intercultural Relations, 2*, 383–393.

Hammer, M. R., Hart, W. and Rogan, R. (1998). 'Can you go home again? An analysis of the repatriation of corporate managers and spouses'. *Management International Review, 38*, 67–86.

Hampton, M. P. (1998). 'Backpacker tourism and economic development'. *Annals of Tourism Research, 25*, 639–660.

Hanna, J. M. and Fitzgerald, M. H. (1993). 'Acculturation and symptoms: A comparative study of reported health symptoms in three Samoan communities'. *Social Science and Medicine, 36*, 1169–1180.

Hannigan, T. (1990). 'Traits, attitudes, and skills that are related to intercultural effectiveness and their implications for cross-cultural training: A review of the literature'. *International Journal of Intercultural Relations, 14*, 89–111.

Hannigan, T. (1997). 'Homesickness and acculturation stress in the international student'. In M. A. L. Van Tilburg and A. J. J. M. Vingerhoets (Eds), *Psychological aspects of geographic movement* (pp. 71–81). Tilburg, The Netherlands: University of Tilburg Press.

Harari, H., Jones, C. and Sek, H. (1988). 'Stress syndromes and stress predictors in American and Polish college students'. *Journal of Cross-Cultural Psychology, 19*, 243–255.

Harris, A. C. and Verven, R. (1996). 'The Greek-American Acculturation Scale: Development and validity'. *Psychological Reports, 78*, 599–610.

Harris, H. and Brewster, C. (1999). 'The coffee-machine system: How international selection really works'. *The International Journal of Human Resource Management, 10*, 488–500.

Harris, J. G. (1973). 'A science of the South Pacific: Analysis of the character structure of the Peace Corps volunteer'. *American Psychologist, 28*, 232–247.

Harris, P. R. and Moran, R. T. (1991). *Managing cultural differences* (3rd edn). Houston, TX: Gulf.

Harrison, D. (1994). 'Tourism and prostitution: Sleeping with the enemy?'. *Tourism Management, 15*, 435–443.

Harrison, E. (1990). 'Searching for the causes of schizophrenia: The role of migrant studies'. *Schizophrenia Bulletin, 16*, 663–671.

Harrison, J. K. (1992). 'Individual and combined effects of behavior modeling and the cultural assimilator in cross-cultural management training'. *Journal of Applied Psychology, 77*, 952–962.

Harrison, J. K., Chadwick, M. and Scales, M. (1996). 'The relationship between cross-cultural adjustment and the personality variables of self-efficacy and self-monitoring'. *International Journal of Intercultural Relations, 20*, 167–188.

Harvey, M. (1995). 'The impact of dual-career families on international relocation'. *Human Resource Management Review, 5*, 279–304.

Harvey, M. (1996). 'Dual-career couples: The selection dilemma in international relocation'. *International Journal of Selection and Assessment, 4*, 215–227.

Harvey, M. (1997a). 'Dual-career expatriates: Expectation, adjustment, and satisfaction with international relocation'. *Journal of International Business Studies, 28*, 627–658.

Harvey, M. (1997b). '"Inpatriation" training: The next challenge for international human resource management'. *International Journal of Intercultural Relations, 21*, 393–428.

Harvey, M. (1998). 'Dual-career couples during international relocation: The trailing spouse'. *The International Journal of Human Resource Management, 9*, 309–331.

Harvey, M., Buckley, M. R., Novicevic, M. M. and Wiese, D. (1999). 'Mentoring dual-career expatriates: A sense-making and sense-giving social support process'. *The International Journal of Human Resource Management, 10*, 808–827.

Harvey, M., Speier, C. and Novicevic, M. N. (1999). 'The role of inpatriation in global staffing'. *The International Journal of Human Resource Management, 10*, 459–476.

Harvey, R. J. (1991). 'Job analysis'. In M. D. Dunnette and L. M. Hough (Eds), *Handbook of industrial and organizational psychology* (2nd edn, pp. 71–163). Palo Alto, CA: Consulting Psychologists Press.

Hauff, E. and Vaglum, P. (1993). 'Vietnamese boat refugees: The influence of war and flight traumatization on mental health on arrival in the country of resettlement'. *Acta Psychiatrica Scandinavia, 88*, 162–168.

Hauff, E. and Vaglum, P. (1995). 'Organized violence and the stress of exile: Predictors of mental health in a community cohort of Vietnamese refugees three years after resettlement'. *British Journal of Psychiatry, 166*, 360–367.

Hawaii Department of Business and Economic Development, Tourism Branch (1989). *1988 statewide tourism impact core study*. Honolulu: Department of Business and Economic Development.

Hawes, F. and Kealey, D. (1980). *Canadians in development*. Ottawa: Canadian International Development Agency.

Hayes, C. (1998). 'World class learning'. *Black Enterprise, 28* (10), 85–90.

Hede, A. and O'Brien, E. (1996). 'Affirmative action in the Australian private sector: A longitudinal analysis'. *International Review of Women and Leadership, 2*, 15–29.

Heine, S. J. and Lehman, D. R. (1997, August). 'Acculturation and self-esteem change: Evidence for a Western cultural foundation in the construct of self-esteem'. Paper presented at the Second Conference of the Asian Association of Social Psychology, Kyoto, Japan.

Heiss, J. and Nash, D. (1967). 'The stranger in laboratory culture revisited'. *Human Organization, 26*, 47–51.

Hemsi, L.K. (1967). 'Psychiatric morbidity of West Indian immigrants'. *Social Psychiatry, 2*, 95–100.

Henderson, G., Milhouse, V. and Cao, L. (1993). 'Crossing the gap: An analysis of Chinese students' culture shock in an American university'. *College Student Journal, 27*, 380–389.

Henderson, J. C. (1997). 'Singapore's wartime heritage attractions'. *The Journal of Tourism Studies, 8*, 39–49.

Heras, P. and Revilla, L. A. (1994). 'Acculturation, generational status, and family environment of Pilipino Americans: A study in cultural adaptation'. *Family Therapy, 21*, 129–138.

Hesketh, B. (1997). 'Dilemmas in training for transfer and retention'. *Applied Psychology: An International Review, 46*, 317–386.

Hesketh, B. and Bochner, S. (1994). 'Technological change in a multicultural context: Implications for training and career planning'. In H. C. Triandis, M. D. Dunnette and L. M. Hough (Eds), *Handbook of industrial and organizational psychology* (2nd edn, Vol. 4, pp. 191–240). Palo Alto, CA: Consulting Psychologists Press.

Hester, R. T. (1990). 'The sacred structure of small towns: A return to Manteo, North Carolina'. *Small Town, 20*, 5–21.

Hewstone, M. and Ward, C. (1985). 'Ethnocentrism and causal attribution in Southeast Asia'. *Journal of Personality and Social Psychology, 48*, 614–623.

Hicks, R., Lalonde, R. and Pepler, D. (1993). 'Psychosocial considerations in the mental health of immigrant and refugee children'. *Canadian Journal of Community Mental Health, 12*, 71–87.

Hickson, J. (1994). 'Re-entry shock: Coming "home" again'. In W. J. Lonner and R. Malpass (Eds), *Psychology and culture* (pp. 253–257). Needham Heights, MA: Allyn & Bacon.

Hinkle, L. L. (1998). 'Teacher nonverbal immediacy behaviors and student-perceived cognitive learning in Japan'. *Communication Research Reports, 15*, 45–56.

Ho, R., Niles, S., Penney, R. and Thomas, A. (1994). 'Migrants and multiculturalism: A survey of attitudes in Darwin'. *Australian Psychologist, 29*, 62–70.

Hocoy, D. (1996). 'Empirical distinctiveness between cognitive and affective elements of ethnic identity and scales for their measurement'. In H. Grad, A. Blanco and J. Georgas (Eds), *Key issues in cross-cultural psychology* (pp. 128–137). Lisse, The Netherlands: Swets & Zeitlinger.

Hoffman, R. C. (1999). 'Organizational innovation: Management influence across cultures'. *Multinational Business Review, 7*, 37–49.

Hofman, J. E. (1982). 'Social identity and readiness for social relations between Jews and Arabs in Israel'. *Human Relations, 35*, 727–741.

Hofstede, G. (1980). *Culture's consequences: International differences in work-related values.* Beverly Hills, CA: Sage.

Hofstede, G. (1983). 'Dimensions of national cultures in fifty countries and three regions'. In J. Deregowski, S. Dzuirawiec and R. C. Annis (Eds), *Expiscations in cross-cultural psychology* (pp. 335–355). Lisse, The Netherlands: Swets & Zeitlinger.

Hofstede, G. (1991). *Cultures and organizations: Software of the mind.* London: McGraw-Hill.

Hofstede, G. (1998). 'Think locally, act globally: Cultural constraints in personnel management'. *Management International Review, 38*, 7–26.

Holdaway, S. (1998). 'Police relations in England: A history of policy'. *International Journal of Intercultural Relations, 22*, 329–349.

Hollander, E. P. (1985). 'Leadership and power'. In G. Lindzey and E. Aronson (Eds), *The handbook of social psychology* (3rd edn, Vol. 2, pp. 485–537). New York: Random House.

Hollander, E. P. and Offermann, L. R. (1990). 'Power and leadership in organizations: Relationships in transition'. *American Psychologist, 45*, 179–189.

Holmes, T. H. and Rahe, R. H. (1967). 'The Social Readjustment Rating Scale'. *Journal of Psychosomatic Research, 11*, 213–218.

Holmes, T. S. and Holmes, T. H. (1970). 'Short term intrusions into the life style routine'. *Journal of Psychosomatic Research, 14*, 121–132.

Home Office. (1998). *Immigration statistics in the United Kingdom.* Available: http://www.homeoffice.gov.uk/rds.pdfs/hosb2498.pdf.

Horenczyk, G. (1996). 'Migrant identities in conflict: Acculturation attitudes and perceived acculturation ideologies'. In G. Breakwell and E. Lyons (Eds), *Changing European identities: Social psychological analyses of social change* (pp. 241–250). Oxford: Butterworth-Heinemann.

Huang, K., Leong, F. T. L. and Wagner, N. S. (1994). 'Coping with peer stressors and associated dysphoria: Acculturation differences among Chinese-American children'. *Counselling Psychology Quarterly, 7*, 53–68.

Hudson, B. J. (1998).'Waterfalls: Resources for tourism'. *Annals of Tourism Research, 25*, 958–973.

Hung, Y. Y. (1974). 'Sociocultural environment and locus of control'. *Psychologica Taiwanica, 16*, 187–198.

Hurtado, A., Gurin, P. and Peng, T. (1994). 'Social identities – A framework for studying the adaptations of immigrants and ethnics: The adaptations of Mexicans in the United States'. *Social Problems, 41*, 129–151.

Hurtado, A., Rodríguez, J., Gurin, P. and Beals, J. L. (1993).' The impact of Mexican descendants' social identity on the ethnic socialization of children'. In M. E. Bernal and G. P. Knight (Eds), *Ethnic identity* (pp. 131–162). Albany: State University of New York Press.

Husbands, W. C. (1986). 'Periphery resort tourism and tourist-resident stress: An example from Barbados'. *Leisure Studies, 5*, 175–188.

Hutnik, N. (1986). 'Patterns of ethnic minority identification and modes of social adaptation'. *Ethnic and Racial Studies, 9*, 150–167.

Huxley, A. (1925). *Along the road: Notes and essays of a tourist.* London: Chatto & Windus.

Icduygu, A. (1994). 'Facing changes and making choices: Unintended Turkish immigrant settlement in Australia'. *International Migration, 32*, 71–93.

Ima, K. and Rumbaut, R. G. (1989). 'Southeast Asian refugees in American schools: A comparison of fluent-English proficient and limited-English proficient students'. *Topics in Language Disorders, 9*, 54–77.

Imahori, T. T. and Cupach, W. R. (1994). 'A cross-cultural comparison of the inter-pretation and management of face: U.S. American and Japanese responses to embarrassing predicaments'. *International Journal of Intercultural Relations, 18,* 193–219.

Inkeles, A. (1975). 'Becoming modern: Individual change in six developing countries'. *Ethos, 3,* 323–342.

Irvine, J. J. and York, D. E. (1995). 'Learning styles and culturally diverse students: A literature review'. In J. A. Banks and C. A. M. Banks (Eds), *Handbook of research on multicultural education* (pp. 484–497). New York: Macmillan.

Isajiw, W. W. (2000). 'Approaches to ethnic conflict resolution: Paradigms and prin-ciples'. *International Journal of Intercultural Relations, 24,* 105–124.

Isogai T. Y., Hayashi, Y. and Uno, M. (1999). 'Identity issues and re-entry training'. *International Journal of Intercultural Relations, 23,* 493–525.

Jackson, M. S., White, G. N. and Schmierer, C. (1996). 'Tourism experiences within an attributional framework'. *Annals of Tourism Research, 23,* 798–810.

Jackson, S. E. (1992). 'Team composition in organizational settings: Issues in managing an increasingly diverse work force'. In S. Worchel, W. Wood and J. Simpson (Eds), *Group process and productivity* (pp. 138–173). Newbury Park, CA: Sage.

Jacobson, E. H. (1963). 'Sojourn research: A definition of the field'. *Journal of Social Issues, 19,* 123–129.

Jaspars, J. and Hewstone, M. (1982). 'Cross-cultural interaction, social attribution and intergroup relations'. In S. Bochner (Ed.), *Cultures in contact: Studies in cross-cultural interaction* (pp. 127–156). Oxford: Pergamon.

Jayasuriya, L., Sang, D. and Fielding, A. (1992). *Ethnicity, immigration and mental illness: A critical review of Australian research.* Canberra: Bureau of Immigration Research.

Jensen, S. B., Schaumberg, E., Leroy, B., Larsen, B. Ø. and Thorup, M. (1989). 'Psy-chiatric care of refugees exposed to organized violence'. *Acta Psychiatrica Scandi-navia, 80,* 125–131.

Jochems, W., Snippe, J., Smid, H. J. and Verweij, A. (1996). 'The academic progress of foreign students: Study achievement and study behaviour'. *Higher Education, 31,* 325–340.

Jones, E. E. and Nisbett, R. E. (1971). 'The actor and observer: Divergent perceptions of the causes of behavior'. In E. E. Jones, D. E. Kanouse, H. H. Kelley, R. E. Nisbett, S. Valins and B. Weiner (Eds), *Attribution: Perceiving the causes of behavior* (pp. 79–94). Morristown, NJ: General Learning Press.

Jones, J. M. (1994). 'The African American: A duality dilemma?'. In W. J. Lonner and R. Malpass (Eds), *Psychology and culture* (pp. 17–21). Needham Heights, MA: Allyn & Bacon.

Jones, S. E. (1971). 'A comparative proxemics analysis of dyadic interaction in selected subcultures of New York City'. *Journal of Social Psychology, 84,* 35–44.

Jou, Y. H. (1993). 'The comparisons of social support between Chinese students in Japan and Japanese students'. *Bulletin of the Faculty of Education, Hiroshima University, 42,* 63–69. (In Japanese, English summary)

Jou, Y. H. and Fukada, H. (1996). 'Comparison of differences in the association of social support and adjustment between Chinese and Japanese students in Japan: A research note'. *Psychological Reports, 79,* 107–112.

Jou, Y. H. and Fukada, H. (1997). 'Stress and social support in mental and physical health of Chinese students in Japan'. *Psychological Reports, 81*, 1301–1312.

Jung, D. I. and Avolio, B. J. (1999). 'Effects of leadership style and followers' cultural orientation on performance in group and individual task conditions'. *Academy of Management Journal, 42*, 208–218.

Juthani, N. V. (1992). 'Immigrant mental health: Conflicts and concerns of Indian immigrants in the U.S.A.'. *Psychology and Developing Societies, 4*, 133–148.

Kagan, H. and Cohen, J. (1990). 'Cultural adjustment of international students'. *Psychological Science, 1*, 133–137.

Kâğitçibaşi, C. (1994). 'A critical appraisal of individualism and collectivism: Toward a new formulation'. In U. Kim, H. C. Triandis, C. Kâğitçibaşi, S.-C. Choi and G. Yoon (Eds), *Individualism and collectivism: Theory, methods and applications* (pp. 52–64). Thousand Oaks, CA: Sage.

Kalin, R. and Berry, J. W. (1979). 'Determinants and attitudinal correlates of ethnic identity in Canada'. Paper presented at the Annual Meeting of the Canadian Psychological Association, Quebec, Canada.

Kalin, R. and Berry, J. W. (1982). 'The social ecology of ethnic attitudes in Canada'. *Canadian Journal of Behavioral Science, 14*, 97–109.

Kao, G. and Tienda, M. (1995). 'Optimism and achievement: The educational performance of immigrant youth'. *Social Science Quarterly, 76*, 1–19.

Kaplan, M. S. and Marks, G. (1990). 'Adverse effects of acculturation: Psychological distress among Mexican American young adults'. *Social Science and Medicine, 31*, 1313–1319.

Kashima, E. S., Hardie, E. A. and Kashima, Y. (1998). 'Effects of stable and temporary social contexts on personal, relational, and collective selves'. *Australian Journal of Psychology, 50*, (Abstracts Supplement), 26.

Kashima, Y. and Callan, V. J. (1994). 'The Japanese work group'. In H. C. Triandis, M. D. Dunnette and L. M. Hough (Eds), *Handbook of industrial and organizational psychology* (2nd edn, Vol. 4, pp. 609–646). Palo Alto, CA: Consulting Psychologists Press.

Kashima, Y., Kokubo, T., Kashima, E. S., Yamaguchi, S., Boxall, D. and MacRae, K. (1998). Culture, social network, and self: Can urban-rural differences in social networks explain differences in self-construals?'. *Australian Journal of Psychology, 50*, (Abstracts Supplement), 26.

Kato, H. and Kato, J. S. (1992). *Understanding and working with the Japanese business world*. Englewood Cliffs, NJ: Prentice-Hall.

Katz, D. and Braly, K. (1933). 'Racial stereotypes of one hundred college students'. *Journal of Abnormal and Social Psychology, 28*, 280–290.

Katz, P.A. (Ed.). (1976). *Towards the elimination of racism*. New York: Pergamon.

Katzell, R. A. and Thompson, D. E. (1990). 'Work motivation: Theory and practice'. *American Psychologist, 45*, 144–153.

Kealey, D. J. (1989). 'A study of cross-cultural effectiveness: Theoretical issues and practical applications'. *International Journal of Intercultural Relations, 13*, 387–428.

Kealey, D. J. (1996). 'The challenge of international personnel selection'. In D. Landis and R. S. Bhagat (Eds), *Handbook of intercultural training* (2nd edn, pp. 81–105). Thousand Oaks, CA: Sage.

Kealey, D. J. and Protheroe, D. R. (1996). 'The effectiveness of cross-cultural training for expatriates: An assessment of the literature on the issue'. *International Journal of Intercultural Relations, 20*, 141–165.

Kearney, G. E. and McElwain, D. W. (Eds). (1976). *Aboriginal cognition: Retrospect and prospect.* Canberra: Australian Institute of Aboriginal Studies.

Kee, P. K. and Skeldon, R. (1994). 'The migration and settlement of Hong Kong Chinese in Australia'. In R. Skeldon (Ed.), *Reluctant exiles: Hong Kong communities overseas* (pp. 260–280). Hong Kong: Hong Kong University Press.

Keefe, S. (1992). 'Ethnic identity: The domain of perceptions and attachment to ethnic groups and cultures'. *Human Organizations, 51,* 35–43.

Keefe, S. and Padilla, A. M. (1987). *Chicano ethnicity.* Albuquerque, NM: University of New Mexico Press.

Kelley, C. and Meyers, J. E. (1989). *The Cross-cultural Adaptability Inventory.* Minneapolis: National Computer Systems.

Kelley, H. H. (1972). *Causal schemata and the attribution process.* Morristown, NJ: General Learning Press.

Kennedy, A. (1994). 'Personality and psychological adjustment during cross-cultural transitions: A study of the cultural fit proposition'. Unpublished master's thesis, University of Canterbury, New Zealand.

Kennedy, A. (1998, April). 'Acculturation and coping: A longitudinal study of Singaporeans studying abroad'. Paper presented at the Annual Meeting of the Society of Australasian Social Psychologists, Christchurch, New Zealand.

Kennedy, A. (1999). 'Singaporean sojourners: Meeting the demands of cross-cultural transition'. Unpublished doctoral thesis, National University of Singapore.

Kennedy, R. F. (1963, February 16). 'A free trade in ideas'. *Saturday Review,* 43–44.

Kenny, M. and Florida, R. (1993). *Beyond mass production: The Japanese system and its transfer in the United States.* New York: Oxford University Press.

Khamouna, M. and Zeiger, J. (1995). 'Peace through tourism'. *Parks and Recreation, 30,* 80–86.

Kidder, L. H. (1992). 'Requirements for being "Japanese:" Stories of returnees'. *International Journal of Intercultural Relations, 16,* 383–394.

Kim, J. (1981). 'The process of Asian American identity development: A study of Japanese American women's perceptions of their struggle to achieve positive identities'. Unpublished doctoral dissertation, University of Massachusetts.

Kim, M.-S. (1995). 'Toward a theory of conversational constraints: Focussing on individual-level dimensions of culture'. In R. L. Wiseman (Ed.), *Intercultural communication theory* (pp. 148–169). Thousand Oaks, CA: Sage.

Kim, U. (1984). 'Psychological acculturation of Korean immigrants in Toronto: A study of modes of acculturation, identity, language and acculturative stress'. Unpublished master's thesis, Queen's University, Kingston, Canada.

Kim, U. (1988). 'Acculturation of Korean immigrants to Canada'. Unpublished doctoral thesis, Queen's University, Kingston, Canada.

Kim, U. (1995). *Individualism and collectivism: A psychological, cultural and ecological analysis.* Copenhagen: NIAS Publications.

Kim, U., Cho, W.-C. and Harajiri, H. (1997). 'The perception of Japanese people and culture: The case of Korean nationals and sojourners'. In K. Leung, U. Kim, S. Yamaguchi and Y. Kashima (Eds), *Progress in Asian social psychology* (Vol. 1, pp. 321–344). Singapore: John Wiley.

Kim, U., Triandis, H. C., Kâğitçibaşi, C., Choi, S.-C. and Yoon, G. (Eds). (1994). *Individualism and collectivism: Theory, methods and applications.* Thousand Oaks, CA: Sage.

Kinzie, J. D., Boehnlein, J. K., Leung, P. K., Moore, L. J., Riley, C. and Smith, D.

(1990). 'The prevalence of Posttraumatic Stress Disorder and its clinical significance among Southeast Asian refugees'. *American Journal of Psychiatry, 147*, 913–917.

Kinzie, J. D., Fredrickson, R. H., Ben, R., Fleck, J. and Karls, W. (1984). 'Post-traumatic Stress Disorder among survivors of Cambodian concentration camps'. *American Journal of Psychiatry, 141*, 645–650.

Kinzie, J. D. and Manson, S. (1983). 'Five-years' experience with Indochinese refugee psychiatric patients'. *Journal of Operational Psychiatry, 14*, 105–111.

Kinzie, J. D., Sack, W. H., Angell, R. H., Manson, S. and Rath, B. (1986). 'The psychiatric effects of massive trauma on Cambodian children'. *Journal of the American Academy of Child Psychiatry, 25*, 370–376.

Kirkman, B. J. and Shapiro, D. L. (1997). 'The impact of cultural values on employee resistance to teams: Toward a model of globalized self-managing work team effectiveness'. *Academy of Management Review, 22*, 730–757.

Klineberg, O. (1971). 'Black and white in international perspective'. *American Psychologist, 26*, 119–128.

Klineberg, O. (1976). *International educational exchange: An assessment of its nature and prospects.* Paris: Mouton.

Klineberg, O. (1981). 'The role of international university exchanges'. In S. Bochner (Ed.), *The mediating person: Bridges between cultures* (pp. 113–135). Cambridge, MA: Schenkman.

Klineberg, O. (1982). 'Contact between ethnic groups: A historical perspective of some aspects of theory and research'. In S. Bochner (Ed.), *Cultures in contact: Studies in cross-cultural interaction* (pp. 45–55). Oxford: Pergamon.

Klineberg, O. and Hull, W. F. (1979). *At a foreign university: An international study of adaptation and coping.* New York: Praeger.

Kluckhohn, C. (1949). *Mirror for man.* New York: McGraw-Hill.

Kluckhohn, F. and Strodbeck, F. L. (1961). *Variations in value orientations.* Evanston, IL: Row Peterson.

Kogut, B. and Singh, H. (1988). 'The effect of national culture on the choice of entry mode'. *Journal of International Business Studies, 19*, 411–432.

Kohls, L. R. (1995). *Training know-how for cross-cultural diversity trainers.* Duncanville, TX: Adult Learning Systems.

Kohls, L. R. and Knight, J. M. (1994). *Developing intercultural awareness: A cross-cultural training handbook* (2nd edn). Yarmouth, MN: Intercultural Press.

Kontogeorgopoulos, N. (1998). 'Accommodation employment patterns and opportunities'. *Annals of Tourism Research, 25*, 314–339.

Kopp, R. (1994). 'International human resource policies and practices in Japanese, European, and United States multinationals'. *Human Resource Management, 33*, 581–599.

Koretz, G. (1998, December 21). 'U.S. colleges look overseas'. *Business Week, Iss. 3609*, 22.

Korn-Ferry International (1981). *The repatriation of the American international executive.* New York: Author.

Kosmitzki, C. (1996). 'The reaffirmation of cultural identity in cross-cultural encounters'. *Personality and Social Psychology Bulletin, 22*, 238–248.

Kram, K. E. (1985). *Mentoring at work.* Glenview, IL: Scott Foresman.

Krause, N. and Goldenhar, L. M. (1992). 'Acculturation and psychological distress in three groups of elderly Hispanics'. *Journal of Gerontology, 47*, S279-S288.

Krishnan, A. and Berry, J. W. (1992). 'Acculturative stress and acculturation attitudes among Indian immigrants to the United States'. *Psychology and Developing Societies, 4*, 187–212.

Kroll, J., Habenicht, M., Mackenzie, T., Yang, M., Chan, S., Vang, T., Nguyen, T., Ly, M., Phommasouvanh, B., Nguyen, H., Vang, Y., Souvannasoth, L. and Cabugao, R. (1989). 'Depression and Posttraumatic Stress Disorder in Southeast Asian refugees'. *American Journal of Psychiatry, 146*, 1592–1597.

Krupinski, J. and Burrows, G. (1986). *The price of freedom: Young Indochinese refugees in Australia*. Sydney: Pergamon.

Kuhn, M. H. and McPartland, T. S. (1954). 'An empirical investigation of self-attitudes'. *American Sociological Review, 19*, 68–76.

Kumar, K. (1979). *Bonds without bondage: Explorations in transcultural interactions*. Honolulu: University of Hawaii Press.

Kuo, W. H., Gray, R. and Lin, N. (1976). 'Locus of control and symptoms of distress among Chinese-Americans'. *International Journal of Social Psychiatry, 22*, 176–187.

Kuo, W. H. and Tsai, V.-M. (1986). 'Social networking, hardiness, and immigrants' mental health'. *Journal of Health and Social Behavior, 27*, 133–149.

LaFromboise, T., Coleman, H. L. K. and Gerton, J. (1993). 'Psychological impact of biculturalism: Evidence and theory'. *Psychological Bulletin, 114*, 395–412.

LaFromboise, T. and Rowe, W. (1983). 'Skills training for bicultural competence: Rationale and application'. *Journal of Counselling Psychology, 30*, 589–595.

Lai, J. and Linden, W. (1993). 'The smile of Asia: Acculturation effects on symptom reporting'. *Canadian Journal of Behavioral Science, 25*, 303–313.

Lalonde, R. N. and Cameron, J. E. (1993). 'An intergroup perspective on immigrant acculturation with focus on collective strategies'. *International Journal of Psychology, 28*, 57–74.

Lalonde, R. N., Taylor, D. M. and Moghaddam, F. M. (1988). 'Social integration strategies of Haitian and Indian immigrant women in Montreal'. In J. W. Berry and R. C. Annis (Eds), *Ethnic psychology: Research and practice with immigrants, refugees, native peoples, ethnic groups and sojourners* (pp. 114–124). Lisse, The Netherlands: Swets & Zeitlinger.

Lambert, R. D. (1966). 'Some minor pathologies in the American presence in India'. *Annals of the American Academy of Political and Social Science, 368*, 157–170.

Lambert, R. D. and Bressler, M. (1956). *Indian students on an American campus*. Minneapolis: University of Minnesota Press.

Lambert, W. E. (1974). 'Culture and language as factors in learning and education'. In F. E. Aboud and R. D. Mead (Eds), *Cultural factors in learning and education* (pp. 91–122). Bellingham, WA: Fifth Washington Symposium on Learning.

Lambert, W. E. (1978). 'Some cognitive and sociocultural consequences of being bilingual'. In J. E. Alatis (Ed.), *International dimensions of bilingual education* (pp. 214–229). Washington, DC: Georgetown University Press.

Lambert, W. E., Mermigis, L. and Taylor, D. M. (1986). 'Greek Canadians' attitudes toward own group and other Canadian ethnic groups: A test of the multiculturalism hypothesis'. *Canadian Journal of Behavioral Sciences, 18*, 35–51.

Lambert, W. E., Moghaddam, F. M., Sorin, J. and Sorin, S. (1990). 'Assimilation versus multiculturalism: Views from a community in France'. *Sociological Forum, 5*, 387–411.

Lanca, M., Alksnis, C., Roese, N. J. and Gardner, R. C. (1994). 'Effects of language choice on acculturation: A study of Portuguese immigrants in a multicultural setting'. *Journal of Language and Social Psychology, 13*, 315–330.

Lance, C. E. and Richardson, D. (1985). 'Correlates of work and non-work related stress and satisfaction among American insulated sojourners'. *Human Relations, 10*, 725–738.

Landis, D. and Bhagat, R. S. (Eds). (1996). *Handbook of intercultural training* (2nd edn). Thousand Oaks, CA: Sage.

Landis, D., Brislin, R. W. and Hulgus, J. F. (1985). 'Attributional training versus contact in acculturative learning: A laboratory study'. *Journal of Applied Social Psychology, 15*, 466–482.

Lasry, J. C. (1977). 'Cross-cultural perspective on mental health and immigrant adaptation'. *Social Psychiatry, 12*, 49–55.

Lasry, J. C. and Sayegh, L. (1992). 'Developing an acculturation scale: A bidimensional model'. In N. Grizenko, L. Sayegh and P. Migneault (Eds), *Transcultural issues in child psychiatry* (pp. 67–86). Montreal: Editions Douglas.

Lavik, N. J., Hauff, E., Skrondal, A. and Solberg, Ø. (1996). 'Mental disorder among refugees and the impact of persecution and exile: Some findings from an outpatient population'. *British Journal of Psychiatry, 169*, 726–732.

Law, C. M. (1994). *Urban tourism: Attracting visitors to large cities.* London: Mansell.

Laws, E., Moscardo, G. and Faulkner, B. (Eds). (1998). *Embracing and managing change in tourism: International case studies.* London: Routledge.

Lawton, L. J., Weaver, D. and Faulkner, B. (1998). 'Customer satisfaction in the Australian timeshare industry'. *Journal of Travel Research, 37*, 30–38.

'Lay-offs soar to record high'. (1999, February 26). *The Straits Times*, p. 2.

Lazarus, R. S. and Folkman, S. (1984). *Stress, coping and appraisal.* New York: Springer.

Lea, J. (1988). *Tourism and development in the Third World.* New York: Routledge.

Leach, M. M. (1997). 'Training global psychologists: An introduction'. *International Journal of Intercultural Relations, 21*, 161–174.

Leach, M. M. and Carlton, M. A. (1997). 'Toward defining a multicultural training philosophy'. In D. B. Pope-Davis and H. L. K. Coleman (Eds), *Multicultural counselling competencies: Assessment, education and training, and supervision* (pp. 184–208). Thousand Oaks, CA: Sage.

Lee, W.-N. (1993). 'Acculturation and advertising communication strategies: A cross-cultural study of Chinese and Americans'. *Psychology and Marketing, 10*, 381–397.

Lefcourt, H. M. (Ed.). (1984). *Research with the locus of control construct: Extensions and limitations* (Vol. 3). New York: Academic Press.

Leff, J. (1977). 'The cross-cultural study of emotions'. *Culture, Medicine and Psychiatry, 1*, 317–350.

Leheny, D. (1995). 'A political economy of Asian sex tourism'. *Annals of Tourism Research, 22*, 367–384.

Leong, C.-H. (1997). 'Where's the cognition in acculturation? A cognitive model of acculturation of the P.R.C. Chinese in Singapore'. Unpublished honours thesis, National University of Singapore.

Leong, C.-H., and Ward, C. (1999). 'The effects of enhancing and effacing attributions for success and failure on Chinese person perceptions in self and group referent conditions'. In T. Sugiman, M. Karasawa, J. Liu and C. Ward (Eds), *Progress in Asian Social Psychology* (Vol. 2, pp. 75–85). Seoul, South Korea: Educational Science Publishers.

Leong, C.-H. and Ward, C. (2000). 'Identity conflict in sojourners'. *International Journal of Intercultural Relations, 24*, 763–776

Leong, C.-H., Ward, C. and Low, M.-L. (2000, July). 'Revisiting the "Cultural Fit" proposition: Personality and adjustment in two cultures'. Paper presented at the XVth International Congress of the International Association for Cross-cultural Psychology, Pultusk, Poland.

Leong, F. T. L. and Kim, H. H. W. (1991). 'Going beyond cultural sensitivity on the road to multiculturalism: Using the intercultural sensitizer as a counsellor training tool'. *Journal of Counselling and Development, 70*, 112–118.

Leopold, M. and Harrell-Bond, B. (1994). 'An overview of the world refugee crisis'. In A. J. Marsella, T. Bornemann, S. Ekblad and J. Orley (Eds), *Amidst the peril and pain: The mental health and well-being of the world's refugee*s (pp. 17–31). Washington, DC: American Psychological Association.

Lerner, Y., Mirsky, J. and Barasch, M. (1994). 'New beginnings in an old land: Refugee and immigrant mental health in Israel'. In A. J. Marsella, T. Bornemann, S. Ekblad and J. Orley (Eds), *Amidst the peril and pain: The mental health and well-being of the world's refugees* (pp. 153–189). Washington, DC: American Psychological Association.

Lese, K. P. and Robbins, S. B. (1994). 'Relationship between goal attributes and the academic achievement of Southeast Asian adolescent refugees'. *Journal of Counselling Psychology, 41*, 45–52.

Leung, S. (1995). 'The implication of China's economic reforms for economic legislation'. In H. Davies (Ed.), *China business: Context and issues* (pp. 65–97). Hong Kong: Longman.

LeVine, R. and Bartlett, K. (1984). 'Pace of life, punctuality and coronary heart disease in six countries'. *Journal of Cross-cultural Psychology, 15*, 233–255.

LeVine, R., West, L. J. and Reis, H. T. (1980). 'Perceptions of time and punctuality in the United States and Brazil'. *Journal of Personality and Social Psychology, 38*, 541–550.

Levy, J., Wubbels, T., Brekelmans, M. and Morganfield, B. (1997). 'Language and cultural factors in students' perceptions of teacher communication style'. *International Journal of Intercultural Relations, 21*, 29–56.

Liberman, K. (1994). 'Asian student perspectives on American university instruction'. *International Journal of Intercultural Relations, 18*, 173–192.

Liebkind, K. (1994). 'Ethnic identity and acculturative stress – Vietnamese refugees in Finland'. *Migration, 23–24*, 155–174.

Liebkind, K. (1996). 'Acculturation and stress: Vietnamese refugees in Finland'. *Journal of Cross-cultural Psychology, 27*, 161–180.

Lim, A. and Ward, C. (in press). 'The effects of nationality, length of residence and type of occupational skills on the perceptions of "foreign talent" in Singapore'. In K.-S. Yang, I. Daibo, P. Pederson and K.-K. Hwang (Eds), *Progress in Asian social psychology, Vol. 3*. New York: Wiley.

Lin, K.-M. (1986). 'Psychopathology and social disruption in refugees'. In C. Williams and J. Westermeyer (Eds), *Refugee mental health in resettlement countries* (pp. 61–73). Washington, DC: Hemisphere.

Lin, K.-M., Masuda, M. and Tazuma, L. (1982). 'Problems of Vietnamese refugees in the United States'. In R. C. Nann (Ed.), *Uprooting and surviving* (pp. 11–24). Boston: Reidel.

Lin, K.-M., Tazuma, L. and Masuda, M. (1979). 'Adaptational problems of Vietnamese refugees I: Health and mental status'. *Archives of General Psychiatry, 36*, 955–961.

Lin, Z. (1997). 'Ambiguity with a purpose: The shadow of power in communication'. In P. C. Earley and M. Erez (Eds), *New perspectives on international industrial/ organizational psychology* (pp. 363–376). San Francisco: The New Lexington Press.

Lindsley, S. L. and Braithwaite, C. A. (1996). '"You should 'wear a mask:'" Facework norms in cultural and intercultural conflict in maquiladoras'. *International Journal of Intercultural Relations, 20*, 199–225.

Lippman, W. (1922). *Public opinion.* New York: Harcourt & Brace.

Litvin, S. W. (1998). 'Tourism: The world's peace industry?'. *Journal of Travel Research, 37*, 63–66.

Liu, W., Lamanna, M. and Muratta, A. K. (1979). *Transition to nowhere, Vietnamese refugees in America.* Nashville, TN: Charter House.

Locke, S. A. and Feinsod, F. (1982). 'Psychological preparation for young adults travelling abroad'. *Adolescence, 17*, 815–819.

Loker-Murphy, J. and Pearce, P. (1995). 'Young budget travelers: Backpackers in Australia'. *Annals of Tourism Research, 22*, 819–843.

Long, P. T., Perdue, R. R. and Allen, L. (1990). 'Rural resident tourism perceptions and attitudes by community level of tourism'. *Journal of Travel Research, 28*, 3–9.

Lonner, W. J. (1990). 'An overview of cross-cultural testing and assessment'. In R. W. Brislin (Ed.), *Applied cross-cultural psychology* (pp. 56–76). Newbury Park, CA: Sage.

Lonner, W. J. (1997). 'Three paths leading to culturally competent psychological practitioners'. *International Journal of Intercultural Relations, 21*, 195–212.

Lonner, W. J. and Malpass, R. (Eds). (1994). *Psychology and culture.* Needham Heights, MA: Allyn & Bacon.

Lowe, K. B., Downes, M. and Kroeck, K. G. (1999). 'The impact of gender and location on the willingness to accept overseas assignments'. *The International Journal of Human Resource Management, 10*, 223–234.

Lu, L. (1990). 'Adaptation to British universities: Homesickness and mental health of Chinese students'. *Counselling Psychology Quarterly, 3*, 225–232.

Lunt, I. and Poortinga, Y. H. (1996). 'Internationalizing psychology: The case of Europe'. *American Psychologist, 51*, 504–508.

Luzar, E. J., Diagne, A., Gan, C. E. C. and Henning, B. R. (1998). 'Profiling the nature-based tourist: A multinomial logit approach'. *Journal of Travel Research, 37*, 48–55.

Lykes, M. B. (1985). 'Gender and individualistic vs. collectivistic bases for notions about the self'. *Journal of Personality, 53*, 356–383.

Lynskey, M., Ward, C. and Fletcher, G. J. O. (1991). 'Stereotypes and intergroup attributions in New Zealand'. *Psychology and Developing Societies, 3*, 113–127.

Lysgaard, S. (1955). 'Adjustment in a foreign society: Norwegian Fulbright grantees visiting the United States'. *International Social Science Bulletin, 7*, 45–51.

McAllister, I. and Moore, R. (1991). 'The development of ethnic prejudice: An analysis of Australian immigrants'. *Ethnic and Racial Studies, 14*, 127–151.

MacCannell, D. (1973). 'Staged authenticity: Arrangements of social space in tourist settings'. *American Journal of Sociology, 79*, 589–603.

McCargar, D. F. (1993). 'Teacher and student role expectations: Cross-cultural differences and implications'. *The Modern Language Journal, 77*, 192–207.

MacCarthy, B. and Craissati, J. (1989). 'Ethnic differences in response to adversity'. *Social Psychiatry and Psychiatric Epidemiology, 24*, 196–201.

McCroskey, J. C., Sallinen, A., Fayer, J. M., Richmond, V. P. and Barraclough, R. A.

(1996). 'Nonverbal immediacy and cognitive learning: A cross-cultural investigation'. *Communication Education, 45*, 200–211.

McDaniel, C. O., McDaniel, N. C. and McDaniel, A. K. (1988). 'Transferability of multicultural education from training to practice'. *International Journal of Intercultural Relations, 12*, 19–33.

McDaniel, E. and Andersen, P. A. (1998). 'International patterns of interpersonal tactile communication: A field study'. *Journal of Nonverbal Behavior, 22*, 59–75.

MacDonald, M. R. and Kuiper, N. A. (1983). 'Cognitive-behavioral preparations for surgery: Some theoretical and methodological concerns'. *Clinical Psychological Review, 3*, 27–39.

McGregor, D. (1944). 'Conditions of effective leadership in the industrial organization'. *Journal of Consulting Psychology, 8*, 55–63.

McGuire, M. and McDermott, S. (1988). 'Communication in assimilation, deviance, and alienation states'. In Y. Y. Kim and W. B. Gudykunst (Eds), *Cross-cultural adaptation: Current approaches* (pp. 90–105). Newbury Park, CA: Sage.

McIntosh, A. J. and Prentice, R. C. (1999). 'Affirming authenticity: Consuming cultural heritage'. *Annals of Tourism Research, 26*, 589–612.

McLennan, W. (1996). *Year book Australia*. Number 78. Canberra: Australian Bureau of Statistics.

Mainous, A. G. (1989). 'Self-concept as an indicator of acculturation in Mexican Americans'. *Hispanic Journal of Behavioral Sciences, 11*, 178–189.

Majodina, Z. (1989). 'Exile as a chronic stressor'. *International Journal of Mental Health, 18*, 87–94.

Mak, A. (1991). 'From elites to strangers: Employment coping styles of Hong Kong immigrants'. *Journal of Employment Counselling, 28*, 144–156.

Mak, A. and Chan, H. (1995). 'Chinese family values in Australia'. In R. Hartley (Ed.), *Families and cultural diversity in Australia* (pp. 70–95). St. Leonard's, NSW: Allen & Unwin.

Mak, A., Westwood, M. J., Ishiyama, F. I. and Barker, M. C. (1999). 'Optimising conditions for learning sociocultural competencies for success'. *International Journal of Intercultural Relations, 23*, 77–90.

Malewska-Peyre, H. (1982). 'L'expérience du racisme et de la xénophobie chez jeunes immigrés'. In H. Malewska-Peyre (Ed.), *Crise d'identité et déviance chez jeunes immigrés* (pp. 53–73). Paris: La Documentation Française.

Malzberg, B. (1936). 'Mental disease among native and foreign-born whites in New York State'. *American Journal of Psychiatry, 93*, 127–137.

Malzberg, B. (1940). *Social and biological aspects of mental disease*. New York: State Hospital Press.

Mamak, A. (1990). 'Urban native American Samoan employment, human services and organization development issues in the United States of America'. Paper presented at the Conference on Pacific Islander Migration and Settlement: Australia, New Zealand and the United States. Centre for Pacific Studies, University of New South Wales, Sydney, Australia.

Mansfeld, Y. (1992). 'From motivation to actual travel'. *Annals of Tourism Research, 19*, 399–419.

Marín, G., Sabogal, F., Marín, B., Otero-Sabogal, R. and Perez-Stable, E. J. (1987). 'Development of a short acculturation scale for Hispanics'. *Hispanic Journal of Behavioral Science, 2*, 21–34.

Markus, H. R. and Kitayama, S. (1991). 'Culture and the self: Implications for cognition, emotion, and motivation'. *Psychological Review, 98*, 224–253.

Marshall, R. (1997). 'Variances in levels of individualism across two cultures and three social classes'. *Journal of Cross-cultural Psychology, 28*, 490–495.

Martin, G. and Beaumont, P. (1998). 'Diffusing "best practice" in multinational firms: Prospects, practice and contestation'. *The International Journal of Human Resource Management, 9*, 671–695.

Martin, J. N. (1984). 'The intercultural re-entry: Conceptualization and directions for future research'. *International Journal of Intercultural Relations, 8*, 115–134.

Martin, J. N. (1986a). 'Training issues in cross-cultural orientation'. *International Journal of Intercultural Relations, 10*, 103–116.

Martin, J. N. (1986b). 'Communication in the intercultural re-entry: Student sojourners' perceptions of change in re-entry relationship'. *International Journal of Intercultural Relations, 10*, 1–22.

Martin, J. N., Bradford, L. and Rohrlich, B. (1995). 'Comparing predeparture expectations and postsojourn reports: A longitudinal study of U.S. students abroad'. *International Journal of Intercultural Relations, 19*, 87–110.

Martin, J. N. and Harrell, T. (1996). 'Re-entry training for intercultural sojourners'. In D. Landis and R. S. Bhagat (Eds), *Handbook of intercultural training* (2nd edn, pp. 307–326). Thousand Oaks, CA: Sage.

Martin, R. A. and Lefcourt, H. M. (1983). 'Sense of humor as a moderator of the relation between stressors and moods'. *Journal of Personality and Social Psychology, 45*, 1313–1324.

Martinez, J. I. and Jarillo, C. (1991). 'Coordination demands of international strategies'. *Journal of International Business Studies, 22*, 429–444.

Masuda, M., Lin, K.-M. and Tazuma, L. (1982). 'Life changes among the Vietnamese refugees'. In R. C. Nann (Ed.), *Uprooting and surviving* (pp. 25–33). Boston: Reidel.

Mathieson, A. and Wall, G. (1982). *Tourism: Economic, physical and social impacts*. New York: Longman Scientific & Technical.

Matsubara, T. and Ishikuma, T. (1993). 'A study of the counselling and guidance of foreign students in Japan'. *Japanese Journal of Counselling Services, 26*, 146–155.

Matsuoka, J. K. (1990). 'Differential acculturation among Vietnamese refugees'. *Social Work, 35*, 341–345.

Matsuoka, J. K. and Ryujin, D. (1989–90). 'Vietnamese refugees: An analysis of contemporary adjustment issues'. *Journal of Applied Social Sciences, 14*, 23–44.

Mattausch, J. (1998). 'From subjects to citizens: British "East African Asians"'. *Journal of Ethnic and Migration Studies, 24*, 121–141.

Matute-Bianchi, M. E. (1986). 'Ethnic identities and patterns of school success and failure among Mexican-descent and Japanese-American students in a California high school: An ethnographic analysis'. *American Journal of Education, 95*, 233–255.

Mavreas, V. and Bebbington, P. (1990). 'Acculturation and psychiatric disorder: A study of Greek Cypriot immigrants'. *Psychological Medicine, 20*, 941–951.

Mavreas, V., Bebbington, P. and Der, G. (1989). 'The structure and validity of acculturation: Analysis of an acculturation scale'. *Social Psychiatry and Psychiatric Epidemiology, 24*, 233–240.

Mayada, N. S. (1983). 'Psychosocial welfare of refugees: An expanding service area of social work'. *International Social Work, 26*, 47–55.

Mead, G. H. (1934). *Mind, self, and society: From the standpoint of a social behavior-ist.* Chicago: University of Chicago Press.

Mead, M. (1928). 'The role of the individual in Samoan culture'. *The Journal of the Royal Anthropological Institute of Great Britain, 57,* 481–495.

Mehrabian, D. (1972). *Nonverbal communication.* Chicago: Aldine.

Mena, F. J., Padilla, A. M. and Maldonado, M. (1987). 'Acculturative stress and specific coping strategies among immigrant and later generation college students'. *Hispanic Journal of Behavioral Sciences, 9,* 207–225.

Mendenhall, M. and Oddou, G. (1985). 'The dimensions of expatriate acculturation'. *Academy of Management Review, 10,* 39–47.

Mendoza, R. H. (1984). 'Acculturation and sociocultural variability'. In J. L. Mar-tínez and R. H. Mendoza (Eds), *Chicano psychology* (pp. 61–75). Orlando, FL: Academic Press.

Mendoza, R. H. (1989). 'An empirical scale to measure type and degree of accultur-ation in Mexican American adolescents and adults'. *Journal of Cross-cultural Psychology, 20,* 372–385.

Merritt, A. C. and Helmreich, R. L. (1996). 'Human factors on the flight deck: The influence of national culture'. *Journal of Cross-cultural Psychology, 27,* 5–24.

Mghir, R., Freed, W., Raskin, A. and Katon, W. (1995). 'Depression and Post-traumatic Stress Disorder among a community sample of adolescent and young adult Afghan refugees'. *Journal of Nervous and Mental Disease, 183,* 24–30.

Milliken, F. J. and Martins, L. L. (1996). 'Searching for common threads: Understand-ing the multiple effects of diversity in organizational groups'. *Academy of Manage-ment Review, 21,* 402–433.

Milman, A. and Pizam, A. (1988). 'Social impacts of tourism on Central Florida'. *Annals of Tourism Research, 15,* 191–204.

Milman, C. D. (1999). 'Merger and acquisition activity in China: 1985–1996'. *Multi-national Business Review, 7,* 106–110.

Minde, T. (1985). 'Foreign student adaptation'. Unpublished honours thesis, Queen's University, Kingston, Canada.

Ministry of Education [Mombusho Kyoiku Joseikyoku] (1999). *Kaigaishijo Kyoiku no Genjo [A report on the educational conditions of Japanese children overseas].* Tokyo: Ministry of Education.

Mitchell, T. R., Dossett, D. L., Fiedler, F. E. and Triandis, H. C. (1972). 'Culture training: Validation evidence for the culture assimilator'. *International Journal of Psychology, 7,* 97–104.

Mitchell, T. R. and Foa, U. G. (1969). 'Diffusion of the effect of cultural training of the leader in the structure of heterocultural task groups'. *Australian Journal of Psychology, 21,* 31–43.

Moghaddam, F. M. (1998). *Social psychology: Exploring universals across cultures.* New York: Freeman.

Moghaddam, F. M., Ditto, B. and Taylor, D. M. (1990). 'Attitudes and attributions related to symptomatology in Indian immigrant women'. *Journal of Cross-cultural Psychology, 21,* 335–350.

Moghaddam, F. M., Taylor, D. M. and Lalonde, R. N. (1987). 'Individualistic and collective integration strategies among Iranians in Canada'. *International Journal of Psychology, 22,* 301–313.

Moghaddam, F. M., Taylor, D. M. and Wright, S.C. (1993). *Social psychology in cross-cultural perspective.* New York: Freeman.

Mole, J. (1990). *When in Rome . . .* New York: AMACOM.

Mollica, R. F. (1989). 'What is a case?'. In M. Abbott (Ed.), *Refugee resettlement and well-being* (pp. 87–100). Auckland: Mental Health Foundation of New Zealand.

Mollica, R. F. (1990). 'Refugee trauma: The impact of public policy on adaptation and disability'. In W. H. Holtzman and T. H. Bornemann (Eds), *Mental health of immigrants and refugees* (pp. 251–260). Austin, TX: University of Texas.

Mollica, R. F., Lavelle, J., Tor, S. and Elias, C. (1989). *Turning point in Khmer mental health: Immediate steps to resolve the mental health crisis in Khmer border camps.* Alexandria, VA: World Federation for Mental Health.

Mollica, R. F., Wyshak, G. and Lavelle, J. (1987). 'The psychosocial impact of war trauma and torture on Southeast Asian refugees'. *American Journal of Psychiatry, 144*, 1567–1572.

Monroe, S. M. (1982). 'Life events and disorder: Event-symptom associations and the course of disorder'. *Journal of Abnormal Psychology, 91*, 14–24.

Montgomery, G. T. (1992). 'Comfort with acculturation status among students from South Texas'. *Hispanic Journal of Behavioral Sciences, 14*, 201–223.

Montgomery, J. R. (1996). 'Components of refugee adaptation'. *International Migration Review, 30*, 679–702.

Moon, J.-H. and Pearl, J. H. (1991). 'Alienation of elderly Korean American immigrants as related to place of residence, gender, age, years of education, time in the U.S., living with or without children and living with or without a spouse'. *International Journal of Aging and Human Development, 32*, 115–124.

Moore, L. J. and Boehnlein, J. K. (1991). 'Posttraumatic stress disorder, depression and somatic symptoms in U.S. Mien patients'. *Journal of Nervous and Mental Disease, 179*, 728–733.

Morgan, M. C., Wingard, D. L. and Felice, M. E. (1984). 'Subcultural differences in alcohol use among youth'. *Journal of Adolescent Health Care, 5*, 191–195.

Morris, D., Collett, P., Marsh, P. and O'Shaughnessy, M. (1979). *Gestures: Their origins and distribution.* London: Jonathan Cape.

Morris, R. T. (1960). *The two-way mirror.* Minneapolis: University of Minnesota Press.

Morrison, A. M., Yang, C-H., O'Leary, J. T. and Nadkarni, N. (1996). 'Comparative profiles of travelers on cruises and land-based resort vacations'. *The Journal of Tourism Studies, 7*, 15–27.

Moscardo, G. and Pearce, P. L. (1999). 'Understanding ethnic tourists'. *Annals of Tourism Research, 26*, 416–434.

'Most neutral to foreign talent'. (1998, August 19). *The Straits Times*, p. 33.

Mouanoutoua, V. L., Brown, L. G., Cappelletty, G. G. and Levine, R. V. (1991). 'A Hmong adaptation of the Beck Depression Inventory'. *Journal of Personality Assessment, 57*, 309–322.

Moyerman, D. R. and Forman, B. D. (1992). 'Acculturation and adjustment: A meta-analytic study'. *Hispanic Journal of Behavioral Sciences, 14*, 163–200.

Muecke, M. A. and Sassi, L. (1992). 'Anxiety among Cambodian refugee adolescents in transit and in resettlement'. *Western Journal of Nursing Research, 14*, 267–291.

Muhlin, G. L. (1979). 'Mental hospitalization of the foreign-born and the role of cultural isolation'. *International Journal of Psychiatry, 25*, 258–266.

Mumford, D. (1998). 'The measurement of culture shock'. *Social Psychiatry and Psychiatric Epidemiology, 33*, 149–154.

Mumford, D., Whitehouse, A. and Platts, M. (1990). 'Sociocultural correlates of eating disorders among Asian schoolgirls in Bradford'. *British Journal of Psychiatry, 158*, 222–228.

Muralidharan, R. (1998). 'Control of foreign subsidiaries over time: A conceptual analysis'. *Journal of Global Business, 10*, 25–36.

Murphy, H. B. M. (1973). 'Migration and the major mental disorders.: A reappraisal'. In C. A. A. Zwingmann and M. Pfister-Ammende (Eds), *Uprooting and after* (pp. 221–231). New York: Springer-Verlag.

Murphy, H. B. M. (1977). 'Migration, culture and mental health'. *Psychological Medicine, 7*, 677–684.

Naidoo, J. (1985). 'A cultural perspective on the adjustment of South Asian women in Canada'. In I. R. Lagunes and Y. H. Poortinga (Eds), *From a different perspective: Studies of behavior across cultures* (pp. 76–92). Lisse, The Netherlands: Swets & Zeitlinger.

Napier, N. K. and Peterson, R. B. (1991). 'Expatriate re-entry: What do repatriates have to say?'. *Human Resource Planning, 14*, 19–28.

Nash, D. (1991). 'The cause of sojourner adaptation: A new test of the U-curve hypothesis'. *Human Organization, 50*, 283–286.

Nash, D. and Wolfe, A. (1957). 'The stranger in laboratory culture'. *American Sociological Review, 22*, 149–167.

Neffe, J. A. and Hoppe, S. K. (1993). 'Race/ethnicity, acculturation, and psychological distress: Fatalism and religiosity as cultural resources'. *Journal of Community Psychology, 21*, 3–20.

Nehru, J. (1936; Reprinted 1958). *An autobiography*. London: Bodley Head.

Nesdale, D., Rooney, R. and Smith, L. (1997). 'Migrant ethnic identity and psychological distress'. *Journal of Cross-cultural Psychology, 28*, 569–588.

Neto, F. (1988). 'Migration plans and their determinants among Portuguese adolescents'. In J. W. Berry and R. C. Annis (Eds), *Ethnic psychology: Research and practice with immigrants, refugees, native peoples, ethnic groups and sojourners* (pp. 308–314). Lisse, The Netherlands: Swets & Zeitlinger.

Neto, F. (1995). 'Predictors of satisfaction with life among second generation migrants'. *Social Indicators Research, 35*, 93–116.

Nettekoven, L. (1979). 'Mechanisms of intercultural interaction'. In E. de Kadt (Ed.), *Tourism: Passport to development?* (pp. 135–145). Washington, DC: Oxford University Press.

Neuliep, J. W. and Ryan, D. J. (1998). 'The influence of intercultural communication apprehension and socio-communicative orientation on uncertainty reduction during initial cross-cultural interaction'. *Communication Quarterly, 46*, 88–99.

New Zealand Immigration Service (1999). *People approved for residence by region*. Available: http://www.immigration.govt.nz/about/statistics/faq/resid_region. html.

Nguyen, H. H., Messé L. A. and Stollak, G. E. (1999). 'Toward a more complex understanding of acculturation and adjustment'. *Journal of Cross-cultural Psychology, 30*, 5–31.

Nguyen, L. T. and Henkin, A. B. (1982). 'Vietnamese refugees in the United States: Adaptation and transitional status'. *Journal of Ethnic Studies, 9*, 101–116.

Nguyen, S. D. (1982). 'The psychosocial adjustment and the mental health needs of Southeast Asian refugees'. *Psychiatric Journal of University of Ottawa, 7*, 26–35.

Nicassio, P. M. (1983). 'Psychosocial correlates of alienation: The study of a sample of Southeast Asian refugees'. *Journal of Cross-cultural Psychology, 14*, 337–351.

Nicassio, P. M. (1985). 'The psychological adjustment of the Southeast Asian refugee: An overview of empirical findings and theoretical models'. *Journal of Cross-cultural Psychology, 16*, 153–173.

Nicassio, P. M. and Pate, J. K. (1984). 'An analysis of problems of resettlement of the Indochinese refugees in the United States'. *Social Psychiatry, 19*, 135–141.

Nicassio, P. M., Solomon, G. S., Guest, S. and McCullough, J. E. (1986). 'Emigration stress and language proficiency as correlates of depression in a sample of Southeast Asian refugees'. *International Journal of Social Psychiatry, 32*, 22–28.

Niles, F. S. (1995). 'Cultural differences in learning motivation and learning strategies: A comparison of overseas and Australian students at an Australian university'. *International Journal of Intercultural Relations, 19*, 369–386.

Nitsche, R. A. and Green, A. (1977). *Situational exercises in cross-cultural awareness.* Columbus, OH: Charles E. Merrill.

Noesjirwan, J. (1978). 'A rule-based analysis of cultural differences in social behaviour: Indonesia and Australia'. *International Journal of Psychology, 13*, 305–316.

Noh, S. and Avison, W. R. (1996). 'Asian immigrants and the stress process: A study of Koreans in Canada'. *Journal of Health and Social Behavior, 37*, 192–206.

Noh, S., Speechley, M., Kaspar, V. and Wu, Z. (1992). 'Depression in Korean immigrants in Canada: I. Method of the study and prevalence'. *Journal of Nervous and Mental Disease, 180*, 578–582.

Noronha, R. (1979). *Social and cultural dimensions of tourism.* World Bank Staff Working Paper No. 326. Washington, DC: The World Bank.

Nowak, R. and Weiland, R. (1998, April). 'Culture shock coming undone: Social selection in the international student sojourn'. Paper presented at the Society for Australasian Social Psychology, Christchurch, New Zealand.

Nwadiora, E. and McAdoo, H. (1996). 'Acculturative stress among Amerasian refugees: Gender and racial differences'. *Adolescence, 31*, 477–487.

Oakley, R. (1989). 'Community and race relations training for the police: A review of developments'. *New Community, 16*, 61–80.

Oakley, R. (1993). 'Race relations training in the police'. In L. R. Gelsthorpe (Ed.), *Minority ethnic groups in the criminal justice system* (pp. 49–67). Cambridge: Cambridge University Press.

Oberg, K. (1960). 'Cultural shock: Adjustment to new cultural environments'. *Practical Anthropology, 7*, 177–182.

O'Brien, G. E., Fiedler, F. E. and Hewett, T. (1971). 'The effects of programmed culture training upon the performance of volunteer medical teams in Central America'. *Human Relations, 24*, 209–231.

O'Brien, G. E. and Plooij, D. (1976). 'Development of culture training manuals for medical workers with Pitjantjatjara Aboriginals: The relative effect of critical incident and prose training upon knowledge, attitudes and motivation'. In G. E. Kearney and D. W. McElwain (Eds), *Aboriginal cognition: Retrospect and prospect* (pp. 383–396). Canberra: Australian Institute of Aboriginal Studies.

O'Connor, N. G. and Chalos, P. (1999). 'The challenge for successful joint venture management in China: Lessons from a failed joint venture'. *Multinational Business Review, 7*, 50–61.

Oddou, G. R. (1991). 'Managing your expatriates: What the successful firms do'. *Human Resource Planning, 14*, 301–308.

Ødegaard, O. (1932). 'Emigration and insanity: A study of mental disease among the

Norwegian-born population of Minnesota'. *Acta Psychiatrica et Neurologica,* Supplement 4.

Oetting, E. R. and Beauvais, F. (1991). 'Orthogonal cultural identification theory: The cultural identification of minority adolescents'. *International Journal of Addictions, 25,* 655–685.

Office of Multicultural Affairs (1988). *Multiculturalism and immigration.* Canberra: AGPS.

Oliver, N. and Wilkinson, B. (1992). *Japanization of British industry.* Oxford: Blackwell.

Olmeda, E. L. (1979). 'Acculturation: A psychometric perspective'. *American Psychologist, 34,* 1061–1070.

Olmeda, E. L. and Padilla, A. M. (1978). 'Empirical and construct validation of a measure of acculturation for Mexican Americans'. *Journal of Social Psychology, 105,* 179–187.

Ong, S.-J. (2000). 'The construction and validation of a social support scale for sojourners – The Index of Sojourner Social Support (ISSS)'. Unpublished master's thesis, National University of Singapore.

Opper, S., Teichler, U. and Carlson, J. (1990). *Impacts of study abroad programmes on students and graduates.* London: Jessica Kingsley Publishers.

Oppermann, M. (1999). Sex tourism. *Annals of Tourism Research, 26,* 251–266.

Orasanu, J., Fischer, U. and Davison, J. (1997). 'Cross-cultural barriers to effective communication in aviation'. In C. S. Granrose and S. Oskamp (Eds), *Cross-cultural work groups* (pp. 134–160). Thousand Oaks, CA: Sage.

O'Reilly, C. A., Caldwell, D. F. and Barnett, W. P. (1989). 'Work group demography, social integration, and turnover'. *Administrative Science Quarterly, 34,* 21–37.

Ostroff, C. and Kozlowski, S. (1993). 'The role of mentoring in the information gathering processes of newcomers during early organizational socialization'. *Journal of Vocational Behavior, 42,* 170–183.

Ostrowska, A. and Bochenska, D. (1996). 'Ethnic stereotypes among Polish and German Silesians'. In H. Grad, A. Blanco and J. Georgas (Eds), *Key issues in cross-cultural psychology* (pp. 102–113). Lisse, The Netherlands: Swets & Zeitlinger.

Padilla, A. M. (1986). 'Acculturation and stress among immigrants and later-generation individuals'. In D. Frick (Ed.), *Urban quality of life: Social, psychological and physical conditions* (pp. 41–60). Berlin: Walter de Gruyter.

Padilla, A. M., Cervantes, R. C., Maldonado, M. and Garcia, R. E. (1988). 'Coping responses to psychosocial stressors among Mexican and Central American immigrants'. *Journal of Community Psychology, 16,* 418–427.

Padilla, A. M., Wagatsuma, Y. and Lindholm, K. J. (1985). 'Acculturation and personality as predictors of stress in Japanese and Japanese-Americans'. *Journal of Social Psychology, 125,* 295–305.

Paige, R. M. (1986). 'Trainer competencies: The missing conceptual link in orientation'. *International Journal of Intercultural Relations, 10,* 135–158.

Paige, R. M. and Martin, J. N. (1996). 'Ethics in intercultural training'. In D. Landis and R. S. Bhagat (Eds), *Handbook of intercultural training* (2nd edn, pp. 35–60). Thousand Oaks, CA: Sage.

Pak, A. W., Dion, K. L. and Dion, K. K. (1991). 'Social-psychological correlates of experienced discrimination: Test of the double jeopardy hypothesis'. *International Journal of Intercultural Relations, 15,* 243–254.

Palin, M. (1997). *Full circle.* London: BBC Books.

Palmer, D. L. (1996). 'Determinants of Canadian attitudes toward immigration: More than just racism?'. *Canadian Journal of Behavioural Science, 28*, 180–192.

Park, R. E. (1928). 'Human migration and the marginal man'. *The American Journal of Sociology, 33*, 881–893.

Parker, B. and McEvoy, G. M. (1993). 'Initial examination of a model of intercultural adjustment'. *International Journal of Intercultural Relations, 17*, 355–379.

Parker, F. (1965). 'Government policy and international education: A selected and partially annotated bibliography'. In S. Fraser (Ed.), *Government policy and international education* (pp. 295–373) . New York: Wiley.

Parkes, L. P., Bochner, S. and Schneider, S. K. (1998). 'The power of one: Individualism, collectivism and power'. Poster presented at the XIV Congress of the International Association for Cross-Cultural Psychology, Bellingham, Washington.

Parkes, L. P., Schneider, S. K. and Bochner, S. (1999). 'Individualism–collectivism and self-concept: Do collectivists construct the self in more contextual or simply more social terms?'. *Society of Australian Social Psychologists Abstracts, 4*, 6.

Parsons, T. and Shils, E. A. (1951). *Toward a general theory of action*. Cambridge, MA: Harvard University Press.

Partridge, K. (1987). 'How to become Japanese: A guide for North Americans'. *Kyoto Journal, 4*, 12–15.

Partridge, K. (1988). 'Acculturation attitudes and stress of Westerners living in Japan'. In J. W. Berry and R. C. Annis (Eds), *Ethnic psychology: Research and practice with immigrants, refugees, native peoples, ethnic groups and sojourners* (pp. 105–113). Lisse, The Netherlands: Swets & Zeitlinger.

Pasmore, W. A. (1988). *Designing effective organisations: The sociotechnical systems perspective*. London: Wiley.

Pasmore, W. A. (1995). 'Social science transformed: The sociotechnical perspective'. *Human Relations, 48*, 1–21.

Patel, N., Power, T. G. and Bhavnagri, N. P. (1996). 'Socialization values and practices of Indian immigrant parents: Correlates of modernity and acculturation'. *Child Development, 67*, 302–313.

Patel, V. and Mann, A. (1997). 'Etic and emic criteria for non-psychotic mental disorders'. *Social Psychiatry and Psychiatric Epidemiology, 32*, 84–87.

Pawliuk, N., Grizenko, N., Chan-Yip, A., Gantous, P., Mathew, J. and Nguyen, D. (1996). 'Acculturation style and psychological functioning in children of immigrants'. *American Journal of Orthopsychiatry 66*, 111–121.

Pearce, D. (1997). 'Analysing the demand for urban tourism: Issues and examples from Paris'. *Tourism Analysis, 1*, 5–18.

Pearce, D. (1999). 'Tourism in Paris: Studies at the microscale.' *Annals of Tourism Research, 26*, 77–97.

Pearce, P. L. (1981). 'Environmental shock:' A study of tourists' reactions to two tropical islands. *Journal of Applied Social Psychology, 11*, 268–280.

Pearce, P. L. (1982a). 'Tourists and their hosts: Some social and psychological effects of intercultural contact'. In S. Bochner (Ed.), *Cultures in contact: Studies in cross-cultural interaction* (pp. 199–221). Oxford: Pergamon.

Pearce, P. L. (1982b). *The social psychology of tourist behaviour*. Oxford: Pergamon.

Pearce, P. L. (1988). *The Ulysses factor: Evaluating visitors in tourist settings*. New York: Springer-Verlag.

Pearce, P. L., Kim, E. and Lussa, S. (1998). 'Facilitating tourist–host social interactions: An overview and assessment of the Culture Assimilator'. In E. Laws,

G. Moscardo and B. Faulkner (Eds), *Embracing and managing change in tourism: International case studies* (pp. 347–364). London: Routledge.

Pearson, V. M. S. and Stephan, W. G. (1998). 'Preferences for styles of negotiation: A comparison of Brazil and the U.S.'. *International Journal of Intercultural Relations, 22,* 67–83.

Pedersen, P. B. (1991). 'Multiculturalism as a generic approach to counselling'. *Journal of Counselling and Development, 70,* 3–14.

Pedersen, P. B. (1994a). 'A culture-centered approach to counselling'. In W. L. Lonner and R. Malpass (Eds), *Psychology and culture* (pp. 291–295). Needham Heights, MA: Allyn & Bacon.

Pedersen, P. B. (1994b). *A handbook for developing multicultural awareness* (2nd edn). Alexandria, VA: American Counselling Association.

Pedersen, P. B. (1995). *The five stages of culture shock: Critical incidents around the world.* Westport, CT: Greenwood Press.

Pedersen, P. B. (Ed.). (1999). *Multiculturalism as a fourth force.* Washington, DC: Taylor & Francis.

Pedersen, P. B., Draguns, J. G., Lonner, W. J. and Trimble, J. E. (Eds). (1996). *Counselling across cultures* (4th edn). Thousand Oaks, CA: Sage.

Pelly, R. (1997). 'Predictors of international student cultural adjustment: An intergroup perspective'. Unpublished honours thesis, University of Queensland, Brisbane, Australia.

Pelto, P. J. (1968). 'The difference between "tight" and "loose" societies'. *Transaction, 5,* 37–40.

Perkins, C. S., Perkins, M. L., Guglielmino, L. M. and Reiff, R. F. (1977). 'A comparison of adjustment problems of three international student groups'. *Journal of College Student Personnel, 18,* 382–388.

Pernice, R. and Brook, J. (1994). 'Relationship of migrant status (refugee or immigrant) to mental health'. *International Journal of Social Psychiatry, 40,* 177–188.

Pervin, L. A. (1968). 'Performance and satisfaction as a function of individual–environment fit'. *Psychological Bulletin, 69,* 56–68.

Pettigrew, T. F. (1964). *A profile of the Negro American.* Princeton, NJ: Van Nostrand.

Pettigrew, T. F. (1969). 'Racially separate or together?'. *Journal of Social Issues, 25,* 43–69.

Phinney, J. S. (1989). 'Stages of ethnic identity in minority group adolescents'. *Journal of Early Adolescence, 9,* 34–49.

Phinney, J. S. (1990). 'Ethnic identity in adolescents and adults: Review of research'. *Psychological Bulletin, 108,* 499–514.

Phinney, J. S. (1991). 'Ethnic identity and self-esteem: A review and integration'. *Hispanic Journal of Behavioral Sciences, 13,* 193–208.

Phinney, J. S. (1992). 'The Multigroup Ethnic Identity Measure: A new scale for use with diverse groups'. *Journal of Adolescent Research, 7,* 156–176.

Phinney, J. S. (1993). 'A three stage model of ethnic identity development in adolescence'. In M. E. Bernal and G. P. Knight (Eds), *Ethnic identity* (pp. 61–79). Albany: State University of New York Press.

Phinney, J. S. (1996). 'When we talk about American ethnic groups, what do we mean?'. *American Psychologist, 51,* 918–927.

Phinney, J. S., Chavira, V. and Williamson, L. (1992). 'Acculturation attitudes and self-esteem among high school and college students'. *Youth and Society, 23,* 299–312.

Phinney, J. S., Lochner, B. T. and Murphy, R. (1990). 'Ethnic identity development and psychological adjustment in adolescence'. In A. Stiffman and L. Davis (Eds), *Ethnic issues in adolescent mental health* (pp. 53–72). Newbury Park, CA: Sage.

Phinney, J. S. and Nakayama, S. (1991, April). 'Parental influences on ethnic identity formation in adolescents'. Paper presented at the Meeting of the Society for Research in Child Development, Seattle, WA.

Pizam, A. (1999). 'A comprehensive approach to classifying acts of crime and violence at tourism destinations'. *Journal of Travel Research, 38*, 5–12.

Pizam, A. and Mansfeld, Y. (Eds). (1996). *Tourism, crime and international security issues*. Chichester, UK: Wiley.

Porte, Z. and Torney-Purta, J. (1987). 'Depression and academic achievement among Indochinese refugee unaccompanied minors in ethnic and non-ethnic placements'. *American Journal of Orthopsychiatry, 57*, 536–547.

Portes, A. and Rumbaut, R. G. (1990). *Immigrant America: A portrait*. Berkeley: University of California Press.

Poortinga, Y. H. (1997). 'Towards convergence?'. In J. W. Berry, Y. H. Poortinga and J. Pandey (Eds), *Handbook of cross-cultural psychology: Vol. 1. Theory and method* (pp. 347–387). Boston: Allyn & Bacon.

Powell, R. G. and Andersen, J. (1994). 'Culture and classroom communication'. In L. A. Samovar and R. E. Porter (Eds), *Intercultural communication: A reader* (pp. 322–330). Belmont, CA: Wadsworth.

Pratt, D. D. (1991). 'Conceptions of self within China and the United States: Contrasting foundations for adult education'. *International Journal of Intercultural Relations, 15*, 285–310.

Pratt, M. (1992). *Imperial eyes: Travel writing and transculturation*. London: Routledge.

Prokop, H. (1970). 'Psychiatric illness of foreigners vacationing in Innsbruck'. *Neurochirugie und Psychiatrie, 107*, 363–368.

Pruegger, V. J. and Rogers, T. B. (1994). 'Cross-cultural sensitivity training: Methods and assessment'. *International Journal of Intercultural Relations, 18*, 369–387.

Pruitt, F. J. (1978). 'The adaptation of African students to American society'. *International Journal of Intercultural Relations, 21*, 90–118.

Ptak, C. L., Cooper, J. and Brislin, R. (1995). 'Cross-cultural training programs: Advice and insights from experienced trainers'. *International Journal of Intercultural Relations, 19*, 425–453.

Punnett, B. J., Singh, J. B. and Williams, G. (1994). 'The relative influence of economic development and Anglo heritage on expressed values: Empirical evidence from a Caribbean country'. *International Journal of Intercultural Relations, 18*, 99–115.

Rai, S. (1988). 'Perception of changes and difficulties by older and younger Tibetan refugees in India'. *Indian Journal of Current Psychological Research, 3*, 90–94.

Ralston, D. A., Gustafson, D. J., Elsass, P. M., Cheung, F. and Terpstra, R. H. (1992). 'Eastern values: A comparison of managers in the United States, Hong Kong, and the People's Republic of China'. *Journal of Applied Psychology, 77*, 664–671.

Ramirez, M. (1984). 'Assessing and understanding biculturalism–monoculturalism in Mexican-American adults'. In J. L. Martínez and R. H. Mendoza (Eds), *Chicano psychology* (2nd edn, pp. 77–94). New York: Academic Press.

Rao, G. L. (1979). *Brain drain and foreign students*. St. Lucia, Australia: University of Queensland Press.

Raschio, R. A. (1987). 'College students' perceptions of reverse culture shock and re-entry adjustments'. *Journal of College Student Personnel, 28*, 156–162.

Rashid, H. M. (1984). 'Promoting biculturalism in young African-American children'. *Young Children, 39*, 13–23.

Reagan, R. (1985, April 18). *Correspondence to the 25th session of the executive council of the World Tourism Organisation*. Washington, DC: The White House.

Redding, S. G., Norman, A. and Schlander, A. (1994). 'The nature of individual attachment to the organization: A review of East Asian variations'. In H. C. Triandis, M. D. Dunnette and L. M. Hough (Eds), *Handbook of industrial and organizational psychology* (2nd edn, Vol. 4, pp. 647–688). Palo Alto, CA: Consulting Psychologists Press.

Redfield, R., Linton, R. and Herskovits, M. J. (1936). 'Memorandum for the study of acculturation'. *American Anthropologist, 38*, 149–152.

Redmond, M. V. (2000). 'Cultural distance as a mediating factor between stress and intercultural communication competence'. *International Journal of Intercultural Relations, 24*, 151–159.

Redmond, M. V. and Bunyi, J. M. (1993). 'The relationship of intercultural communication competence with stress and the handling of stress as reported by international students'. *International Journal of Intercultural Relations, 17*, 235–254.

Reykowski, J. (1994). 'Collectivism and individualism as dimensions of social change'. In U. Kim, H. C. Triandis, C. Kâğitçibaşi, S.-C. Choi, and G. Yoon (Eds), *Individualism and collectivism: Theory, methods and applications* (pp. 276–292). Thousand Oaks, CA: Sage.

Richardson, A. (1974). *British immigrants and Australia: A psycho-social inquiry*. Canberra: Australian National University Press.

Richman, J. A., Gaviria, M., Flaherty, J. A., Birz, S. and Wintrob, R. M. (1987). 'The process of acculturation: Theoretical perspectives and an empirical investigation in Peru'. *Social Science and Medicine, 25*, 839–847.

Richmond, A. H. (1993). 'Reactive migration: Sociological perspectives on refugee movements'. *Journal of Refugee Studies, 6*, 7–24.

Rick, K. and Forward, J. (1992). 'Acculturation and perceived intergenerational differences among Hmong youth'. *Journal of Cross-cultural Psychology, 23*, 85–94.

Riesman, D. (1964). *Individualism reconsidered*. New York: The Free Press.

Riley, R., Baker, D. and Van Doren, C. S. (1998). 'Movie induced tourism'. *Annals of Tourism Research, 25*, 919–935.

Ritchie, J. E. (1981). '*Tama tu, tama ora*: Mediating styles in Maori culture'. In S. Bochner (Ed.), *The Mediating person: Bridges between cultures* (pp. 221–245). Cambridge, MA: Schenkman.

Robb, J. G. (1998). 'Tourism and legends: Archeology of heritage'. *Annals of Tourism Research, 25*, 579–596.

Robertson, J. W. (1903). 'The prevalence of insanity in California'. *American Journal of Insanity, 60*, 81–82.

Roebers, C. and Schneider, W. (1999). 'Self-concept and anxiety in immigrant children'. *International Journal of Behavioral Development, 23*, 125–147.

Rogers, J. and Ward, C. (1993). 'Expectation–experience discrepancies and psychological adjustment during cross-cultural re-entry'. *International Journal of Intercultural Relations, 17*, 185–196.

Rogler, L., Cooney, R. and Ortiz, V. (1980). 'Intergenerational change in ethnic identity in the Puerto Rican family'. *International Migration Review, 14*, 193–214.

Rogler, L., Cortés, D. and Malgady, R. (1991). 'Acculturation and mental health status among Hispanics: Convergence and new directions for research'. *American Psychologist, 46*, 585–597.

Rohrlich, B. F. and Martin, J. N. (1991). 'Host country and re-entry adjustment of student sojourners'. *International Journal of Intercultural Relations, 15*, 163–182.

Rondinelli, D. A. (1993). 'Resolving U.S.–China trade conflicts: Conditions for trade and investment expansion in the 1990s'. *Columbia Journal of World Business, 28*, 66–81.

Rose, E. and Felton, W. (1955). 'Experimental histories of culture'. *American Sociological Review, 20*, 383–392.

Rosenberg, S. W. and Wolsfeld, G. (1977). 'International conflict and the problem of attribution'. *Journal of Conflict Resolution, 21*, 75–103.

Rosenthal, D. (1984). 'Intergenerational conflict and culture: A study of immigrant and non-immigrant adolescents and their parents'. *Genetic Psychology Monographs, 109*, 53–75.

Rosenthal, D., Bell, R., Demetriou, A. and Efklides, A. (1989). 'From collectivism to individualism? The acculturation of Greek immigrants in Australia'. *International Journal of Psychology, 24*, 57–71.

Rosenthal, D. and Chicello, A. (1986). 'The meeting of two cultures: Ethnic identity and psychosocial adjustment of Italian-Australian adolescents'. *International Journal of Psychology, 21*, 487–501.

Rosenthal, D. and Hrynevich, C. (1985). 'Ethnicity and ethnic identity: A comparative study of Greek-, Italian-, and Anglo-Australian adolescents'. *International Journal of Psychology, 20*, 723–742.

Ross, D. N. (1999). 'Culture as a context for multinational business: A framework for assessing the strategy-culture "fit"'. *Multinational Business Review, 7*, 13–19.

Rotheram-Borus, M. J. (1993). 'Biculturalism among adolescents'. In M. E. Bernal and G. P. Knight (Eds), *Ethnic identity* (pp. 81–102). Albany: State University of New York Press.

Rothman, R. (1978). 'Residents and transients: Community reactions to seasonal visitors'. *Journal of Travel Research, 16*, 8–13.

Ruben, B. D. (1976). 'Assessing communication competency for intercultural adaptation'. *Group and Organization Studies, 1*, 334–354.

Ruben, B. D. and Kealey, D. J. (1979). 'Behavioral assessment of communication competency and the prediction of cross-cultural adaptation'. *International Journal of Intercultural Relations, 3*, 15–47.

Rumbaut, R. G. (1985). 'Mental health and the refugee experience: A comparative study of Southeast Asian refugees'. In T. C. Owan (Ed.), *Southeast Asian mental health: Treatment, services, prevention and research* (pp. 433–486). Rockville, MD: National Institute of Mental Health.

Rumbaut, R. G. (1991). 'The agony of exile: A study of migration and adaptation of Indochinese refugee adults and children'. In F. L. Ahearn and J. Garrison (Eds), *Refugee children: Theory, research and services* (pp. 53–91). Baltimore: Johns Hopkins University.

Russel, S. S. and Teitelbaum, M. (1992). *International migration and international trade*. Washington, DC: World Bank.

Ryan, C. (1997). 'Maori and tourism: A relationship of history, constitutions and rites'. *Journal of Sustainable Tourism, 5*, 257–278.

Ryan, C. (1998). 'Saltwater crocodiles as tourist attractions'. *Journal of Sustainable Tourism, 6*, 314–327.

Sack, W. H. (1985). 'Posttraumatic stress disorders in children'. *Integrative Psychiatry, 3*, 162–164.

Sagiv, L. and Schwartz, S. H. (1995). 'Value priorities and readiness for out-group social contact'. *Journal of Personality and Social Psychology, 69*, 437–448.

Sagiv, L. and Schwartz, S. H. (1998). 'Determinants of readiness for out-group social contact: Dominance relations and minority group motivations'. *International Journal of Psychology, 33*, 313–324.

Sahin, N. H. (1990). 'Re-entry and the academic and psychological problems of the second generation'. *Psychology and Developing Societies, 2*, 165–182.

Salt, J. (1995). 'International migration report'. *New Community, 21*, 443–464.

Sam, D. L. (1994). 'The psychological adjustment of young immigrants in Norway'. *Scandinavian Journal of Psychology, 35*, 240–253.

Sam, D. L. (1995). 'Acculturation attitudes among young immigrants as a function of perceived parental attitudes toward cultural change'. *Journal of Early Adolescence, 15*, 238–258.

Sam, D. L. (1998). 'Predicting life satisfaction among adolescents from immigrant families in Norway'. *Ethnicity and Health, 3*, 5–18.

Sam, D. L. (2000). 'Psychological adaptation of adolescents with immigrant backgrounds'. *Journal of Social Psychology, 140*, 5–25.

Sam, D. L. and Berry, J. W. (1995). 'Acculturative stress and young immigrants in Norway'. *Scandinavian Journal of Psychology, 36*, 10–24.

Sam, D. L. and Eide, R. (1991). 'Survey of mental health of foreign students'. *Scandinavian Journal of Psychology, 32*, 22–30.

Samovar, L. A. and Porter, R. E. (1988). *Intercultural communication: A reader*. Belmont, CA: Wadsworth.

Samuelowicz, K. (1987). 'Learning problems of overseas students: Two sides of a story'. *Higher Education Research and Development, 6*, 121–134.

Sandhu, D. S. and Asrabadi, B. R. (1994). 'Development of an acculturative stress scale for international students: Preliminary findings'. *Psychological Reports, 75*, 435–448.

Sands, E. and Berry, J. W. (1993). 'Acculturation and mental health among Greek-Canadians'. *Canadian Journal of Community Mental Health, 12*, 117–124.

Saphiere, D. M. H. (1995). 'Ecotonos: A multicultural problem-solving simulation'. In S. M. Fowler and M. G. Mumford (Eds), *Intercultural sourcebook: Cross-cultural training methods* (Vol. 1, pp. 117–125). Yarmouth, MN: Intercultural Press.

Sarason, I. G., Levine, H. M., Basham, R. B. and Sarason, B. (1983). 'Assessing social support: The Social Support Questionnaire'. *Journal of Personality and Social Psychology, 44*, 127–139.

Sayegh, L. and Lasry, J. C. (1993). 'Immigrants' adaptation to Canada: Assimilation, acculturation, and orthogonal cultural identification'. *Canadian Psychology, 34*, 98–109.

Scarbrough, H. (1995). 'The social engagement of social science: A Tavistock anthology'. *Human Relations, 48*, 23–33.

Scherer, S. E. (1974). 'Proxemic behavior of primary school children as a function of their socioeconomic class and subculture'. *Journal of Personality and Social Psychology, 29*, 800–805.

Schild, E. O. (1962). 'The foreign student, as stranger, learning the norms of the host culture'. *Journal of Social Issues, 18*, 41–54.

Schmitz, P. G. (1992). 'Immigrant mental and physical health'. *Psychology and Developing Societies, 4*, 117–131.

Schnapper, D. (1995). 'The significance of French immigration and integration policy'. In F. Heckmann and W. Bosswick (Eds), *Migration policies: A comparative perspective* (pp. 91–103). Stuttgart: Enke.

Schneider, S. C. and Asakawa, K. (1995). 'American and Japanese expatriate adjustment: A psychoanalytic perspective'. *Human Relations, 48*, 1109–1127.

Schönpflug, U. (1997). 'Acculturation, adaptation or development?'.*Applied Psychology: An International Review, 46*, 52–55.

Schrage, C. R., Chao, P., Wuehrer, G. and Koeslich, D. (1999). 'The role of cultural differences in joint venture activities in selected East European and Central Asian countries'. *Journal of Global Business, 10*, 23–32.

Schreier, A. R. and Abramovitch, H. (1996). 'American medical students in Israel: Stress and coping'. *Medical Education, 30*, 445–452.

Schwartz, S. H. and Bilsky, W. (1990). 'Toward a theory of the universal content and structure of values: Extensions and cross-cultural replications'. *Journal of Personality and Social Psychology, 58*, 878–891.

Schwarzer, R., Jerusalem, M. and Hahn, A. (1994). 'Unemployment, social support and health complaints: A longitudinal study of stress in East German refugees'. *Journal of Community and Applied Social Psychology, 4*, 31–45.

Scott, F. D. (1956). *The American experience of Swedish students: Retrospect and aftermath.* Minneapolis, MN: University of Minnesota Press.

Scott, W. A. and Scott, R. (1991). 'Adaptation of immigrant and native Australians'. *Australian Psychologist, 26*, 43–48.

Searle, W. and Ward, C. (1990). 'The prediction of psychological and sociocultural adjustment during cross-cultural transitions'. *International Journal of Intercultural Relations, 14*, 449–464.

Seaton, A. V. (1996). 'From thanatopsis to thanatourism: Guided by the dark'. *Journal of International Heritage Studies, 2*, 234–244.

Seaton, A. V. (1999). 'War and thanatourism: Waterloo 1815–1914'. *Annals of Tourism Research, 26*, 130–158.

Seelye, H. N. (Ed.). (1996). *Experiential activities for intercultural learning* (Vol. 1). Yarmouth, MN: Intercultural Press.

Seidel, G. (1981). 'Cross-cultural training procedures: Their theoretical framework and evaluation'. In S. Bochner (Ed.), *The mediating person: Bridges between cultures* (pp. 184–213). Cambridge, MA: Schenkman.

Seipel, M. M. O. (1988). 'Locus of control as related to life experiences of Korean immigrants'. *International Journal of Intercultural Relations, 12*, 61–71.

Seiter, J. S. and Waddell, D. (1989, February). 'The intercultural re-entry process: Re-entry shock, locus of control, satisfaction and interpersonal uses of communication'. Paper presented at the Annual Meeting of the Western Speech Communication Association, Spokane, WA.

Selby, H. A. and Woods, C. M. (1966). 'Foreign students at a high pressure university'. *Sociology of Education, 39*, 138–154.

Seligman, M. E. P. (1975). *Helplessness: On depression, development and death.* San Francisco: Freeman.

Selltiz, C., Christ, J. R., Havel, J. and Cook, S. W. (1963). *Attitudes and social relations of foreign students in the United States.* Minneapolis, MN: University of Minnesota Press.

Selltiz, C. and Cook, S. W. (1962). 'Factors influencing attitudes of foreign students towards the host country'. *Journal of Social Issues, 18*, 7–23.

Selmer, J. and Shiu, L. S. C. (1999). 'Coming home? Adjustment of Hong Kong Chinese expatriate business managers assigned to the People's Republic of China'. *International Journal of Intercultural Relations, 23*, 447–465.

Semin, G. R. and Fiedler, K. (Eds). (1996). *Applied social psychology*. London: Sage.

Sethi, R. (1990, July). 'Intercultural communication and adaptation among first generation Asian-Indian immigrants'. Paper presented at the Korean Psychological Association International Conference, Individualism–Collectivism: Psychocultural Perspectives from East and West, Seoul, Korea.

Sewell, W. H. and Davidsen, O. M. (1961). *Scandinavian students on an American campus*. Minneapolis, MN: University of Minnesota Press.

Sewell, W. H., Morris, R. T. and Davidsen, O. M. (1954). 'Scandinavian students' images of the United States: A study in cross-cultural education'. *Annals of the American Academy of Political and Social Science, 295*, 126–135.

Shade, B. J. and New, C. A. (1993). 'Cultural influences on learning: Teaching implications'. In J. A. Banks and C. A. M. Banks (Eds), *Multicultural education: Issues and perspectives* (pp. 317–331). Boston: Allyn & Bacon.

Shadur, M. A., Rodwell, J. J., Bamber, G. J. and Simmons, D. E. (1995). 'The adoption of international best practices in a Western culture: East meets West'. *The International Journal of Human Resource Management, 6*, 735–757.

Shenkar, O. and Ronen, S. (1993). 'The cultural context of negotiations: The implications of Chinese interpersonal norms'. In L. Kelley and O. Shenkar (Eds), *International business in China* (pp. 191–207). London: Routledge.

Shields, J. J. (1968). 'A selected bibliography'. In D. G. Scanlon and J. J. Shields (Eds), *Problems and prospects in international education* (pp. 371–399). New York: Teachers College Press.

Shimoda, K., Argyle, M. and Ricci Bitti, P. (1978). 'The intercultural recognition of emotional expression by three national groups – English, Italian and Japanese'. *European Journal of Social Psychology, 8*, 169–179.

Shirts, R. G. (1973). *BAFA BAFA: A cross-cultural simulation*. Delmar, CA: Simile II.

Shirts, R. G. (1995). 'Beyond ethnocentrism: Promoting cross-cultural understanding with BAFA BAFA'. In S. M. Fowler and M. G. Mumford (Eds), *Intercultural sourcebook: Cross-cultural training methods* (Vol. 1, pp. 93–100). Yarmouth, MN: Intercultural Press.

Shisana, O. and Celentano, D. D. (1987). 'Relationship of chronic stress, social support and coping style to health among Namibian refugees'. *Social Science and Medicine, 24*, 145–157.

Siefen, G., Kirkcaldy, B. D. and Athanasou, J. A. (1996). 'Parental attitudes: A study of German, Greek and second generation Greek migrant adolescents'. *Human Relations, 49*, 837–851.

Singapore Tourist Promotion Board (1996). *Tourism 21: Vision of a tourism capital*. Singapore: Singapore Tourist Promotion Board.

Singelis, T. M. (1994). 'The measurement of independent and interdependent self-construals'. *Personality and Social Psychology Bulletin, 20*, 580–591.

Singelis, T. M. and Brown, W. J. (1995). 'Culture, self, and collectivist communication: Linking culture to individual behaviour'. *Human Communication Research, 21*, 354–389.

Singelis, T. M., Triandis, H. C., Bhawuk, D. and Gelfand, M. J. (1995). 'Horizontal and vertical dimensions of individualism and collectivism: A theoretical and measurement refinement'. *Cross-Cultural Research, 29,* 240–275.

Singh, A. K. (1963). *Indian students in Britain.* Bombay: Asia Publishing House.

Singh, A. K. (1989). 'Impact of acculturation on psychological stress: A study of the Oraon tribe'. In D. M. Keats, D. Munro and L. Mann (Eds), *Heterogeneity in cross-cultural psychology* (pp. 210–215). Lisse, The Netherlands: Swets & Zeitlinger.

Sisk, D. A. (1995). 'Simulation games as training tools'. In S. M. Fowler and M. G. Mumford (Eds), *Intercultural sourcebook: Cross-cultural training methods* (Vol. 1, pp. 81–92). Yarmouth, MN: Intercultural Press.

Sitwell, O. (1925). *Discursions on travel, art and life.* London: Greenwood Press.

Skhiri, D., Annabi, S. and Allani, D. (1982). 'Enfants d'immigres: Facteurs de lines ou de rupture?'. *Annales Medico Psychologiques, 140,* 597–602.

Skinner, Q. (1968). *American industry in developing economies: The management of international manufacturing.* New York: Wiley.

Smith, C. D. (1991). *The absentee American.* New York: Praeger.

Smith, G. (1997). *Building on Egerton Ryerson's legacy: Bringing education to the world.* Ottawa: Department of Foreign Affairs and International Trade.

Smith, M. B. (1966). 'Explorations in competence: A study of Peace Corps in Ghana'. *American Psychologist, 21,* 555–566.

Smith, M. D. and Krannich, R. S. (1998). 'Tourism dependence and resident attitudes'. *Annals of Tourism Research, 25,* 783–802.

Smith, P. B. and Bond, M. H. (1998). *Social psychology across cultures* (2nd edn). London: Prentice Hall.

Smith, P. B., Dugan, S., Peterson, M. F. and Leung, K. (1998). 'Individualism–collectivism and the handling of disagreement – A 23 country study'. *International Journal of Intercultural Relations, 22,* 351–367.

Smith, V. (1989). 'Introduction'. In V. Smith (Ed.), *Hosts and guests: The anthropology of tourism* (2nd edn, pp. 1–17). Philadelphia: University of Pennsylvania Press.

Smith, V. and Eadington, W. (Eds). (1992). *Tourism alternatives: Potentials and problems in the development of tourism.* Philadelphia: University of Pennsylvania Press.

Smither, R. and Rodriguez-Giegling, M. (1979). 'Marginality, modernity and anxiety in Indochinese refugees'. *Journal of Cross-cultural Psychology, 10,* 469–478.

Snell, S. A. (1992). 'Control theory in strategic human resource management: The mediating effect of administrative information'. *Academy of Management Journal, 35,* 292–327.

Sodowsky, G. R. and Plake, B. S. (1991). 'Psychometric properties of the American-International Relations Scale'. *Educational and Psychological Measurement, 51,* 207–216.

Sodowsky, G. R. and Plake, B. S. (1992). 'A study of acculturation differences among international people and suggestions for sensitivity to within-group differences'. *Journal of Counselling and Development, 71,* 53–59.

Solomon, C. M. (1999). 'Short term assignments and other solutions'. *Global Workforce, 4,* 38–40.

Sommer, R. (1969). *Personal space: The behavioral basis of design.* Englewood Cliffs, NJ: Prentice-Hall.

Sonmez, S. F. and Graefe, A. R. (1998). 'Influence of terrorism risk on foreign tourism decisions'. *Annals of Tourism Research, 25,* 112–144.

Sorimachi, A. (1994). 'Subjective feelings of cultural adjustment among Japanese high school students returning from foreign countries'. *Japanese Journal of Counselling Science, 27*, 1–10. [In Japanese, English summary]

Sorti, C. (1994). *Cross-cultural dialogues: 74 brief encounters with cultural difference.* Yarmouth, MN: Intercultural Press.

Spiess, E. and Wittmann, A. (1999). 'Motivational phases associated with the foreign placement of managerial candidates: An application of the Rubicon model of action phases'. *The International Journal of Human Resource Management, 10*, 891–905.

Spradley, J. P. and Phillips, M. (1972). 'Culture and stress: A quantitative analysis'. *American Anthropologist, 74*, 518–529.

Starke, M. (1802). *Travels in Italy.* London: R. Phillips.

Stein, B. N. (1986). 'The experience of being a refugee: Insights from the research literature'. In C. L. Williams and J. Westermeyer (Eds), *Refugee mental health in resettlement countries* (pp. 5–23). Washington, DC: Hemisphere.

Steinwachs, B. (1995). 'Barnga: A game for all seasons'. In S. M. Fowler and M. G. Mumford (Eds), *Intercultural sourcebook: Cross-cultural training methods* (Vol. 1, pp. 101–108). Yarmouth, MN: Intercultural Press.

Stening, B. W. and Hammer, M. R. (1992). 'Cultural baggage and the adaption of expatriate American and Japanese managers'. *Management International Review, 32*, 77–89.

Stephan, C. W. and Stephan, W. G. (1992). 'Reducing intercultural anxiety through intercultural contact'. *International Journal of Intercultural Relations, 16*, 89–106.

Stephan, W. G., Ybarra, O. and Bachman, G. (1999). 'Prejudice towards immigrants: An integrated threat theory'. *Journal of Applied Social Psychology, 29*, 2221–2237.

Stephan, W. G., Ybarra, P., Martínez, C. M., Schwarzwald, J. and Tur-Kaspa, M. (1998). 'Prejudice toward immigrants to Spain and Israel: An integrated threat theory analysis'. *Journal of Cross-cultural Psychology, 29*, 559–576.

Stevens, F. S. (Ed.). (1971). *Racism: The Australian experience: Vol. 1. Prejudice and xenophobia.* Sydney: Australia and New Zealand Book Company.

Stevens, F. S. (Ed.). (1972). *Racism: The Australian experience: Vol. 2. Black versus white.* Sydney: Australia and New Zealand Book Company.

Stewart, S. and DeLisle, P. (1994). 'Hong Kong expatriates in the People's Republic of China'. *International Studies of Management and Organization, 24*, 105–118.

Stoller, A. (Ed.). (1966). *New faces: Immigration and family life in Australia.* Melbourne: Chesire.

Stoller, A. and Krupinski, J. (1973). 'Immigration to Australia: Mental health aspects'. In C. A. A. Zwingmann and M. Pfister-Ammende (Eds), *Uprooting and after* (pp. 252–268). Berlin: Springer-Verlag.

Stone, R. (1991). 'Expatriate selection and failure'. *Human Resource Planning, 14*, 9–18.

Stone Feinstein, E. and Ward, C. (1990). 'Loneliness and psychological adjustment of sojourners: New perspectives on culture shock'. In D. M. Keats, D. Munro and L. Mann (Eds), *Heterogeneity in cross-cultural psychology* (pp. 537–547). Lisse, The Netherlands: Swets & Zeitlinger.

Stonequist, E. V. (1937). *The marginal man.* New York: Scribner.

Storey, B. (1991). 'History and homogeneity: Effects of perceptions of membership groups on interpersonal communication'. *Communication Research, 18*, 199–221.

Stoynoff, S. (1997). 'Factors associated with international students' academic achievement'. *Journal of Instructional Psychology, 24*, 56–68.

Strand, P. J. and Jones, W. (1985). *Indochinese refugees in America: Problems of adaptation and assimilation.* Durham, NC: Duke University Press.

Stroebe, W., Lenkert, A. and Jonas, K. (1988). 'Familiarity may breed contempt: The impact of student exchange on national stereotypes and attitudes'. In W. Stroebe, D. Bar-Tal and M. Hewstone (Eds), *The social psychology of intergroup relations* (pp. 167–187). New York: Springer.

Sue, D. (1997). 'Multicultural training'. *International Journal of Intercultural Relations, 21,* 175–193.

Sue, D. W., Ivey A. and Pedersen, P. B. (1996). *A theory of multicultural counselling and therapy.* Pacific Grove, CA: Brooks/Cole.

Sue, D. W. and Sue, D. (1990). *Counselling the culturally different* (2nd edn). New York: Wiley.

Sugimoto, N. (1998). 'Norms of apology depicted in U.S. American and Japanese literature on manners and etiquette'. *International Journal of Intercultural Relations, 22,* 251–276.

Suinn, R. M., Ahuna, C. and Khoo, G. (1992). 'The Suinn–Lew Asian Self-Identity Acculturation Scale: Concurrent and factorial validation'. *Educational and Psychological Measurement, 52,* 1041–1046.

Suinn, R. M., Rickard-Figueroa, K., Lew, S. and Vigil, P. (1987). 'The Suinn-Lew Asian Self-Identity Acculturation Scale: An initial report'. *Educational and Psychological Measurement, 47,* 401–402.

Sundquist, J. (1993). 'Ethnicity as a risk factor for mental illness: A population-based study of 338 Latin American refugees and 996 age-, sex-, and education-matched Swedish controls'. *Acta Psychiatrica Scandinavia, 87,* 208–212.

Sundquist, J. (1994). 'Refugees, labor migrants and psychological distress: A population-based study of 338 Latin American refugees, 161 South European and 396 Finnish labor migrants, and 996 Swedish age-, sex- and education-matched controls'. *Social Psychiatry and Psychiatric Epidemiology, 29,* 20–24.

Sundquist, J. and Johansson, S. E. (1997). 'Long-term illness among indigenous and foreign-born people in Sweden'. *Social Science and Medicine, 44,* 189–198.

Swan, N., Auer, L., Chenard, D., dePlaa, A., deSilva, A., Palmer, D. and Serjak, J. (1991). *Economic and social impacts of immigration.* Ottawa: Economic Council of Canada.

Sykes, I. J. and Eden, D. (1987). 'Transitional stress, social support and psychological strain'. *Journal of Occupational Behavior, 6,* 293–298.

Symonds, J., Santhai, S., Farr, H., Vidmar, M., Lekhyananda, D. and Chemers, M. (1966). *Culture assimilator: IB Arab culture.* University of Illinois, Urbana: Training Research Laboratory.

Szapocznik, J. and Kurtines, W. M. (1980). 'Acculturation, biculturalism and adjustment among Cuban Americans'. In A. M. Padilla (Ed.), *Psychological dimensions of the acculturation process: Theory, models and some new findings* (pp. 139–160). Boulder, CO: Westview Press.

Szapocznik, J., Kurtines, W. M. and Fernandez, T. (1980). 'Bicultural involvement and adjustment in Hispanic-American youths'. *International Journal of Intercultural Relations, 4,* 353–365.

Szapocznik, J., Santisteban, D., Kurtines, W., Perez-Vidal, A. and Hervis, O. (1984). 'Bicultural effectiveness training: A treatment intervention for enhancing intercultural adjustment in Cuban American families'. *Hispanic Journal of Behavioral Sciences, 6,* 317–344.

Szapocznik, J., Scopetta, M. A., Kurtines, W. M. and Aranalde, M. A. (1978). 'Theory and measurement of acculturation'. *Interamerican Journal of Psychology, 12*, 113–130.

Taft, R. (1966). *From stranger to citizen*. London: Tavistock.

Taft, R. (1973). 'Migration: Problems of adjustment and assimilation in immigrants'. In P. Watson (Ed.), *Psychology and race* (pp. 224–239). Harmondsworth, UK: Penguin.

Taft, R. (1986). 'Methodological considerations in the study of immigrant adaptation in Australia'. *Australian Journal of Psychology, 38*, 339–346.

Taft, R. and Steinkalk, E. (1985). 'The adaptation of recent Soviet immigrants in Australia'. In I. R. Lagunes and Y. H. Poortinga (Eds), *From a different perspective: Studies of behavior across cultures* (pp. 19–28). Lisse, The Netherlands: Swets & Zeitlinger.

Tajfel, H. (1970). Experiments in intergroup discrimination. *Scientific American, 223*, 92–102.

Tajfel, H. (Ed.). (1978). *Differentiation between social groups: Studies in the psychology of intergroup relations*. London: Academic Press.

Tajfel, H. (1981). *Human groups and social categories*. Cambridge: Cambridge University Press.

Tajfel, H. and Dawson, J. L. (Eds). (1965). *Disappointed guests*. London: Oxford University Press.

Tajfel, H. and Turner, J. (1979). 'An integrated theory of intergroup conflict'. In W. Austin and S. Worchel (Eds), *The social psychology of intergroup relations* (pp. 33–48). Monterey, CA: Brooks/Cole.

Tajfel, H. and Turner, J. (1986). 'The social identity theory of intergroup behavior'. In W. Austin and S. Worchel (Eds), *The social psychology of intergroup relations* (pp. 7–24). Chicago: Nelson-Hall Publishers.

Takai, J. (1989). 'The adjustment of international students at a third culture-like academic community in Japan: A longitudinal study'. *Human Communication Studies, 17*, 113–120.

Tanaka, T., Takai, J., Kohyama, T. and Fujihara, T. (1994). 'Adjustment patterns of international students in Japan'. *International Journal of Intercultural Relations, 18*, 55–75.

Tanaka, T., Takai, J., Kohyama, T., Fujihara, T. and Minami, H. (1997). 'Effects of social networks in cross-cultural adjustment'. *Japanese Psychological Research, 39*, 12–24.

Tanaka-Matsumi, J. and Draguns, J. G. (1997). 'Culture and psychopathology'. In J. W. Berry, M. H. Segall and C. Kâğitçibaşi (Eds), *Handbook of cross-cultural psychology: Vol. 3. Social behavior and applications* (2nd edn, pp. 449–491). Boston: Allyn & Bacon.

Tang, J. and O'Brien, T. P. (1990). 'Correlates of vocational success in refugee work and adaptation'. *Journal of Applied Social Psychology, 20*, 1444–1452.

Tayeb, M. (1999). 'Foreign remedies for local difficulties: The case of three Scottish manufacturing firms'. *The International Journal of Human Resource Management, 10*, 842–857.

Taylor, D. M. and Jaggi, V. (1974). 'Ethnocentrism in a South Indian context'. *Journal of Cross-cultural Psychology, 5*, 162–172.

Taylor, D. M., Moghaddam, F. M. and Bellerose, J. (1989). 'Social comparison in an intergroup context'. *Journal of Social Psychology, 129*, 499–515.

Taylor, D. M., Wright, S., Moghaddam, F. M. and Lalonde, R. N. (1990). 'The personal/group discrimination discrepancy: Perceiving my group but not myself to be a target for discrimination'. *Personality and Social Psychology Bulletin, 16*, 254–262.

Taylor, S. and Brown, J. (1988). 'Illusion and well-being: A social psychological perspective on mental health'. *Psychological Bulletin, 103*, 193–210.

Testa, M. R., Williams, J. M. and Pietrzak, D. (1998). 'The development of the cruise line job satisfaction questionnaire'. *Journal of Travel Research, 36*, 13–19.

Textor, R. B. (1966). *Cultural frontiers of the Peace Corps.* Cambridge, MA: MIT Press.

Theobald, W. (Ed). (1994). *Global tourism: The next generation.* Oxford: Butterworth.

Theroux, P. (1988). *Riding the iron rooster: By train through China.* London: Hamish Hamilton.

Thomas, D. C. (1999). 'Cultural diversity and work group effectiveness: An experimental study'. *Journal of Cross-cultural Psychology, 30*, 242–263.

Thomas, E. E. (Ed.). (1994). *International perspectives in culture and schooling: A symposium proceedings.* London: Institute of Education, University of London.

Thomas, T. N. (1995). 'Acculturative stress in the adjustment of immigrant families'. *Journal of Social Distress and the Homeless, 4*, 131–142.

Throssell, R. P. (1981). 'Toward a multicultural society: The role of government departments and officials in developing cross-cultural relations in Australia'. In S. Bochner (Ed.), *The Mediating person: Bridges between cultures* (pp. 246–272). Cambridge, MA: Schenkman.

Tietze, C., Lemkau, P. and Cooper, M. (1942). 'Personality disorder and spatial mobility'. *American Journal of Sociology, 48*, 29–39.

Ting-Toomey, S. (1981). 'Ethnic identity and close friendship in Chinese-American college students'. *International Journal of Intercultural Relations, 5*, 383–406.

Ting-Toomey, S. (1988). 'Intercultural conflict styles: A face negotiation theory'. In Y. Y. Kim and W. B. Gudykunst (Eds), *Theories in intercultural communication* (pp. 213–238). Newbury Park, CA: Sage.

Ting-Toomey, S. and Kurogi, A. (1998). 'Facework competence in intercultural conflict: An updated face-negotiation theory'. *International Journal of Intercultural Relations, 22*, 187–225.

Topalova, V. (1997). 'Individualism/collectivism and social identity'. *Journal of Community and Applied Social Psychology, 7*, 53–64.

Torbiorn, I. (1982). *Living abroad: Personal adjustment and personnel policy in the overseas setting.* Chichester, UK: Wiley.

Torbiorn, I. (1994). 'Operative and strategic use of expatriates in new organizations and market structures'. *International Studies of Management and Organizations, 24*, 5–17.

Torres-Rivera, M. A. (1985). 'Manifestations of depression in Puerto Rican migrants to the United States and Puerto Rican residents of Puerto Rico'. In I. R. Lagunes and Y. H. Poortinga (Eds), *From a different perspective: Studies of behavior across cultures* (pp. 63–75). Lisse, The Netherlands: Swets & Zeitlinger.

Trafimow, D., Triandis, H. C. and Goto, S. G. (1991). 'Some tests of the distinction between the private self and the collective self'. *Journal of Personality and Social Psychology, 60*, 649–655.

Tran, T. V. (1987). 'Ethnic community supports and psychological well-being of Vietnamese refugees'. *International Migration Review, 21*, 833–844.

Tran, T. V. (1991). 'Family living arrangement and social adjustment among three ethnic groups of elderly Indochinese refugees'. *International Journal of Aging and Human Development, 32*, 91–102.

Tran, T. V. (1993). 'Psychological traumas and depression in a sample of Vietnamese people in the United States'. *Health and Social Work, 18*, 184–194.

Tran, T. V., Wright, R. and Mindel, C. H. (1987). 'Alienation among Vietnamese refugees in the United States: A causal approach'. *Journal of Social Service Research, 11*, 59–75.

Triandis, H. C. (1967). 'Interpersonal relations in international organizations'. *Organizational Behavior and Human Performance, 2*, 26–55.

Triandis, H. C. (1975). 'Culture training, cognitive complexity and interpersonal attitudes'. In R. W. Brislin, S. Bochner and W. J. Lonner (Eds), *Cross-cultural perspectives on learning* (pp. 39–77). New York: Wiley.

Triandis, H. C. (1984). 'A theoretical framework for the more efficient construction of culture assimilators'. *International Journal of Intercultural Relations, 8*, 301–330.

Triandis, H. C. (1988). 'Collectivism and individualism: A reconceptualization of a basic concept in cross-cultural psychology'. In G. K. Verma and C. Bagley (Eds), *Personality, attitudes and cognitions* (pp. 60–95). London: Macmillan.

Triandis, H. C. (1989). 'The self and social behavior in differing cultural contexts'. *Psychological Review, 96*, 506–520.

Triandis, H. C. (1990). 'Theoretical concepts that are applicable to the analysis of ethnocentrism'. In R. W. Brislin (Ed.), *Applied cross-cultural psychology* (pp. 34–55). Newbury Park, CA: Sage.

Triandis, H. C. (1994a). *Culture and social behavior.* New York: McGraw-Hill.

Triandis, H. C. (1994b). 'Cross-cultural industrial and organizational psychology'. In H. C. Triandis, M. D. Dunnette and L. M. Hough (Eds), *Handbook of industrial and organizational psychology* (2nd edn, Vol. 4, pp. 103–172). Palo Alto, CA: Consulting Psychologists Press.

Triandis, H. C. (1995a). *Individualism and collectivism.* Boulder, CO: Westview Press.

Triandis, H. C. (1995b). 'Culture-specific assimilators'. In S. M. Fowler and M. G. Mumford (Eds), *Intercultural sourcebook: Cross-cultural training methods* (Vol. 1, pp. 179–186). Yarmouth, MN: Intercultural Press.

Triandis, H. C. (1997). 'Where is culture in the acculturation model?'. *Applied Psychology: An International Review, 46*, 55–58.

Triandis, H. C., Dunnette, M. D. and Hough, L. M. (Eds). (1994). *Handbook of industrial and organizational psychology* (Vol. 4, 2nd edn). Palo Alto, CA: Consulting Psychologists Press.

Triandis, H. C., Kashima, Y., Shimada, E. and Villareal, M. (1986). 'Acculturation indices as a means of confirming cultural differences'. *International Journal of Psychology, 21*, 43–70.

Triandis, H. C., Kurowski, L. L. and Gelfand, M. J. (1994). 'Workplace diversity'. In H. C. Triandis, M. D. Dunnette and L. M. Hough (Eds), *Handbook of industrial and organizational psychology* (2nd edn, Vol. 4, pp. 769–827). Palo Alto, CA: Consulting Psychologists Press.

Triandis, H. C., McCusker, C. and Hui, C. H. (1990). 'Multimethod probes of individualism and collectivism'. *Journal of Personality and Social Psychology, 59*, 1006–1020.

Triandis, H. C. and Singelis, T. M. (1998). 'Training to recognize individual differences in collectivism and individualism within culture'. *International Journal of Intercultural Relations, 22*, 35–47.

Triandis, H. C. and Vassiliou, V. (1967). 'Frequency of contact and stereotyping'. *Journal of Personality and Social Psychology, 7*, 316–328.

Triandis, H. C., Vassiliou, V., Vassiliou, G., Tanaka, Y. and Shanmugam, A. V. (1972). *The analysis of subjective culture*. New York: Wiley.

Trimble, J. E. (1976). 'Value differences among American Indians: Concerns for the concerned counsellor'. In P. B. Pedersen, W. J. Lonner and J. G. Draguns (Eds), *Counselling across cultures* (pp. 203–226). Honolulu: University of Hawaii Press.

Trower, P., Bryant, B. and Argyle, M. (1978). *Social skills and mental health*. London: Methuen.

Truss, C., Gratton, L., Hope-Hailey, V., McGovern, P. and Stiles, P. (1997). 'Soft and hard models of human resource management: A reappraisal'. *Journal of Management Studies, 34*, 53–73.

Tsai, H. Y. (1996). 'Concept of "Mien Tzu" (Face) in East Asian societies: The case of Taiwanese and Japanese'. In H. Grad, A. Blanco and J. Georgas (Eds), *Key issues in cross-cultural psychology* (pp. 309–315). Lisse, The Netherlands: Swets & Zeitlinger.

Tung, R. (1987). 'Expatriate assignments: Enhancing success and minimizing failure'. *Academy of Management Executive, 1*, 117–125.

Tung, R. (1988a). *The new expatriates: Managing human resources abroad*. New York: Ballinger.

Tung, R. (1988b). 'Career issues in international assignments'. *The Academy of Management Executive, 2*, 241–244.

Tung, R. (1997). 'International and intranational diversity'. In C. S. Granrose and S. Oskamp (Eds), *Cross-cultural work groups* (pp. 163–185). Thousand Oaks, CA: Sage.

Turban, D. B. and Dougherty, T. W. (1994). 'Role of protege personality in receipt of mentoring and career success'. *Academy of Management Journal, 37*, 668–702.

Turner, J. C. (1982). 'Toward a cognitive redefinition of the social group'. In H. Tajfel (Ed.), *Social identity and intergroup relations* (pp. 15–40). Cambridge: University of Cambridge Press.

Turner, L. and Ash, J. (1975). *The golden hordes*. London: Constable.

Tyhurst, L. (1977). 'Psychosocial first aid for refugees'. *Mental Health and Society, 4*, 319–343.

Tyson, G. A. and Duckitt, J. (1989). 'Racial attitudes of British immigrants to South Africa: A longitudinal study'. In D. M. Keats, D. Munro and L. Mann (Eds), *Heterogenity in cross-cultural psychology* (pp. 194–203). Lisse, The Netherlands: Swets & Zeitlinger.

Uehara, A. (1986). 'The nature of American student re-entry adjustment and the perceptions of the sojourn experience'. *International Journal of Intercultural Relations, 10*, 415–438.

Ullah, P. (1987). 'Self-definition and psychological group formation in an ethnic minority'. *British Journal of Social Psychology, 26*, 17–23.

United Nations (1951, July). *United Nations Convention Relating to the Status of Refugees*, Conference of Plenipotentiaries, Article 1, Paragraph A Clause (2). Cited in M. Beiser (1999). *Strangers at the gate* (p. 37). Toronto: University of Toronto Press.

United Nations (1994). *International Migration Bulletin, 4* (1).

United Nations High Commission on Refugees (1993). *The state of the world's refugees*. New York: Penguin.

United Nations High Commission on Refugees (1996). *UNHCR by numbers, basic facts (as of August 1996)*. Available: http://www.unhcr.ch.

United Nations High Commission on Refugees (1998). *Statistics: Refugees and others of concern to UNHCR*. Available: http://www.unhcr.ch/statist/98oview/ch1.htm.

United States Committee for Refugees (1992). *World refugee survey, 1992*. Washington, DC: USCR.

United States Immigration and Naturalization Service (1999). *Immigration statistics*. Available: http://www.ins.usdoj.gov/graphics/publicaffairs/ newsrels/98Legal.pdf.

Urry, J. (1990). *The tourist gaze: Leisure and travel in contemporary societies*. London: Sage.

Van de Vijver, F. J. R., Helms-Lorenz, M. and Feltzer, M. J. A. (1999). 'Acculturation and cognitive performance of migrant children in the Netherlands'. *International Journal of Psychology, 34*, 149–162.

Van den Broucke, S., De Soete, G. and Bohrer, A. (1989). 'Free response self-description as a predictor of success and failure in adolescent exchange students'. *International Journal of Intercultural Relations, 13*, 73–91.

Van Pelt, P. and Wolniansky, N. (1990). 'The high cost of expatriation'. *Management Review, 79*, 40–41.

Vaux, A., Riedel, S. and Stewart, D. (1987). 'Modes of social support: The Social Support Behaviors (SS-B) Scale'. *American Journal of Community Psychology, 15*, 209–235.

Vega, W. A., Gil, A. G., Warheit, G. J., Zimmerman, R. S. and Apospori, E. (1993). 'Acculturation and delinquent behavior among Cuban-American adolescents'. *American Journal of Community Psychology, 21*, 113–125.

Vega, W. A., Khoury, E. L., Zimmerman, R. S., Gil, A. G. and Warheit, G. J. (1991). 'Cultural conflicts and problem behaviors of Latino adolescents in home and school environments'. *Journal of Community Psychology, 23*, 167–179.

Vellas, F. and Becherel, L. (1995). *International tourism: An economic perspective*. London: Macmillan.

Verkuyten, M. (1990). 'Self-esteem and the evaluation of ethnic identity among Turkish and Dutch adolescents in the Netherlands'. *Journal of Social Psychology, 130*, 285–297.

Volet, S. E. and Renshaw, P. D. (1995). 'Cross-cultural differences in university students' goals and perceptions of study settings for achieving their own goals'. *Higher Education, 30*, 407–433.

Wagner, J. (1995). 'Studies of individualism–collectivism: Effects of cooperation in groups'. *Academy of Management Journal, 38*, 152–172.

Wall, T. D., Kemp, N. J., Jackson, P. R. and Clegg, C. W. (1986). 'Outcomes of autonomous workgroups: A long-term field experiment'. *Academy of Management Journal, 29*, 280–304.

Waller, J. and Lea, S. E. G. (1999). 'Seeking the real Spain?: Authenticity in motivation'. *Annals of Tourism Research, 26*, 110–129.

Walmsley, D. J. and Jenkins, J. M. (1993). 'Appraising images of tourist areas: An application of personal constructs'. *Australian Geographer, 24*, 1–13.

Walmsley, D. J. and Young, M. (1998). 'Evaluative images and tourism: The use of personal constructs to describe the structure of destination images'. *Journal of Travel Research, 36*, 65–69.

Wang, N. (1999). 'Rethinking authenticity in tourism experience'. *Annals of Tourism Research, 26*, 349–370.

Ward, C. (1996). 'Acculturation'. In D. Landis and R. S. Bhagat (Eds), *Handbook of intercultural training* (2nd edn, pp. 124–147). Thousand Oaks, CA: Sage.

Ward, C. (1999). 'Models and measurements of acculturation'. In W. J. Lonner, D. L. Dinnel, D. K. Forgays and S. Hayes (Eds), *Merging past, present and future: Selected proceedings of the XIVth International Congress of the International Association for Cross-cultural Psychology* (pp. 221–229*)*. Lisse, The Netherlands: Swets & Zeitlinger.

Ward, C., Berno, T., and Main, A. (2000, July). 'Can the Cross-cultural Adaptability Inventory (CCAI) predict cross-cultural adjustment?'. Paper presented at the XV International Congress of the International Association for Cross-cultural Psychology, Pultusk, Poland.

Ward, C. and Chang, W. C. (1994). [Adaptation of American sojourners in Singapore]. Raw unpublished data.

Ward, C. and Chang, W. C. (1997). '"Cultural fit:" A new perspective on personality and sojourner adjustment'. *International Journal of Intercultural Relations, 21*, 525–533.

Ward, C., Chang, W. C. and Lopez-Nerney, S. (1999). 'Psychological and sociocultural adjustment of Filipina domestic workers in Singapore'. In J. C. Lasry, J. G. Adair and K. L. Dion (Eds), *Latest contributions to cross-cultural psychology* (pp. 118–134*)*. Lisse, The Netherlands: Swets & Zeitlinger.

Ward, C. and Kennedy, A. (1992). 'Locus of control, mood disturbance and social difficulty during cross-cultural transitions'. *International Journal of Intercultural Relations, 16*, 175–194.

Ward, C. and Kennedy, A. (1993a). 'Psychological and sociocultural adjustment during cross-cultural transitions: A comparison of secondary students at home and abroad'. *International Journal of Psychology, 28*, 129–147.

Ward, C. and Kennedy, A. (1993b). 'Where's the culture in cross-cultural transition? Comparative studies of sojourner adjustment'. *Journal of Cross-cultural Psychology, 24*, 221–249.

Ward, C. and Kennedy, A. (1993c). 'Acculturation and cross-cultural adaptation of British residents in Hong Kong'. *Journal of Social Psychology, 133*, 395–397.

Ward, C. and Kennedy, A. (1994). 'Acculturation strategies, psychological adjustment and sociocultural competence during cross-cultural transitions'. *International Journal of Intercultural Relations, 18*, 329–343.

Ward, C. and Kennedy, A. (1996a). 'Crossing cultures: The relationship between psychological and sociocultural dimensions of cross-cultural adjustment'. In J. Pandey, D. Sinha and D. P. S. Bhawuk (Eds), *Asian contributions to cross-cultural psychology* (pp. 289–306). New Delhi: Sage.

Ward, C. and Kennedy, A. (1996b). 'Before and after cross-cultural transition: A study of New Zealand volunteers on field assignments'. In H. Grad, A. Blanco and J. Georgas (Eds), *Key issues in cross-cultural psychology* (pp. 138–154). Lisse, The Netherlands: Swets & Zeitlinger.

Ward, C. and Kennedy, A. (1999). 'The measurement of sociocultural adaptation'. *International Journal of Intercultural Relations, 23*, 659–677.

Ward, C. and Kennedy, A. (in press). 'Coping with cross-cultural transition'. *Journal of Cross-Cultural Psychology*.

Ward, C., Leong, C.-H. and Kennedy, A. (1998, April). 'Self construals, stress, coping and adjustment during cross-cultural transition'. Paper presented at the Annual Conference of the Society of Australasian Social Psychologists, Christchurch, New Zealand.

Ward, C., Okura, Y., Kennedy, A. and Kojima, T. (1998). 'The U-curve on trial: A longitudinal study of psychological and sociocultural adjustment during cross-cultural transition'. *International Journal of Intercultural Relations, 22*, 277–291.

Ward, C. and Rana-Deuba, A. (1999). 'Acculturation and adaptation revisited'. *Journal of Cross-cultural Psychology, 30*, 372–392.

Ward, C. and Rana-Deuba, A. (2000). 'Home and host culture influences on sojourner adjustment'. *International Journal of Intercultural Relations, 24*, 291–306.

Ward, C. and Searle, W. (1991). 'The impact of value discrepancies and cultural identity on psychological and sociocultural adjustment of sojourners'. *International Journal of Intercultural Relations, 15*, 209–225.

Watkins, D., Adair, J., Akande, A., Cheng, C., Fleming, J., Gerong, A., Ismail, M., McInerney, D., Lefner, K., Mpofu, E., Regmi, M., Singh-Sengupta, S., Watson, S., Wondimu, H. and Yu, J. (1998). 'Cultural dimensions, gender, and the nature of self-concept. A fourteen-country study'. *International Journal of Psychology, 33*, 17–31.

Watson, J. L. (Ed.). (1977). *Between two cultures: Migrants and minorities in Britain.* Oxford: Blackwell.

Watson, O. M. (1970). *Proxemic behavior: A cross-cultural study.* The Hague, The Netherlands: Mouton.

Watson, O. M. and Graves, T. D. (1966). 'Quantitative research in proxemic behavior'. *American Anthropologist, 68*, 971–985.

Wehrly, B. (1990). 'Indochinese refugees in schools in the United States of America – Challenges and opportunities for counsellors'. *International Journal for the Advancement of Counselling, 13*, 155–167.

Weinreich, P. (1989). 'Conflicted identifications: A commentary on Identity Structure Analysis concepts'. In K. Liebkind (Ed.), *New identities in Europe* (pp. 219–236). Aldershot, UK: Gower Publishing.

Weinreich, P. (1998, August). 'From acculturation to enculturation: Intercultural, intracultural and intrapsychic mechanisms'. Paper presented at the XIV International Congress of the International Association for Cross-cultural Psychology, Bellingham, WA.

Weiss, S. E. (1996). 'International negotiations: Bricks, mortar, and prospects'. In B. J. Punnett and O. Shenkar (Eds), *Handbook for international management research* (pp. 209–266). Cambridge, MA: Blackwell.

Weissman, D. and Furnham, A. (1987). 'The expectations and experiences of a sojourning temporary resident abroad: A preliminary study'. *Human Relations, 40*, 313–326.

Weisz, J. R., Rothbaum, F. M. and Blackburn, T. C. (1984). 'Standing out and standing in: The psychology of control in America and Japan'. *American Psychologist, 39*, 955–969.

Weldon, D. E., Carlston, D. E., Rissman, A. K., Slobodin, L. and Triandis, H. C. (1975). 'A laboratory test of effects of culture assimilator training'. *Journal of Personality and Social Psychology, 32*, 300–310.

Wellins, R. S., Wilson, R., Katz, A. J., Laughlin, P., Day, C. R. and Price, D. (1990). *Self-directed teams: A study of current practice.* Pittsburgh, PA: DDI.

Wesseley, S., Castle, D., Der, E. and Murray, R. (1991). 'Schizophrenia and Afro-Caribbeans: A case-control study'. *British Journal of Psychiatry, 159*, 795–801.

Westermeyer, J. (1987). 'Cultural factors in clinical assessment'. *Journal of Consulting and Clinical Psychology, 55*, 471–478.

Westermeyer, J., Callies, A. and Neider, J. (1990). 'Welfare status and psychosocial adjustment among 100 Hmong refugees'. *Journal of Nervous and Mental Disease,* *178*, 300–306.

Westermeyer, J., Neider, J. and Callies, A. (1989). 'Psychosocial adjustment of Hmong refugees during their first decade in the United States – A longitudinal study'. *Journal of Nervous and Mental Disease, 177*, 132–139.

Westermeyer, J., Vang, T. F. and Neider, J. (1983). 'Refugees who do and do not seek psychiatric care: An analysis of premigratory and postmigratory characteristics'. *Journal of Nervous and Mental Disease, 171*, 86–91.

Westermeyer, J., Vang, T. F. and Neider, J. (1984). 'Symptom change over time among Hmong refugees: Psychiatric patients versus non-patients'. *Psychopathology, 17*, 168–177.

Westwood, M. J. and Barker, M. (1990). 'Academic achievement and social adaptation among international students: A comparison groups study of the peer-pairing program'. *International Journal of Intercultural Relations, 14*, 251–263.

Westwood, M. J., Lawrence, W. S. and Paul, D. (1986). 'Preparing for re-entry: A program for the sojourning student'. *International Journal for the Advancement of Counselling, 9*, 221–230.

Wibulswadi, P. (1989). 'The perception of group self-image and other ethnic group images among the Thai, Chinese, Thai Hmong hilltribes and American in the province of Chiang Mai'. In D. M. Keats, D. Munro and L. Mann (Eds), *Heterogeneity in cross-cultural psychology* (pp. 204–209). Lisse, The Netherlands: Swets & Zeitlinger.

Wiesner, L. A. (1988). *Victims and survivors: Displaced persons and other war victims in Vietnam, 1954–75.* Westport, CT: Greenwood Press.

Wight, A. R. (1995). 'The critical incident as a training tool'. In S. M. Fowler and M. G. Mumford (Eds), *Intercultural sourcebook: Cross-cultural training methods* (Vol. 1, pp. 127–140). Yarmouth, MN: Intercultural Press.

Wilkinson, P. and Pratiwi, W. (1995). 'Gender and tourism in an Indonesian village'. *Annals of Tourism Research, 22*, 283–299.

Williams, C. L. and Westermeyer, J. (1983). 'Psychiatric problems among adolescent Southeast Asian refugees: A descriptive study'. *Journal of Nervous and Mental Disease, 171*, 79–85.

Williams, G. and Bent, R. (1996). 'Developing expatriate managers for Southeast Asia'. In D. Landis and R. S. Bhagat (Eds), *Handbook of intercultural training* (2nd edn, pp. 383–399). Thousand Oaks, CA: Sage.

Williams, J. E. and Best, D. L. (1990). *Measuring sex stereotypes: A multination study.* Newbury Park, CA: Sage.

Wilson, A. H. (1993). 'A cross-national perspective on re-entry of high school exchange students'. *International Journal of Intercultural Relations, 17*, 465–492.

Wilson, A. T. M. (1961). 'Recruitment and selection for work in foreign cultures'. *Human Relations, 14*, 3–21.

Wilson, D. (1997). 'Paradoxes of tourism in Goa'. *Annals of Tourism Research, 24*, 52–75.

Winchie, D. B. and Carment, D. W. (1988). 'Intention to migrate: A psychological analysis'. *Journal of Applied Social Psychology, 18*, 727–736.

Winter-Ebmer, R. (1994). 'Motivation for migration and economic success'. *Journal of Economic Psychology, 12*, 269–284.

Wiseman, H. (1997). 'Far away from home: The loneliness experience of overseas students'. *Journal of Social and Clinical Psychology, 16*, 277–298.

Wiseman, R. L. (Ed.). (1995). *Intercultural communication theory.* Thousand Oaks, CA: Sage.

Witherell, S. (1996). *Foreign students in the U.S.* New York: Institute of International Education.

Witte, K. and Morrison, K. (1995). 'Intercultural and cross-cultural health communication: Understanding people and motivating healthy behaviors'. In R. L. Wiseman (Ed.), *Intercultural communication theory* (pp. 216–246). Thousand Oaks, CA: Sage.

Wong, G. and Cochrane, R. (1989). 'Generation and assimilation as predictors of psychological well-being in British-Chinese'. *Social Behavior, 4,* 1–14.

Wong-Rieger, D. and Quintana, D. (1987). 'Comparative acculturation of Southeast Asian and Hispanic immigrants and sojourners'. *Journal of Cross-cultural Psychology, 18,* 345–362.

Worchell, S. and Mitchell, T. (1972). 'An evaluation of the culture assimilator in Thailand and Greece'. *Journal of Applied Psychology, 56,* 472–479.

Yamada, A. M., Marsella, A. J. and Yamada, S. (1998). 'The development of the Ethnocultural Identity Behavioral Index (EIBI): Psychometric properties and validation with Asian-American and Pacific Islanders'. *Asian-American and Pacific Islanders Journal of Health, 6,* 35–45.

Yamaguchi, S. (1994). 'Collectivism among the Japanese: A perspective from the self'. In U. Kim, H. C. Triandis, C. Kâğitçibaşi, S.-C. Choi and G. Yoon (Eds), *Individualism and collectivism: Theory, method, and applications* (pp. 175–188). Thousand Oaks, CA: Sage.

Yang, B. and Clum, G. A. (1995). 'Measures of life stress and social support specific to an Asian student population'. *Journal of Psychopathology and Behavioral Assessment, 17,* 51–67.

Yang, K.-S. (1988). 'Will societal modernization eventually eliminate cross-cultural psychological differences?'. In M. H. Bond (Ed.), *The cross-cultural challenge to social psychology* (pp. 67–85). Newbury Park, CA: Sage.

Yau, J. and Smetana, J. G. (1993). 'Chinese-American adolescents' reasoning about cultural conflicts'. *Journal of Adolescent Research, 8,* 419–438.

Ybarra, O. and Stephan, W. G. (1994). 'Perceived threat as a predictor of stereotypes and prejudice: Americans' reactions to Mexican immigrants'. *Boletín de Psicología, 42,* 39–54.

Yee, B. W. K. (1990). 'Elders in Southeast Asian refugee families'. *Generations,* Summer, 24–27.

Yee, B. W. K. (1992). 'Markers of successful aging among Vietnamese refugee women'. *Women and Therapy, 13,* 221–238.

Ying, Y.-W. (1996). 'Immigration satisfaction of Chinese Americans: An empirical examination'. *Journal of Community Psychology, 24,* 3–16.

Ying, Y.-W. and Liese, L. (1990). 'Initial adaptation of Taiwan foreign students to the U.S.: The impact of pre-arrival variables'. *American Journal of Community Psychology, 18,* 825–845.

Ying, Y.-W. and Liese, L. H. (1991). 'Emotional well-being of Taiwan students in the U.S.: An examination of pre- to post-arrival differential'. *International Journal of Intercultural Relations, 15,* 345–366.

Yoshida, Y., Sauer, L., Tidwell, R., Skager, R. and Sorenson, A. G. (1997). 'Life satisfaction among the Japanese living abroad'. *International Journal of Intercultural Relations, 21,* 57–70.

Yoshikawa, M. J. (1988). 'Cross-cultural adaptation and perceptual development'. In

Y. Y. Kim and W. B. Gudykunst (Eds), *Cross-cultural adaptation: Current approaches* (pp. 140–148). Newbury Park, CA: Sage.

Young, M. and Evans, D. R. (1997). 'The well-being of Salvadoran refugees'. *International Journal of Psychology, 32*, 289–300.

Young, M. and Gardner, R. C. (1990). 'Modes of acculturation and second language proficiency'. *Canadian Journal of Behavioral Sciences, 22*, 59–71.

Zaidi, S. M. H. (1975). 'Adjustment problems of foreign Muslim students in Pakistan'. In R. W. Brislin, S. Bochner and W. J. Lonner (Eds), *Cross-cultural perspectives on learning* (pp. 117–130). New York: Wiley.

Zapf, M. K. (1991). 'Cross-cultural transitions and wellness: Dealing with culture shock'. *International Journal for the Advancement of Counselling, 14*, 105–109.

Zeiger, J. and Caneday, L. (Eds). (1991). *Tourism and leisure: Dynamics and diversity*. Alexandria, VA: National Recreation and Parks Association.

Zeira, Y. and Banai, M. (1981). 'Attitudes of host-country organizations towards MNC's staffing policies: A cross-country and cross-industry analysis'. *Management International Review, 2*, 38–47.

Zheng, X. and Berry, J. W. (1991). 'Psychological adaptation of Chinese sojourners in Canada'. *International Journal of Psychology, 26*, 451–470.

Zilber, A. and Lerner, Y. (1996). 'Psychological distress among recent immigrants from the former Soviet Union to Israel, I: Correlates of level of distress'. *Psychological Medicine, 26*, 493–501.

Zimmerman, S. (1995). 'Perceptions of intercultural communication competence and international student adaptation to an American campus'. *Communication Education, 44*, 321–335.

Zwingmann, C. A. A. and Gunn, A. D. G. (1983). *Uprooting and health: Psychosocial problems of students from abroad.* Geneva: World Health Organization.

Author index

Subject index